Foreign Aid as Foreign Policy

Foreign Aid as Foreign Policy

The Alliance for Progress in Latin America

Jeffrey F. Taffet

Routledge
Taylor & Francis Group
New York   London

Routledge
Taylor & Francis Group
711 Third Avenue
New York, NY 10017

Routledge
Taylor & Francis Group
2 Park Square
Milton Park, Abingdon
Oxon OX14 4RN

International Standard Book Number-10: 0-415-97771-1 (Softcover) 0-415-97770-3 (Hardcover)
International Standard Book Number-13: 978-0-415-97771-5 (Softcover) 978-0-415-97770-8 (Hardcover)

Library of Congress Cataloging-in-Publication Data

Taffet, Jeffrey F.
    Foreign aid as foreign policy : the Alliance for Progress in Latin America / Jeffrey F. Taffet.
        p. cm.
    ISBN 0-415-97770-3 (hardback : alk. paper) -- ISBN 0-415-97771-1 (pbk.
    : alk. paper)
    1. Alliance for Progress. 2. Economic assistance, American--Latin America.
3. United States--Foreign relations--Latin America. 4. Latin America--Foreign
relations--United States. I. Title.

HC125.T294 2007
327.1'11--dc22   2006032180

Visit the Taylor & Francis Web site at
http://www.taylorandfrancis.com

and the Routledge Web site at
http://www.routledge.com

For Benjamin and Micah

Contents

Acknowledgments

I would like to thank the staff at the National Archives in College Park, Regina Greenwell and the archivists at the Lyndon B. Johnson Library in Austin, William Johnson and the archivists at the John F. Kennedy Library in Boston, and the staff at the Library of Congress in Washington, DC. I also received help from Jim Huttlinger at the World Bank and Michele Dolbec at the International Monetary Fund (IMF) in Washington, DC. Gloria Carmen deHart aided me at the Ministry of Foreign Relations in Santiago, Chile. Librarians at the University of Rochester, Georgetown University, Canisius College, Princeton University, Yale University, Dickinson College, the New York Public Library, and the United States Merchant Marine Academy all tracked down materials for me. Wayne Fuhrman at the New York Public Library was gracious in offering space in the Wertheim Study and Allen Rooms where I wrote most of the text.

I received financial assistance from the John F. Kennedy Library Foundation, the Lyndon B. Johnson Library Foundation, and Georgetown University.

David Painter of Georgetown University has been a constant source of support. Many of the best ideas in this work came from our discussions. John Tutino, also from Georgetown, started me thinking about these issues more than a decade ago. The number of scholars who commented on conference papers that became part of this manuscript is far too long to list, but I would like to especially thank Stephen Rabe and William Walker. These historians of U.S.–Latin American relations set a very high standard in their writing. Stephen Rabe's book on U.S.–Latin American relations in the 1960s will long be the definitive word on the topic, and was instrumental in guiding my thinking about the Alliance for Progress. Mark Hove, Matt Loyaza, and Jim Siekmeier read the text and offered suggestions that made the book far better. Toward the end of the writing process, Alan McPherson reviewed the manuscript. His pointed questions about my arguments pushed me to rethink many of my analyses. Richard Greenwald was instrumental in encouraging me to move forward with this book and Jennifer Hammer gave me wonderful advice at key moments during the writing process. My editor at Routledge, Kimberly Guinta, has been enthusiastic and always helpful. Nevertheless, though I wish it were not so, I remain responsible for all errors, omissions, and poor analytic decision making.

I also must thank family and friends for their support as I wrote this book. I especially need to thank my parents Bertram and Barbara Taffet and my friends in the Department of Humanities at the United States Merchant Marine Academy. My students also provided me with inspiration; through the writing process I had them in mind.

Last, but certainly not least, I must thank my wife Heather. She has been a source of encouragement and loving reassurance that made this book possible. My sons, Benjamin and Micah, to whom I dedicate this text, provide me more joy than I can ever express in words.

Foreign Aid as Foreign Policy

Introduction
The Politics of Foreign Aid

During its 2004 fiscal year, the United States Agency for International Development (AID) made $26.6 billion in economic assistance loans and grants. Of this foreign aid, just under 30 percent went to Iraq and Afghanistan ($6.4 billion and $1.4 billion, respectively). This massive spending should not be surprising. Following the invasions of these two countries, President George W. Bush's administration determined that rebuilding them, or perhaps even creating self-sustaining economic growth in them, should be a national priority.[1]

They are not the only two nations lavished with hefty aid programs. Colombia has recently been a major target because of U.S. efforts to fight the international drug trade. Between fiscal years (FY) 2000 and 2004, Colombia received $3.2 billion in aid, and the year it got its largest aid packages, FY2000, it accounted for more than 10 percent of all U.S. foreign economic aid. Israel and Egypt have also been among the largest aid recipients. Though both saw cuts in aid during the late 1990s, from FY1995 to FY2004 the two received more than $17.1 billion, or about 12 percent of all U.S. aid funds. The United States sent aid to these countries to ensure that they remained devoted to peaceful relations with each other and to creating stability in the Middle East.[2]

So much spending in these five countries raises important questions about the nature of foreign aid. The U.S. government is, and has long been, dedicated to the improvement of living conditions in poorer countries and to the creation of effective economic systems around the world, but that interest is not spread evenly. Some poverty is more important than other poverty, and helping some countries develop is more important than helping other countries. Foreign aid is not, and cannot be, divorced from foreign policy goals. Foreign aid is a tool that policymakers use, and have used, to achieve their larger aims of dominating, pacifying, protecting, strengthening, or changing certain countries. This book describes that process.[3]

With the exception of Colombia, aid to Latin America has not been a recent high priority for the United States. This was not always the case. At the start of the 1960s, Latin American aid programs were a top, if not *the top*, U.S. concern.

Under the program assessed in this book, the Alliance for Progress, the United States attempted to use economic aid to ensure that Latin America developed in ways that strengthened pro-U.S. politicians and created economic conditions that would limit the appeal of anti-U.S. or pro-Communist forces. Understanding these policies helps explain how inter-American relationships developed in the 1960s. As significantly, study of aid to Latin America during this period is valuable for understanding contemporary international relations and the larger historical connection between aid and international power. The world has changed a great deal since the 1960s, but the logic and application of foreign aid has not.

The Attractions of Foreign Aid

One example of the lack of change in ideas about foreign aid comes from a 2003 AID study, *Foreign Assistance in the National Interest: Promoting Freedom, Security, and Opportunity*. This document explained why the United States needed to make economic aid central to its foreign policy today. The authors suggested that poverty and ineffective government were indicators of instability, which was an indicator that conflict might emerge that could threaten the United States. By promoting democracy and effective governance, they argued, economic development would be more likely to occur. Prosperity would then strengthen democracy. Ultimately, the elimination of poverty would mean the elimination of instability. The authors wrote, "When development and governance fail in a country, the consequences engulf entire regions and leap around the world. . . . They endanger the security and well-being of all Americans. . . ." If their argument can be accepted—that foreign aid is vital to secure domestic peace and reduce the chances of a terrorist attack—it becomes easy to accept the argument that eliminating global poverty is a worthwhile endeavor.[4]

Throughout the Cold War period, policymakers similarly imagined that foreign aid could create stability abroad. They believed that Communists would be unable to threaten countries with healthy economies. They also assumed that foreign leaders who received aid would be willing to support the United States in the international arena. Though the Cold War is over, the idea that economic aid can be used as a foreign policy tool to create a particular kind of world lives on.[5]

The idea persists, in part, because of perceptions about the overwhelming success of the Marshall Plan. Dedicated to rebuilding Europe in the years following World War II, the Marshall Plan represented the first major U.S. foreign aid program. Though some scholars have challenged the argument that U.S. aid was vital (or even helpful) in promoting European recovery, at first glance the program seems to have been a spectacular success. World War II devastated Western European countries and its aftermath left chaos. In response, the United States developed a massive European aid program, and a similar one for Japan, and in the succeeding years economic, social, and political conditions improved. That there may not be a direct line between cause (the granting of aid) and effect (recovery) has mattered little to subsequent policymakers. The simplistic formulation that aid led to stability has inspired leaders over the past half-century to attempt to recreate the programs elsewhere.[6]

The idea of using aid to create growth and stability remains driven by notions about the relationship between wealth and political moderation. Americans believe that financially secure people are unlikely to become revolutionaries and that economic stability in the United States strengthens political stability. They imagine that if only the rest of the world's people would become like those in the United States (relatively well off, that is), there would be no conflicts. Further, it seems easy for Americans to know exactly what kinds of conditions can create economic growth. If educational opportunities are good, if there is a market system, and if governments are fair, it seems obvious that development should occur. If medical care is available, if water is clean and inexpensive, if transportation systems are efficient, if sewer systems exist, and if there is a stock of affordable and safe housing, growth can be accelerated.[7]

Aid is also attractive because it allows the U.S. government to express a set of Judeo-Christian ideas held by most Americans about the moral responsibilities the rich have to the poor. Aid is a way to demonstrate that the country is not simply a powerful nation, but a powerful nation committed to a higher purpose. Helping people build homes, schools, and medical facilities is a way to ensure that the inequalities of history are addressed, and that the United States fulfills its mission as a nation dedicated to peace and justice.[8] That said, it must be noted that many nations give aid, and most of the richer ones give far more than the United States on a per capita basis. In 2005, the United States gave less than 0.2 percent of its gross national income to foreign aid; this ranked twentieth in the world. Nevertheless, the idea that the United States helps the poor in the rest of the world suggests to the American people that their government is good. Economic aid programs are thus both a foreign policy tool and a window into the national political soul.[9]

Though there is a moral component to economic aid programs, practically speaking, one of their central attractions is the power they give policymakers over other governments. If the goal of foreign policy is to get other nations to do what U.S. policymakers want, there are essentially only two options—the use of threats or violence (or the threats of violence) and enticements. Political scientists and historians often refer to this as *carrot and stick diplomacy*. Employing the stick is sometimes necessary, but it can lead to foreign resentment and domestic opposition. While the U.S. government has used threats and violence on many occasions, many citizens feel that there is something unseemly about this approach for a representative democracy. On the other hand, creating consent with enticements (carrots) can produce a far more satisfying relationship and a deeper level of cooperation. It is a tool, perhaps the best tool that exists, to get other governments, especially poor and weak ones, to act in the "right way."

Economic aid can also serve as a powerful lever to encourage change beyond influencing other governments. Given with appropriate conditions, it can get ordinary people to conform to the ideals of U.S. policymakers. Perhaps the best recent example is the way the U.S. government has made funding decisions based on family planning, abortion, and condom distribution. In 1973, the U.S. Congress passed legislation banning any foreign aid recipient from providing abortion services with U.S. funds. At a 1984 conference in Mexico City, President Ronald Reagan's administration announced it would strengthen this policy by forbidding aid recipients from providing abortion services or educating women about abortion, even if the funds they used to do so did not come from the United States. This policy, known by its supporters as the Mexico City Policy, and opponents as the Global Gag Rule, has been divisive in the United States. Congress failed to sign any legislation approving the policy, allowing President Bill Clinton to rescind it immediately on taking office in 1993. Clinton argued that given U.S. support for population control and women's health, the law did not make sense. But Congress passed a bill in November 1999 in favor of the rule, and on his first day in office President Bush reversed Clinton's decision. The Bush administration also pushed for restrictions on aid to fight HIV/AIDS in Africa. United States' rules state that one-third of all money dedicated to combating HIV/AIDS must be spent on sexual abstinence and monogamy/fidelity programs, even though the evidence suggests that condom distribution and safe sex education are far more effective at slowing the rate of new infections. This demonstrates that U.S. leaders use aid to push a particular set of ideas in which they believe.[10]

The Alliance for Progress

Ideas about using aid as a political and moral tool, and the problems inherent in doing so, are illustrated by the Alliance for Progress experience. Introduced by President John F. Kennedy in 1961, it was to be a ten-year, $20 billion foreign aid program for Latin American nations. This was an extraordinary commitment, equivalent to over $100 billion in 2004.[11] The goal of the program was to promote economic growth and political reform in Latin America. Funding by the United States would allow the Latin Americans to build port facilities, hospitals, roads, housing, power plants, and schools. In return, Latin American governments would commit themselves to instituting tax reform, promoting land redistribution, and extending political freedom.

The program was not a success. Latin American countries did not experience economic development because of U.S. aid, and the program did not strengthen democratic governance. Perhaps the most important reason the Alliance for Progress failed was an inherent conflict between lofty humanitarian goals and a desire to fight the Cold War. While U.S. policymakers had a sincere commitment to nation building, political considerations proved far more important in developing aid priorities. Rather than committing money to the most worthy humanitarian projects, the United States funneled its money to explicitly political projects. This book will suggest that attempting to use aid to achieve moral goals and long-term economic development will always fail if aid is also used to advance short-term foreign policy aims.

In assessing the Alliance for Progress, this book will examine larger themes in U.S.–Latin American relations during the 1960s. The years following the Cuban Revolution were the most significant in the Cold War for inter-American relations. In the early part of the Cold War, before Fidel Castro's successes and the development of a Communist government in Cuba, the United States did not focus much attention on Latin America. Concerns about potential Soviet expansion in Europe and the regional impact of the Chinese Revolution left little energy to deal with the seemingly stable and anti-Communist countries in the Western Hemisphere. Although by the end of the 1950s evidence of growing unrest in Latin America began to emerge, it was not until the Cuban Revolution that U.S. policymakers began to panic about trends in the region. They had little difficulty in recognizing that Castro's success was a result of political corruption and poor material conditions in Cuba. Though the Cuban

Revolution was disturbing, a more sobering realization was that repressive government and widespread poverty existed throughout Latin America. The Alliance for Progress was the solution to this problem. The hope was that by promoting growth and democracy the U.S. had its best chance of containing communism.

The Alliance for Progress changed the dynamics of U.S.–Latin American relations. Instead of seeing the region as safe, and thus not worthy of attention, U.S. policymakers made it a top priority. If the United States could eliminate poverty, or at least reduce it, then it would become difficult for Communists to take power.

For Kennedy, as for leading economists and political scientists who supported the program, the Alliance for Progress was not only a means of containing global Communism, it was intended to be a model of U.S. values. It was not just a program to stop the spread of the Cuban Revolution, it was a program to build alliances and spread the positive vision at the heart of U.S. democracy. Success in the Alliance for Progress would demonstrate that U.S. ideas about political organization were universally applicable and would naturally lead to economic growth. That is, in formulating the program, the developers of the Alliance for Progress expressed a connection between national ideology and the role of the United States in the world. They suggested that the ideas inherent in the foundation of the nation could, and should, be exported. If U.S. power was going to be moral (which was the hope of Kennedy era policymakers), it needed to serve as a force for global good. Aid provided the best way to achieve that end. It was a creative and positive foreign policy action, and contrasted with negative foreign policy actions such as military intervention that might help the United States defeat the Soviet Union but not necessarily create a better world.[12]

The Alliance for Progress embodied a classic approach to problems for 1960s thinkers. Policymakers in the United States believed that committing enormous amounts of money, along with the technical expertise of leading intellectuals, would solve problems. They had faith in the perfectibility of society and the ability of social scientists to engineer change. The Alliance for Progress was thus part of Kennedy's New Frontier, but even more significantly, it mirrored President Lyndon Johnson's Great Society. It was a foreign policy counterpart to the development of social welfare programs for the poor within the United States.

The program ran into significant problems almost immediately because of the flawed assumption that foreign aid, or the promise of aid, would lead Latin American leaders to change their policies and accept U.S. ideas about development. The Alliance for Progress, as the name suggested, was to be a partnership between the United States and Latin Americans, but it did not work out that way. Aid became a way to push governments to adopt policies developed in Washington. Latin Americans wanted money, but they did not want to be told what to do.

Although the Alliance for Progress was a regional program, the United States allocated funds on a country by country basis. There was little connection between levels of poverty and aid distribution. Four countries—Chile, Brazil, the Dominican Republic, and Colombia received almost 60 percent of all U.S. funding during the period.[13] A major portion of this book will explain the way the Alliance for Progress affected bilateral relations with these countries. In each case the United States sent most of its money to deal with short-term political issues. Helping economic development was important in all situations, but it was less important than political concerns. The cases demonstrate that the Alliance for Progress, as initially conceived, was simply too idealistic for policymakers to implement.

In Chile, the Alliance for Progress became the main conduit for supporting politicians opposed to the Marxist parties and their leader, Salvador Allende. The story of anti-Allende CIA interventions in the 1964 and 1970 presidential elections has long been public knowledge thanks to the efforts of U.S. Senate investigators in the mid-1970s. Before the 1964 election, the CIA distributed money to Allende's rival, the reform-minded Christian Democrat, Eduardo Frei. The Senate also found that the CIA had been involved in funding anti-Allende candidates throughout the later part of the decade.[14] But this is only a small part of the story. The United States spent almost $600 million on aid programs dedicated to the same goals. CIA programs were miniscule compared to the economic aid coming through the Alliance for Progress. Aid programs ensured that the economy was in strong shape in 1964 and provided the funding that allowed Frei to pursue an extended period of state spending. Nevertheless, the Alliance for Progress did not achieve its goals. Frei actually became more antagonistic to the United States as the decade wore on because he tired of the extensive restrictions linked to AID loans. Perhaps more significantly, the aid did little to weaken the appeal of the Marxist parties because they were able to convince enough people that foreign aid was a form of economic imperialism. In 1970, after a full decade of aid programs, Chileans elected Salvador Allende as president.

In Brazil, the United States used Alliance for Progress funds in a more disturbing manner. From the moment João Goulart assumed the presidency in 1961, U.S. policymakers feared that his sympathy with the poor and his close connections to radical labor unions might mean he would create conditions that would allow for a Communist takeover. To stop this from happening the United States tried to use restrictive aid loans to control him. When it determined that this effort was not working, the U.S. government halted Alliance for Progress funding. This fostered conditions that led the military to overthrow Goulart in 1964. The coup d'état ushered in one of the more brutal military dictatorships in Latin America during the Cold War, and served as a model for the even more bloodthirsty Chilean and Argentine military interventions in 1973 and 1976. Though military leaders consistently violated the basic human rights of the Brazilian people, the U.S. government, in the name of backing a solid ally in the Cold War, used the Alliance for Progress to funnel aid to them. Rather than serving to promote political reform, Alliance for Progress money strengthened a dictatorship. This case demonstrates how the Alliance for Progress lost its reformist goals and moral compass.

In the Dominican Republic, the U.S. government was not willing to send economic aid to help the dictatorship of the repressive Rafael Trujillo, but after his assassination in 1961 and a transition to democracy highlighted by Juan Bosch's victory in 1962 presidential elections, U.S. policymakers did send economic aid. Like Goulart, Bosch soon appeared to be a problem. He was a reformer and just the kind of leader Alliance for Progress theorists had hoped to see come to power, but some U.S. officials thought his government might welcome Communist participation in national politics. When the military ousted Bosch in 1963 they were pleased, but again became worried when Bosch supporters tried to take power in 1965. To keep this from happening, President Johnson had U.S. soldiers invade the country. In the aftermath of this intervention, the United States supported a return to conservative rule as a way of making the Dominican Republic stable. Under conservative leaders, the country became a leading recipient of Alliance for Progress funds. Although it did develop political stability, the loans and grants did not create economic development. Aid was mostly a way to secure the peace.

Finally, this book will examine aid to Colombia. This case represents a different kind of Alliance for Progress story. During the 1960s, Colombia was relatively stable and there was no serious threat of Communist or anti-American leaders taking power, but it did have the most pro–Alliance for Progress leadership in Latin America. In large part because of the interest in reform, and the fact that the leaders elsewhere were resistant to change, U.S. policymakers wanted Colombia to become a model for the program. Though the reasons for offering aid were dramatically different, the ways in which the United States developed its policies were similar to other cases. Kennedy and Johnson administration officials hoped that they could control Colombian economic policy and force leaders to adopt policies developed in Washington. In large part this policy worked, yet as elsewhere it created resentment that undermined Colombia's overall relationship with the United States.

The Alliance for Progress began to lose momentum in the mid- and late-1960s. The Communist threats that seemed to exist when Kennedy took office did not materialize, and worrying about Latin America became less essential. The U.S. government also faced a growing budgetary problem as the decade wore on. Johnson hoped to fund both his Great Society social programs and his own foreign policy priority, the Vietnam War. Money for these efforts had to come from somewhere, and the Alliance for Progress became a target. Policymakers working on Latin America continually asked for more economic aid, but high-level Johnson administration officials repeatedly cut their requests. Although the program had lofty goals, the necessities of day-to-day policymaking trumped a long-term approach.

The Alliance for Progress was even less of a priority for President Richard Nixon. He had no desire to connect himself to what most observers saw as a failed Kennedy and Johnson program. Right-wing dictatorship had proven a reasonably effective bulwark against communism elsewhere, and for the Nixon administration, supporting it became an efficient approach to Latin America. It may not have been attractive, but it was cheap and effective.

Questions Asked, Questions Unanswered, Questions Not Asked

The Alliance for Progress was a massive program. U.S. government agencies made hundreds of loans to Latin American nations, held dozens of planning meetings, and produced thousands upon thousands of pages of economic reports. Through the program, U.S. policymakers had to become involved in the changing economic situation of every recipient nation. Because it was so large, assessing every aspect of the program is impossible. Instead, this book focuses on why Latin America became a priority, how that interest manifested itself in the making of loans, what problems existed in the United States in making loans, and how each of these factors changed during the 1960s.

The spending of so much money in Latin America begs an important question about the impact of the program. Assessment of regional and national economic indicators reveals that there was no dramatic quantitative or qualitative progress. Yet there was change. Previous studies of the Alliance for Progress have fixated on the issue of how much was achieved in an economic sense, and in what ways the effort fell short. Two factors make this focus a mistake. First, it presumes that there can be a direct line drawn between aid given and economic change. In very basic cases, some kind of proof might exist, but Alliance for Progress funds were sent in a haphazard way using a variety of theoretical approaches. It is not possible to expect meaningful economic results when there is no consistency in the application of policy. Further, in many countries, even when economic aid was substantial, government revenue or spending was far more dependent on shifting prices for exports than aid (copper in Chile, sugar in the Dominican Republic, and coffee in Colombia). That is, the United States may have given money, and that money may have been important, but it was only one of a number of things influencing a national economy. Second, and more significantly, a purely economic analysis misses the point. The Alliance for Progress was not an economic program; it was a political program designed to create certain types of political outcomes. Examining these results is far more important in determining where the program succeeded and failed.[15]

Some analyses of the Alliance for Progress have focused on the question of when the program ended. This is a difficult problem, especially as this work will argue that the nature and application of the Alliance for Progress shifted constantly and that changes were usually gradual, rather than sharp. While the program had a clearly defined start, it withered in such a way that makes determining the moment of its end impossible. Suggesting that there was one such moment simplifies a series of complex trends and distorts their meaning.[16]

This theme—the complexity in the Alliance for Progress—runs through the text. As the first half of the work will show, there was no shared or simple definition of what the Alliance for Progress meant, how it would be implemented, or even who was in charge. There was not one factor that led to the program, and there were a wide variety of reasons that understandings of it changed over time. Some U.S. leaders saw connections between loans, idealism, and a set of economic theories, but others thought of the Alliance for Progress only as a way to use aid to influence Latin American politics. In general, by the end of the 1960s, though U.S. policymakers still talked about the Alliance for Progress, it is difficult to understand exactly what they meant.

As the case studies show, although there were consistencies in the United States' approach, its goals, methods, and timing varied by country. This often makes the Alliance for Progress hard to classify, but it also makes it a good window into the minds of policymakers. It would be nice to suggest that U.S. policy was consistent, coherent, and well thought out, but this is not the case.

CHAPTER 1

Changing Course in Latin America

Influences from Eisenhower, Modernization
Theorists, Kennedy, and the Cuban Revolution

President John F. Kennedy introduced the Alliance for Progress upon assuming the presidency. He suggested that the program would be a dramatic break with the past, and if successful, would permanently transform Latin American economies, societies, and politics. The effort, which Kennedy said would be massive, reflected the young president's long-held notions about the importance of poorer parts of the world as the key battleground in the Cold War. However, the idea for the Alliance for Progress, and the particular form it took, had deeper foundations. Much of the logic for the program came from scholars who believed in a concept known as *modernization theory*. This theory suggested that properly administered aid could create the growth that Kennedy promised. The program also built upon changes in President Dwight Eisenhower's administration in the late 1950s. The idea that aid programs to Latin American governments needed to be more aggressive had become accepted logic in Washington by 1960. Finally, while it was not the only reason, fear about Fidel Castro and the Cuban revolution was a consistent anxiety that motivated U.S. policymakers to pay greater attention to Latin America.

Introducing the Alliance for Progress

On the evening of March 13, 1961, less than two months into his term, Kennedy held an unusual event at the White House for the Latin American diplomatic corps. He used a formal social reception as an opportunity to make his first major foreign policy address. The evening was a dramatic signal of change in Washington life. Reporters accustomed to the stuffiness of the Eisenhower years gleefully noted the "happy informality" of the new White House, and explained that contrary to past practice, guests ate and drank in the Blue and Green rooms and everyone smoked as they wished. The president's wife, Jacqueline, also served as a dramatic symbol of the new White House. She wore a stunning sleeveless blue dress with a black geometric pattern and only one piece of jewelry, an impressive diamond bracelet. Kennedy and his wife knew how to throw an elegant party, dress in high-fashion clothes, and were willing to dispense with the staid traditions of the Eisenhower administration. The White House was a changed place and had, in the words of the day, a "New Gleam." Reporters wrote that everything was new, even the jokes.[1]

Change was also obvious for those paying attention to the speech, the unveiling of a new ten-year development program for Latin America that Kennedy called the Alliance for Progress. The following morning, the lead editorial in the *Washington Post* noted, "the president abandoned the stand-pat rhetoric used too often in years past." Kennedy announced that he would take a much more active approach in dealing with dangerous problems in Latin America.[2] New policies were necessary because the successes of the Cuban Revolution suggested that the entire region was vulnerable to communism.

In 1959 and 1960, Fidel Castro's efforts to gain control of the Cuban economy and his fiery rhetoric about independence and nationalism increased tensions with the United States. These tensions, and the increasingly obvious antipathy U.S. policymakers had for Cuba's revolutionary new leaders, encouraged Castro to forge a relationship with the Soviet Union. For the United States, a Soviet ally next door was an embarrassing signal of the failure of U.S. Cold War policies and potentially dangerous.[3] But the Cuban revolution and Castro's movement toward the Soviet Union was scary not only because of what was happening in that country. Castro's movement was terrifying because it could serve as a model for others in Latin America. The poverty that existed in Cuba was ubiquitous in Latin America, and Castro's example could encourage more anti-American/pro-Communist movements throughout the hemisphere. Kennedy implied that a continuation of Eisenhower's ineffective reaction to these developments would lead to disastrous results for both Latin America and the United States.

Kennedy's speech, which he based on ideas suggested during his 1960 presidential campaign and in his inaugural address, called for "a vast cooperative effort, unparalleled in magnitude and nobility of purpose, to satisfy the basic needs of the [Latin] American people for homes, work and land, health and schools." For emphasis, he then repeated these key themes in Spanish, "*techo, trabajo y tierra, salud y escuela.*" He argued that if the "effort is bold enough and determined enough... the living standards of every American family will be on the rise, basic education will be available to all, hunger will be a forgotten experience, the need for massive outside help will have passed, most nations will have entered a period of self-sustaining growth, and though there will still be much to do, every American republic will be the master of its own revolution and its own hope and progress." To get this effort started, Kennedy said he would call for a meeting of the Inter-American Economic and Social Council (IA-ECOSOC), an organ of the Organization of American States (OAS), to begin formulating long-range development plans. He would also push Congress to appropriate $500 million promised by Eisenhower in 1960 for Latin American development, and would encourage talks on economic integration and stabilization of prices for Latin American exports. Kennedy pledged to expand the Food for Peace program, encourage cooperation with Latin American scientists, and enlarge technical training programs. As part of the Alliance for Progress, Kennedy would attempt to convince Latin American nations to reduce spending on expensive weaponry, and finally, he would encourage Latin Americans to share their culture with people in the United States (see Appendix A)[4] (see Figure I.1 following page 148).

Thus, the Alliance for Progress was not only about eliminating poverty in Latin America. It was to be a grand effort to help the nations of Latin America with a push forward so they could join the industrialized and developed nations of the world. Latin America had been poor, but that would begin to change because of his plan.

Eisenhower's Initial Latin American Policy

The Alliance for Progress was in many ways the ultimate step in a series of changes set in motion by the Eisenhower administration. Though the United States did not have an extensive economic aid program for Latin America during most of the 1950s, by the end of the decade Eisenhower had begun to move toward an Alliance for Progress–like approach. Kennedy certainly did bring important new inspirations and energy to U.S. policy, but key elements of his proposals were part the Eisenhower administration's vision in its last years.[5]

Between 1953 and 1957, the consensus within the Eisenhower administration was that private banks and international organizations should take the lead in promoting economic development in Latin America. Officials in Washington believed that they should not help with substantial loans, but should encourage nations to improve their investment climate to attract private capital. That is, the United States should push Latin Americans to create conditions that would make businesses want to invest in their countries. Private corporations had built the United States, Eisenhower administration officials believed, and they expected that the same thing would work in Latin America.[6]

Between mid-1953 and mid-1958 (FY1954 to FY1958) the United States government made loans and grants totaling $12.6 billion worldwide. Of this, Latin America received only $783 million, or less than 7 percent. Funding for Latin America in this period paled in comparison to spending in other regions. Asian countries received $6.6 billion, over 52 percent of the total. South Korea and India each received more than all of Latin America. The Middle East and North Africa, and even Western Europe, presumably a less needy area, also received greater sums than Latin America. (see Figure 1.1)

Because of the Eisenhower administration's ideas about Latin American economic development and private business, the region received significant Export-Import Bank loans. This U.S. government institution made (and still makes) loans directly to foreign companies to promote purchases of U.S. goods. The bank is not supposed to make loans directly to foreign governments for development programs. From FY1954 to FY1958, the Export-Import Bank made $1.49 billion in loans, more than 64 percent of which went to Latin America[7] (see Figure 1.2).

Eisenhower administration priorities in Latin America, codified in a 1953 National Security Council (NSC) policy paper (NSC 144/1), were to ensure that Latin Americans supported the United States at the United Nations, to work to protect the hemisphere from Communist invasion, to continue to have them produce raw materials, and to eliminate the "menace of internal Communist or other anti-U.S. subversion." Although the Eisenhower staff attempted to develop inter-American military cooperation programs and tried to improve relations with key nations, it ruled out underwriting a major economic aid program to promote Latin America's economic development.[8]

Eisenhower administration officials began to question some of these policies in the mid-1950s as they watched the Soviet Union develop a more sophisticated Cold War strategy. Following the death of Joseph Stalin in 1953, Soviet leaders shifted from emphasizing military power to more subtle and diplomatic means to achieve foreign policy goals. Perhaps the most dangerous element of this strategy was Soviet economic overtures to poorer parts of the world. Under Nikita Khrushchev, the Soviet Union began making trade deals and offering aid programs in Latin America, Asia, and Africa.[9]

By 1956, Eisenhower and some of his top officials began to think that greater development spending might be a way to fight this new Soviet

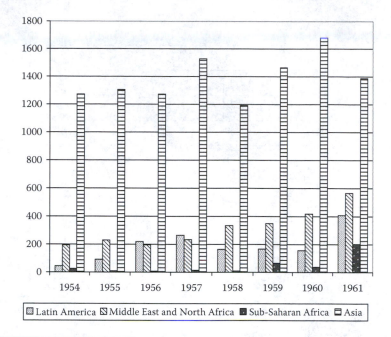

Figure 1.1 U.S. Economic Assistance Loans and Grants, FY1954–FY1961 (in millions of U.S. dollars; data not adjusted for inflation). From the United States Agency for International Development Web site, The Greenbook (http://qesdb.cdie.org/gbk).

threat. However, State Department officials argued that the real problems were only in places like India, Burma, and Japan, and not in Latin America. While reports to Eisenhower suggested that his administration needed to stop the Soviets from supplanting the United States as the primary aid donor throughout the world, Latin America, because of the limited threat of Communist expansion, did not become a priority.[10]

As late as 1958, Eisenhower administration officials thought they had succeeded in keeping Latin America free of communism. Both internal government reports and speeches by people such as Secretary of State John Foster Dulles asserted that Marxist groups would not take power in any Latin American country. While problems in Asia did require an aggressive approach, the Eisenhower administration remained confident that Latin America was safe.[11]

Seeing Threats in Latin America

In the final years of the Eisenhower administration, confidence about Latin American security eroded. The first major sign of problems came during Vice President Richard Nixon's goodwill trip to Latin America in May 1958. The

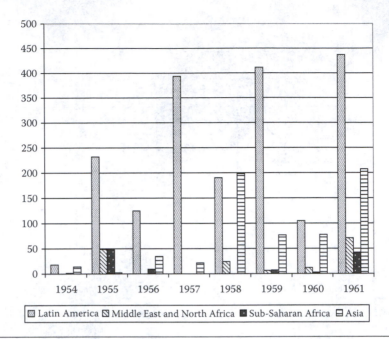

Figure 1.2 U.S. Export-Import Bank Loans, FY1954–FY1961 (in $US millions; data not adjusted for inflation)..

key stop on this trip was Argentina, where Nixon attended the inauguration of Arturo Frondizi as president. Because of Argentina's regional importance, and because Frondizi's inauguration marked the end of years of military rule, sending a high-level delegation seemed appropriate.[12]

The Nixon trip started reasonably peacefully in Uruguay and Argentina, though in small rallies student groups protested the mission while carrying signs with anti-American slogans.[13] Private meetings with government officials were generally positive, but there were tensions because of the lack of U.S. support for development programs. The trip started to look like a disaster in Peru however. Nixon endured a night of listening to students chant "*Muera Nixon*" (Death to Nixon) outside his hotel and the next day, a visit to the San Marcos University turned violent as students spat at Nixon and threw rocks at his entourage.[14]

After peaceful meetings in Ecuador and Colombia, Nixon again faced large and angry crowds in Caracas, Venezuela. The visit began with a protest at the airport in which large crowds of demonstrators spat on the vice president and his wife, Pat. From there the trip only got worse. On the drive into the city center, a mob stopped his car and attacked it with metal pipes. Then, as Nixon would later write, "we heard the [lead] attacker shout a command and our car began to rock. . . . For an instant, the realization passed through my mind—we might be killed." Escaping the mob, Nixon changed his itinerary and ordered the motorcade to speed to the United States embassy. Following these episodes, the vice president spent the rest of his stay in Venezuela within the safety of the embassy walls and even considered taking a helicopter to the airfield to fly home. To ensure a safe exit, the Venezuelan government arranged for an extensive army escort for the drive to the airport. President Eisenhower's reaction made the attacks even more embarrassing. Fearing for Nixon's life, and just plain angry, the president mobilized troops and sent naval vessels toward the Venezuelan coast to prepare a small rescue invasion. This plan, dubbed Operation Poor Richard, served to increase tensions as the Venezuelans foresaw a new attempt to carry out "big stick" diplomacy.[15]

The existence of anti-Americanism in Latin America was certainly not new or limited to a few places. As Alan McPherson, a historian of U.S.–Latin American relations explains,

> From the days of independence to the middle of the twentieth century, anti-U.S. sentiment touched every major social group in Latin America, especially in the Caribbean. Peasants, workers, and members of the middle class and the elite all resented being exploited or disdained by the United States at some point. Yet social divisions and ambivalence largely inhibited cross-class alliances among Latin Americans, who were left to resist U.S. imperialism in atomized, isolated groups. Eventually the United States government spread its influence even further. As a result, anti-Americanism seeped down from literary and other elites into the political consciousness of ordinary people as it also percolated up from the poor to shape mainstream politics.[16]

Yet because anti-American sentiments had not led to a unified political movement, there seemed to be little need for the United States to respond. Long present anti-Americanism had done little to hinder U.S. influence in the region.

The intense hatred toward the United States demonstrated on the Nixon trip caught policymakers by surprise and pushed them to think about ways to improve relations. One idea came from the Senate Foreign Relations Committee, which in August 1958 (just three months after the Nixon trip) studied U.S. economic aid. Arguing that the amount of military and development assistance was inadequate given world realities, seven of eight Democratic members of the committee, including Kennedy, and one Republican member, sent a letter to Eisenhower asking for a reappraisal of aid programs. In response, the president selected William H. Draper, the chairman of the Mexican Power and Light Company, to head a committee to examine this issue. The Draper committee was an early step in Eisenhower's willingness to reconsider aid policy; however, the committee did not report its findings that the United States needed to increase aid levels until 1959, and ultimately it had little impact on aid programs.[17]

One change that did result from the Nixon trip was support for the creation of the Inter-American Development Bank (IADB). Using U.S. funds, the bank would make loans across Latin America to help infrastructure projects in transportation, health, and education. In 1889, Secretary of State James G. Blaine had proposed such an institution, and in the almost seventy years following that suggestion, Latin Americans had argued for its creation. Since Blaine, however, the United States had consistently opposed its establishment. Part of the reluctance came from general opposition to development aid for Latin America, and part came from a fear that a regional bank would lead to a loss of control over foreign aid spending. Nixon's trip forced the administration to come up with some immediate response, but even this step forward did not signify a full commitment to development spending in Latin America. The Eisenhower administration hoped to keep the bank small, and at the time was supporting a development bank for the Near East. It would have been very difficult to explain why the administration was creating a bank for one region, but not the other.[18]

Nixon's trip did not merely prod Washington into thinking about how to restructure development policies. The embarrassment also offered Latin Americans a chance to suggest ideas. Juscelino Kubitschek, the Brazilian president, wrote to Eisenhower in May 1958 to suggest that more economic aid would improve inter-American relationships. He argued, "something must be done to restore composure to continental unity."[19] Eisenhower warmly received Kubitschek's letter as a way to salvage U.S. prestige and sent Secretary of State John Foster Dulles and Assistant Secretary of State for Inter-American Affairs Roy Rubottom to Rio de Janeiro to discuss the Brazilian ideas. Kubitschek sketched the outlines of a development plan that became known as Operation Pan America. The plan, which was similar to the Alliance for Progress, suggested a vast economic partnership between the United States and Latin America in the coming decade. However, while U.S. officials did begin to talk more positively about enacting something along these lines, there was little movement in Washington. Both Eisenhower and Dulles still resisted the development of a broad multilateral aid program.[20]

Though the Brazilian plan failed to gain enough support in 1958 at the highest levels, it did not completely die. Throughout 1959 State Department analysts repeatedly presented memos calling for a greater focus on development assistance. Eisenhower finally began to change his mind following a goodwill trip to Latin America in February 1960. Friendly crowds greeted Eisenhower, yet in private conversations with Latin American leaders he found a great deal of unhappiness with U.S. policy. He decided that the United States needed to do more for Latin America.[21] To that end, in July 1960, Eisenhower sent Congress a request for the creation of what became known as the Social Progress Trust Fund. This fund was the centerpiece in what State Department officials called "Operation Pan America (non-Brazilian)" or "The President's New Positive Program for Latin America." Conceived by Rubottom, and actively supported by Undersecretary of State Douglas Dillon, this plan called for the appropriation of a $500 million grant for development spending in Latin America.[22]

A commitment to large-scale development funding, along the lines the Alliance for Progress would take, was an indication that the administration was finally willing to admit to itself that its earlier policies had failed. The need for action was so compelling that State Department officials ignored the fact that Eisenhower was about to leave office. They commented that while it was odd to speak "of bold new initiatives in the dying days of an administration," the need to go on the offensive seemed obvious by 1960.[23]

The legislation authorizing the Social Progress Trust Fund passed Congress on September 8, 1960 as Public Law 735. The timing for this vote coincided with an OAS meeting in Bogotá to discuss Operation Pan America as a framework for encouraging economic development within the region. The final report of the meetings, which became known as the Act of Bogotá, spelled out many of the concerns that would also guide the development of the Alliance for Progress: promoting a more equitable distribution of land, the creation of agricultural credit institutions, improvements in agricultural productivity, reform of tax systems, creation of urban housing programs, development of stronger educational systems, and the extension of health services to all. The Act of Bogotá did not set up a mechanism to guide policy or even suggest a framework for how the United States would make funding decisions. However, the Act of Bogotá and the Social Progress Trust Fund were dramatic changes in approaches to Latin American development.[24] These changes occurred too late in the Eisenhower administration to have an impact on spending. Assistance to Latin America between mid-1958 and mid-1960 was almost a mirror of the earlier part of the 1950s: 5.6 percent of all aid spending abroad. There was only a notable increase in 1961 to 12 percent[25] (see Figure 1.1).

The Modernization Theorists and Self-Help

Kennedy's policies for greater economic aid to Latin America built on the foundations set in the last years of the Eisenhower administration. Like his predecessor, the new president wanted to fight anti-Americanism and stem the growth of Castro-inspired revolutionaries, but he also hoped to create massive change in Latin America and use U.S. power as a force for international good. His ideas in this respect built upon the theories of a community of academics, mostly located in Boston, known as the Charles River group. Many of these scholars, including the two most prominent, Walt Rostow and Max Millikan, worked at the Center for International Studies (CENIS) at MIT (Massachusetts Institute of Technology).[26]

As early as 1952, faculty at CENIS had begun focusing on the importance of economic aid programs in U.S. foreign policy. As economists, they attempted to create models and theories to explain how economic aid programs could create lasting growth. Initially they studied India, believing that aid could be critical in helping that country's development. In the mid-1950s, CENIS scholars began extensive efforts to influence members of the U.S. government. Kennedy became a natural ally for the scholars because of his own ideas about foreign aid. Writing much later, Rostow recalled the situation: "Kennedy sought out and found in CENIS a group whose ardent commitment was to enlarged development aid rather than to party or political personality. He understood this clearly and used us well . . ."[27]

To publicize their views, the CENIS group wrote and distributed to members of Congress a blueprint for a comprehensive foreign aid program. They then published the document, giving it the confident title, *A Proposal: Key to an Effective Foreign Policy*. The basic premise of *A Proposal* was that the United States should use its aid program as a tool to promote positive change. The CENIS scholars wrote, "one of the highest priority tasks is to use our influence to promote the evolution of societies that are stable in the sense that they are capable of rapid change without violence, effective in the sense that they can make progress in meeting the aspirations of their citizens, and democratic in the sense that ultimate power is widely shared through society." These types of societies would "promote the evolution of a world in which threats to our security and, more broadly, our way of life are less likely to arise." The CENIS scholars were not only making an economic argument. They were suggesting that aid could have overtly political goals. If Washington wanted to fight the Cold War effectively, it had to create societies that shared its values. The CENIS group suggested that economic growth alone was not enough; some kind of qualitative change had to occur in the way people lived.[28]

The Charles River group's key contribution to ideas about economic aid was the development of modernization theory. This theory offered an explanation about why some areas and peoples had advanced economically and others had not. Nils Gilman, a historian of the Modernization Theorists, explains that:

> The central thread that ran through all of modernization theory was a particular rendition of the dichotomy of "the traditional" and "the modern." According to modernization theorists, modern society was cosmopolitan, mobile, secular, welcoming of change, and characterized by a complex division of labor. Traditional society, by contrast, was inward looking, inert, passive toward nature, superstitious, fearful of change, and economically simple.[29]

This model of the world was attractive to policymakers because it suggested a way to create economic development. Study of how rich nations had moved from *traditional* to *modern* and then application and repetition of these same processes in poorer countries would lead to the extension of modern societies. Modernization theory was thus not only an explanation of how the world had come to be divided into "haves" and "have-nots," it also suggested the means to fix the world of the "have-nots."[30]

In 1960 Rostow popularized these ideas in *The Stages of Economic Growth: A Non-Communist Manifesto*. This study proposed a theory of economic "take-off" based on the tenets of modernization theory. According to Rostow there were five stages of economic development: (1) a traditional society, (2) a society in the preconditions for take-off, (3) the take-off, (4) the drive to maturity, and (5) the age of high mass consumption. To Rostow, the United States was entering the last phase, and the Europeans, Japanese, and Soviets were all well on their way there. However, the Latin American nations were still in the second period, the preconditions-for-take-off stage. In each of the "successful" cases there had been some kind of "sharp stimulus" that provided a push leading to rapid movement from stage two to stage three. Rostow argued that a well-funded economic aid program could serve as this sharp stimulus and move Latin American countries into the "take-off" phase. From this phase, movement to the later stages would be inevitable.[31]

Following Kennedy's 1960 victory, Rostow became a member of the new administration and was able to offer more pointed advice about aid programs. Writing in the weeks before the Alliance for Progress speech, Rostow sent Kennedy a long memo calling for an abandonment of Eisenhower administration policies. Rostow explained that the old aid policy funded military spending and programs designed to avoid short-run political or military collapse. He argued, "We begin with a program that is almost wholly defensive in character and one that commands neither the resources, the administration, nor the criteria designed to move the underdeveloped countries toward sustained economic growth." To Rostow, the problem with the Eisenhower program was its focus on the short run. The new program, he wrote, should be a "Free World effort with enough resources to move forward those nations prepared to mobilize their own resources for development purposes. The goal is to help other countries learn how to grow." This strategy, according to Rostow, "will take some time and the greatest discipline in our whole establishment. . . . but it is the only path that makes sense." For Rostow, the long run was crucial. He suggested "a major and ruthless overhaul of existing programs is necessary with a new emphasis on basic education; on bringing modern science to bear in the undeveloped areas; on technological training to complement economic programs; and the financing of projects aimed at modernizing social institutions."[32]

To turn these theoretical ideas into policy recommendations, Kennedy created the Task Force for Latin America to refine the Alliance for Progress idea. He asked Adolf Berle, a veteran diplomat, to chair the group. Other members with significant experience in Latin American affairs joined the committee. These included Teodoro Moscoso and Arturo Morales Carrion, both of whom had been involved in Puerto Rican development planning. Professors Robert Alexander of Rutgers University, Arthur Whitaker from the University of Pennsylvania, and Lincoln Gordon of Harvard also joined the Task Force. This group worked with White House aide Richard Goodwin, whom Kennedy charged with writing the March 13 speech.[33]

The Task Force recommendations, though less theoretical than the advice given by modernization theorists, covered much of the same ground. The group suggested that the central theme of a development program for Latin America needed to be "a sustained effort for development and social progress, combining vigorous measures of self-help with the provision of complementary outside resources." They agreed that the United States "should embark on a decade of democratic progress, to demonstrate in this hemisphere that economic growth, social equity, and the democratic development of societies can proceed hand in hand." The Task Force argued that although this type of program was reminiscent of the Marshall Plan, the Latin American initiative would be different because of the need to overcome "an ancient heritage of poverty, widespread illiteracy, and grave social, economic, and geographical imbalances." This meant there would be a slower rate of progress than the Marshall Plan had. Because of the vast hurdles, the Task Force insisted Latin American governments needed to create national development plans and set targets for internal investment, monetary stability, and external payments equilibrium. The Task Force also noted that these countries should be encouraged to pass legislative reforms and to mobilize their own domestic resources to improve performance in tax collection, land reform, banking, and education.[34]

A fundamental aspect of the recommendations, which Kennedy accepted, was that the United States, while offering financial support, would only work with nations committed to joint goals. A program of self-help would be a signal that a nation was ready for the Alliance for Progress partnership, and following that step, the United States would offer assistance. As Kennedy would later put it in explaining the Alliance for Progress, "only the most determined efforts of the American nations themselves can bring success to this effort. They, and they alone, can mobilize their resources—enlist the energies of their people—and modify their social patterns so that all, and not just a privileged few share the fruits of growth. If the effort is made, then outside assistance will give a vital impetus to progress . . ."[35]

Kennedy's Evolving Vision About the Developing World

The Alliance for Progress built upon the foundations set by the Eisenhower administration and the ideas presented by modernization theorists, but its initial style reflected Kennedy's own sense of purpose and philosophy. Kennedy's goals were essentially the same as Eisenhower's, yet he wanted to try new ways to achieve them.

In his inaugural address, Kennedy explained that fighting communism would drive his foreign policy and that there would be continuity with the past. Making a call to the world, he proclaimed, "Let every nation know, whether it wishes us well or ill, that we shall pay any price, bear any burden, meet any hardship, support any friend, oppose any foe to assure the survival and success of liberty." Like Eisenhower, he would fight the Cold War, but the methods used would be different. Kennedy announced, "Let the word go forth from this time and place, to friend and foe alike, that the torch has been passed to a new generation of Americans." This was his way of suggesting that his administration would provide new solutions to old problems.[36]

Kennedy's intent to depart from past practice was obvious in early 1961. Most symbolically, the inaugural festivities demonstrated that Kennedy would be more experimental and exciting than his stodgy predecessor. The presence of people like Frank Sinatra and his Rat Pack friends, as well as the poet Robert Frost, suggested that Kennedy was much more worldly, cultured, and lively. The guest lists also indicated that Kennedy would be more attentive to intellectuals and artists. Beyond the scholars from Harvard and MIT who joined his administration, Kennedy symbolically invited people to the inauguration like the modernist composer Igor Stravinsky and authors who had challenged literary conventions, such as Arthur Miller, John Steinbeck, W. H. Auden, William Faulkner, Ernest Hemingway, and Thornton Wilder. He invited influential religious scholars Paul Tillich and Reinhold Niebuhr and the abstract expressionist painter Mark Rothko.[37] The interest in new ideas led to optimism that Kennedy would make real changes in Washington.

The Alliance for Progress reflected this new spirit of governance, but also advanced ideas the new president had long held about the role of foreign aid and the developing world. As a young member of Congress, Kennedy initially had not believed foreign aid was important or that the United States should focus on Africa, Asia, or Latin America. He opposed President Harry Truman's efforts to fight the Cold War outside Europe and was critical of the Korean War, fearing that it would leave the United States unprepared to fight a larger war against the Soviet Union. Kennedy also voted against funding for Truman's Point Four program, a plan to use foreign aid to help poorer countries develop their economies. Until the Point Four program, U.S. development assistance was essentially limited to the Marshall Plan and aid to Japan. Kennedy supported the Marshall Plan, but thought the Point Four program was wasteful.[38]

Kennedy's ideas changed during an extended international trip in 1951 to Israel, Pakistan, India, Indochina, Malaya, and Korea. During his travels he came to believe that the growth of communism in Asia was a threat to the United States and that foreign aid could be an important mechanism for helping to protect friendly governments.[39] When he returned to Washington, Kennedy made a national radio address in which he explained that Communists took advantage of the "fires of nationalism" and were able to offer an alternative to the colonial situation. In this radio address Kennedy criticized U.S. policy, noting, "It is tragic to report that not only have we made no new friends, but we have lost old ones." He said that the United States had not stood up for the weak, but allowed the strong, who were often "sinister and subversive" to be successful. Kennedy also argued that the presence of European colonies in Asia and Africa would lead to problems for the United States. He suggested that the West's failure to recognize that "every country is entitled to its independence" would allow the Communists an easy road to the domination of nationalist movements.[40]

Kennedy continued to push for a greater focus on the developing world following his election to the Senate in 1952. In that body he became a leading voice calling for greater aid programs and for encouraging independence movements fighting European colonialism. This led to perhaps his most famous action in the Senate—support for Algerian independence from France. Taking a stand against a strong U.S. ally, and at odds with much of Congress and his own party, Kennedy made the case that Algerian independence was in the best interests of the United States. In a speech on July 2, 1957, Kennedy explained that "the most powerful single force in the world today is neither communism nor capitalism, neither the H-bomb nor the guided missile—it is man's desire to be free and independent." The Eisenhower administration, he argued, had made a grave error in backing France, an error that "affected our standing in the eyes of the Free World, our leadership in the fight to keep that world free, our prestige, and our security, as well as our moral leadership in the fight against Soviet imperialism . . ." The United States needed to accept and embrace change, especially change that would lead to greater freedom around the world. Support for revolution and independence movements was not only morally correct, Kennedy said, it was geopolitically prudent. Opposition to these movements would demonstrate to the world that the United States was not a force for positive change, but a defender of the generally unpleasant status quo. Embracing change and revolution was consistent with U.S. values and would help win the Cold War. This speech was the first of several on the issue and helped establish Kennedy as a national figure.[41]

To Kennedy, a basic way to win the Cold War in the developing world would be through an expanded foreign aid program. In a 1954 speech about Vietnam, Kennedy proposed that the United States develop an aid program that would offer "a revolution—a political, economic, and social revolution far superior to anything the communists can offer—far more peaceful, far more democratic, and far more locally controlled."[42] The United States had to accept and even promote dramatic change as the only alternative to nationalistic movements that would find communism appealing. Aid was useful because it would create economic growth and undercut Communist arguments about the inequalities inherent in a capitalist system. It could also ensure that nations and peoples would embrace Western and capitalist values. Though he spoke of problems in Vietnam in 1954, these ideas would form the backbone for the Alliance for Progress.

During the late 1950s Kennedy continued to talk about foreign aid. In an article for the October 1957 issue of *Foreign Affairs*, "A Democrat Looks at Foreign Policy," Kennedy gave special attention to developing areas. He wrote, "In the years ahead we face a challenge in how to help the new and underdeveloped nations bear their economic burdens. Again we must strike a balance between 'the illusion of American omnipotence' and a somber contemplation of the impossibility of absolute solutions." Kennedy argued that "deteriorating economic conditions and steeply rising populations" were indicators that the Communists would be successful in a particular region. U.S. policy needed to be more effective, Kennedy argued, at addressing these conditions.[43]

Reflecting these concerns, Kennedy, with the collaboration of Senator John Sherman Cooper (R-KY), introduced a resolution calling for greater assistance to India in March 1958. Kennedy explained that successful Indian economic growth, and by extension democratic life, would be in jeopardy without U.S. action. The best way to help would be to support "programs of real economic development," which would allow the "Asian and African nations . . . [to] find the political balance and social stability which provide the true defense against Communist penetration."[44]

Thus, well before Kennedy won the 1960 Presidential election, economic development in poor countries was key to his ideas about foreign policy. His leadership on this issue also provided a useful tool for distinguishing himself from the policies of the Eisenhower administration, and by implication, the likely policies of Richard Nixon who ran against him in 1960. To the extent that Kennedy could argue that Eisenhower's foreign policy was a failure, emphasis on foreign aid provided him with an opportunity for explaining how he could do a better job.

Cuba as a Motivating Factor

These three elements, Kennedy's ideas and energy, the influence of modernization theorists, and the Eisenhower legacy, all played central roles in the development of the Alliance for Progress. As noted at the outset however, the Cuban situation loomed over the project and guaranteed that it would have a high priority within the Kennedy White House. The growing evidence that Cuba would become the first Communist nation in the Western Hemisphere, and Castro's eventual declaration that he was a Marxist-Leninist frustrated U.S. officials.[45]

Castro challenged Washington's domination in a region that the United States had seen as its ward. Focusing on the long history of interventionism and economic domination, Castro offered the Cuban people the chance to develop their independence from foreign (notably U.S.) control. Fears about the appeal of this message caused the United States to spend an incredible amount of time and energy on developing responses to Castro's movement. Most conspicuously, these fears led to the Bay of Pigs invasion.[46] In April 1961, the U.S. Navy delivered 1,100 Cuban exiles trained by the Central Intelligence Agency (CIA) to a remote part of southern Cuba called the Bay of Pigs as part of a plan to create a mass uprising against Castro. The invasion was a failure. Castro's armies were able to keep the exiles from moving out of a tidal swamp and captured most of them.[47]

Obviously the Alliance for Progress was dramatically different in tone and scope, but it was an extension of the ideology driving the invasion. Kennedy's aides were careful not to talk about the Cuban revolution's link to the Alliance for Progress, and explicitly went out of their way to keep Castro's name out of public remarks about the program. Yet the Cuban experience drove it forward. Castro was successful because he appealed to the poor and middle classes who suffered at the hands of the traditional Latin American oligarchy. If the United States could not do something to eliminate the conditions that fueled Castro's successes, the entire region might be consumed in a dangerous radical revolution.

The connection between Cuba and the Alliance for Progress is vital to understanding why the program became a priority and remained one. Those involved with the development of policy toward Latin America reported that Kennedy, especially following the Bay of Pigs embarrassment, was obsessed with Cuba. Kennedy saw the Bay of Pigs fiasco as a blow to his honor, and his antipathy toward Castro turned into a personal quest for revenge. Castro remained a problem throughout his presidency, and as the Cuban Missile Crisis demonstrated, it was a problem that became ever more connected to the larger fight against the Soviet Union. Yet Kennedy understood that Cuba was only one part of a larger Latin American picture. Expanded Soviet penetration deep into Washington's sphere of influence, beyond Cuba, would demonstrate that Washington was losing the Cold War. As historian Stephen Rabe argues, Kennedy repeatedly emphasized the centrality of Latin America to his entire foreign policy. Rabe explains:

> Fighting and winning the Cold War in Latin America was Kennedy's paramount concern. He believed that the Soviet Union's drive for global supremacy included subverting the region. Throughout his presidency he predicted trouble. In January 1961 he [said] . . . "the whole place could blow up on us." . . . In June 1963 [he said] Latin America was only "the most dangerous area in the world." In October 1963, less than a month before his death, Kennedy warned that Latin America posed "the greatest danger to us."

The Alliance for Progress became, in effect, the solution to this problem. Kennedy was often pessimistic in private about the potential of his aid program. As Rostow noted, it needed to focus on the long term, and thus would necessarily be slow in bringing change. Yet there appeared to be no other options. Only improvements in social and economic conditions, Kennedy reasoned, could stabilize the region.

CHAPTER 2

Implementing the Alliance for Progress
The Initial Theoretical, Political, Management, and Marketing Problems

Following President John F. Kennedy's introduction of the Alliance for Progress, U.S. policymakers had to figure out the best way to implement the program. There were major problems in doing this. Within the United States, creating a nimble and effective bureaucracy proved difficult, as did securing support from Congress for the massive appropriations necessary to fund loans and grants. Another challenge involved developing partnerships with Latin American governments. Latin Americans needed to see the program as a new beginning in inter-American relations and an alliance among equals. It would be a new kind of imperialism if the United States simply told Latin Americans that they needed to change their societies. At the same time, because Washington was providing the funds, aid had to reflect U.S. political interests. The Kennedy administration could not allow the Latin Americans to control spending. This undercut the idea of a partnership. Each of these issues made getting the program under way difficult and forced the U.S. government to develop a considerable marketing effort to sell the program at home and in Latin America.

Who Should Be in Control?

Central to the Alliance for Progress was the idea of a new beginning in inter-American relations. Kennedy understood that if Latin Americans continued to resent U.S. power, communism would find fertile ground even if economic development did occur. Therefore, he thought it was important to manage the Alliance for Progress with a light touch, especially in public. The U.S. government had to get Latin Americans to believe that the Alliance for Progress was their own program. They needed to be confident that the United States would help them with development needs but also that they could determine on their own how to proceed. By stepping back, the United States would demonstrate that it was respectful of differences in Latin American societies and of local leaders and that it was repudiating its own past behavior.

The first step was to develop a set of shared understandings about what the Latin Americans were to do and what support the United States would offer. To produce these, the Kennedy administration called a meeting of Latin American leaders in August 1961 at the Uruguayan resort town of Punta del Este. There, the assembled diplomats wrote a document outlining the goals of the Alliance for Progress. By signing the document, which became known as the Charter of Punta del Este, Latin American governments publicly declared that they would reform their own societies to create economic development.[1]

Stepping back from a dominant position and avoiding any suggestion of coercion became even more important following the botched Bay of Pigs invasion. The invasion was not only an embarrassment in execution, but also raised questions about a "new" approach. Kennedy appeared to be acting exactly as earlier U.S. leaders had in attempting to dominate the region. Although most Latin American governments worried about Castro and accepted the idea that he represented a threat to hemispheric security, they did not like the unilateral and covert action. As Walt Rostow, newly appointed as deputy national security advisor, explained in a note to Kennedy, the Bay of Pigs jeopardized the Alliance for Progress because it forced Latin American leaders to reject U.S. policy, and thus to question a close partnership with Washington. He wrote, "for those politicians whose success and collaboration we need most" the United States could not force a choice between "working with us against Castro or in working with us in development business."[2] Success in collaborating with the Latin Americans to create a development program became Kennedy's only way of demonstrating that the Bay of Pigs was an aberrant mistake and that he really did care about a new approach to inter-American relations.

At the same time, because Kennedy introduced the Alliance for Progress and committed his prestige to it, the United States could not simply sit back and allow Latin Americans to do what they wished. Because the United States would ultimately be funding the programs discussed at Punta del Este, it had an obvious interest in ensuring that the charter reflected its concerns. The United States could not dominate the program, but at the same time it *had to* dominate the program. White House aide

Richard Goodwin wrote, in explaining the planning for Punta del Este to Kennedy, "there are more than twenty countries involved and we have to talk to them first to make sure everyone understands what's supposed to happen; otherwise we'll just end up with two weeks of speeches."[3]

Making It Look Latin American

It was easy to give the Punta del Este meetings a veneer of Latin American control. The Charter of Punta del Este presented the Alliance for Progress as an heir to Brazilian President Juscelino Kubitschek's Operation Pan America and as a product of the inter-American meetings in 1960 in Bogotá, Colombia. Before the sessions at Punta del Este, the Kennedy administration also went out of its way to obtain Latin American input. In late March 1961, Kennedy met with Felipe Herrera, the president of the new IADB (Inter-American Development Bank) to begin discussions about the bank's role in supporting the Alliance for Progress.[4] Conversations followed in Rio de Janeiro between Herrera, Goodwin, and Task Force member Professor Lincoln Gordon in April. These meetings also included two of the most important figures in Latin American development: Jorge Sol, the IA-ECOSOC (The OAS Inter-American Economic and Social Council) chief of staff, and Raúl Prebisch, the longtime principal intellectual at the United Nations Economic Commission for Latin America/*Comisión Económica para América Latina* (CEPAL). Prebisch, especially, had been important in the 1950s in encouraging Latin American nations to pursue economic policies that would lead to industrialization, and thus, along with Sol, was supportive of the Alliance for Progress concept. The April meetings among Goodwin, Gordon, Sol, Prebisch, and Herrera led to further sessions in Rio de Janeiro in July to develop position papers to guide the Punta del Este meetings.[5]

This was not the only effort to ensure that the Alliance for Progress reflected Latin American ideas. Kennedy's representative to the United Nations, Adlai Stevenson, spent most of June 1961 visiting Latin American capitals in an effort to develop enthusiasm for the program and determine what Latin Americans wanted. Stevenson, who had run for president in 1952 and 1956, commanded great international respect and was an ideal choice to serve as the administration's public face in the wake of the Bay of Pigs disaster. In the UN debate about the invasion it became clear that he did not know the full extent of U.S. involvement, which meant he obviously played no part in its planning. His lack of "tarnish" meant that he could still effectively represent the ideals of inter-Americanism.[6]

Stevenson found that Latin American governments had different ideas about the Alliance for Progress and the goals for the Punta del Este conference. In a memo to Kennedy he noted that the Peruvians "appeared to believe that the meeting would be the occasion for the cutting of an aid 'melon.'" Other nations, according to Stevenson, had developed shopping lists of projects they hoped the United States would fund. He reported that while some nations, notably Chile, Brazil, and Colombia, had created development plans, most others had done little.[7]

Though Latin Americans were involved in planning, and the Alliance for Progress was built on Kubitschek's Operation Pan America and the Act of Bogotá, U.S. policymakers made the real decisions on their own. Just a week after Kennedy's White House speech, Bromley Smith, the acting executive secretary of the National Security Council, produced an extensive planning checklist to get the Alliance for Progress running. Smith called for a prompt meeting of IA-ECOSOC and suggested detailed plans about the priorities for a new aid program, all of which Kennedy had mentioned in his speech to the Latin American diplomatic corps. Smith focused on the need for agreements on regional market integration, commodity price stabilization planning, and improving the quality of Latin American educational institutions. His agenda also called for the development of country-by-country plans to guide future efforts.[8]

Smith's key concern was encouraging self-help. The United States could only commit to plans that demonstrated a readiness to make institutional improvements and that promised lasting social progress. The United States would only work with nations pursuing reform on their own; otherwise it would be wasting its money. This concern also reflected the emphasis on allowing Latin Americans a measure of control over the program. The U.S. government could not know what was possible in each country, or even what was right for each country. This focus on self-help was remarkable because it was a sign that the United States understood there were limits to its power in Latin America—it was a rejection of imperial hubris. This is curious because as the United States was rejecting imperial hubris at the tactical level, the Alliance for Progress was the product of incredible hubris on a broader level. To imagine that the United States could make Latin America change simply by giving financial aid suggested a fairly confident vision of U.S. power.

Dillon's Big Financial Promise

Because money was the principal reason Latin Americans were interested in the program, the key issue at Punta del Este was how much the United States would offer. Douglas Dillon, Kennedy's treasury secretary and the leader of the United States delegation at the conference, never had complete instructions on how to handle this. Before the meeting, Kennedy issued a written declaration that the United States would offer more than $1 billion in aid in the year following the March 13 speech. Less than half of the $500 million promised by the Eisenhower administration would be included in this commitment. Kennedy's statement noted that this promise represented a threefold increase over appropriations in the previous year, and did not include the money that other institutions might offer Latin America. There had been discussions among administration officials about suggesting $2 billion as an initial commitment, but offering "more than one billion" seemed a safer, and perhaps more fiscally realistic, course.[9]

At Punta del Este, Dillon keenly understood that longer-term promises would be necessary. In a memo to Washington he explained that in numerous and lengthy talks with the Latin Americans, the "Single overriding preoccupation of all is [the] extent of U.S. commitment." Not every member of the United States delegation shared Dillon's belief that a big promise was necessary. Edwin Martin represented the State Department and suggested that offering a concrete sum was a mistake because Congress had to approve any spending. Martin, a notoriously by-the-book State Department career officer who would become Kennedy's assistant secretary of state for inter-American affairs, also worried about making statements without backing from Washington. But Dillon and Goodwin (who served as Kennedy's personal representative) believed that waiting for Congress or the State Department to authorize a spending level would be a mistake. The Latin Americans needed to know that the United States was willing to make a massive investment. Failure to make this clear would mean widespread and immediate disillusionment.[10]

Dillon made the big promise in a speech to the delegates on the third day of the conference. He noted that Kennedy had already pledged $1 billion, but emphasized that this was just a start. Using careful language Dillon explained, "Looking to the years ahead, and to all sources of external financing—from international institutions, from Europe and Japan as well as from North America, from new private investment as well as from public funds—Latin America, if it takes the necessary internal measures, can reasonably expect its own efforts to be matched by an inflow of capital during the next decade amounting to at least $20 billion." The Latin American delegates responded with delight, as this figure was exceedingly high, especially given previous U.S. aid. It is important to note that Dillon's statement was not much of a promise. The United States did not commit to funding the $20 billion alone, and aid would be contingent on the local financing of projects. The United States, as Dillon seemed to put it, would offer matching funds. Nevertheless, putting Dillon's legalistic language aside, that Latin Americans might receive $20 billion for development projects over ten years was dramatic.[11]

The delegates spent most of the conference drafting and revising the Charter of Punta del Este. Understandably and predictably, the text suggested an ambitious vision for change, but it presented few specifics. For example, one goal was to raise "the level of agricultural productivity and output and to improve related storage, transportation, and marketing services." The charter did not explain how this would happen or set quantifiable goals for the increases. In some places, the text did spell out more concrete ambitions. The most important of these was an expectation that "the rate of growth in any country of Latin America should not be less than 2.5 percent per capita per year." There were other specific goals. The charter called for an elimination of adult illiteracy by 1970 and for assuring, "as a minimum, access to 6 years of primary education." Another goal was to increase life expectancy at birth by five years by 1970. Part of the means to this goal included a commitment to providing clean water and sewage services to at least 70 percent of all urban areas and 50 percent of rural areas (see Appendix B).[12]

The charter also laid out a series of mechanisms for granting aid. It urged each nation to write proposals for review by a nine-member panel of experts. These experts, who came to be called the Wise Men (and they were all men) would be selected by the IADB, CEPAL, and the secretary of the OAS (Organization of American States). The panel would be part of the IA-ECOSOC and each member could hold his position for three-year periods with the option of renewal. The Wise Men were to judge national proposals to see if they were in accord with the Charter of Punta del Este and the Act of Bogotá. Their recommendations would be sent to the IADB and beyond to "other governments and institutions that may be prepared to extend external financial and technical assistance."[13] This meant primarily, of course, the U.S. government. There was also an expectation that the major international financial organizations, the International Monetary Fund (IMF) and the International Bank for Reconstruction and Development (World Bank), and other wealthy nations might become involved. The recommendations of the nine Wise Men were not binding. The U.S. government and other donors retained their freedom to control aid disbursements.[14]

Some leaders were initially skeptical about the Alliance for Progress as yet another in a long line of U.S. attempts to control the region, but more simply saw the program as a way to get money from the United States.[15] Perhaps most notable was the effort of the Uruguayan host, President Eduardo Haedo. According to Dillon, Haedo, who only had a year left in office, wanted the United States to commit emergency funding to him. Haedo threatened that if he did not get an aid promise he would walk out of the conference, which because Uruguay was the host country, would have been embarrassing. Dillon called this effort "pure blackmail," but had little choice but to accede. To satisfy Haedo, Dillon pushed into the charter a statement that the United States would make some aid decisions on an emergency basis. Though the charter did not spell it out, the United States used this mechanism to make a significant loan for schools, roads, and medical facilities in Uruguay.[16] While Haedo's scheming was annoying, it suggested that Latin Americans had leverage over the United States. If the United States wanted the Alliance for Progress to be successful, the Kennedy administration occasionally had to buy support.

Guevara's Challenge to Kennedy's Vision

Perhaps the most fascinating event at Punta del Este had little to do with the writing of the charter. The Cuban government, then still a member of the OAS, decided to send Ernesto "Che" Guevara to Uruguay to represent its interests. Guevara had been one of the leaders of the Cuban Revolution, and his presence provided much of the excitement at the sessions. Reporters followed Guevara closely. Watching a bunch of diplomats and finance ministers hanging around a beach town during the winter talking about "development" was not particularly dramatic, but the unshaven Guevara who, in his military fatigues, attacked the United States at every opportunity, made a great newspaper story.[17]

Guevara's presence at Punta del Este was doubly interesting because of his ability to counter the Kennedy narrative that the Alliance for Progress represented a partnership of equals. The Kennedy administration had set up the program to be, at least in part, a rejection of previous U.S. policy in the region—and at least in part it was. However, because the United States was going to control funding, it was still easy to see the program as a continuation of U.S. domination. The Cuban government most aggressively, successfully, and predictably made this critique.

Although Cuba was the only country to oppose the Charter of Punta del Este, Guevara received a fair hearing. In a long and rambling two-and-a-half-hour speech he applauded the desire of Latin American leaders to attempt reform programs and reminded the delegates that Cuba's government was also organized around the principle of improving the well-being of its people. He said that he hoped for peace and growth, but noted, "if there were not urgent measures to meet the demands of the people, the example of Cuba can take root in the countries of Latin America."[18] In making this point, Guevara indicated that he saw the connections between social and economic development and political change in the same way as U.S. policymakers. The difference was that for the United States poverty was a problem. It was an opportunity for Castro, who had previously predicted that revolutions would occur throughout South America, and for Guevara, who would ultimately die fighting to replicate the Cuban experience in the mountains of Bolivia.

Guevara was not without sympathizers. The Cuban revolution had been popular in parts of Latin America, and many delegates held deep concerns about U.S. power. Late in the meetings, the head of the Brazilian delegation, Minister of Finance Clemente Mariani, argued that Cuba was not an enemy of other Latin American nations. Cuba needed to remain part of the inter-American community, even though it obviously would not receive Alliance for Progress funding. Mariani's statements were just one part of a Brazilian effort to promote good relations with Cuba. On his way home, Guevara stopped in Brasilia, the Brazilian capital, where President Jânio Quadros gave him the nation's highest honor, the Order of the Southern Cross. Guevara also met with Argentine President Arturo Frondizi for long talks. These sessions were remarkable because the United States was doing everything in its power to isolate Cuba and ensure that Latin Americans saw Castro as a threat. Yet Frondizi and Quadros believed, as many others in Latin America did, that Cuba was not a significant problem and that accommodation rather than confrontation would be the best way to handle Castro.[19]

Guevara welcomed the Brazilian and Argentine approach and hoped that it could translate into better relations with Washington. At Punta del Este he called for a nonaggression pact with the United States and repeatedly argued that Cuba only wanted peace and economic growth. Given Guevara's statements, Dillon feared that the Cubans might actually approve the charter and request Alliance for Progress funding. This was a problem because although it would have been easy enough to reject Cuban appeals, it would have undercut the fundamental point of the charter. The Alliance for Progress was supposed to be a way to fight communism. The charter would have lost much of its symbolic value if Cuba signed on.[20]

Guevara also tried to improve United States–Cuban relations through secret talks. During the course of the meetings he determined that Goodwin was personally close to Kennedy and he hoped to use that connection to explain Cuban positions to the U.S. president. But simply arranging a meeting was difficult because U.S. delegates ignored the Cubans. After Guevara's first attempt to set up a meeting failed, a Brazilian delegate helped by inviting Goodwin and Guevara to the same party. Talking from 2:00 to 6:00 a.m., Guevara and Goodwin discussed ways to stabilize the relationship between the countries. According to Goodwin, Guevara offered a deal for an informal settlement: Cuba would pay for all the properties that the Castro government had expropriated during the revolution, would not ally itself with the Soviet Union, would have elections, and would not attempt to export its revolution throughout the hemisphere. In return, the United States would agree to stop trying to overthrow the Castro regime. While nothing came of the meetings, and Goodwin eventually had to testify before Congress to explain how he had ended up talking with Guevara, the proposals suggested that the Cubans feared more U.S. aggression following the Bay of Pigs.[21]

After talking with Guevara, Goodwin concluded that Cuba was extremely weak and suffering through a period of economic chaos. As a result, he recommended more efforts to topple the Cuban government. He suggested that the United States increase economic pressure on Havana by sabotaging industrial plants and forcing U.S. companies to stop trading with Cuba. Goodwin argued that the United States should engage in "frequent unpublicized naval maneuvers off the Cuban coast" and use agents to spread false intelligence about potential U.S. actions. This would make the Cuban government expend valuable resources on its military. He argued for increased covert action aimed at supporting anti-Castro groups in Cuba, and a massive propaganda effort throughout Latin America to discredit Castro. He also recommended following up on his meeting with Guevara, but only as a means for probing weaknesses and splits among Cuban leaders.[22]

Failure to Set Up an Effective Administrative Structure

The Charter of Punta del Este suggested goals and basic structures, but it did not actually create any organization to control and manage the program. Indeed, there never was any organizational entity called the Alliance for Progress. The failure to develop an effective bureaucracy to manage U.S. efforts was a significant impediment to the program. In the United States the management of the Alliance for Progress was lodged inside the Agency for International Development, which itself was an entity within the Department of State.

To run the U.S. part of the program, Kennedy appointed Teodoro Moscoso as the coordinator of the Alliance for Progress and assistant administrator of the Agency for International Development in November 1961. Moscoso, who at the time was U.S. ambassador to Venezuela, was an excellent candidate on paper.[22] A native of Puerto Rico, he had been the founder of the island's industrial development agency, *Fomento*, and the driving force behind the successful Operation Bootstrap. Through this program, in the 1940s and 1950s, Moscoso was able to wean Puerto Rico off its dependence on agriculture by aggressively promoting industrialization. As a direct result of his efforts, Puerto Rico began to attract significant commercial investment from the United States. *Fomento*'s efforts helped boost the number of large factories from fewer than ten in the early 1940s to almost six hundred by the late 1950s. Moscoso's acumen at marketing the island's advantages to U.S.-based firms and his ability to navigate between Puerto Rican and U.S. government officials were the keys to Operation Bootstrap's success and a model for Alliance for Progress. Further, Moscoso served on Adolf Berle's Latin American Task Force at the outset of the Kennedy administration, and was thus intimately familiar with the logic and goals of the program.[24]

Moscoso never got the power he needed to manage the Alliance for Progress effectively. He was subordinate to the AID director and to the assistant secretary of state for inter-American affairs. This setup ensured that Moscoso, the government figure most responsible for guiding the Alliance for Progress, had little clout.[25] The Alliance for Progress was supposed to have its own identity, but Moscoso's lack of power meant that it would remain subject to the whims of other bureaucrats.[26] He also had little influence with Latin American leaders. Plans about what projects to fund did not originate in his office and he was therefore unable to develop a commanding presence in the region. Despite his impressive title, Moscoso could not compel other U.S. policymakers to do anything and was unable to successfully pressure Latin Americans to commit to Alliance for Progress goals.[27]

In large part because of this administrative structure, complaints about the lack of movement in the Alliance for Progress emerged almost immediately. They continued throughout Kennedy's presidency. Though not the only target, Moscoso received much of the blame for the bureaucratic confusion, and eventually Kennedy concluded he had made a mistake in appointing him. At regular intervals Kennedy demanded to know why the Alliance for Progress was not moving forward, and Moscoso had few answers.[28]

The bureaucratic problems occasionally forced Kennedy to become involved in the minutiae of the program. A meeting on February 16, 1962, just seven months after the Punta del Este conference, between Kennedy, Moscoso, and other State Department officials turned into a heated conversation about what had gone wrong with the management of the program. Kennedy ended up spending hours reviewing Alliance for Progress loans. Seeing chaos, he pushed Moscoso to bring in more staff, even to the point of hiring temporary secretaries if necessary. In despair, Kennedy suggested creating a new, more powerful position to manage the Alliance for Progress. In a later meeting, without Moscoso, who had come off quite badly in the earlier discussions, Kennedy suggested that Moscoso needed a good deputy who would be able to handle administrative matters.[29] Reports of Kennedy's frustration with Moscoso leaked to the press, which led to stories in the media about the failure of the Alliance for Progress. These stories set the tone for negative media coverage of the Alliance for Progress in the coming years. Moscoso's reputation never completely recovered, which further reduced his ability to build a power base within the U.S. government. Though Kennedy wanted the program to be independent, he was not necessarily willing to allow it to become independent under Moscoso.[30]

While Moscoso may have been in over his head, the lack of movement was not necessarily his fault. The cumbersome mechanisms, and even more important, the lack of Latin American efforts to pursue reform programs (self-help), made progress difficult. All countries committed to submitting long-range development plans to the Wise Men as quickly as possible after the Punta del Este conference. As of January 1962, only Colombia had made a plan, but the Wise Men did not approve it until August 1962. By April 1963, four other countries, Chile, Venezuela, Mexico, and Bolivia, had submitted plans to the Wise Men, though only Chile and Colombia did much to implement them. Moscoso blamed the Latin Americans for the lack of initiative. In an interview he explained, "We are ready to move, but there is no sense in fooling ourselves that we are ready to finance the plan of a certain country that requires 80 percent local resources, when there are no local resources [that have been committed]."[31]

An additional problem was the role of the Wise Men. While in theory this group should have served to make sure only the best proposals moved to AID personnel, there was no formal mechanism designed to stop countries from presenting their proposals directly to the Department of State. Especially because the Kennedy administration wanted quick movement on development projects, the process of going to the panel made little sense. If the United States was going to make the loans, asking the United States seemed appropriate.[32] Indeed, Washington made huge loans in 1961, 1962, and 1963 to countries that had not developed long-range development plans or received approval from the Wise Men. In reality, there was little connection between aid programs and the Alliance for Progress structure. The Wise Men had only a symbolic role.

The U.S. Congress Gets in the Way

While inefficient and weak bureaucratic machinery was a problem, a bigger hurdle on the U.S. side was Congressional reluctance to spend money on foreign aid. Although AID could negotiate loans and top officials like Dillon could promise billions of dollars, only Congress could actually appropriate the money to make the loans. Throughout his administration, Kennedy was in constant conflict with Congressional leaders about the size of appropriations and the speed of their approval, and he consistently lost these battles. By far the most important of Kennedy's opponents was the chairman of the Foreign Operations Subcommittee of the House Appropriations Committee, Otto Passman (D-LA). Believing that foreign aid was a waste of money, the powerful representative repeatedly slowed the appropriations process and cut money out of legislation that came before his subcommittee. Passman and his supporters consistently argued that the president was being an irresponsible and reckless spender. It helped that foreign aid requests were easy to attack. Passman argued effectively that each dollar spent in Latin America or elsewhere abroad meant one less potential dollar spent in the United States.[33]

As its long-serving chair, Passman had developed a free hand within his subcommittee to decide what spending bills should reach the full House of Representatives. He also served as a key player in legislative negotiations with the Senate. Generally, the House of Representatives and Senate passed different bills on the same issue. To resolve the differences between the Senate and House legislation, leaders from both chambers would meet in a conference committee to work out the differences and write legislation that could pass in both chambers. In the meetings with Senate negotiators, Passman insisted on keeping spending down. Though merely a single representative from Louisiana, he was able to force the House, and eventually the Senate, to keep cutting aid bills. Part of his power came from Congress's tendency to put off discussions of aid bills until other legislation, perceived to be more important, had passed. This meant that often it became useful for Congress or the president to use changes in aid legislation as a bargaining chip to help other bills move forward.[34]

In May 1961, Kennedy asked Congress for a $4.8 billion military and economic foreign aid appropriation. Passman insisted on cuts. The Senate passed a $4.2 billion appropriations bill, but in conference committee negotiations Passman pushed the final total down further. Eventually, in late September 1961, Kennedy had no choice by to sign a $3.9 billion appropriation. This process was slow and created questions about the ability of the United States government to make commitments to foreign governments, especially since the 1962 fiscal year began on July 1, 1961. The same thing happened in 1962. Kennedy requested $4.9 billion in March, and in September, again after the fiscal year had begun, the House passed a $3.6 billion appropriation bill. The Senate had passed a $4.4 billion appropriation, but Passman fought the Senate hard, leading to an eventual compromise bill of $4 billion. In 1963 it was more of the same. Following Kennedy's request for $4.9 billion, Passman insisted that he would cut the bill by half. Not only had the fiscal year begun, but Kennedy was dead by the time Congress passed a $3 billion foreign aid appropriations bill. Passman's intransigence and his unwillingness to negotiate with the Senate, which had eventually voted on a $3.3 billion bill, kept Congress from adjourning on its Christmas break until December 23, 1963. Lyndon Johnson was more successful in dealing with Passman after Kennedy's death. To push the 1964 foreign aid budget request, a modest $3.6 million, he made an unusual and unexpected visit to meet the speaker of the House of Representatives, John W. McCormack (D-MA). In that meeting, Johnson indicated that if Passman fought his request he would attempt to push the battle to the House floor. This was enough to ensure that House leaders reigned in Passman. In later years, Johnson continued to be more successful than Kennedy had been in reducing cuts to his foreign aid appropriations, but he presented much smaller bills.[35] (see Table 2.1)

The cuts were a disaster for Kennedy's foreign aid agenda. In a dramatic statement about the FY1963 bill, Kennedy called reduction of foreign aid "a threat to world security." He continued, "It makes no sense at all to make speeches against the spread of communism, to deplore instability in Latin America and Asia, to call for an increase in American prestige or an initia-

Table 2.1 Cuts in Foreign Aid Appropriations from the Presidential Request to the Final Appropriation

Year	Presidential Request	House Appropriation	Senate Appropriation	Final Appropriation
FY1962 7/1/61–6/30/62	$4.8 billion on 5/26/61	$3.6 billion on 9/5/61	$4.2 billion on 9/15/61	$3.9 billion on 9/26/61
FY1963 7/1/61–6/30/62	4.9 billion on 3/13/62	3.6 billion on 9/21/62	4.4 billion on 10/1/62	4.0 billion on 10/8/62
FY1964 7/1/61–6/30/62	4.9 billion on 1/16/63	2.8 billion on 12/16/63	3.3 billion on 12/19/63	3.0 billion on 12/23/63

Note: In U.S. dollars; data not adjusted for inflation, rounded to the nearest $100 million.

Source: Data from "Self Help Policy Pegged to U.S. Aid," *NYT*, June 1, 1961; "House Restores Most Arms Aid Committee Cut," *NYT*, September 6, 1961; "Senate Restores Most of Aid Cuts," *NYT*, September 16, 1961; "Congress Votes Aid Compromise of 3,900,000,000," *NYT*, September 27, 1961; "President Urges Congress to Vote $4.878 Billion in Aid," *NYT*, March 14, 1962; "Rusk Bids Senate Restore Aid Cuts to Protect U.S.," *NYT*, September 22, 1962; "Senate Rejects Aid Cuts," *NYT*, October 2, 1962; "News Summary and Index," *NYT*, October 9, 1962; "Kennedy to Ask $4.9 Billion Fund for Foreign Aid," *NYT*, January 16, 1963; "House Approves $2.8 Billion in Aid," *NYT*, December 17 1963; "Senate Kills Ban on Grain Credit; Votes Aid Funds," *NYT*, December 20, 1963; "Democrats United But Fail to Force Show Down on Aid," *NYT*, December 24, 1963.

tive in Eastern Europe—and then vote to cut back the Alliance for Progress, to hamper the Peace Corps, to repudiate our long term commitments of last year and to undermine those who are seeking to stave off chaos and communism in the most vital areas of the world." He concluded, "The aid program is just as important as any military spending we do abroad. You cannot separate guns from roads and schools when it comes to resisting Communist subversion in under-developed countries."[36]

Congressional leaders were not only concerned about reigning in spending and preserving control over appropriations. They also were worried that foreign aid might hurt U.S. businesses. As Western Europeans and the Japanese were developing stronger economies in the 1950s and early 1960s, there was a fear that aid recipients might use U.S. funds to purchase goods from competitors. To stop this, Congress inserted into the Foreign Assistance Act of 1962, and subsequent aid appropriations, requirements on the spending of U.S. aid funds. Their laws stipulated that all purchases made possible by foreign aid occur in the United States. Moreover, at least 50 percent of the purchases made with foreign aid had to be carried on merchant vessels registered in the United States[37] (see Figure I.2 following 148).

These stipulations are important to consider because they help in understanding the aid process. While the United States government wanted to help Latin American countries grow through loans for development, the loans also served as a boon to exporters, the shipping industry, and others hoping to do business in Latin America.

For Kennedy, the rationale that aid would help the United States economy was vital in attempting to sell the idea that foreign aid was necessary. He argued, "American business needed to realize how important aid had been in assisting them" and that "11 percent of [U.S.] exports were financed under our aid program." As aid increased, he insisted, exports would increase. He asserted, "We are not giving away money, we are giving away goods ... on a loan basis which will be paid back and which must be spent ... in the United States." Kennedy continued, "Almost one-fourth of the railroad equipment exported by the United States was paid for by AID, ten percent of the trucks and buses sold abroad were sold under AID. One-third of the fertilizer shipped abroad was under AID contracts." Aid would continue to help U.S. business, he argued, because as countries developed and could grow without aid they would become regular customers. Kennedy insisted that aid was important in competition as well. He claimed that in some countries it had been difficult for U.S. businesses to bid effectively on foreign contracts, but because of aid, these businesses had become much more successful in winning contracts.[38]

To further make the case that aid was not a giveaway, AID regularly issued press releases on the amount of business created within the United States. For example, a statement from June 26, 1962 highlighted the earnings of ninety three New Jersey companies that received $57,042,722 in foreign aid spending from January 1954 to December 1961. The press release even broke down income by community, pointing out that some towns had received millions, and others, like Arlington, New Jersey, had received $342.[39]

Trying to Sell the Program in Latin America

The theory behind the Alliance for Progress suggested that the United States could not, and should not, implement the program on its own. In Latin American nations, both leaders and the common people needed to see that the work was worth it. To that end, the United States developed a significant propaganda effort to sell the Alliance for Progress. Kennedy administration staffers were keenly aware that merely lending money to Latin Americans would not create enthusiasm for the program and it reinforced the United States' role as the promoter of the Alliance for Progress. Although the U.S. government tried to create publicity around loan signings, this did not generate any groundswell of support. As Deputy Assistant Secretary of State for Inter-American Affairs Arturo Morales-Carrion aptly put it, even after Punta del Este and all the rhetoric about self-help, Latin Americans still saw the United States as a moneylender, and remarked that "no moneylender in history had ever evoked great enthusiasm."[40]

This vision of the Alliance for Progress existed even at the highest levels. At the beginning of a state visit to Washington in June 1962, Panamanian President Roberto Chiari said, in his response to Kennedy's welcome, "Being here in Washington [allows me] to wish you . . . success in your program." These words echoed Morales-Carrion, who said that the Alliance "still looks 'foreign' and 'imported,' it still looks as a 'Made in the USA' product."[41] This failure was also a key theme in a powerful critique of the Alliance for Progress by former Colombian president Alberto Lleras Camargo in the October 1963 edition of *Foreign Affairs*. Lleras Camargo was among the strongest initial supporters of the program, yet he came to believe that its failure stemmed from a perception that it was just a U.S. program.[42]

To attempt to create enthusiasm in Latin America, the United States Information Agency (USIA) tried to promote Kennedy's grand vision for the Alliance for Progress.[43] USIA used a number of media, including radio, TV, film, pamphlets, and traveling speakers, and planted news stories to explain how the program would help ordinary people. One interesting effort was the publication of comic books. Inexpensive to produce, easy to distribute, and with a visual appeal that might speak to a broad audience, they were an excellent medium for explaining the program.

A good example of these comic books was *Arriba Muchachos*. In this story, young students come together to convince Communist students that violence is not necessary to promote positive change. The Alliance for Progress concept would lead to a revolution without fighting. At the end of the comic book, a full-page illustration explained the basics of the Alliance for Progress using the Charter of Punta del Este. Other Alliance for Progress comics had stories about how the program helped communities, focusing on workers such as agronomists trained with U.S. funds that were helping people produce more food (See Figure 1.3 following page 148).

The counterpart to the comic books on the Alliance for Progress was a series designed to scare Latin Americans about the Cuban Revolution. In theory, if Latin Americans were worried about Cuba they would have been more amenable to U.S. policies. The comic book *El Despertar* told the story of Pepe and Blanca, two lovers facing the evils of the Castro regime. Pepe and Blanca had been initial supporters of the revolution, but they came to realize that Castro's dictatorship was even more insidious than Fulgencio Batista's. Hunted by Castro's agents because of their opposition, the couple escaped into the mountains to join anti-Communist revolutionary movements. The comics *Los Expoliadores* and *La Punalada* had similar themes that reinforced the message that the Alliance for Progress and the United States were, in the simplest possible word, good, and that Cuban alternatives were bad. The total number of comics printed was fairly large. For example, USIA printed 366,000 copies of *Arriba Muchachos* in May 1967 and 500,000 copies of *La Punalada* in May 1962. Cartoons were also translated into Portuguese for distribution in Brazil[44] (see Figure I.4 following page 148).

Films were also important. Nicholas Cull, a historian of USIA, has identified at least five films produced to sell the Alliance for Progress: *The School of Rincón Santo, Letter from Columbia, Evil Wind Out, Bridges of the Barrios,* and *Progress through Freedom*. Some of these films addressed themes of development, such as the Paul Newman–narrated *Bridges of the Barrios*, and others, like *Progress through Freedom*, were more straightforward explanations of what the program was doing. Though television ownership in Latin America was low, USIA also produced a twenty-six-part miniseries, *Nuestro Barrio*, to explain the Alliance for Progress. Initially shown in Mexico City in 1965 and extraordinarily popular, USIA later distributed it in sixteen countries.[45]

Another attempt to market the Alliance for Progress was a people-to-people program that linked various U.S. states to Latin American countries. Chile, because of its important role in the Alliance for Progress, was the initial target country and linked with California, which had areas of similar climate and natural resources. There were other programs between Idaho and Ecuador, Oregon and Costa Rica, Utah and Bolivia, Texas and Peru, and Arizona and Guatemala. The Partners in the Alliance program, as it became known, also sponsored the efforts of smaller communities such as Oakland County, Michigan, and its counterpart, the Colombian state of Valle del Cauca, and Pensacola, Florida, with Chimbote, Peru. The goal of this program was to bring expertise that may have existed in U.S. states to Latin American nations with similar problems. The programs had fairly insignificant results. Mostly it energized high school students, like those in Austin, Texas, who raised money to send a cement mixer to a Peruvian village and others in Arlington, Virginia, who raised money for a rural school in Peru. Other civic groups in the United States also became involved. The Boise, Idaho, Junior Chamber of Commerce sent four sewing machines to an orphanage in Conocoto, Ecuador. Though it is unclear how many partnerships were actually functional, there were plans for more than twenty.[46]

Kennedy himself did his part to publicize the program. He regularly touted the promise and successes of the Alliance for Progress in speeches to audiences that had a connection to Latin America, and often to those that did not. On his trips to Latin America—a visit to Puerto Rico, Venezuela, and Colombia in December 1961, a trip to Mexico in 1962, and a trip to Costa Rica in 1963—he visited a series of Alliance for Progress projects. The aim was to attract as much attention as possible to the effort. But no matter how much the United States publicized the program, Latin Americans still tended to view the Alliance for Progress as Kennedy's plan, rather than a multilateral partnership[47] (see Figure I.5 following page 148).

The Initial Problems Foreshadow Bigger Failures

From the outset, three problems made implementation of the Alliance for Progress difficult: (1) Kennedy failed to ensure that Teodoro Moscoso, the coordinator for the Alliance for Progress, had enough power within the U.S. government, (2) influential congressional leaders, most notably Otto Passman, resisted larger foreign aid appropriations, (3) and convincing Latin Americans that the program was theirs proved difficult because directions came from Washington. The last of these issues points to a fourth and much larger theoretical problem. As the preparations for Punta del Este demonstrated, the Alliance for Progress could not be U.S. directed, but at the same time had to be U.S. directed. In order for the program to live up to its idealistic goals, it truly had to be an alliance in which both the U.S. government and Latin Americans committed to respecting each other's priorities. This was almost impossible because most of the power, in this case in the form of money, came from the United States. U.S. policymakers could not, and would not, relinquish control over spending. The tension between these political and economic realities kept the Alliance for Progress from achieving its initial vision.

CHAPTER 3

Kennedy to Johnson
Giving Up on Idealism and Worrying
About Political Instability

The Alliance for Progress was in a state of constant reevaluation in the early 1960s as U.S. policymakers and Latin Americans bemoaned the lack of dramatic achievements and came to understand its inherent problems. One early fundamental change was a recognition that the United States needed to abandon some of its ambitious and idealistic expectations and deal with Latin American problems in a more practical way. Rather than imagine that the Alliance for Progress would guarantee positive changes by creating growth, U.S. policymakers came to believe that it should be used to influence particular politicians to adjust their policies. These changes continued and accelerated in the Johnson administration. The grand rhetoric remained, but few policymakers continued to see the program as such. Rather than the start of a revolution, it became simply a means to guide political and economic change in Latin America.

Developing a More Practical Alliance for Progress

In mid-January 1962 President Kennedy created the Working Group on the Problems of the Alliance for Progress, composed of high-level State Department and administration officials to study the program. This group, which included Coordinator for the Alliance for Progress Teodoro Moscoso, White House aide Richard Goodwin, Deputy National Security Advisor Walt Rostow, and Harvey Perloff, the U.S. representative on the committee of Wise Men, argued that reform was unpopular because most Latin American leaders could not pursue the Alliance for Progress and stay in power. Throughout the region, traditional elites who feared change remained influential and often controlled national governments. The elites worried, for example, that land reform would break up their large estates and give their property to the poor. They worried that tax reforms would mean they would have to pay more. In general, for those favored by the status quo, there were not enough incentives to support change. Leftist parties were not much help either. For the radical left, Alliance for Progress reforms would not fundamentally alter structures of power. They would be a half measure for those hoping for a revolution.

The Working Group argued that the United States would have to change how it thought about aid because of this lack of enthusiasm. Money should not always go directly to funding development projects, it could also help politicians establish reformist governments. The United States needed to focus on improving political conditions and helping centrist, pro-reform politicians take power. The Working Group did insist that when aid was given for "political reasons," it also had to have some "economically sensible purpose," but it concluded that the economic reason could be connected to change in the distant future.[1]

The Working Group also undertook a frank discussion about the limitations of the concept of partnership within the Alliance for Progress. They understood that the United States was creating criteria for development loans, and therefore essentially making decisions about internal policies of Latin American nations. It was not a partnership and it never had been. The members of the Working Group admitted that the Alliance for Progress had become simply another form of interventionism. It was not necessarily a bad kind of interventionism, but nonetheless it was interventionism.[2]

Using Nongovernmental Groups to Promote the New Ideals

The idea that aid should focus on creating political conditions undercut Kennedy's initial idea about creating a social revolution. It also meant self-help was not particularly important. If the goal was to get pro-reform centrist politicians into power, self-help need not be expected from the anti-reform politicians the United States eventually hoped to see leave office.

A second problem related to self-help became apparent as Latin American leaders resisted reform. The United States simply had to give money to demonstrate that the Alliance for Progress was a going concern. Failure to send aid would have signaled that the Kennedy administration had given up on Latin America. This made self-help less and less essential as the program evolved.

The consensus arising from a February 1963 meeting between Kennedy and State Department officials was that there was "no correlation between per capita assistance received by countries and their performance in terms of self-help and reform criteria." The State Department report of the meeting explained, "Indeed, the most irresponsible countries, those which get into balance-of-payments or other major financial difficulties, are the ones which have received the most assistance." The United States had developed a policy to "reward the irresponsible and discriminate against the responsible." Kennedy, of course, could not state this publicly. In the 1963 State of the Union speech he claimed, "Whenever nations are willing to help themselves, we stand ready to help them build new bulwarks of freedom. We are not purchasing votes for the Cold War."[3]

One solution to the self-help problem was to sidestep national governments and attempt to partner with special interest groups more likely to embrace reformist goals.[4] Among the largest effort in this area involved Latin American labor unions. Labor unions were important because if they were effective they could help in the creation of a middle class, which would likely back centrist and reformist politicians. To connect with unions the Kennedy administration worked with the American Institute for Free Labor Development (AIFLD), an organization created by the AFL-CIO to promote non-Communist unionization movements outside the United States.

In 1962, the United States government gave AIFLD two grants totaling $460,000 to train union leaders. Other funds went to union organization and to helping improve labor–management relations. Part of the goal was helping AIFLD-supported unions compete with Communist unions. In many Latin American countries, Communists had either formed their own trade unions or infiltrated others. Strong, well-funded and well-organized pro-U.S. unions would not only support reformist politicians, but could help fight the Communist threat. As part of this effort, AIFLD also received funding to develop a social projects division to help set up food cooperatives and assist low-cost housing construction. The United States also made relatively small loans directly to specific unions. In 1962, the United States sent $350,000 to Ecuadorian unions and $640,000 to Uruguayan meatpackers. Some of these small loans had very specific goals. A $400,000 loan to a Honduran railway union, for example, was for the building of 120 three-bedroom homes for workers.[5]

Along with labor unions, institutions of higher education became a target for the Alliance for Progress. There was an understanding in Washington that Latin America needed to have more college graduates, especially with technical degrees, to help ensure long-term growth. At the same time, policymakers believed that developing a positive influence on university campuses would strengthen the prospects of reformist and centrist politicians, or at least challenge the power of Communists. As with unions, many Latin American universities had become hotbeds of Communist activity, and Alliance for Progress programs were one way to deal with this problem. Internal State Department reports suggested that "Improvement in the quality and quantity of education can contribute powerfully to weaning students from extreme leftist philosophies if aid is directed to strengthening universities and faculties which have moderate political leanings." Thus, by concentrating aid on schools, political aims would intersect with economic ones. As with the greater program though, political decisions would guide spending. State Department officials insisted that the United States offer support primarily "to those institutions . . . which include the fewest far left agitators."[6]

There was also extensive discussion in the State Department about attempting to use Latin American military forces as agents of the Alliance for Progress. U.S. policymakers reasoned that troops, funded by Washington, could be put to work in a civic action role by providing services such as building schoolhouses and providing teachers to rural districts.[7] This initiative had a political angle as well. While there was no concern about Communist activity within militaries (as existed with the unions and universities), U.S. policymakers wanted to make sure that they retained close relationships with military leaders in case Communist political strength grew in Latin America.

Steps Latin Americans Did Take

Frustration with the pace of self-help, the lack of interest among Latin American politicians, and a willingness to seek out additional partners should not suggest complete failure. Although rarely as dramatic as the United States hoped they would be, most countries did begin some kind of Alliance for Progress program.

During the first year of the Alliance for Progress, every Latin American nation reported to IA-ECOSOC that they either had implemented a broad array of political reforms and new social welfare programs, or at least had made plans to do so. Countries like Colombia and Brazil were among the most ambitious, but they were not alone. Argentina reported that it planned to double investment in health services, that it would create a national housing agency and build 55,000 new homes, that it simplified tax codes to prevent tax evasion, and that it cut 200,000 unnecessary civil service jobs. The Peruvians reported that they had 21 new hospitals under construction, instituted new clean water programs, developed antituberculosis, malaria, and malnutrition programs, had a long-range housing plan under way that called for the creation or repair of more than 1.1 million units, and started to work on administrative and agrarian reform programs. Ecuador reported that it had begun studying water supply and sanitation in the country, created a national housing agency and had a plan to build 9,100 homes, passed a progressive tax code, and that it had created an agency to curb government inefficiency and manage administration of state funds.[8]

The smaller Central American nations also reported that they had been active in establishing Alliance for Progress programs. Honduras, for example, reported it was making a 19 percent increase in public health spending and improvements to thirty-one health facilities. It also claimed it had developed clean water programs and that an anti-malaria and tuber-culosis program was under way. Beyond these health programs, Honduras also claimed it would have its new housing agency manage construction of 1,500 units annually and it was moving forward with agrarian, tax, and government efficiency reforms.[9]

While many of these programs showed concrete results, other reports appeared merely to trumpet the virtues of progress and cooperation with-out taking any action. Repressive dictatorships claimed they were pursu-ing change, but were the least likely to do anything. Haiti announced plans to construct new medical facilities and classrooms, and claimed that it was discussing the creation of a new development agency. The Paraguayan government similarly announced it planned to create a national housing agency and that it would increase spending on health care and education. But these were just plans to make plans and did not amount to much.[10]

It is also important to note that in some areas problems were so severe that reforms and government projects could never solve them. In 1961, for example, the Ecuadorian government estimated that it needed 580,000 new housing units. The cost of these units would total roughly $1 billion. The 9,100 units they proposed to build, some of which U.S. money funded, would not have much of an impact. This kind of problem remained an issue throughout the 1960s and beyond. Even with substantial efforts made to improve conditions they often got worse because of high popula-tion growth. This is visible, for example, in the number of hospital beds per capita. Latin Americans constructed 151,670 new hospital beds during the 1960s, but the number of hospital beds per person actually dropped from 3.2 to 3.0 per 1,000 persons. One solution to this issue would have been making population control an element of the Alliance for Progress, yet Kennedy had little interest in this kind of policy.[11]

Tracking all the loans and grants made by AID or other agencies that distributed Alliance for Progress funds is difficult because information was not kept in a single place. But starting in September 1962, the OAS began to compile weekly lists of all new loans and grants, which makes it easier to assess spending. A sample from the January and February 1963 reports indicates the various kinds of loans and grants the United States funded. This list, reproduced in Table 3.1, demonstrates that much U.S. aid was targeted at helping specific individuals improve their lives.[12]

Kennedy's Attempt to Make the Alliance Work by Adding More Committees

Despite all the funding and some improvements in living conditions, it became obvious that the structure of the Alliance for Progress was not effective. In October 1962, IA-ECOSOC officials met in Mexico City to review the achievements of the Alliance for Progress in its first year. In preparatory meetings, the United States decided that a series of committees should be formed to encourage Latin Americans to, in the words of one State Department official, "promote as much responsibility as possible in each of the Latin American countries for the rate of progress in each of the others." These committees, or really subcommittees within the IA-ECOSOC, would be responsible for reviewing progress in specific areas and making recommendations for further actions. The State Department also hoped to create a supercommittee consisting of the former president of Colombia, Alberto Lleras Camargo, and former Brazilian president Juscelino Kubitschek. The purpose of this supercommittee was not necessarily relevant. The hope was that if these well-respected figures signed on, the supercommittee would be able to "strengthen the mystique of the Alliance for Progress" through the "virtue of their public stature." This was to be essentially a marketing device. U.S. officials insisted it was important that the supercommittee not be "given too much responsibility" because they could quite easily get in the way of technical experts. It would be important to develop with Lleras Camargo and Kubitschek, "very careful understandings" about the "limitations of their responsibilities."[13]

In limiting the role of the supercommittee, U.S. policymakers missed an ideal opportunity to make the Alliance for Progress more Latin American. Because of his efforts to promote Operation Pan America in 1958, Kubitschek had established himself as a regional leader in pushing for economic reform. Lleras Camargo had been a strong Alliance for Progress supporter as president of Colombia. The two could have been useful in organizing inter-American committees, and had they received the power, in pushing the U.S. government to live up the original ideals of the program. But U.S. policymakers did not want to relinquish control, only give the appearance of doing so.

At the Mexico City meetings the Latin American governments dutifully discussed and agreed to the U.S. proposals. They created six working committees with titles reflecting their focus: Planning and Project Formulation; Agricultural Development and Agrarian Reform;

Table 3.1 Alliance for Progress Loans and Grants Announced in January and February 1963

Country	Amount	Granting Agency[a]	Purpose and Other Key Information
Brazil	$1.8 million	AID	For a water supply project in northeast Brazil to develop and improve conditions in 58 cities; total project cost $3.16 million
Colombia	$60 million	AID	For general development projects; loan to be repaid in 40 years without interest (.75% to be paid annually for administrative costs), first payment due in 10 years
Ecuador	No amount specified	EXIM	For purchase of 200 dairy cattle and 400 beef cattle from the U.S. to improve Ecuadorian herds
Honduras	$1 million	IADB	For construction of 716 homes for low-income families in Tegucigalpa; loan part of the $500 million Social Progress Trust Fund
Paraguay	$2.9 million	IADB	For providing credits to small farmers to purchase livestock and machinery; total project cost $4.593 million; loan part of the Social Progress Trust Fund
Costa Rica	$765,000	IADB	For project to strengthen basic science departments and improving general studies programs at the University of Costa Rica; loan part of the Social Progress Trust Fund
Guatemala	$785,000	IADB	For project to strengthen basic science departments and improving general studies programs at the University of San Carlos; loan part of the Social Progress Trust Fund
El Salvador	$675,000	IADB	For project to strengthen basic science departments and improving general studies programs at the University of El Salvador; loan part of the Social Progress Trust Fund
Honduras	$350,000	IADB	For project to strengthen basic science departments and improving general studies programs at the University of Honduras; loan part of the Social Progress Trust Fund

Table 3.1 Alliance for Progress Loans and Grants Announced in January and February 1963 (continued)

Country	Amount	Granting Agency[a]	Purpose and Other Key Information
Nicaragua	$350,000	IADB	For project to strengthen basic science departments and improving general studies programs at the University of Nicaragua; loan part of the Social Progress Trust Fund
Chile	$35 million	AID	For general development projects; this loan was the first allocation of a promised $60 million in loans; balance of loans, $25 million, to come from EXIM and the U.S. Treasury
Panama	$9 million	AID	For general development projects
Central American nations	$310,000	AID	For publication and distribution of 800,000 first- and second-grade textbooks; all textbooks to carry the Alliance for Progress logo
Dominican Republic	$4 million	EXIM	For purchase of highway maintenance equipment; loan to be paid back in five years starting in 1965
Dominican Republic	$1 million	EXIM	For purchase of industrial equipment by small companies
Bolivia	$9.5 million	FFP	Food for Peace program to provide government with 4.2 million bushels of wheat to sell to Bolivian people; proceeds from sale to be used for general development projects; amount includes transportation costs
Bolivia	$9.1 million	IADB	For resettlement of 8,000 low income farm families from densely populated areas to sparsely populated, but fertile areas; total project cost $21.5 million.
Dominican Republic	$3.5 million	IADB	For construction of 5,000 houses for low-income families; total project cost $6.375 million; loan part of the Social Progress Trust Fund
Mexico	$1.2 million	IADB	For an irrigation project in the Temascalcingo valley; total project cost $3 million; 15,000 people to benefit
Bolivia	$2.5 million	AID	For purchase of sugar, aviation fuel, and railroad equipment

Table 3.1 Alliance for Progress Loans and Grants Announced in January and February 1963 (continued)

Country	Amount	Granting Agency[a]	Purpose and Other Key Information
Brazil	$3.7 million	AID	For improvement or construction of 769 health centers in Brazilian northeast; total project cost $8 million
Brazil	$2 million	AID	For construction of a synthetic rubber factory; total project cost $6.19 million; Phillips Petroleum to license factory and provide assistance; loan to be repaid in 8 years at 5.75%
Argentina	$6.7 million	AID	For construction of a 400-mile road between Corrientes and Posadas; total project cost $12.7 million; loan to be repaid in 25 years at 3.5%
Colombia	$3.3 million	EXIM	For purchase of machinery to expand a cement factory; total project cost $5 million; Allis-Chambers and Westinghouse to provide equipment
Bolivia	$300,000	AID	For establishment of a national industrial development bank
Bolivia	$200,000	AID	For design of highway from La Paz to new international airport and a customs warehouse; contract awarded to Stanley Engineering Company, Iowa City
Colombia	$9 million	AID	For construction of 6,000 homes; total project cost $18 million
Ecuador	$2.7 million	AID	For construction to complete the highway between Quito and Guayaquil; $13 million previously borrowed for project; loan to be repaid in 40 years without interest (.75% to be paid annually for administrative costs), first payment due in 10 years
Honduras	$12,000	AID	For construction of runway lighting system at Toncontín airport in Tegucigalpa; total project cost $35,000
Venezuela	$49,418	AID	For consulting services to industrial firms; contract awarded to Bruce Payne and Associates, New York City

Table 3.1 Alliance for Progress Loans and Grants Announced in January and February 1963 (continued)

Country	Amount	Granting Agency[a]	Purpose and Other Key Information
Paraguay	$1.3 million	FFP	Food for Peace to provide government with 20,500 metric tons of wheat for sale within the country
Argentina	$30.5 million	AID	For national road construction and improvement project; total project cost $690 million; loan to be repaid in 40 years without interest (.75% to be paid annually for administrative costs), first payment due in 10 years
Uruguay	$6 million	AID	For construction of new housing units; total project cost $27 million; loan to be repaid in 40 years without interest (.75% to be paid annually for administrative costs), first payment due in 10 years
Bolivia	$638,000	FFP	Food for Peace to provide 10,000 metric tons of wheat for sale within the country
Bolivia	$1.4 million	FFP	Food for Peace to provide wheat flour (12 million lbs.) and rice (123,000 hundredweight) for distribution as payment to miners; amount includes transportation costs
Chile	$5.4 million	FFP	Food for Peace to provide 85,000 metric tons of wheat for sale within the country
Brazil	$2 million	IADB	For purchase of farm machinery equipment, fertilizers and insecticides, seeds, and livestock by small farmers in the state of Espirito Santo; loan part of the Social Progress Trust Fund
Guatemala	$3.5 million	IADB	For construction of water and sewage systems in 25 towns; total project cost $5 million
Brazil	$3.85 million	AID	For construction of 8,500 low-income homes in the state of Pernambuco
Ecuador	$97,000	AID	For expansion of Central University; University of Pittsburgh to collaborate on the project
Ecuador	$2.54 million	IADB	For national rural integration program

Table 3.1 Alliance for Progress Loans and Grants Announced in January and February 1963 (continued)

Country	Amount	Granting Agency[a]	Purpose and Other Key Information
Panama	$6 million	AID	For expansion of the Panama City water and sewage systems; $2.7 to be spent on U.S. products; total project cost $7.8 million; loan to be repaid in 40 years without interest (.75% to be paid annually for administrative costs), first payment due in 10 years
Argentina	$22.5 million	AID	For financing home savings and loan associations and housing construction
Paraguay	$2.9 million	IADB	For loans to small farmers; total project cost $4.38 million

[a] Abbreviations: AID (Agency for International Development), EXIM (Export-Import Bank), IADB (Inter-American Development Bank), FFP (Food for Peace/PL480)

Source: Data from Alliance for Progress Clearinghouse for Information, *The Alliance for Progress: A Weekly Report on Activities and Public Opinion* 19, January 7, 1963 (Washington, DC: Pan American Union); also Vol. 20, January 14, 1963; Vol. 21, January 21, 1963; Vol. 22, January 28, 1963; Vol. 23; February 4, 1963; Vol. 24, February 11, 1963; and Vol. 25, February 18, 1963.

Fiscal and Financial Policies and Administration; Industrial Development and Financing of the Public Sector; Education and Training; and Health, Housing, and Community Development. They also created the Lleras Camargo and Kubitschek supercommittee.[14]

Kennedy met with the two ex-presidents in December 1962 and expressed his hope that they would focus on the idea that the Alliance for Progress was not "a US run or inspired undertaking, but rather a true cooperative effort that had had its inception with Operation Pan America and earlier aid programs." Kennedy stressed his desire that the Latin Americans "make a decided effort, singly and collectively, to improve their lot with the assistance of the United States, but never losing sight of the fact that the Alliance is basically a Latin American concept and reality, instead of being some abstract scheme imposed from the United States by remote control."[15] These kinds of sentiments demonstrate that Kennedy continued to talk about the Alliance for Progress as a partnership well after he supported programs that ensured it would not be. He understood that the supercommittee was a marketing effort, but he could not admit that to Lleras Camargo or Kubitschek.

In the weeks before Kennedy's death there was a second IA-ECOSOC meeting, this time in São Paulo, to review the Alliance for Progress after two years. At the meetings U.S. policymakers attempted to explain that they had done their part in funding the program, and echoed Alliance for Progress coordinator Teodoro Moscoso's earlier criticism that the fault for lack of movement lay with Latin Americans. Undersecretary of State W. Averell Harriman, who led the U.S. delegation, noted that the United States had given "$2.3 billion in development assistance to Latin America since the establishment of the Alliance for Progress in August 1961." He emphasized, however, that Latin American governments needed "to develop well-conceived and technically sound projects within the framework of the Alliance" for funding to continue.[16]

The solution was another committee, which emerged out of the Lleras Camargo-Kubitschek supercommittee, to help Latin Americans again see that the Alliance for Progress was not simply a U.S. program. Both Kubitschek and Lleras Camargo had prepared reports in advance of the São Paulo meetings calling for a new committee that would give the Alliance for Progress more direction. Most significantly, their reports suggested that this committee, which would become known as the Inter-American Committee for the Alliance for Progress (CIAP), should have the power to allocate funding. Kubitschek and Lleras Camargo wanted CIAP to wield power never given to the Wise Men.[17] Latin American diplomats discussed this idea in the weeks before the São Paulo meeting, and countries such as Chile, Colombia, and Venezuela vehemently argued for it, but Washington's opposition ensured that it would not move forward. While the United States hoped CIAP would have more power than the Wise Men, there was a limit. Truly allowing the Alliance for Progress to become a Latin American–dominated program was unacceptable. The United States could not give up its power to determine what programs had the highest priority or relinquish its leverage. Political needs trumped idealism.[18]

In a memo to Secretary Dean Rusk about the conference, Assistant Secretary of State for Inter-American Affairs Edwin Martin explained that CIAP "is designed to implement the Alliance as a cooperative development, and destroy its image as just another US aid program." It was to review country plans and "within the limits of what is available, it is to make proposals on the distribution of the totals of the external resources which each country can use effectively and meaningfully in support of its own development efforts." CIAP was driven by the ideal of Latin American governance of the Alliance for Progress, as the Wise Men has been, but as with the earlier structures, U.S. unilateral decision making limited CIAP's role. The São Paulo meetings essentially added yet another powerless committee to an aid program that was already laden with powerless committees.[19]

Johnson and Mann Focus Even More on Politics

On one hand, during Kennedy's presidency the Alliance for Progress was in a constant state of flux. Its mechanisms, leadership, and structure kept changing. On the other hand, there was a healthy degree of consistency to U.S. aims. Certainly the refrain that Latin Americans were not doing enough persisted, but more significantly, the Alliance for Progress reflected the political concerns of the Kennedy administration. It was a way to appear multilateral while increasing U.S. leverage over short-run, and theoretically long-run, conditions in the region.

Kennedy's tragic death and Lyndon Johnson's ascension to the presidency had great symbolic impact for the Alliance for Progress. It was Kennedy's program, but Johnson argued early on that he would be as committed as Kennedy to Latin American development. On November 26, 1963, the day after Kennedy's funeral, Johnson spoke to the Latin American diplomatic corps and the many Latin American government representatives who had traveled to Washington for the ceremony. The new president reaffirmed Kennedy's commitment to Latin America. He stated, "We all know that there have been problems within the Alliance for Progress, but the accomplishments of the past three years have proven the soundness of our principles. The accomplishments of the years to come will vindicate our faith in the capacity of free men to meet the challenges of a new day." Inspired by Kennedy's commitment to the ideals of the program, he promised, "we will carry out the job," and concluded, "Let the Alliance for Progress be his living memorial." Although Johnson my have wanted to fulfill this vision, given the close connection between Kennedy and the Alliance for Progress, he was unable to counter a feeling that it could never fully succeed with someone else at the helm[20] (See Appendix B).

Johnson did move quickly to fix some of the problems inherent in the structure of the Alliance for Progress. As Kennedy had before him, Johnson understood that the program was stuck in the bureaucracy and that a new administrator with more clout would be necessary. Throughout his presidency, Kennedy attempted to get the Alliance for Progress to operate more quickly and aggressively, but with few results. The bureaucracy was simply too cumbersome to move nimbly on vast plans that dealt with multiple governments. Just before his death, Kennedy wanted to appoint an undersecretary of state for inter-American affairs. This position would have more power than an assistant secretary, and Latin America would be the only region with an official with this title and authority.[21] Kennedy and Johnson knew that the extant setup, and the key personnel, including Moscoso, had failed.

Johnson asked Thomas Mann, who was then ambassador to Mexico, to take on the position that Kennedy had been considering. Mann became Johnson's key link in the Alliance for Progress. He served both as assistant secretary of state for inter-American affairs, replacing Martin, but also as special assistant to the president and coordinator of the Alliance for Progress, replacing Moscoso. Mann, who had served Eisenhower as assistant secretary of state for economic affairs, would be able to ensure that the program received the highest attention. Also, because Mann was not part of the original development of the Alliance for Progress and owed his position to Johnson alone, he could be considerably tougher than Moscoso. [22]

Mann, in looking at the program and its results, argued that U.S. policy needed to focus on Latin American political change. He was less idealistic than the Kennedy appointees and less willing to obscure the fact that the motivation of the Alliance for Progress was to fight communism. To explain this vision he convened a meeting of U.S. ambassadors in Latin America in March 1964. Tad Szulc, a reporter for the *New York Times*, reported that Mann outlined a four-point policy for Latin America, which soon became known as the Mann Doctrine. He argued that (1) the United States should focus on economic development and leave social development to Latin Americans, (2) it should protect private U.S. businesses in Latin America, (3) it should not show preference for democratic governments over nondemocratic ones, and (4) it should focus on fighting communism. Mann's basic philosophy was that economic aid dedicated to social programs would not create economic conditions leading to peace and prosperity. He believed that political stability would create conditions that would spur prosperity. These ideas were controversial at the time because they signified to some the abandonment of Alliance for Progress idealism. But they were essentially a step forward, albeit a big one, in how the Kennedy administration and the Working Group had hoped the program could push political changes.[23]

A concern that Latin American political systems were spiraling out of control in places like the Dominican Republic, Guatemala, Nicaragua, Panama, Colombia, Ecuador, Bolivia, Venezuela, and Brazil drove Mann's policy. He feared that instability in any form could create openings for Communists, and therefore the United States had to focus on short-term political conditions before economic growth. Mann's new policies did not completely abandon economic development programs because he understood that they were necessary. He suggested that the United States needed to give aid for a series of reasons; among them was that, in the absence of aid, other more sinister forces might offer assistance.[24] (see Figure 3.1)

Many Kennedy administration officials saw Mann's assumption of responsibility as a repudiation of the slain president's legacy. Arthur

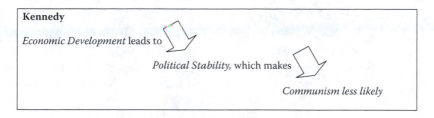

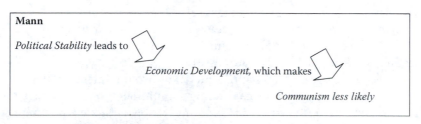

Figure 3.1 A Comparison between Kennedy's and Mann's Visions of the Alliance for Progress.

Schlesinger, a Kennedy administration insider, on hearing that Mann was taking control, declared that the Alliance for Progress was dead. Schlesinger, and others, were deeply offended that Johnson had turned over one of Kennedy's signature programs to an outsider. Ultimately many Kennedy appointees would continue to work on the Alliance for Progress, but others would argue that Johnson and Mann simply did not have the vision or capability to manage the program.[25]

Because Johnson understood the failures in effectively organizing the Alliance for Progress, bringing in an outsider who could push for rapid change was the best option. The program was directionless, and handing it over to another Kennedy loyalist would mean more of the same. Although Mann's appointment is important in understanding how the Alliance for Progress evolved, he was not the sole actor involved in making Latin American policy in the Johnson administration and he was only on the job little more than a year. In early 1965, Jack Hood Vaughn, an experienced foreign service officer, took over, only to leave the job the following year as Lincoln Gordon, one of the key players in the formulation of the Alliance for Progress and a former ambassador to Brazil, assumed the post. In 1967 Covey Oliver, another foreign service officer with experience in Latin America, became the assistant secretary of state for inter-American affairs. Mann did make changes, but those changes need to be understood as evolutionary rather than revolutionary.[26]

Johnson Markets Continuity

While Mann's appointment can be read as a shift in the Alliance for Progress, Johnson also took steps to ensure continuity, and more importantly the perception of continuity, in his Latin American policies. Beyond Mann, in May 1964 Johnson tapped Walt Rostow to serve as the U.S. representative to CIAP. Rostow had been heavily involved in developing the Alliance for Progress in the months before Kennedy's March 1961 speech and was a key player in formulating broader ideas about the role of foreign aid in U.S. foreign policy. As importantly, Rostow served as the chairman of the State Department's Policy Planning Council, and in that position, had been a leading figure in the Kennedy administration.

Johnson expected that Latin Americans would interpret Rostow's appointment as a sign of his continuing commitment to the Alliance for Progress and its high priority in his administration. He hoped the appointment served to offset the concerns raised by Mann's selection. On the day of the announcement, and as part of the effort to show his ongoing dedication, Johnson met a number of Latin American ambassadors in Washington to explain his support for the program. William Rogers, a staffer at the Department of State who handled much of the day-to-day administration of the Alliance for Progress, explained that the Rostow appointment was an opportunity to "try to convince the Latin Americans that we are committed to the Alliance for Progress." Rostow's involvement with CIAP did ensure that there was high-level concern for the Alliance for Progress, but it did little to either empower CIAP to become strong enough to create a new sense of purpose in the program or to shift it back to the kind of effort Kennedy and Rostow had initially hoped it would become.[27]

The Rostow appointment was part of a series of public and private efforts to demonstrate that Johnson had a forward-looking plan for Latin America. This use of the Alliance for Progress became especially important following the intervention in the Dominican Republic. The story of the intervention will be told in a later chapter, but it is important to note here that the landing of U.S. Marines in April 1965, in an effort the United States claimed was dedicated to promoting stability, was massively unpopular in Latin America. There were protests in a number of cities as citizens from both the left and center objected to the repudiation of the ideal of nonintervention. A series of governments, notably Argentina, Mexico, Uruguay, and Chile, formally and publicly announced their opposition to the military landings, and they adamantly refused to support OAS action legitimizing the intervention.

Given the public relations problem caused by the intervention, efforts to focus attention back on the Alliance for Progress seemed like a reasonable strategy. At the beginning of a June 1965 press conference, Johnson explained that U.S. intervention was entirely consistent with the Alliance for Progress because it was designed to fight Communism. The Alliance for Progress, to Johnson, though perhaps not to Latin Americans, suggested the idea that there were good and bad types of intervention. As long as the goals were good and supported the aim of fighting communism, Johnson considered the intervention a good one.[28]

Other marketing ideas followed. In July 1965, Johnson administration staffers contemplated an Alliance for Progress Week, during which top officials would travel throughout Latin America to sign loans and visit projects (some completed and some just underway). While it is unclear that much came from this idea, it was not the only one of its type. In early 1966, William Bowdler, a State Department official in the Bureau of Public Affairs, suggested the United States develop a "slick pamphlet" in Spanish and English containing Johnson's statements on the Alliance for Progress. Bowdler also suggested encouraging a friendly U.S. columnist to write a story on what Johnson had done for the Alliance for Progress, and pressing State Department officials to give a series of speeches lauding Johnson's record on getting money for Latin America.[29] In these efforts to sell the Alliance for Progress and promote the program as a way of shifting attention from the Dominican Republic, there was a consistency with the way the Kennedy administration understood the public relations aspects of the program. That said, these were quite small efforts compared to Kennedy's.

The Alliance Adrift

Maintaining excitement and energy within the Johnson administration proved difficult. At least initially, Johnson seemed to believe that aid to Latin America should be a priority. Throughout his administration he used Kennedy's terminology and often talked about fulfilling the promises of Punta del Este, but over time his focus on the Alliance for Progress receded. As historian Stephen Rabe explains, Johnson "did not share President Kennedy's apocalyptic vision that the Cold War would be decided in Latin America." It was important, but not vital, and certainly not something to establish as the centerpiece of his administration.[30]

Focus on the Alliance for Progress was also difficult to maintain because it was hard to say if it was succeeding or failing. A March 1966 comprehensive study of achievements suggested that while there were improvements in Latin American social conditions, it was not clear that the Alliance for Progress had caused them. Further, there had not been wholesale regional change, and in some respects there remained as much to do in 1966 as there had been in 1961. In reviewing the key elements of the Charter of Punta del

Este, the report suggested that in fields like agrarian reform there had been success in passing legislation, organization of governmental agencies, and planning of land redistribution, but precious little land had actually been distributed. Indeed, per capita agricultural production had improved, on average, only .8 percent annually between 1960 and 1965.[31]

In the area of educational reform, the report suggested that there were "attitude changes" as Latin Americans came to accept their public responsibility for secondary school education, and enrollments were up in the early 1960s. Nevertheless, in the mid-1960s, 50 percent of the population was illiterate and only 8 percent of those who entered primary schools completed secondary schools. Life expectancy in most countries was rising, and it was reasonable to suggest that the hundreds of millions of dollars the United States had loaned Latin American nations might have helped in this area. On the other hand, life expectancy at birth had been rising in most Latin American countries since the 1930s and its rate of growth appeared to be slowing in the early 1960s. This did not necessarily mean failure, but it may not have been progress either. In short, while change was happening, it was not obvious that the Alliance for Progress had much to do with it. Poverty, illiteracy, poor services, and ineffective government remained massive problems.[32]

There was a general feeling by 1966 that somehow the Alliance for Progress had missed achieving its idealistic goals. U.S. policymakers, journalists, and Latin American leaders all bemoaned its failure to achieve its potential. Reflecting this sensibility, and the lack of cooperation, the Wise Men all resigned together in April 1966. They stated simply that the Alliance for Progress had not lived up to the spirit of Punta del Este. Inter-American meetings became occasions for routine and predictable statements. A meeting of the IA-ECOSOC in Buenos Aires in March 1966 produced the rather bland Buenos Aires Action Program for the Alliance for Progress, which called on nations to do such things as "carry out concrete agricultural development measures" and "unify agencies responsible for public health programs."[33] U.S. government officials remained hopeful that IA-ECOSOC could achieve something, but they knew and certainly admitted to each other, that the body would not be able to do much.[34]

Economic aid programs for Latin America increasingly became less connected to the Alliance for Progress. Following passage of the FY1965 foreign aid appropriations bill, AID director David Bell reviewed the major U.S. spending in the region for President Johnson. In detailed explanations of $170 million in loans to Brazil, $75 million to Chile, and $65 million to Colombia, there was not a single mention of the Alliance for Progress. Even in describing $46 million in loans to other Latin American countries, there was no mention of the program. The aid was still there, and it was still significant, but the use of the Alliance for Progress terminology grew increasingly rare.[35]

Moving on to the Four Case Studies

To this point, discussions of the Alliance for Progress have focused on the bureaucracy associated with the program and the key regional issues driving concern with Latin America. Although the program was a regional one at the outset, broad discussions turned very quickly to specific countries and needs for economic aid. The Alliance for Progress was not implemented in the same way throughout the region. Certain countries became high priorities and others received very little funding.[36] Almost from the outset, U.S. policymakers viewed Chile, Brazil, and Colombia as priorities. The Dominican Republic became a priority later, and thus it is illustrative of the ways the Alliance for Progress changed.

By carefully examining the Alliance for Progress in these four countries, a clearer picture about the program will emerge. Most significantly, it will become apparent that the U.S. government came to envision economic aid programs as a foreign policy tool; aid was used as a means to promote U.S. interests, encourage friends, and punish enemies.

CHAPTER 4

Chile and the Alliance for Progress
Fighting Allende and Pushing Frei

From FY1962 to FY1969 (July 1, 1961 to June 30, 1969), Chile received $743 million in U.S. economic aid, 11.8 percent of all the Alliance for Progress money sent to Latin America. (see Table 4.1) It was the third highest recipient of U.S. funding behind only Brazil and Colombia. Chile was also an early target. The $165.5 million distributed in FY1962 was the largest amount sent to any country, other than Brazil, in a single year during the period.[1] The United States had two priorities in Chile during the 1960s. Both were political. The first was to ensure that Salvador Allende and his coalition of Marxist parties would not win the 1964 presidential election. The second was to help the winner of that election, the reformist Eduardo Frei, create conditions that would ensure long-term stability in Chile. Foreign aid through the Alliance for Progress was the means to achieve both goals.

The use of aid in Chile to achieve political ends demonstrates how the Alliance for Progress changed from being an idealistic program with a philosophy to simply being a foreign policy tool. In many ways the shifts in aid policy towards Chile conform with the larger narrative of the program. At first the United States faced a resistant conservative government and decided to use aid to help pro-reform politicians. Though it later helped Frei's reformist government, by the mid-1960s there was a declining will to remain engaged. As in most of the rest of Latin America, U.S. policymakers slowly let the Alliance for Progress fade away in the late 1960s. Because aid to Chile fits the larger trends so well, it serves as a fine control study.

Table 4.1 U.S. Economic Assistance Loans and Grants to Chile, FY1962–FY1969 (in millions of U.S. dollars; data not adjusted for inflation)

Year	FY1962 7/1/61– 6/30/62	FY1963 7/1/62– 6/30/63	FY1964 7/1/63– 6/30/64	FY1965 7/1/64– 6/30/65	FY1966 7/1/65– 6/30/66	FY1967 7/1/66– 6/30/67	FY1968 7/1/67– 6/30/68	FY1969 7/1/68– 6/30/69
Loans and Grants	165.5	68.8	111.8	125.4	111.3	25.8	82.9	51.5

Source: United States Agency for International Development website, The Greenbook (http://qesdb. cdie.org/gbk).

The Problem of Chilean Marxists

Chile stretches 2,630 miles along the Pacific Ocean. Long and thin, it averages only 100 miles in width, and at no point is the country more than 250 miles wide. The vast majority of the population lives in the center of the country, from the area around Valparaiso in the north to the Bío Bío River in the south, an area stretching less than 300 miles. Though small, with only 7,698,000 people in 1960, Chile nevertheless emerged as one of the more powerful and dynamic Latin American states in the nineteenth century.[2]

Following independence, Chile was one of the only nations in the region to escape the pattern of repeated civil wars and government instability that plagued Latin America. Partially because of its size, and partially because of an understanding of the problems that existed in other nations, the Chilean elite was able to come together to govern the country, and even to humiliate the larger forces of Bolivia and Peru in the War of the Pacific (1879–1884). There were internal conflicts, most notably the civil war of 1891 and a period of tumult at the start of the 1930s, but with the exception of these, Chile was stable.[3]

Political calm helped lead to economic growth, especially through the exploitation of the nation's extensive mineral resources, which then led to improvements in social conditions. By the 1960s Chile was among the most successful countries in Latin America. This does not mean that it was a wealthy country—it was not. It also does not mean that serious social and political conflicts did not exist—they did, but Chile had done well relative to its neighbors.[4]

Chilean successes allowed for the emergence of a vibrant and complex political system. Through much of the twentieth century, parties from the ideological right, left, and center competed with each other and developed short-term alliances to govern the state. The most powerful group in the 1940s and the 1950s was the Radical Party/*Partido Radical*. Like other radical parties in Latin America, the Chilean Radicals were not particularly radical. They were a centrist, middle-class party. They were also, histori-cally, a secular party opposed to the power of the Catholic Church. By the end of the 1950s the power of the Radicals appeared to be weakening as more ideological parties emerged.

There was a sharp increase in migration from rural areas to the cities in the 1950s and 1960s as poorer Chileans hoped to take advantage of bet-ter job opportunities in factories. Many migrants became attracted to the two Marxist parties, the Socialists and the Communists (*Partido Socialista* and *Partido Comunista*). Both advocated massive structural change and were critical of U.S. economic and political influence in the country. Other poorer Chileans, and many middle class and some wealthy people, became supporters of the Christian Democratic Party/*Partido Demócrata Cris-tiano*. A centrist party, like the Radicals, the Christian Democrats were more aggressive than the Radicals in calling for social change. They shared the Marxist goal of eliminating the vast disparities in wealth that existed in Chile, but they hoped to do so within a reformist, peaceful, democratic, and Christian framework. These groups competed with the parties of the old elite, the Conservatives and Liberals (*Partido Conservador* and *Partido Liberal*). By virtue of their connections to the wealthiest Chileans, these two original political parties retained considerable power.[5]

In the late 1950s it had become clear that the Marxist parties might eventually gain enough votes to take power. In the 1958 presidential elec-tion, their candidate, Salvador Allende, a Socialist, narrowly lost to a right-wing candidate, Jorge Alessandri. This demonstrated a good possibility that the country might soon have a Marxist leader. Unlike Cuba, where Communists took power through an armed revolution, in Chile the radi-cal leftist revolution could take place through the ballot box. This pos-sibility, which U.S. policymakers understood, made Chile one of the key targets of the Alliance for Progress. The country was not among the poor-est or neediest in Latin America. Relative to the economic problems that existed elsewhere it did not need support, but it was one of the most likely to become Communist.[6]

Alessandri's Resistance to Alliance for Progress Ideas

Implementing the Alliance for Progress in Chile was not easy. Alessandri was a member of the elite and had little interest in pursuing most of the reforms called for by the Charter of Punta del Este. He did not want more equitable distribution of wealth, nor did he support land reform, and he did not want to allow the masses to have greater political or social power. He did accept the need for more schools, hospitals, roads, and other infrastructure, but he wanted to ensure that change would not mean a loss of elite economic and political control.[7]

Though he was not committed to reform, Alessandri hoped for, and expected to receive, significant economic aid. In part, the United States response to a major earthquake in southern Chile in May 1960 conditioned his thinking about aid. In this vast and tragic natural disaster at least one thousand people died and the financial loss was well over $350 million. The United States quickly joined other nations in offering assistance. The U.S. armed forces airlifted field hospitals and staff, medicines, ambulances, jeeps, tents, cots, blankets, and food to the devastated region. The U.S. government also lent the Chileans ships and planes for rescue missions. In part, because the earthquake occurred just as the Eisenhower administration was reassessing its policies toward Latin America, Alessandri was the beneficiary of overcompensation for years of neglect. A week after the earthquake the Export-Import Bank opened a $10 million line of credit for the purchase of construction materials, and within a month President Dwight Eisenhower authorized a $20 million grant to the Chilean government. The Eisenhower administration ultimately promised a $100 million loan for reconstruction expenses in the earthquake zone. Alessandri's government received this money even though it had not made a commitment to reform.[8]

After Kennedy took office, and after the initial Alliance for Progress speech, little changed in Chilean moves toward reform. Although Alessandri's government signed the Charter of Punta del Este, it did not pursue self-help. Consequently there was little interest in sending new economic aid to the country. Policymakers in the United States, to the extent they focused on Chile, were frustrated at the lack of willingness to implement Alliance for Progress–style programs.[9]

By the end of 1961, however, Alessandri's government had begun to develop a serious need for economic assistance because of a balance-of-payments problem. The need to buy foreign goods to pursue reconstruction programs in earthquake zones led to a 45 percent increase in imports between 1960 and 1961. Imports also rose because of an unrealistic fixed exchange rate between the U.S. dollar and the Chilean currency, the escudo. The exchange rate made imported goods less expensive than domestic goods, which further increased imports and led to a draining of currency from the country. At the same time, Chilean goods became more expensive in international markets, and as their price rose fewer foreign customers were interested in buying them. The problem did not suggest weakness in the Chilean economy. During 1961 it actually grew roughly 13 percent over 1960; unemployment was down and the cost of living remained stable. Yet in January 1962 Chilean foreign reserves dropped to between $3 million and $5 million. The problem with the balance-of-payments gap meant that the country was running out of cash quickly.[10]

Economists use the term *balance of payments* to refer to the difference in monetary flows in and out of a country created by exports and imports. Countries that export goods with more value than those they import run a national *trade surplus*; the money entering the nation (akin to profit) creates a *positive balance-of-payments* situation. Countries that import more high-value goods than they export have a *trade deficit* and a *negative balance-of-payments* situation (a loss). This means that relative to its trading partners, a country is getting poorer while others get richer. It also means that a country with a positive balance-of-payments situation will accumulate foreign currency. A nation with a negative situation will lose currency. As in the Chilean case, a negative balance-of-payments situation becomes a crisis when a country runs out, or fast appears to be running out of funds to pay for imports. It means, essentially, that they are broke or will soon be broke.[11]

As this problem emerged, the Alessandri administration had little choice but to approach the United States for a loan because an influx of money could solve the problem, albeit temporarily. But there was little sympathy in Washington for Alessandri. He could have adjusted the unrealistic exchange rates and fixed the problem on his own. Though this would have been politically unpopular because it would have caused inflation, it was the best solution. More importantly, U.S. policymakers felt that Alessandri did not deserve special consideration because of his lack of commitment to the Alliance for Progress. There was frustration on the part of U.S. government officials about Chile. In a policy paper prepared in early 1962, disappointed State Department staffers lamented the lack of progress on reform in frank terms. The report explained: "Despite lip service by the Alessandri administration to the concepts implicit in the Alliance for Progress. . . . there have been no real achievements to date which meet Alliance criteria." Thus, the report concluded, without real change, "We should provide only the minimum of assistance to the present government."[12]

Using Aid to Make Alessandri Pursue Reform

As policymakers in Washington resisted Chilean requests for assistance, the U.S. ambassador in Santiago, Charles Cole, suggested an alternative strategy. Cole, who arrived in Chile in October 1961, had been the vice president of the Rockefeller Foundation, and before that the president of Amherst College. As an outsider, he was able to see the situation quite differently than his superiors in the State Department. Cole argued that the Chilean financial crisis was an opportunity for the Alliance for Progress. He admitted that the Chilean government had "done things it should not have, and left undone things it should have done," but because Alessandri desperately needed support, he would have to be much more amenable to moving forward with the Alliance for Progress. The United States could force him to pursue reform as a quid pro quo for aid. Cole also argued that if Alessandri failed, the Marxist parties would gain strength. Alliance for Progress funds could ensure that Alessandri stayed strong and the Chilean economy remained healthy, both of which would ensure political stability.[13]

Cole's suggestions appealed to policymakers in Washington desperate to see Latin American countries pursue self-help, and came at just the moment that Kennedy's Working Group was making similar suggestions on a more theoretical level. It was deeply frustrating that only Colombia seemed to be moving forward with an Alliance for Progress–style development program. Cole suggested that rather than requiring self-help as a precondition for giving aid, the Kennedy administration could grant aid to spur change. That is, the United States could give money in ways that would hopefully force Alessandri to pursue self-help reforms. Cole and the Working Group members saw that Alliance for Progress funds needed to be used, not as a reward for reform, but to impel it. (See Figure 4.1)

To execute the new strategy, White House aide Richard Goodwin and Teodoro Moscoso, the coordinator for the Alliance for Progress, traveled to Santiago in March 1962. Following a series of meetings with Chilean officials, they offered $120 million as an incentive to pursue reform. One third, or $40 million, of the loan would come from Food for Peace shipments. This program, also known as PL480, was a mechanism in which surplus food shipments generated funds in local currency (and it remains so today). In this case, U.S. merchant vessels would bring surplus grain to Chile. The Chilean government would take possession of this grain, sell it internally at market or below market prices for $40 million in Chilean escudos, and use the money for government spending projects. The procedure helped U.S. farmers by providing a guaranteed market for their grain and U.S. shippers by providing guaranteed customers for their vessels. It helped the Chilean government by providing funds, and to the extent that Chilean farmers were unable to provide enough grain for the country, it would lessen the need for food imports.

Program loans made up the rest of Moscoso and Goodwin's commitment. These types of loans were, along with *project loans*, the most important kinds of loans used by the U.S. government. Project loans were designed specifically to fund costs associated with a single specific effort. Funds for construction of new schools, hospitals, roads, housing, water plants, and sewage facilities all generally came from project loans. Program loans, in contrast, went straight to a recipient nation's national bank

Initial Idea	**Cole's Idea**
Reforms rewarded with offers of Foreign Aid	*Foreign Aid offered to encourage reforms*

Figure 4.1 A Comparison between the Initial Alliance for Progress Idea in Chile and the Strategy Suggested by Ambassador Cole.

or budget to help improve a government's overall balance sheet. Program loans, which only Chile, Brazil, and Colombia received, were also usually significantly larger than project loans. To ensure its money was being used wisely, the United States made loans in tranches. A *tranche* is a portion of a loan distributed at regular intervals following a review of the recipient's actions with respect to earlier portions of the loan. Most loan agreements specified that a portion (usually well less than half) of the loan would be made available on the signing of a loan agreement and the rest would be made available at three- or four-month intervals, assuming the spending reviews were positive. As part of the Moscoso-Goodwin loan package, the Chileans agreed to develop a more effective foreign exchange system. Failure to do so would mean that Chile would not receive all the funds possible under the agreement.[14]

The Moscoso-Goodwin agreement was a major victory for Alessandri; the United States agreed to make a large commitment to help keep his government stable. But Alessandri apparently failed to completely understand the message. In return for the loan he was supposed to move forward with reform. He made a series of promises to Goodwin and Moscoso, but did not follow through in any substantive way. Thus, most of the monies promised in the loan (the later tranches) were not released.[15]

Failure to comply with the terms of the Moscoso-Goodwin agreement led to frustration at the State Department, especially from the assistant secretary of state for inter-American affairs, Edwin Martin. In early May 1962, reflecting his disillusionment with Alessandri, Martin sent Cole a memo attacking the lack of Chilean achievements. Martin wrote that among all the nations he had to deal with, the Chileans were "the poorest performers" in the region. Secretary of State Dean Rusk agreed that there was "an urgent requirement for prompt and decisive action" on the part of the Chilean government to develop social and economic reform programs. Without such action, the Alliance for Progress could not move forward. Lack of Chilean compliance suggested to Martin that the United States should focus its energies elsewhere.[16]

Allowing Concerns with the 1964 Presidential Elections to Guide Policy

As Martin and Rusk argued from Washington for more Chilean reforms before making new commitments, Cole, in Santiago, consistently argued that the United States should ignore the lack of self-help and develop a more supportive policy anyway. Cole contended that aid was necessary to keep the Chilean economy growing and, more importantly, to help ensure political stability. In July 1962, Cole wrote to Martin that a real threat of economic turmoil existed, and that this type of crisis could weaken Chilean institutions and allow Marxists to win the September 1964 presidential elections. In asking for some change in policy Cole wrote, "You and I are going to feel a little odd if Chile lapses into economic chaos and . . . [the radical left] takes over and makes another Cuba out of Chile." The stakes were high in Chile. It was, according to Cole, the one country where the U.S. aid program could make a real difference in supporting democracy and stability. Cole admitted that "the Chilenos don't do things our way . . . [and] they are short on follow-through," but this, he suggested, should not jeopardize the whole program. Cole argued that even though Alessandri had not pursued reform, and even though he had failed to live up to the commitments made to Moscoso and Goodwin, the United States still needed to help.[17]

Cole and Martin had a difference of opinion that was fundamental to the Alliance for Progress. There was no question in anyone's mind in Washington or in the U.S. embassy in Santiago that Alessandri had failed to pursue reform and really did not deserve foreign aid. Yet Cole insisted the failure to offer assistance might be ultimately counterproductive to U.S. regional goals. The most important thing for the United States was ensuring that the Marxists lost the 1964 election. It would have been preferable if Alessandri had moved forward with reform, but that was less important than the immediate political situation. In short, anti-Communism should trump economic development.

In mid-1962, Cole's position about using aid for political reasons began to gain adherents. Walt Rostow, who initially had focused on self-help as the core of the Alliance for Progress, began thinking that a change in U.S. policy was necessary. In a telling memo to Ralph Dungan, one of the Kennedy aides most responsible for tracking the Alliance for Progress, Rostow explained, "Chile may prove to be the first real test of our Alliance strategy and at the moment the success of that program is subject to grave doubt. The burden of evidence suggests that tactical flexibility at the present time is essential to the realization of our longer range objective."[18]

Discussions within the U.S. government began referring to the 1964 election as the central issue in Chile. In a June 1962 memo, Cole summed up his major concerns: "leaving aside our many other objectives, such as prosperity and democracy for Chile, good relations with the U.S., etc., etc., it seems clear to me that our short-run political interest or hope is clear— that the FRAP [Popular Action Front/*Frente de Acción Popular*—a coalition of Communist and Socialist parties] should not win in 1964." David Bell, the AID director, put it similarly when he wrote that the United States would be "walking an edge" in Chile until after the 1964 elections.[19]

As U.S. policymakers were arguing for greater flexibility, Alessandri, still needing financial support, again began to talk more seriously about broad reform programs. He also began to intervene in financial markets in an effort to fix the problems with the overvalued escudo. He even pushed a weak land reform bill through the Chilean congress. Opposition parties called the bill *flowerpot land reform* because of its extremely meager provisions, the slowness in the passage of necessary enabling legislation, the limited funds allocated for payment of expropriated properties, and the Alessandri administration's lack of enthusiasm for implementation. Still, it was reform, and a step, albeit a tentative one, toward the Alliance for Progress.[20]

Alessandri was also able to convince Cole to push Kennedy to extend him an invitation to visit Washington in December 1962. During this trip Alessandri, who was highly deferential and respectful of Kennedy, continued to talk about reform. This more cooperative attitude, though mostly on the rhetorical level, combined with growing fears about the 1964 election, were enough to shift U.S. policy dramatically and make Chile a major priority for the Alliance for Progress.[21]

Abandoning Self-Help and Developing Impact Projects

Kennedy administration officials understood that in supporting Chile they were undermining key concepts behind the Alliance for Progress, but they believed they had little choice. A memo from Dungan's office in the White House to the State Department on aid strategy suggested bluntly that the Chilean development program was "essentially a fiction," but that in order to keep some chance for future progress, the United States "should finance on a massive scale those reforms which are essential to avoid a victory of the FRAP and achieve victory for a non-Marxist government." A program presented by aid officials working in Santiago, and approved by Dungan, began to guide policy. Under this plan, "designed with a definite view toward Chile's presidential elections," the U.S. government would fund programs that would have a direct and rapid impact on the lives of the poor, aiming "to prove . . . that their aspirations for a better life can become a reality under a non-Marxist government."[22]

As officials in the U.S. embassy and in Washington looked on, the basic contours of the 1964 election developed in the first few months of 1963. The leftist parties, the Communists and the Socialists, agreed in January that they would continue their coalition (FRAP) and run Allende again. The centrist Radical Party, with support from the right wing parties, the Liberals and the Conservatives, offered Julio Durán. The final major candidate, Eduardo Frei, came from the Christian Democratic Party. The U.S. government initially supported Durán, believing that he would be the strongest anti-Marxist candidate, but his campaign faltered and the United States began to support Frei.[23] This was risky. The Christian Democrats called for a "revolution" in Chile, and their goals were often indistinguishable from FRAP positions, but their commitment to reform within a democratic framework, and their ability to compete with the Marxists for the votes, hearts, and minds of the poor, made them appealing.[24]

To help Durán and Frei, or more accurately to hurt Allende, the United States began employing *impact projects*, a new kind of aid mechanism. Project and program loans continued, but they were supplemented by small loans and grants, generally less than $500,000, distributed by the U.S. embassy in electorally significant areas. These small loans funded projects such as the purchasing and equipping of a mobile health unit for poor urban areas, repairing school buildings, and funding a cooperative education program. Total spending on these impact projects was roughly $30 million, or one-third of all money spent in Chile during 1963.[25]

In 1964, the United States continued its strategy of using aid to help promote general stability and to influence particular key wards through impact projects. Some aid spending was fairly straightforward. For example, the State Department was extremely concerned about food supply and made sure enough PL480 shipments arrived in Chile during the pre-election period to avoid shortages, scarcity, and excessive prices. The U.S. government also tried to help Alessandri curb inflation, which rose in 1964 after years of relatively low annual rates.[26]

United States embassy officials worked hard to ensure that the Chilean people knew about U.S. support. Throughout the pre-election period, especially in June, July, and August 1964, they traveled to southern Chile to participate in ceremonies inaugurating projects made possible by the $100 million earthquake reconstruction loan. Prominent among these were openings of rural communities named after U.S. states. For example, in late June, officials from the U.S. embassy traveled to areas near Fruitillar and Casma to open the communities of Vermont and Kentucky. At these ceremonies, embassy officials distributed flags with the Alliance for Progress logo and Alliance for Progress comic books. They called these openings an "all-out national drive through means of all communications

media to publicize the Alliance for Progress and U.S. economic cooperation with Chile"[27] (see Figure I.7 following page 148).

The propaganda effort stressed that the funding had come from "the
people of the United States," and that this was done "within the spirit of
the Alliance for Progress." The embassy claimed that they ultimately distributed over 25,000 small flags, 55,000 lapel pins with the Alliance for
Progress logo, and 10,000 comic books. Efforts to publicize the Alliance
for Progress did not stop there. The U.S. embassy distributed films and
arranged for two large photo exhibits, one on Kennedy and one on Chile
and the Alliance for Progress, to travel throughout the country. They estimated that approximately 250,000 people saw the films and 770,000 people
saw the exhibits.[28]

U.S. involvement in the 1964 election was not restricted to aid projects.
The CIA became involved in extensive covert actions to ensure Allende
would not win. Part of this campaign relied on direct mailings, radio
advertisements, posters, leaflets, and wall paintings to scare voters about
a potential Communist dictatorship. The CIA also produced and distributed counterpropaganda, falsely attributed to the FRAP, "revealing" Communist "plans" for eliminating democratic processes following an Allende
victory. The CIA also sent money directly to the Frei campaign. Between
1962 and 1964, a secret U.S. government committee, the Special Group,
authorized the spending of almost $4 million to support Frei's campaign.
Although this funding was important in helping the Christian Democratic
campaign, it paled next to the massive economic aid the United States had
used to influence the election.[29]

The election on September 4, 1964 was a stunning victory for Frei. He
received 56.1 percent of the vote compared to 38.9 percent for Allende.
The Conservative and Liberal parties abandoned Durán, who ran a poor
campaign and finished well back with 4.9 percent of the vote. The failure
of Durán's candidacy, and the willingness of the Conservative and Liberal parties to back Frei, was the key factor in explaining the victory. Had
the Radicals, Conservatives, and Liberals joined in presenting an effective candidate, the non-Marxist vote would have split more evenly, giving
Allende a chance to win. U.S. support was not central to Frei's victory, but
it likely helped increase his margin. It helped the Alessandri government
create economic stability in Chile during 1963 and 1964, which likely made
Allende's radical critique of the extant system less attractive to Chileans.[30]

Policymakers in Washington were ecstatic about Frei's victory. Because
they could simplify the 1964 election into terms such as Marxist and anti-
Marxist, Frei's landslide could be interpreted as a mandate for the United
States in the entire region. Tad Szulc, a *New York Times* reporter, captured
this sentiment in writing, "The elections in Chile were watched here [in

Washington] as the most crucial test since the Cuban revolution in 1959 of whether the hemisphere was prepared to follow the moderate democratic way of reform under the Alliance for Progress, or preferred extreme leftist solutions." The issue to Szulc was "whether a Western nation would voluntarily choose a Marxist or Communist government."[31]

Supporting Frei the Reformer

Following Frei's victory, the United States increased aid funding to Chile. This occurred for three reasons. First, although Frei's margin of victory was huge, careful observers noted that in the 1964 election Allende had significantly improved upon his showing from 1958 (38.9 percent vs. 28.8 percent). The result suggested that the Marxist left remained a growing power in Chile. Second, the extraordinary spending in Chile in the early 1960s ensured that Washington would continue to view the country as a priority. Having spent so much to help the Chilean economy develop, it made little sense to abandon it. Finally, and most importantly, Eduardo Frei and his Christian Democratic Party appeared to be just the kind of pro-reform leaders that the United States had hoped for in Chile, and indeed throughout Latin America. Chile could become an Alliance for Progress showcase.[32]

Frei presented himself as an heir to Kennedy's legacy and suggested that they shared the same economic and political goals. To Frei, Kennedy was important because he understood "the different evolution, and the creation of distinct communities" in Latin America, but he also appreciated "the need to readjust international commercial mechanisms to help underdeveloped countries accelerate their economies." Frei claimed that Kennedy believed that police or military action did not protect democracy, but that it was ensured through an "internal conviction of the people that they exist in a system that permits a rational life and can lead to their own liberation."[33]

Frei said that just as the Kennedy administration represented the beginning of a new era in the United States, the Christian Democratic leadership would open a new age in Chile. As Kennedy represented a change from the old order to the new, Frei similarly believed that he spoke for a "new generation formed through a new way of looking at the world, and a new philosophy." Frei explained that he intended to promote sweeping change in Chile to "destroy the rigidities in a social order that does not respond to the problems of the moment, and to open to the people access to a culture, a responsibility in leadership, and a true participation in the riches and advantages that characterize a modern advanced society."[34] Frei called his program a "profound revolution in liberty and law," but it was also unmistakably the Alliance for Progress.

To achieve his goals, Frei emphasized the need to modernize agricultural methods and to increase output. Chile, at the time, was a net importer of food products, which led to inflation and rural poverty. Frei hoped to develop agricultural subsidies and tax breaks, create efficient marketing systems, and promote the building of new roads to lower transportation costs for food. To foster general industrial expansion, Frei proposed import substitution programs that would cut Chile's dependence on external goods. To do this, he suggested special credit programs for industrialists, tax breaks, elimination of laws that created bureaucratic hurdles, and support for loans to small businesses. Additionally, copper companies and other mining concerns would be encouraged to increase production and investment.[35]

Housing and urban planning also played an important role in plans for economic development. Shortages in acceptable and affordable housing had long been a problem in Chile, and low construction rates, estimated at 8,000 homes annually in 1960, did not help the situation. Dramatically, Frei proposed the construction of 60,000 new homes per year for 6 years. This would not only solve housing needs, but would spur the construction industry and create new jobs. The state would support home ownership with loans, flexible financing, and subsidies based on wage levels. To ensure these new houses were in viable communities, Frei promised the construction of shopping areas, parks, theaters, and schools. In education, Frei offered plans to eliminate illiteracy, lower costs for universities, and improve and expand technical and agricultural education programs.

To foster social justice, Frei outlined yet another series of reform programs. Most notable was a plan to redistribute underused and underexploited rural properties to new proprietors, and ultimately to create 100,000 new farms in six years. The state would also promote farming cooperatives to increase production and access to markets. Other proposed reforms included a change in tax laws and the implementation of a progressive system. The state would also increase the investigation and punishment of tax evasion and fraud in an effort to ensure equality. Frei offered a plan for reforming legislation covering labor and unionization. His government would amend the national constitution in order to ensure the rights of workers to a just wage, fair and safe working conditions, and collective bargaining. Finally, Frei also developed proposals for expanding public health services, controlling inflation within three years, and even limiting political contributions. All of these policies suggested that Frei would be an ideal recipient of Alliance for Progress funding.[36]

Frei's Need for Money and U.S. Support

Ideas were not in short supply, but money was. The Chilean government simply did not have enough revenue to fund the kinds of programs Frei envisioned. The Alessandri government had actually made this problem worse by creating massive debt. In total, during the period from 1959 to 1962 alone, the Chileans accepted over $720 million in loans. Of this amount, more than half ($372.5 million) went directly to the Chilean national government. Agencies of the Chilean government and the Central Bank borrowed the rest. The need to repay these debts taxed government resources.[37]

Christian Democratic leaders opened discussions with the U.S. government well before the elections to request support. In discussions in May 1964, and a second set of meetings in October, the Chileans explained that they would need substantial help almost immediately, and wisely posed their requests as part of the Alliance for Progress. Frei's representatives claimed they could double copper exports and develop their fishmeal, wood, steel, and paper industries. This growth would allow for more social spending and allow Chile to make the leap Walt Rostow envisioned in his *Stages of Economic Growth*. But for any of these dreams to become reality, the Chileans needed money in the near term. They hoped to reschedule loans of $100 million due to the United States and receive an additional $150 to $200 million in aid credits.[38]

State Department officials assured Frei that the United States would work to create a debt-rescheduling program, and even assist the Chileans in restructuring their loan repayments to European creditors. U.S. officials also committed to a high level of aid funding, promising to give at least as much to Frei as they had given the Alessandri administration. These discussions eventually led the United States to offer an initial aid package of just under $140 million. Most of this package came from AID program loans, though portions would also come from PL480/Food for Peace shipments, the Export-Import Bank, and other sources.[39]

The Frei program was an opportunity to prove that democracy could succeed in Latin America, and that although Washington supported dictatorships in places like Brazil, it had a strong interest in better alternatives. For the Christian Democrats, working with the United States was more fundamentally important. Without economic assistance and support, reform and growth would not be possible. The Christian Democrats desperately wanted to make substantial changes, but they needed time, and more importantly money, to make their dreams a reality.

Expecting More Political Support from Chile in Return for Aid

Though the United States was initially generous with Frei, by mid-1965 the close relationship began to deteriorate. During most of the Alessandri administration and during the first year of the Frei term, the United States focused intensely on Chile, but by late 1965, the Chilean situation appeared, at least to Washington, to have settled, and the United States began to adopt an aid policy that was ironically more in line with Alliance for Progress ideals and operating procedures than at any other time since early 1962. Unlike earlier periods, the Johnson administration began to require significant evidence of reform before giving aid. The concept of self-help, generally ignored in the Chilean case from mid-1962 to mid-1965, began to guide U.S. policy. Chile remained a priority and continued to garner a disproportionate share of aid, but policymakers in Washington began to feel they had the luxury of using aid to force Chilean leaders to follow U.S. economic advice. Johnson administration officials also recognized that they could demand Chilean cooperation on political issues in return for aid payments. Chile, simply put, was less important to the United States in 1965 without an immediate Communist threat than it had been when the elections loomed on the horizon.

In April 1965, still facing financial difficulties, Frei again looked to the United States. His government asked for $30 to $35 million and State Department support for loans of between $30 and $40 million from major New York banks. In explaining his needs, Frei had to admit that he would be facing a massive budget shortfall, and that if he hoped to try to carry out a reform program, he would simply need more money.[40]

Ralph Dungan, who took over from Cole as U.S. ambassador to Chile in October 1964, did not believe that these loan requests should be approved because the Chileans had not displayed the fiscal responsibility necessary to handle the existing loans. As importantly, they seemed to be wasting money on nonessential items. Frei began a campaign to begin purchasing new high-tech military aircraft Dungan felt were unnecessary for the nation's defense. Even worse, when Frei did have money to spend, he did not always look to the United States. In the early months of 1965, the U.S. embassy in Santiago discovered that the Chilean government was considering signing a contract with the Soviet Union to buy bus chassis. Even though the United States wanted to help, and hoped Frei would succeed, free-flowing aid would not be possible given these actions.[41]

The United States did not give in to Chilean pressure for a loan in mid-1965, but the State Department did begin to consider a program loan for 1966. In September and October 1965, AID officials started looking at Chilean needs and identifying what would be possible from a U.S. standpoint. This study led, one month later, to a State Department suggestion that the United States propose a figure of $80 million in aid for the coming year. Dungan, in Santiago, strongly supported this figure as high enough to give the United States significant leverage over the Chilean development program, but low enough to require Chilean self-help efforts.[42]

The $80 million proposal, though presented as a figure based on a comprehensive study of Chilean development programs, had less to do with Chilean needs and more to do with political considerations in Washington. In a memo to National Security Advisor McGeorge Bundy in the White House, Thomas Mann, who had become undersecretary of state for economic affairs, explained that his support for the $80 million loan "took into account the fact that the Chilean government was most uncooperative in the Dominican crisis." Frei had joined other leading democratic figures in Latin America in denouncing the 1965 U.S. intervention in the Dominican Republic. Mann recommended that the United States explain to Frei that "we expect cooperation to be a two way street and that we are very disturbed about the Chilean government's attitude towards the Dominican crisis." Mann wanted Frei to know that "the United States would not continue to make heavy sacrifices to help Chile unless the Chilean government would cooperate with us on matters we consider vital to hemisphere security."[43]

United States government officials with responsibility for budgetary issues also threatened the $80 million figure. William Bowdler, an assistant to Bundy, explained to his boss that a reduction of $10 million was possible and probably justified. The loan could enter the $60 million range, he suggested, before forcing the Frei government to drastically cut its 1966 investment program or force the Chileans to resort to inflationary financing. Nevertheless, a major loan to Chile was appropriate. The United States, Bowdler explained, could "hardly do less for a strong democracy like Chile than we do for a shaky constitutional government in Colombia and a de facto government in Brazil." Bowdler suggested that Bundy remind President Johnson of Chile's centrality to the "contest between democracy and communism" in Latin America, and that the United States had a "big stake" in Frei's success.[44]

David Bell, the AID administrator, argued that the United States should use the loan to ensure that Frei's development program was in accord with Washington's determinations about what types of changes would be necessary in the Chilean economy. Bell explained, "The U.S. must decide that, on balance, the government's forward progress" will be "sufficient to outweigh any specific shortfalls."[45] In making this case, Bell expressed a central change in policy toward Chile. The days in which the U.S. government was willing to support Chilean development without asking for substantial concessions or seeing evidence of reform had passed.

Deciding to Use Aid to Change Chilean Copper Policy

Before approaching the Chileans, however, changes in the world copper markets, concerns within the Johnson administration about copper supplies for Vietnam, and general worries about inflation in the U.S. economy interceded, shifting U.S. government ideas about the 1966 program loan. During 1964 and 1965, prices for copper began to move steadily higher, mostly because of an increasing gap between the supply and demand in world markets. Chile was the non-Communist world's third-largest copper producer (behind the United States and Zambia), and the Johnson administration became fixated on the idea that it could use its aid program to curb rising copper prices.

The Vietnam War increased U.S. copper consumption. Copper was a basic war good, vital to electrical machinery of all types, and perhaps most importantly, a key ingredient in gun cartridges. As the U.S. military became more involved in fighting the war, its need for copper rose. As a result of growing U.S. demand and turmoil in Zambia, prices, which had already been rising, spiked in October and November 1965. Rapidly increasing copper prices made the effort in Vietnam more expensive, but more disconcertingly to Johnson, appeared likely to have a dramatic impact on the U.S. economy as a whole. Gardner Ackley, the chairman of Johnson's Council of Economic Advisors, argued that keeping copper prices down was vital to the health of the U.S. economy. Ackley claimed in late 1965 that price increases in copper "have contributed significantly to the rise in the index of wholesale industrial prices in the past year which follows several years of complete stability. As copper prices continue to rise, the pressure on the nation's industrial price level becomes greater." The ultimate result would be increases in the cost of living and a potential inflationary spiral in the United States.[46]

The Chilean government had a measure of control over global copper prices. Some trading of its copper occurred on open markets in New York and London, but most was not sold on these exchanges. Rather, companies operating in Chile negotiated long-term contracts at a fixed price. This contract price remained relatively stable at thirty-six cents until October 20, 1965 when the Frei government ordered the two largest companies in Chile to raise their prices by two cents. Copper prices in the United States moved higher immediately.[47]

The Johnson administration hoped it could convince the Chileans to change their policies on their price increase. On November 13, 1965, Thomas Mann sent a memo to Johnson, then at his ranch in Texas, suggesting that Assistant Secretary of State for Economic Affairs Anthony Solomon and Ambassador-at-Large W. Averell Harriman lead a special team to Chile to talk about the foreign aid program and the copper situation.[48] Johnson saw no problem in attempting to use aid to influence copper prices. In a conversation on November 12 with Senator Mike Mansfield (D-MT), he fumed that the timing of the price increases was alarming, just as he was getting ready to call up reserves for Vietnam, and suggested that the United States could cut foreign aid to countries that raised the prices of metals.[49]

These discussions led Bundy to propose a combination of "carrots and sticks" that would persuade the Chileans to reduce their copper price. The biggest stick was the pending $80 million program loan. He argued that the United States should refuse to agree to the loan without Chilean compliance on a price rollback. The United States could also slow approval on $135 million in applications for Export-Import Bank loans to companies operating in Chile. The carrots, essentially, were the mirror images of the sticks—the program loan and "continuing warm political support for Frei on all practicable issues."[50]

Dungan, in Santiago, did not like the idea one bit. He noted that the "Carrot and stick combination . . . might, repeat might, succeed in forcing [a] . . . rollback," but "[t]he cost to the Frei government, and to the extent that it represents the hope of democracy and the Alliance for Progress in Latin America, would be incalculable." Dungan explained that the price "increase to 38 cents [was] strongly supported by all political parties and public opinion." The copper ministry top official, Javier Lagarrigue, was "now struggling against increasing pressure to push [the] price to 40 cents in view of [the] tight market apparently continuing well into the future. In other words, to force [the] Frei government to a rollback might very well bring the government down or so weaken it as to make it difficult or impossible to pursue the reform program on which it is embarked."[51]

On November 15, Harriman and Solomon arrived in Chile. In their initial meeting with Frei, reported in detail to Johnson and other top administration officials (Undersecretary of State George Ball, Secretary of Defense Robert McNamara, Special Assistant to the President Joseph Califano, Mann, and Bundy), they made the case for a Chilean rollback. They started by stressing "Johnson had personally sent [the] mission," and by explaining his fears about inflation in the United States and the possible repercussions to the global economy. They explained that "Johnson feels Chile [is] the bellwether: If Chile brings [the] price back to 36 cents [a] price rise can be prevented." Frei's cooperation was thus necessary to help protect the world economy.[52]

Frei and his staff understood that their financial future was linked to economic aid from the United States, and that without cooperation from the Johnson administration, obtaining sizeable loans was unlikely. The

Chileans had little choice but to act. Frei agreed to cut the price of copper, but only as far as shipments to the United States were concerned. The United States, in turn, would add $10 million to the 1966 program loan, to total $90 million, and would follow through on its other promises of support.[53] Harriman, betraying an understanding of the pressure he had brought to bear, wrote to Johnson "Frei agreed to [the] copper price rollback in spite of serious domestic political difficulties because he clearly appreciates [the] importance to Chile and himself of [the] good will of the president of the U.S. . . . . [Frei] is realistic enough to know that Chile's future depends on [the] U.S."[54]

Pushing Stabilization Programs

The rollback and the commitment to additional funding did not solve Frei's problem because there had been no agreement on the terms of the program loan and U.S. policymakers were not inclined to sign it quickly. Following the Harriman and Solomon mission, U.S. policymakers insisted on a series of changes to the Chilean budget that limited Frei's ability to set fiscal policy, leading to a contentious few months of negotiation. The talks over the 1966 program loan are important because they demonstrate how U.S. ideas about the economic theories behind the Alliance for Progress had changed.

In talks about the 1966 loan, the State Department increasingly focused on encouraging economic stabilization rather than structural development. In Chile, because of the focus on the 1964 election and its aftermath, this shift happened rather late compared to other countries. By late 1965, the kinds of policies U.S. government officials began to encourage in Chile were already central to Washington's broader understanding of what was best for Latin American growth elsewhere.

Initially, the economic theory guiding the Alliance for Progress was that government spending would encourage growth in two ways. First, it would create the structures that would allow for long-term development. By constructing schools, roads, power generation facilities, hospitals, and other infrastructure, nations would have the basic framework upon which a sophisticated economy could grow. Second, government spending would also create jobs and help stagnant economies grow. In this way it relied upon theories developed by John Maynard Keynes, the English economist. Keynes's ideas, often referred to as "pump priming," suggested that putting money into circulation by creating government-sponsored projects would give individuals money (salaries) that would be spent on local goods. This would encourage production and growth. In large part, this theory guided the U.S. government during the New Deal, making it appealing as a strategy for dealing with poverty elsewhere.

These kinds of ideas were attractive to Latin Americans who believed in *structuralism* and *dependency theory*, both of which were popular during the 1950s and 1960s. Dependency theorists argued that Latin America was poor as a result of the history of colonial trade. Because Latin Americans exported inexpensive goods to Europe (raw materials) and imported costly ones (finished goods), the terms of trade kept the region undeveloped. Further, as with other regions, Europeans had colonized Latin America in the hopes of making Europe rather than the colonized areas prosper, and limited technological transfers in the hopes that locals would not be able to compete with them. Latin Americans, at the moment of independence were poorer than Europeans and could not catch up.

Structuralists, led by economists working at the United Nations Economic Commission for Latin America/*Comisión Económica para América Latina*, most notably Raúl Prebish, suggested that the solution would be to develop internal markets and production facilities. They agreed that government construction projects could create the foundation on which a developed economy could grow. They also advocated policies designed to promote import-substitution-industrialization (ISI). If Latin Americans could cut imports, generally by manipulating tariff and exchange rates to make them more expensive, local manufacturers could produce those goods. Consumers would substitute the consumption of internally produced items for externally produced ones, which would create local industrialization.

Policymakers in the United States, though initially attracted to structuralism, instead began to push *stabilization* programs as the Alliance for Progress evolved. In some places in Latin America this shift started as early as 1962; in Chile it was significantly later. Stabilization programs focused on the idea that economic growth was contingent on the existence of favorable investment conditions, these included low levels of inflation, balanced government budgets, and open markets. (See Figure 4.2)

The IMF was central in pushing the United States to change its policies. Founded to ensure stable currency transfers and thus facilitate international trade, the IMF put a premium on limiting inflationary policies in the developing world. IMF economists believed that extensive government spending led to inflation, so in return for help they required that governments give up development projects.[55] U.S. policymakers did not completely abandon structuralism and continued to encourage construction projects, but funding for them had to occur in ways that would not lead to increases in government expenditures.

Using Aid to Control Frei's Budget

The U.S. government entered negotiations over the terms of the 1966 loan focused on IMF concerns about government spending. IMF officials had suggested that Frei's administration, in the name of stabilization, should limit public sector investment, balance government deficits, and work to improve the balance-of-payments situation. A major concern was the use of Central Bank funds to support government spending. To the IMF, this was dangerous because it would increase funds in circulation and lead to inflation.[56] U.S. policymakers also objected to a planned 25 percent wage increase package for public employees. This wage increase would help keep salaries in line with cost-of-living changes and provide a marginal real wage raise, but could ultimately lead to inflation. To Dungan, the spending plan did not comply with the "the philosophy of the Alliance for Progress." Program loan funds could not be spent irresponsibly.[57]

Frei's economic advisors did not necessarily reject United States and IMF positions; they recognized that adopting plans to cut spending could lead to greater stability, increased investment, and a growth in national production. But they also knew that the government needed to improve basic social services such as education, housing, and health care. Spending on these priorities was the only way that Chileans could be successful in meeting the social objectives of the Alliance for Progress. However, U.S. policymakers, even though they understood the Chilean position and had supported social development spending in the past, still pushed hard for a budget that emphasized fiscal priorities.[58]

Structuralism
Government spending on infrastructure will create conditions that will lead to growth. Aggressive government spending is necessary. Connected to Keynes, Dependency Theorists, and CEPAL.

Stabilization
Low inflation and an attractive investment climate will create conditions that will lead to growth. Government spending should be limited.
Connected to The IMF and World Bank

Figure 4.2 Structuralism Versus Stabilization.

It is important to note that the shift in economic policy improved the prospects for U.S. commercial interests. As Dungan put it, "a major objective of [the] U.S. negotiating team has been" to develop "financial incentives for aid-financed U.S. exports to Chile." In the years leading up to 1966, just under 50 percent of all goods imported by Chile came from the United States, but taking advantage of the "significant opportunity to U.S. exporters to increase their share of the Chilean market" offered by the program loan, State Department officials hoped this figure could reach close to 65 percent.[59]

The Chileans found the U.S. position bewildering. It demonstrated that the United States was not paying attention to the dramatic achievements and self-help programs the Frei government had undertaken, which according to the Chilean ambassador in Washington, Radomiro Tomic, confirmed "the sincerity and singleness of purpose" in its commitment to reform. Tomic argued that the United States, where Chile was concerned, was "less understanding now than it was a year ago in spite of the fact that a year ago the United States had to accept them [i.e. promises] on faith alone. Now that they had demonstrated their ability to perform, [and] now that they had achieved significant progress" the United States was "less sympathetic." Tomic also reminded Jack Hood Vaughn, who had become the assistant secretary of state for inter-American affairs, that the Chileans had bent over backwards to accommodate the United States on the copper rollback. Tomic noted that the Chilean sacrifices on copper prices indicated a willingness to understand U.S. problems, but this position seemed to be a one-way street.[60]

The problems in finding a compromise position between the United States and the Chileans stalled the program loan arrangements. In a meeting on the issue in January 1966 with Dungan, Frei signaled his growing frustration about the U.S. position and his realization that his dependency on foreign loans limited his control over his own government. At one point in the conversation Frei agonized, "I hope that no president of Chile ever is [again] in the position in which I find myself. I speak to my country about our dignified position though small and weak, but in my heart I know this is not true." He continued, "I have no dignity. I am a mendicant." Frei then continued to speak with understanding about a recent speech by Socialist Senator Carlos Altimirano, in which he "talked about the U.S. having its knees at the throat of Chile." Frei empathized with this position because he could not understand the U.S. stance, and claimed that "certainly no politician in Chile could . . . [appreciate] why the United States should be inflexible on [a] program loan with a small democratic country trying its best to follow commonly agreed economic policies." The Chileans were doing their part by "following reasonable policies with respect to copper prices in the interests of others," but this flexibility was not returned by the United States. Ultimately the Chilean government had little choice but to present a budget that reflected U.S. and IMF concerns.[61]

Frei Becomes More Nationalistic in Response to Aid Pressure

For Frei, the taking of foreign aid changed his understanding of U.S.–Chilean relations. In a major speech later in 1966, Frei argued, "When shall we really be independent? When we don't have to ask for loans for our development." Frei had come to believe that Chile, if it were to develop true economic independence, which of course meant independence to set budget priorities and other policies, needed to stop taking loans. Though Frei did not fully explain to the public that during 1966 loan negotiation processes the United States had essentially vetoed his budget, an understanding of the events of January make the reasons for the speech apparent.[62]

Frei continued to be critical of the United States. Most notably he wrote an essay in the prestigious journal *Foreign Affairs*, "The Alliance That Lost Its Way," which sharply criticized the Alliance for Progress. Unsurprisingly, the problem with aid relationships Frei found most disappointing was the lack of mutual cooperation. He wrote, "It is unnecessary to point out names and dates, but at some stage the imaginative, dynamic commitment of countries united in a common ideal was gone." Aid programs were not coordinated between states with shared goals in large part because there was no guidance or leadership behind the Alliance for Progress.[63]

Copper provided the key means for Frei to escape the dependence on foreign aid. Through a series of complex financial maneuvers, Frei was able to gain greater control over the assets of the two major U.S. mining firms active in Chile—Anaconda and Kennecott. His ultimate goal was not only greater Chilean control, but also expansion of their operations and greater output. The U.S. government was actually quite supportive of these plans. Frei's program would increase government revenues and obviate the need for continued foreign aid. As importantly, U.S. policymakers understood that the copper mines, and their U.S. ownership, provided a powerful rallying call for Chilean Marxists angry about economic dependence. Even copper company executives came to support greater Chilean ownership, as long as they received adequate payment. They understood that if a leftist government in Chile did take over, it would likely expropriate their properties without much compensation.[64]

As 1966 continued, copper prices remained high. This allowed Frei to follow through on his ideas about economic independence. In a December 24, 1966 Christmas message he announced, dramatically, that because of the high copper prices, no more foreign loans would be necessary or requested.[65]

Pushing to Retry Pre-1964 Aid Policy to Fight Allende Again

Unfortunately for Frei, copper prices peaked in 1966 and began to drop precipitously in 1967. This cut his government's revenues, and once again he faced budgetary problems. He had little choice but to again ask the United States for foreign aid in 1968. There was support in the U.S. government for helping Frei, especially as Allende and the Marxist parties remained powerful. Chilean congressional elections, scheduled for March 1969, and the presidential elections in September 1970, loomed as opportunities for the far left to take control of the government.[66] As a result, in late 1960s, the dynamics of the U.S. aid relationship with Chile began to echo the 1962 to 1964 period. There was a notable difference, however. While some U.S. policymakers, most significantly Edward Korry, who replaced Dungan as U.S. ambassador in August 1967, focused on the need to help promote stability, his concerns failed to resonate as loudly as they had in the early 1960s.

Frei's request for U.S. financial aid led Korry to lobby AID officials in Washington for a new program loan. He explained in mid-June 1968 that "a serious . . . budgetary problem exists" caused by a drop in copper revenues, and that without U.S. action there would be a balance-of-payments deficit in 1969. If the Frei government tried to solve this problem by increasing borrowing from the Central Bank, it would lead to inflation, and as a result, general political instability. This would strengthen Frei's opponents, especially the Marxist parties.[67]

Here, Korry used much the same logic as Cole had in 1962. According to Korry, "The total . . . aspect of U.S. relations with Chile requires that our aid" be dedicated to political conditions. Frei, however, had done much better than Alessandri in pursuing acceptable economic policies. Korry argued, "Whatever its shortcomings have been . . . in terms of excessive government expansion, the Frei government has moved in a direction which U.S. policy should support. It has vastly expanded popular participation in the democratic processes of the country, stressed education and agricultural reform, raised taxes, relied less on foreign credits for its budget, [and] tried at a heavy political cost (albeit without success) to moderate excessive wage increases." Thus, the Chileans had met Alliance for Progress criteria and "earned U.S. support" to the extent that funds were available.[68]

The response to Korry's call for a new program loan was generally well received in the State Department. Covey T. Oliver, the assistant secretary of state for inter-American affairs during this period, indicated almost immediately that he was willing to support the idea and would take Korry's case to higher authorities.[69] To provide Oliver with further ammunition, Korry fired off yet another memo to argue that inflation, and its effects, were the central "overriding issue on the Chilean scene," and that the U.S. loan could have an impact on Frei, keeping him from pursuing inflationary policies. Korry stated flatly, "I am absolutely certain in my own mind that if the Christian Democrats enter the 1969 congressional elections with a massive rate of inflation, they will do badly; that if inflation is more or less out of hand when they enter the 1970 presidential election, the left or the right or both will reap the benefit." Rhetorically, to Korry, controlling inflation would be "primordial." Korry argued, "The program loan can serve a balance of payments and government investment purpose in such a way that no other mix of instruments can for the remainder of 1968. It can strengthen both the resolve and the assets of those persons in this government seeking stabilization and growth objectives."[70]

Focusing almost exclusively on inflation demonstrated a growing inability of U.S. policymakers, especially Korry, to appreciate the complexities in the Chilean situation, Frei's personal goals, or the recent history of U.S.–Chilean relations. In focusing on inflation they started to lose the big picture. The economic stabilization programs necessary to limit inflation were overwhelmingly unpopular because they required cuts in government spending on services, new construction projects, and wages for government workers. Massive inflation, which U.S. officials considered possible, would certainly have been a problem. It would have suggested the incompetence of the Frei government and led to an increase in power for the far left and far right, but it was not the only issue on which Chilean voters were likely to judge Frei.[71]

In a memo to Johnson asking for authority to negotiate a loan, AID director William Gaud similarly emphasized the political motive. Following Korry, Gaud noted that some sort of government budget deficit was almost inevitable in 1968, and the United States needed to step in to keep the Frei government's stabilization programs on track. Gaud argued, "The deterioration of the economic situation with the threat of sharply increased inflation and political opposition from both right and left place the Frei government on the defensive, and it will require a major effort simply to maintain and continue for the balance of his term the substantial achievements already made. While the political alternatives after the end of the Frei administration are as yet unclear, the chances for the continuance of moderate, constructive leadership will depend considerably on what happens in the final period of the Frei government."[72]

Though Korry, Gaud, and others pushed for a loan, it did not move forward. Throughout the latter part of 1968 there was not a definitive negative decision on the loan, but there was also no positive decision. Frei's request hovered in diplomatic limbo. The Chilean situation did not seem urgent, and thus delay was acceptable. Other concerns, including Vietnam and the

U.S. presidential election, made it difficult for U.S. policymakers to focus on Chile, which had seemed relatively safe and remained stable without U.S. aid in 1967. Korry, in Santiago, kept pushing for the loan throughout the second half of 1968 into January 1969. As the loan decision failed to move, Korry feared that if Johnson did not make a decision by the end of his term, it would be too late to help Frei. Even if the incoming president, Richard Nixon, could ultimately be persuaded to make a loan, it would take months as the new administration organized itself.

In the days before Johnson left the White House, Korry sent an impassioned plea directly to the president. Korry wrote, "I am compelled for the first time . . . to appeal directly to you." He explained, "At a time when the lights of democracy and of constitutional order are once again dimming in many parts of Latin America, and at a time when one of the few remaining democracies is suffering from catastrophic drought, do we wish to take an action (by inaction) of grave potential consequence against the Latin American who has most symbolized the democratic purposes and action of the Alliance for Progress?" Korry insisted, "I am persuaded that such adverse action is contrary to your personal philosophy and to the sum and components of your very considerable contributions and commitments to the building of the bulwarks of democratic stability and progress in the world." Korry pointed out that leaving this matter to Nixon would create "ticklish difficulties" all over Latin America.[73] Korry also sent a message to Rostow, asking for help in "facilitating presentation of my cable to the president, and any support you can give." Closing with a short plea, Korry concluded that Rostow's help "would be an act of major political import in Chile."[74]

Johnson did not make the loan. In a letter to Rusk, Korry expressed some of the shock he and other AID officials in Chile felt over the decision. Korry explained that the U.S. decision would likely "be interpreted as a judgment against President Frei and his policies. It will be interpreted economically as a signal that there is no chance whatsoever of accomplishing the difficult task of holding the inflationary rate near the 1968 level (as we intend)." Perhaps more important, Korry insisted that the failure to pass the loan would be a "confirmation that the Alliance for Progress was truly dead, [and] that in a continent where democracy is debilitated if not disappearing, the U.S. really has no, repeat no, commitment to constitutionality nor to reformist-type policies typified by President Frei."[75] U.S. aid to Chile, which had been central to the Alliance for Progress, simply was not important anymore.

Final Thoughts

It is difficult to assess the totality of the U.S. aid program in Chile because of the different ways the U.S. sent aid and the limitations of this study in analyzing domestic Chilean politics. However, three factors stand out to suggest that U.S. policy was not effective. Most notably and dramatically, Salvador Allende won the 1970 presidential election. It would be possible to suggest that all U.S. aid to Chile was dedicated to stopping this from happening, making this failure extremely spectacular. Second, Eduardo Frei moved from being a close supporter of U.S. policy to a frequent critic. Finally, Chile was not able to wean itself from economic aid. The necessary growth to make the leap toward a more developed and healthy economy did not occur. Yet it would be a mistake to suggest that, with the exception of Frei's shift in attitude, a more effective aid program, or even no aid at all, would have had much difference on the Chilean outcomes. U.S. aid was able to have an impact on key political decisions, on budgetary priorities, and on construction of many development projects, but it was unable to transform the country in the ways U.S. policymakers hoped. The Chilean Marxist left was powerful at the start of the 1960s, and powerful at the end of the 1960s and the success of the economy was dependent on the copper industry. These two factors reinforced each other and limited the ability of the Alliance for Progress to achieve the kinds of successes that Kennedy had hoped for.

The Chilean case demonstrates how quickly U.S. policymakers gave up on the idealistic vision inherent in the Charter of Punta del Este, and how they tried to use aid to influence political events. It raises the question, which will be revisited in later chapters, of what the Alliance for Progress actually was. This case suggests that sometimes the program was about supporting actual reform and self-help, as with Frei in his first year. But it was also about creating conditions that would allow Frei to take power, as in the 1962 through 1964 period. In the late 1960s, the Alliance for Progress retained some of its connection to encouraging reform, but it was also a lever to manipulate Frei. Perhaps the only constant was the way U.S. policymakers used Alliance for Progress rhetoric to justify their actions, but even that started to end in the late 1960s. The changes in the Alliance for Progress in Chile, which was supposed to be a model for the program, indicate that it was simply a way to achieve short-run goals. It was not about promoting reform, it was about influence.

CHAPTER 5

Brazil and the Alliance for Progress
Undermining Goulart and Rewarding the Military

From FY1962 to FY1969 (July 1, 1961 to June 30, 1969), Brazil received $1.833 billion in U.S. economic aid. (see Table 5.1) This represented 29.2 percent of all the money sent to Latin America during this period. In every year between FY1961 and FY1968 Brazil was the highest recipient of U.S. aid.[1] Other than being the largest country in the region and having some of the worst poverty, it was a priority in the early 1960s because the United States hoped to force Presidents Jânio Quadros and João Goulart toward economic and political positions acceptable to the United States. When the United States became frustrated at the lack of Brazilian cooperation, it used aid to undermine the national government. After a U.S.-backed military coup d'état in 1964, Washington found it prudent to use financial aid to help the leaders it had supported as an alternative to Goulart. The U.S. government only stopped presenting massive aid packages in the late 1960s as the Brazilian military became spectacularly repressive.

As with Chile, economic aid coming through the Alliance for Progress had more to do with political considerations than humanitarian ones. But the Brazilian program was quite different from the Chilean one. Aid to Chile was political, but the larger goal was helping Frei take power and ultimately promoting reform. In this respect it had at least some connection to the ideals of the Alliance for Progress. In Brazil this is less clear. Washington tried to push reform and self-help in Brazil, yet there was no larger plan for integrating political and Alliance for Progress goals. Policymakers in the United States sometimes had a difficult time remembering why they had made Brazil a priority. This made it easier to push the Brazil-

Table 5.1 U.S. Economic Assistance Loans and Grants to Brazil, FY1962–FY1969 (in millions of U.S. dollars; data not adjusted for inflation)

Year	FY1962 7/1/61– 6/30/62	FY1963 7/1/62– 6/30/63	FY1964 7/1/63– 6/30/64	FY1965 7/1/64– 6/30/65	FY1966 7/1/65– 6/30/66	FY1967 7/1/66– 6/30/67	FY1968 7/1/67– 6/30/68	FY1969 7/1/68– 6/30/69
Loans and Grants	205.6	141.3	336.9	270.8	329	240	280.7	29.2

Source: United States Agency for International Development website, The Greenbook (http://qesdb.cdie.org/gbk).

ians harder and easier to turn against them when they did not fulfill U.S. expectations. It guaranteed an unpleasant relationship. Similarly, support for the military demonstrates the inability to connect Alliance for Progress ideals and actual economic aid spending. It shows not only how far U.S. policymakers could stretch Kennedy's vision, but also how little they cared to try.

Brazilian Exceptionalism and Vargas

Brazil is unique among the Latin American nations. At more than 3.2 million square miles it is three times larger than any other country in the region and its population in 1960, almost 71 million people, was almost half the South American total. Brazil's population is also racially different. Though African slaves went to all parts of the New World, areas that produced sugar, like Brazil, imported many more slaves than areas that did not. Brazil had, and has, a far greater population with African heritage as a result.

Brazil also had a unique political history. It was a Portuguese rather than a Spanish colony and it developed a distinctive government system in the nineteenth century. As other Latin American countries achieved independence and created republics, Brazil became a sovereign state led by the Portuguese royal family. Other Latin American countries made a sharp break with Spain and its monarchy, but in Brazil, Portuguese royals, Emperor Pedro I and Emperor Pedro II, governed until 1889. The empire of Brazil provided a great deal of stability, yet when the royal family moved to end slavery, elites rebelled and Pedro II had to abdicate. Following the empire, these elites, especially from the two richest states of São Paulo and Minas Gerais, colluded to dominate the new republic until a military coup in 1930.

From the coup until 1954, Getúlio Vargas, a populist with fascist leanings, dominated Brazilian politics. Put in place by the military, Vargas slowly developed his own power base, modeling his governance on Benito Mussolini's style in Italy. He attempted to co-opt urban workers by promoting pro-labor legislation, encouraging the growth of a fascist paramilitary, and reducing the power of state governments. In 1937, following a staged coup attempt, he assumed dictatorial powers, only to be ousted in 1945 by military leaders who had tired if his pro-labor positions. However, even after being overthrown he remained popular because of his efforts on behalf of industrial workers. He became a senator in 1946 and won the 1950 presidential election. As a democratically elected president he had difficulty in balancing his populism and the need to work with other elected officials. Facing failure, and a probable coup, he committed suicide in 1954. The tumult of Vargas's dominance kept the country from developing a peaceful and democratic political culture.[2]

The election of Juscelino Kubitschek in 1955 appeared to be the beginning of a period of transition to normalcy, allowing for a focus on pursuing economic growth in the name of making Brazil "modern." Most notably, Kubitschek pursued this vision by supporting the construction of Brasilia, a futuristic capital city, deep in the interior. Wanting rapid development, he famously called for "fifty years of progress in five," and in many respects his programs did begin the process of creating growth. But, the spending needed to fund that growth ultimately created overwhelming debts and fiscal instability. Brazil did not have enough export earnings to balance its borrowing, and by the end of the 1950s the state had developed a balance-of-payments problem. This made foreign investment less attractive, which further exacerbated its fiscal problems. By 1961, the Brazilian economy was in complete disarray.[3]

Trying to Change Brazilian Foreign Policy with Aid

In October 1960, Jânio Quadros, a former mayor of São Paulo, won the Brazilian presidency. He assumed the office on January 31, 1961, just eleven days after Kennedy. Quadros' successful campaign promised reform and the creation of stable and reliable governance, both of which Brazil desperately needed. But instead of being able to focus on reform though, he had little choice but to address the nation's serious financial problems. The Kubitschek government had left $3.8 billion in debt and a widening gap between government revenue and expenditures. Quadros, to solve the problem, pledged himself to an economic austerity and anti-inflation program that would require a drastic cut in state spending.[4]

The Alliance for Progress would have been an ideal mechanism to promote Brazilian economic stability, but working with Quadros proved difficult. Unlike Kubitschek, who had been a strong supporter of U.S. foreign policy, Quadros attempted to pursue an independent foreign policy that assumed a neutral position in the Cold War. During his presidential campaign he visited Fidel Castro and made his support for the Cuban Revolution clear. His position emerged, in part, from internal economic conditions. He hoped that by expanding contacts with the rest of the world Brazil could improve on its balance of trade. Quadros was also attempting to tap into popular and historical nationalism by invoking expectations that Brazil would soon become a global power. To do this, Brazil needed to create distance from the United States.[5]

To stop Quadros from pursuing this policy, the State Department suggested offering a substantial loan package. Policymakers in the United States thought that if the Brazilian leader recognized the seriousness of his fiscal position he would have little choice but to change his foreign policy. The Kennedy administration hoped that its willingness to offer financial assistance, given Quadros's problems, could promote a better working relationship.[6] Quadros viewed U.S. assistance in a radically different way. He understood that because of Brazil's size and its problems, the United States could not ignore his country and claim that the Alliance for Progress represented a meaningful effort in the region. Knowing this, Quadros had a healthy amount of freedom in his relations with the United States.

In March 1961, Adolf Berle, the chair of Kennedy's Task Force responsible for developing the Alliance for Progress, traveled to Rio de Janeiro to offer a $100 million loan. In making the loan offer, Berle encouraged Quadros to join the United States in challenging Cuba. The obvious, albeit unspoken, quid pro quo was that in return for aid, the U.S. government would expect cooperation on international issues. Rather than welcome the U.S. proposal, Quadros pushed for a larger, $500 million loan.

Newspaper reports of the meeting suggested that it went badly. Quadros, the stories suggested, was annoyed that Berle assumed that he could be bought, especially at such a low price. Exactly what occurred is not completely apparent. In a memo to Washington the U.S. ambassador, John Moors Cabot, who had been present, refuted the claim that the meeting had been contentious and claimed that Quadros seemed "to be in complete agreement" with Berle on Cuba. However, Cabot did notice that Quadros had decorated his office with a statue sent by the Cuban revolutionary hero Ernesto "Che" Guevara.[7]

Quadros remained committed to the independent line in public. Immediately after Berle left he announced that the Yugoslavian Communist leader, Josip Tito, would visit Brazil. He reopened diplomatic relations with Communist governments in Hungary, Romania, and Bulgaria, and announced his intention to support the admission of Communist China into the United Nations. He sent trade representatives to the Communist countries in Eastern Europe to negotiate a $1.66 billion, five-year trade agreement and even announced that he would resume diplomatic relations with the Soviet Union. As the United States began gearing up for Punta del Este, it was hard to imagine that Quadros was a friend.[8]

In the hope of securing cooperation, Kennedy decided to offer Quadros exactly what he had asked for, a $500 million loan. This was roughly three times the total aid spending for Latin America during FY1961. Kennedy was offering a massive loan from a position of weakness. He could not ignore Brazil and needed Quadros's support to ensure that the Alliance for Progress had legitimacy.[9]

Goulart Makes a Plea for Alliance for Progress Support

In August 1961, Brazilian politics took a strange turn. Quadros had sent his delegation to Punta del Este, and although friendly with the Cuban delegation, they firmly backed the Alliance for Progress. It became clear that as long as the United States focused on economic development, rather than Cuba, the Brazilians would support the program. Quadros, however, wanted to emphasize his independence from the United States and sent his vice president, João Goulart, on a trade mission to the Soviet Union and Communist China while the Punta del Este conference was in session.[10]

On August 25, 1961, Quadros suddenly and unexpectedly resigned. Scholars of Brazilian history continue to debate exactly why. The most logical argument is that he was making a play for greater power on the assumption that the Brazilian Congress would reject his resignation, allowing him to press them for more authority. He knew that Goulart, the next in line for the presidency, was unpopular with the military because of his connections to Vargas and cooperative relationships with Communist unions.[11] He reasoned that Congressional leaders would not want to risk another coup. He was wrong. A majority in the Brazilian Congress thought they did not have the power to accept or reject resignations and they simply declared the presidency vacant. After some negotiations in which the Brazilian Congress reduced the power of the office, Goulart became president.[12]

Goulart's accession to the presidency in early September 1961 was worrisome for the United States because of his history of working with the Communists. He also quickly announced his intention to continue Quadros's independent foreign policy. Reflecting these concerns, U.S. officials in Brazil suggested that the United States "should be particularly slow in entering into new aid commitments." They continued, "Goulart's past associations with communists and his anti-U.S. positions are a matter of public record and well known throughout Latin America. Haste in offering U.S. aid, in [the] absence of convincing disavowal of those associations and positions would undoubtedly weaken [the] political strength of U.S. friends throughout the hemisphere and particularly in Brazil."[13]

Despite reservations about Goulart, it was difficult to stop sending aid. As Quadros understood, Brazil was far too important. Further, by accepting Goulart, Kennedy could demonstrate that Latin Americans could be different, and perhaps follow diverse ideological lines, and still be part of the program. Thus, there was little the United States could do except make statements that it expected that Brazil would follow through on the promises about self-help made at Punta del Este.[14]

While Goulart did have a long history of association with Vargas and radical leftist politicians, at least initially he appeared to recognize how much he needed the United States. In October 1961, during meetings with Lincoln Gordon, who had become ambassador to Brazil, Goulart explained that he would need more aid in order to maintain stability and ensure that Communists did not take power. The Brazilian financial position was dangerous. Quadros had attempted to fix the balance-of-payments problems by instituting currency exchange rate reforms. Instead of creating stability and promoting economic activity, this led to inflation rates of about 50 percent in late 1961. Quadros's resignation, Goulart argued, had led to internal chaos and civil war was possible. Goulart claimed his government was the only thing keeping the forces of "right and left extremism" under control. He appeared to understand and fear Communist activity, and knew he would have to improve economic conditions to achieve stability. Goulart seemed to have a keen appreciation of the weakness of his own position and the ability of the United States to help him.[15]

In requesting aid, Goulart claimed that because he was a "man of the people," if Washington helped his government, ordinary Brazilians would come to understand that the United States was a force for good. He noted that although the United States had been generous with Brazil in the past, the fruits of that generosity had not filtered down to the common people. Most Brazilians, Goulart claimed, were ignorant about U.S. largesse, and were therefore easy targets of Communist propaganda. Goulart's apparent understanding of Alliance for Progress philosophy helped lessen Washington's fears. As a result, the United States began to release more and more money to help his government.[16]

Distress About Goulart, But Aid Anyway

Goulart remained a mystery. Although he appeared amenable to U.S. concerns and supportive of the Alliance for Progress, Department of State advisors worried about his overall policy decisions. Most distressingly,

Goulart strengthened Quadros's independent foreign policy. In November 1961, Brazil reestablished formal diplomatic relations with the Soviet Union. More disturbing was Brazilian action at the January 1962 OAS meetings in Punta del Este. The Brazilian delegation, led by Foreign Minister Francisco Clementino San Tiago Dantas, refused to support resolutions calling on all Latin American nations to break relations with Cuba and on ousting Cuba from the OAS. The Brazilians hoped Cuba and the rest of the inter-American community could agree to coexist peacefully.[17]

Given Goulart's past associations, these kinds of actions led to fears that he might welcome Communist activity in Brazil. In a stark memo, Haydn Williams, the deputy assistant secretary of defense for international security affairs, wrote, "it would seem that we may be faced in Brazil with a foreign policy oriented increasingly toward the Soviet Bloc in world affairs and toward the Castro regime in inter-American affairs." He continued, saying that Goulart's actions had created "a government in which Communist infiltration and influence exceeded anything of the sort previously known in the country." The worst part, to Williams, was that the Brazilians "apparently plan to force the U.S. to finance this inimical regime."[18]

The CIA's estimate of Goulart was less apocalyptic, but concurred that Brazilian Communists "will benefit by the tolerance . . . of Goulart . . . . They will probably encounter little effective competition or governmental restriction in their efforts to enrich themselves in areas where agrarian and social unrest is most acute and will also benefit to some extent by the entry of additional party members or sympathizers into the bureaucracy." Yet the CIA also noted that right-wing and military hostility to Marxism, as well as Goulart's desire to control Brazilian politics, would limit any gains made by the radical left. The CIA concluded, "it is unlikely that the Communist infiltration of the government will go so far as to give the Communist Party a significant influence on the formulation and execution of policy."[19]

The evidence did suggest that Goulart was giving the radical left more freedom. Most notably, he allowed his brother-in-law, Lionel Brizola, the governor of Rio Grande do Sul, to strengthen his own position as a national leader. More radical than Goulart, Brizola had long associations with Brazilian Communists and a history of spouting vehement anti-U.S. rhetoric.[20]

In February 1962, Brizola expropriated the properties of International Telephone and Telegraph (ITT) in his state. While Brizola pledged to compensate ITT in accordance with international law, his government only offered $400,000 as payment. ITT, a U.S.-based company that controlled utilities throughout Latin America, estimated the value of their assets between $6 and $8 million. Goulart supported Brizola and argued that although foreign investors were welcome, they needed to be responsible to the Brazilian people. This was disturbing to U.S. business leaders and politicians. Most significantly, Harold Geneen, the president of ITT, urged Senator Burke Hickenlooper (R-IA) to introduce an amendment to the Foreign Assistance Act of 1962 to fight this kind of nationalization. The Hickenlooper Amendment, which became a standard part of future foreign assistance acts, ordered that the president suspend foreign assistance to nations that expropriated property of U.S. companies unless they provided adequate compensation within six months of the expropriation.[21]

Some U.S. analyses of Goulart suggested that his actions came not from any desire to develop a meaningful and coherent policy, but from a lack of intelligence and a limited capacity for leadership. A wealthy rancher from the state of Rio Grande do Sul, Goulart was not particularly well educated, and according to U.S. analyses, prone to changing his mind rapidly. Even his Brazilian allies conceded that he lacked the ability to stand firm in his opinions. During the course of his presidency, U.S. advisors were continually frustrated by his personality and claimed his general weakness made it easy for leftist radicals, or indeed whomever had seen him last, to influence him. This made trusting him difficult.[22]

None of these concerns was enough to stall the granting of aid to Goulart. Just as the United States had been willing to fund Quadros, it also lavished aid on Goulart. In FY1962, the United States sent almost $206 million to Brazil, about one-fourth of all aid to Latin America. In February 1962, AID proposed a new series of loans to Brazil, including a $62 million program loan. The United States also committed to a large PL480 Food for Peace program for Brazil. Believing that Brazilian stability was vital, strengthening Goulart appeared to be the only U.S. option. In thinking about Goulart, Kennedy aide Richard Goodwin wrote in early 1962, "The political situation in Brazil is extremely precarious. We have no choice but to work to strengthen this government since there appears to be no viable alternative."[23]

Goulart Tries to Embrace the Alliance for Progress

To gain greater cooperation from Brazil in developing Alliance for Progress programs, the Kennedy administration invited Goulart to Washington for meetings in April 1962. Before he resigned, Quadros had been invited and the Goulart trip was an extension of this earlier invitation. For Goulart, the trip was vital for improving his chances of obtaining significant aid, and as an opportunity to help his domestic reputation. A welcome in Washington would show his opponents in the military that he was acceptable.

In what was likely a bid for Washington's approval before his departure for the United States, Goulart announced a new economic program that would end support for unrealistic exchange rates (which increased imports and cut exports), limit wage increases to government workers, and curb other government spending. In his series of talks with Kennedy, Goulart insisted that these efforts at monetary stabilization and internal reform would put Brazil on healthier ground. On the political front, he attempted to convince Kennedy that his government was trying to solve the Brizola-ITT problem. Goulart also appeared amenable to Kennedy's suggestions about fighting radicalism, especially in labor unions. Kennedy successfully pushed Goulart to allow the AFL-CIO (American Federation of Labor and Congress of Industrial Organizations), through its international agency, AIFLD, to develop contacts with Brazilian labor leaders.[24]

Kennedy agreed to make a four-year $131 million commitment to development programs in the northeastern part of Brazil. The states of Rio Grande do Norte, Paraíba, Pernambuco, Alagoas, Sergipe, Ceará, Bahia, Piaui, and Maranhão had all been part of Brazil's sugar-producing area and faced periodic drought, famines, illiteracy, disease, and malnutrition on a vast scale. Holding about one-third of the national populace, these areas had the lowest per capita income anywhere in Latin America.[25]

Under Kubitschek, the Brazilian government had hoped to bring about change in the region. In 1958, in response to a catastrophic drought, the government had asked a young well-respected economist, Celso Furtado, to create a development plan. This led to the creation of a development agency, the Superintendency of Northeast Development/*Superintendência do Desenvolvimento do Nordeste* (SUDENE). Political conflicts over who would control funding for the organization slowed its final approval, but by mid-December 1961, the Brazilian congress accepted the SUDENE development agenda. The plans called for the creation of a transportation, water, and electric infrastructure that would attract industrialization. SUDENE also provided incentives to investors in the region to shift from sugar production toward diversified agriculture. It also called for the movement of people from overpopulated areas to sparsely settled areas with agricultural promise.[26]

SUDENE's emphasis on development projects made it an attractive venue for Alliance for Progress funding. Policymakers in the United States also believed that because of the massive poverty, the northeast was the one place in Latin America most vulnerable to Communist organization. Indeed, in 1960 there were fears that Communists had been involved in creating rural unions called "peasant leagues" to lay the groundwork for a revolution on the Cuban or Chinese models. These leagues, according to U.S. reports, had mobilized over 25,000 members. The evidence does not support these contentions. The leagues were much smaller and focused on improving local conditions, but fears about them ensured that the Kennedy administration sent Alliance for Progress money to the region.[27]

The problems were substantial enough for Kennedy to decide that, no matter what his misgivings about Goulart, Brazil needed a great deal of help. Kennedy reportedly told Goulart that he wanted U.S. aid to have a major impact in Brazil, especially in the northeast. Much of the aid the United States had given in 1961 and early 1962 had been to help with budgetary and exchange rate problems as opposed to development, and Kennedy said he wanted to really address the problems of ordinary Brazilians. This meeting was the high-water mark in relations between Goulart and the United States. Following the meeting, and as a result of Goulart's commitment to make economic reforms, AID released $35 million in previously committed aid, and indicated that more it would release more money after the implementation of Goulart's new economic program.[28]

Getting Tough with Goulart

Although he generally made a favorable impression in Washington, questions about Goulart remained. On leaving the United States, Goulart traveled to Mexico where he met with President Adolfo López Mateos. The two leaders issued a statement saying that they considered themselves independent of "any political-military group." This statement, which reaffirmed Goulart's independent foreign policy, undercut the satisfaction Kennedy and his advisors had developed about the meetings and reinforced the idea that Goulart was an opportunist.[29]

To better understand what was happening in Brazil, Kennedy wanted a comprehensive report on Brazilian politics. He asked William H. Draper, an Eisenhower administration foreign policy expert, to lead a study team in October 1962. Its report was highly critical of Goulart. Supported by the CIA, State Department, AID, USIA, and the Department of Defense, Draper's team made the observation that "Goulart's political career has been based on demagogic leadership of organized labor, after the fashion of Vargas. . . . His future course is unpredictable. He is essentially a clever opportunist with no strong motivation save his craving for popularity and personal power." Perhaps worse, it was unlikely that he fully understood or was "competent to cope with Brazil's desperate financial situation."[30]

The report suggested the most sensible course of action was continuing "efforts to make [Goulart] realize the gravity of Brazil's financial and economic situation." The United States should "continue to urge the adoption of adequate remedial measures that would justify our large-scale financial help. At the same time we should influence his political orientation in directions better calculated to serve U.S. interests." The report also argued that continuing instability and the historical role of the military as guarantors of the constitutional process meant that the United States "should also intensify its intelligence concerning, and unobtrusively maintain contact with, any military and political elements of a potential and more friendly alternative regime, and should be prepared to act promptly and effectively in support of such a regime, in case the impending financial crisis or some other eventuality should result in the displacement of Goulart."[31]

The conclusions of the Draper report suggested to U.S. policymakers that they needed to be tougher on Goulart and underscored their alarm about "both the political orientation of the Brazilian government and the deterioration of its financial position." Yet it remained difficult to determine exactly how bad he was. The economic problems he faced would have taxed any leader.[32]

To push Goulart, and to indicate to him the seriousness of U.S. concerns about his vacillating stances expressed in the Draper report, Kennedy decided to send his brother, Robert, on a special mission to Brazil in mid-December 1962. The younger Kennedy's task was to insist that Goulart be more cooperative on international issues and more fully embrace the logic behind the Alliance for Progress. His meeting with Goulart did not go well. The younger Kennedy, expressing Washington's frustrations, was extremely harsh in criticizing Goulart's tolerance of Communists in Brazil and the appointment of anti-U.S. politicians to important posts. Goulart emerged from the meeting angry with U.S. presumptuousness, and Robert Kennedy left with the impression that Goulart was irresponsible. Following this meeting, Washington began moving away from Goulart. Shortly after the Kennedy meeting, the United States rejected a Brazilian request for a $30 million emergency loan until Goulart had achieved some "positive constructive steps" on reform.[33]

Goulart Again Tries to Make the Case That He Supports Reform

Goulart was able to strengthen his domestic position in January 1963 through a plebiscite that returned full presidential powers to the office. His victory was massive (9.46 million votes for versus 2.07 million against) because all the leading 1965 presidential election hopefuls also supported the measure. The election results encouraged Goulart to become more active in pushing for economic change. He introduced a new, even larger development plan, making clear his belief that it complied with Alliance for Progress expectations about self-help and priorities. The three-year plan (Three-Year Plan for Economic and Social Development/*Plano Trienial do Desenvolvimento Economico e Social*) focused on attempting to promote growth while controlling inflation and encouraging agrarian and tax reforms. New government spending would be possible by increasing taxes on the wealthy and reducing government subsidies of industry. To make the plan a reality, Brazil would need $1.5 billion in external assistance and $300 million in foreign investment.[34]

Brazil was in dire financial straights by this time. Inflation had exceeded 50 percent in 1962 and the national external debt was skyrocketing. By early 1963 Brazil owed roughly $3 billion to foreigners. Its repayment costs were, as a result, huge; it would have to pay $900 million in debt service in 1963 alone. Of this money, $200 to $300 million was due to the U.S. government and private institutions in the United States. Thus, while Brazil needed money for its development program, it needed U.S. financing simply to stay solvent.[35]

Officials in Washington greeted Goulart's plan with derision and regarded it as a superficial way to comply with Alliance for Progress criteria. The plan did not force Brazil to undergo any stabilization measures nor did it propose cuts in government spending. Analysts in the United States concluded, "the plan appears to have been designed with Goulart's political needs very much in mind and in an effort to solve Brazil's financial problems without austerity. It attempts the difficult feat of reducing the rate of inflation and at the same time maintaining a high rate of economic growth, and it relies on extensive foreign assistance to make these both possible." Policymakers in the United States did hope that the plan could "be a positive and potentially important forward step for the Alliance for Progress and for economic planning in Brazil, particularly as a political document and a base to build upon." But as proposed, it was "technically deficient" and had "gaps and internal contradictions . . . some dubious economic analysis, some shaky assumptions, as well as several unfortunate policy emphases."[36]

Brazilian officials insisted that the plan complied with the sprit and letter of the Alliance for Progress and therefore they were justified in requesting U.S. support. A letter from Goulart reminded Kennedy that the Charter of Punta del Este gave each nation the right to determine its own specific economic destiny and the means to that destiny. The United States had committed itself to support legitimate development programs established within that framework. He wrote, "economic remedies must be adapted to the reality of the social environment in which they are to be used." Goulart had a point. He understandably suggested that he knew what was best for Brazil, that he was committed to reform, and that under the Alliance for Progress aid should have been forthcoming in these circumstances.[37]

Yet opposition to Goulart made support unlikely. In congressional hearings in early 1963, Ambassador Gordon told the House Committee on Foreign Affairs that Communists had infiltrated the government and labor unions. Many congressmen suggested, as a response, that the United States cut all aid to Brazil. The U.S. Congress would also soon receive the Clay Report, a document created by a Kennedy-appointed committee re-examining foreign aid programs. The report from this committee, headed by retired General Lucius D. Clay, suggested that the United States need not only insist on self-help measures, but actually see them in place before committing aid. The United States, according to the report, should not bail out nations, but wait for performance. The report concluded that sometimes U.S. aid was justified, but in many cases it was wasted.[38]

Keeping Aid to Goulart on a "Short Leash"

The U.S. government faced a difficult set of decisions. On one hand, agreeing to underwrite Goulart's development schemes did not guarantee that Brazil would conform to Kennedy's foreign policy positions. On the other hand, refusing to send aid could drive Goulart further to the left and might even prompt him to seek out greater financial aid from the Soviet Union. At the very least, Goulart could blame Brazil's financial position on U.S. stinginess and failure to adhere to the ideals of the Alliance for Progress. To avoid these undesirable outcomes, Gordon recommended to Kennedy that the United States give Brazil financial aid, but "on a 'short-leash' basis, permitting periodic review and making possible the withdrawal of support on either economic or political grounds." Brazil would be expected to "strengthen the private sector . . . and progressively shift the 'independent foreign policy' toward more systemic collaboration with the United States and the free world."[39]

Officials in the United States reluctantly decided that they had little choice but to offer assistance based on Gordon's formula, no matter how much they hoped Goulart would ultimately fail. An agreement between Dantas and AID Administrator David Bell specified a series of steps the Brazilians would need to take in order to receive U.S. funding. The United States agreed to offer Brazil $398.5 million, $84 million of which would be provided immediately as long as Goulart concluded agreements with U.S. companies expecting restitution for expropriation and he implemented an economic stabilization program. Release of the remaining $314.5 million in FY1964 was contingent on Brazil's successful negotiation of assistance programs with the Europeans, Japanese, and the IMF, and its ability to follow through on the implementation of the stabilization programs.[40]

Brazilian officials were disappointed with U.S. offers. They had hoped for a three-year package that would have allowed for long-range planning, and hopefully the development of enough exports that aid would no longer be necessary. They also found U.S. reliance on the IMF a problem. They believed that the terms of the loan essentially gave the IMF veto power over the Brazilian budget. This was a concern because the IMF was likely to be extremely critical if Goulart pursued any policies that seemed inflationary. The plan, to Dantas, was a "global rejection" of what the Goulart government was attempting to do. The Brazilians could accept "suggestions but not instructions." Dantas further explained to Bell that it would not be possible to allow his government to appear to be "agreeing to submit to externally imposed conditions . . . in order to get foreign assistance." Indeed, Dantas and the Brazilian ambassador in Washington, Roberto Campos, discussed not signing the loan because it infringed on Brazilian sovereignty. Nevertheless, they did sign because the three-year plan depended on U.S. support. Moreover, failure to sign a deal would have dramatically weakened the Goulart government because it would have required a severe national austerity program to make up for the needed funds. The Brazilian government would have had to cut back so far on spending that all political support could have disappeared.[41]

Of course from the U.S. perspective, the deal was fair. The United States was simply following through on its stated objectives of connecting aid deals to performance on reform. AID would be able to claim that the deal was based on self-help principles, as called for in the Charter of Punta del Este and the Clay Report. In addition, emphasis on the participation of other countries and other institutions would demonstrate that the United States would not be solely responsible for Brazil's success or failure.[42] Moreover, aiding a government that was uncooperative with U.S. regional foreign policy objectives further demonstrated Washington's generosity.

The Brazilian government did try to implement the plan and improve relations. In April 1963 the Brazilians agreed to settle their dispute with ITT on generous terms. They also agreed to settle differences with another company, the American and Foreign Power Company (AMFORP), an owner of electric utility companies. Brizola's Rio Grande do Sul's state government had expropriated some AMFORP assets in 1959, though at the time the expropriation had received little attention. Losing money because of bad contracts that did not keep pace with inflation, AMFORP hoped to get out of the Brazilian market entirely and cash in on the furor over the ITT case. They convinced the Kennedy administration to push Goulart to purchase the company. Goulart, in accordance with the Dantas-Bell agreement, decided to pay ITT $13.5 million for its assets, plus $7.7 million to settle AMFORP debts. This deal was attractive to the U.S. companies and understandably damaged Goulart's domestic reputation. Brizola and his allies attacked Goulart for capitulating to the United States. Others simply said, correctly, that Goulart was wasting money by overpaying. Only after this point did the United States release funds signed as part of the Dantas-Bell agreement.[43]

Goulart also moved forward on the reform program, first by cutting wheat subsidies to farmers and general subsidies on fuel. He also devalued the cruzeiro, the national currency, to create an exchange rate more in line with market conditions as the IMF required. In addition, he tried to limit wage increases for government workers and the military, but the austerity program and the devaluation created higher inflation. Government workers and the military saw their relative earnings fall dramatically as a result. Needing the support of these two groups to govern, Goulart had no choice but to raise pay. He proposed a 40 percent wage increase, and the Brazilian Congress passed a 70 percent increase.[44]

These last actions indicated, at least to the IMF, that Goulart had given up on the austerity plan, forcing a critical review in May 1963. Goulart also dismissed his entire cabinet, including Dantas, who had become one of the few Brazilians in the Goulart administration that U.S. policymakers felt they could support. The lack of Brazilian commitment to the Dantas-Bell agreement prompted State Department officials to have Kennedy send Goulart a personal letter. The Kennedy letter offered no direct criticism. It stated simply that Kennedy believed that the Dantas-Bell agreement was "very constructive" in that it "laid out a specific course of action" for the Brazilian government to follow in solving its fiscal problems. Goulart had not followed through, and that presented a problem.[45]

Giving Up on Goulart and Undermining Him through Islands of Sanity

Because of its failure to follow the Dantas-Bell agreement, Goulart's government would not see new U.S. aid, nor receive the approximately $144.5 million in loans already promised. But in mid-1963 it was not completely apparent that the halting of aid was permanent as Goulart continued to make promises about reform.[46] Some officials in the State Department, most notably Assistant Secretary of State for Inter-American Affairs Edwin Martin, were not ready to give up on him. In May 1963, Martin approved a memo that called for "a more active effort to win Brazil over." His idea was not to accept Goulart's domestic or international positions, but simply to "treat Brazil's views with respect by resorting to a greater exchange of views for the purpose of achieving a greater meeting of the minds." This would bring "a greater responsiveness on the part of the Brazilian government." Later, in August 1963, Martin even proposed a Kennedy visit to Brazil with the purpose of explaining U.S. intentions and interest in promotion of reform. But Martin's ideas about accommodation did not carry the day, and the U.S. government committed itself to an increasingly anti-Goulart position.[47]

Lincoln Gordon took the lead in developing the new hostile approach. He justified his opposition by suggesting, with little evidence, that Goulart wanted to create a dictatorship in Brazil. In a memo to the State Department he wrote, "As I weigh evidence with maximum objectivity I can command, it seems to be increasingly clear that Goulart's personal aim is to perpetuate himself in power [and to create a] . . . regime of extreme anti-American nationalism. . . . In this effort, Goulart is accepting and even promoting support from communists and fellow travelers." Gordon continued, "The danger of a communist takeover arises from Goulart's own total incompetence to understand or resolve real problems, economic, administrative, or other, so that having served as front man to establish authoritarian mold, he might easily be pushed aside." He concluded, "Brazil under Goulart has become [a] very sick country indeed."[48]

Having given up on Goulart, the question became how to remain engaged in the country while setting the stage for a transition to a better government; the United States could not and did not want to give up on Brazil. For Gordon, the solution was to promote and strengthen anti-Communist state governors that might be able to counteract and challenge the power of the national government. He claimed there were "Islands of Administrative Sanity" within Brazil, and that these could be propped up in a way that would reduce Goulart's control. By mid-1963, under Gordon's leadership, the United States shifted its aid program from the national government to state governments.[49]

The Islands policy was obviously an innovation that revealed some of the new ways Kennedy administration officials had come to think about the Alliance for Progress. Because of the new policy, schools would be built, roads improved, and hospitals supplied. But improving conditions in Brazil was not really the point, the idea was to undermine the Goulart government. The political justification of aid was certainly not new. At roughly the same time the United States was busy developing programs to have an impact on the 1964 Chilean election, and some of the Brazilian programs for state governments were even called "impact projects." The major difference was that in Chile the idea was to use aid to strengthen a government, in Brazil the goal was destabilizing one.[50]

The first beneficiary of the Islands policy was Aluízo Alves, the pro-U.S. governor of Rio Grande do Norte. Alves was among the most ambitious state governors in developing economic and social development plans, and in wooing U.S. policymakers involved in making Alliance for Progress funding decisions. The United States agreed to rebuild and equip the state's school facilities and to pay for the construction of one thousand classrooms and a series of teacher training centers. The United States also provided money for new urban water supply systems, school lunch programs, roads, and electrification programs. [51]

Bahia was another focus. The governor of this state, Antônio Lomanto Junior, was also a strong Alliance for Progress supporter. In Salvador, the capital of the state, U.S. officials argued successfully that "in view of his persistent and outspoken support of democratic ideals and [the Alliance for Progress] . . . Lomanto deserves all the support we are able to give him." In this case the United States focused on water treatment plants, education programs, and road building. Believing that the program was working, AID officials went so far as encouraging Lomanto to make larger requests for funds. [52]

Support for Rio Grande do Norte and Bahia can be contrasted with the state of Pernambuco. Facing similar conditions of poverty, Pernambuco was not an aid priority in large part because of the hostility of the governor, Miguel Arreas, toward the United States. Arreas, a Goulart ally who took office in late January 1963, argued that Alliance for Progress loans destroyed Brazilian sovereignty and created "foreign zones of influence." In his inaugural address he said, "we shall not be able to liquidate underdevelopment without liquidating the exploitation of foreign capital in this country." According to U.S. embassy officials, "the Arreas government is largely dominated by extreme leftists and nationalists," and he was "completely antagonistic to [an] American presence in Brazil." He was "hypersensitive, extremely suspicious, and . . . blindly vindictive." Pernambuco did not receive aid on a scale comparable to its neighbors. [53]

This policy had unmistakable problems. Carlos Lacerda, the governor of Guanabara (encompassing Rio de Janeiro), was among the most powerful anti-Goulart politicians and a major recipient of funding under the Islands policy. Unfortunately, Lacerda was a conservative politician opposed to reform. He was not the kind of politician who showed a willingness to pursue self-help. Nevertheless, he was a Goulart opponent, and thus he received U.S. money. [54]

The program also pushed some of the frustrations the Goulart government had with the Alliance for Progress down to the state level. As with all loans, movement of funds was slow. In FY1963 (July 1, 1962 to June 30, 1963) the United States spent only $1.7 million on loans to state governments. The next year spending reached almost $35.6 million, yet given Brazil's size and the number of projects to fund, this amount was not particularly large. While ultimately the United States would make more than $96 million in loans to state governments, most of that aid would not actually reach Brazil until after the military ousted Goulart.

The case of the state of Matto Grosso is illustrative of this problem. In January 1964 its governor, Fernando Correa da Costa, complained to U.S. aid officials about the slow pace in aid reaching his state. He had developed detailed plans to build a hydroelectric plant, and had received promises of U.S. support, but the funds did not arrive. He did not expect the construction to begin before January 1966 and his general attitude toward the United States worsened because of the delays. Similarly, Lomanto of Bahia complained about the slowness in getting loan money. He argued to AID officials, "If you Americans would only give me more help, I could show up . . . Arreas [of Pernambuco] and demonstrate what can be done under the Alliance for Progress." He insisted the pace of aid disbursements was making that difficult.[55]

No Aid Means the End of the U.S.–Goulart Relationship

As they became frustrated with Goulart, U.S. policymakers increased their efforts to develop friendly contacts with Brazilian military leaders. Officers had intervened in the political system many times in the past, and if the situation merited, could reasonably be expected to intervene again.[56] Understanding this threat, Goulart had attempted to gain control over the armed forces. He promoted officers who supported him and inserted them into positions of authority while holding back promotions for the most outspokenly pro-U.S. commanders, giving them unpleasant assignments and keeping them from commanding troops. To Gordon, this suggested a "plot by Goulart to seize power."[57]

In late 1963, U.S. policymakers, recognizing that a coup might be likely, initially worked to encourage Brazilian military leaders not to rebel. Goulart's government, as long as it did not attempt to seize power, could be tolerated until 1965, the year of new presidential elections. The U.S. goal should be, according to ambassador Lincoln Gordon, "to prepare the most promising possible environment for his [Goulart's] replacement by a more desirable regime in the event that conditions deteriorate to a point where coups or counter-coups are attempted."[58]

The political situation worsened in September 1963 as a group of non-commissioned officers attempted a coup in Brasilia. Their effort failed, but demonstrated the scope and intensity of anti-Goulart sentiment in the military. In response, Goulart had little choice but to request additional powers from Congress to protect his government. This, however, gave opponents the opportunity to claim that he intended to develop a dictatorship. Most notably, Gordon argued even more insistently after this point that "the major threat to Brazilian democracy comes from Goulart himself," and he started to become supportive of military plotting.[59]

Goulart, recognizing the forces arrayed against him, and U.S. backing for those forces, had little choice but to be more assertive in challenging Washington's influence in Brazil. He had come to understand, as Frei would in Chile, that while his government needed foreign aid, taking that aid opened it up to external control. At the meetings of the IA-ECOSOC in November 1963, held in São Paulo, Goulart attacked the United States in his opening speech to the delegates. He had nothing to lose. His speech completely ignored the Alliance for Progress, arguing that more action, notably at the U.N., was necessary to alter basic economic relationships between the wealthy and the poor.[60]

Kennedy's death accelerated the breakdown in the U.S. relationship with Goulart. Phyllis Parker, a historian of U.S.–Brazilian relations, suggests that Goulart's admiration for Kennedy was the last positive association between the two countries. Goulart had respected Kennedy, even though he was often frustrated by U.S. policy. He had considered his trip to Washington to be a highlight of his presidency. Without his personal link, Goulart had fewer reasons to be deferential to the United States.[61]

In December 1963, Goulart began a review of all foreign mining concessions in Brazil, and in January 1964 he signed legislation to enact a "profit remittance" act, which would keep U.S. companies operating in Brazil from sending money out of the country. The Brazilian Congress had passed this law in 1962, but Goulart understood that it would be antagonistic to the United States and lead to a reduction in aid, so he did not sign it. By early 1964 the United States was not sending his government aid and he was emboldened to act independently, or at least with little regard for U.S. concerns. Under the new law, foreign companies had to reinvest profits in Brazil. This move understandably and expectedly, angered the U.S. business community. However, the way Goulart proceeded was most disturbing to Gordon. Before signing the bill, Gordon met with Goulart and requested that the Brazilian leader veto parts of the law. Apparently Goulart indicated to Gordon that he would follow this advice, but he did not. Gordon was angry and believed that he could never trust Goulart's word in the future. Even more irritating, Goulart spoke about Kennedy in justifying the law. He said, "Brazil faces one sole and true dilemma already defined by that young and great statesman John Kennedy. The dilemma is: Reform or Revolution." Invoking Kennedy struck Gordon as inappropriate and offensive, but he failed to recognize that Goulart's rhetoric and focus on domestic production were entirely consistent with Kennedy's initial vision of the Alliance for Progress.[62]

Gordon was not alone in his disappointment. In a personal note to Gordon, Edwin Martin said that although the United States was concerned with issues such as profit remittances, it was more "fundamentally worried by the failure of Goulart to participate in and support the Alliance and its objectives, by the inflationary problem and by the continued political instability in Brazil, preventing it from exercising its normal role of leadership in the hemisphere." Martin concluded that Goulart "has let us down."[63]

Isolated from the United States, Goulart continued to move ahead with a strategic shift toward the radical left. In March 1964 he began calling for a land reform package, and suggested that he would implement this policy by decree, rather than through congressional action. Symbolically, in February 1964, he allowed the Communist Chinese government to open a trade office in Brazil.[64]

As important in enflaming political conflict was the increasingly bad Brazilian economic situation. Inflation had averaged 80 percent in 1963 and in the early months of 1964 it was 100 percent. Incomes were falling and foreign investment had stalled, likely from the effect of the law on foreign profit remittances. Total foreign debt had risen beyond $3 billion, and there was simply no way to pay off the interest due while at the same time paying for necessary imports. Brazil was in a deep financial trap from which there seemed no way out. More foreign aid could have temporarily solved the problems, but that aid was not forthcoming.[65]

The Coup

There was no shortage of coup plots against Goulart, yet moderate factions in the military held enough power to stymie them. In early 1964, a key switch occurred as the Army Chief of Staff General Humberto Castelo Branco decided to join the antigovernment faction. Castelo Branco had maintained a reputation as a legalist and had refused to participate in any previous conspiracies against Goulart or any of his predecessors. Castelo Branco's decision to abandon Goulart meant that even the moderate factions in the military had decided that Goulart was becoming odious.[66]

The rationale for supporting a coup, both for the United States and in the Brazilian military, rested on fears that Goulart intended to destroy the democratic system and establish a dictatorship. Castelo Branco and Gordon would later explain that to defend democracy it was necessary to act offensively. In other words, the only way to save the democratic system was through overthrowing the Goulart government.[67]

On March 31, 1964, Goulart gave his opposition a chance to make the case that he was bent on extending his rule. At a massive rally in Rio de Janeiro, Goulart gave a long speech in which he talked about passage of a law that gave the state more control of the oil industry and another law promoting land reform. Neither were important bills, nor particularly dramatic, yet he framed them as the start of more changes to come. Brizola, at the same rally, gave a speech that advocated a plebiscite to eliminate the Brazilian Congress. This was not Goulart's plan, and he did not refer to it in his speech. Nevertheless, it provided key fodder for the military leaders and Gordon, who by now was making the case that Goulart had to be removed. Castelo Branco, on watching the rally, commented to Vernon Walters, the U.S. military attaché, that Goulart was not going to give up power at the end of his term.[68]

As coup plotting accelerated, U.S. policymakers, including Gordon and Walters, were in close contact with Brazilian officers. In early March, Gordon requested an increase in military aid to Brazil as a means of showing support for the armed forces' expected coup attempt, and in late March, as the action appeared to be imminent, the U.S. embassy formulated plans to help the military with obtaining emergency supplies of petroleum, small arms, and ammunition. They also developed a plan to send a series of U.S. naval vessels, including an aircraft carrier, to Brazilian waters.[69]

These actions were unnecessary because a military coup that began on March 30 overthrew Goulart. By April 1, Goulart had left Brasilia, and the president of the Brazilian Senate declared the office vacant. It is important to recognize that the coup was the result of U.S. pressure, but more significantly the Brazilian military's own initiative. Military leaders, even moderate ones, had enough of Goulart's leadership. They did not need the help of the U.S. government to overthrow Goulart, and certainly did not need to be told that the U.S. government would be happy to see a new Brazilian regime. As Secretary of State Dean Rusk concluded just after the coup, despite U.S. "efforts to persuade Goulart to follow a democratic reform program, and despite . . . efforts to support the Brazilian economy by making large loans, Goulart had moved toward the creation of an authoritarian regime politically far to the left." The military understood the situation in the same way and could not countenance it.[70]

Reopening the Aid Pipeline to Reward the Military

Even before the coup succeeded, U.S. policymakers contemplated sending economic aid to a new government. On the morning of March 31, 1964, while the coup was still going on, Rusk asked Assistant Secretary of State for Inter-American Affairs Thomas Mann to "get someone to put together a task force" to "start working on post coup emergency assistance for Brazil." There was a general agreement in Washington that the United States would need to help the Brazilian military put the state back together.[71]

The Johnson administration was willing to offer increased economic aid despite the military's destruction of democracy. In a meeting on April 3, Johnson assured congressional leaders that the United States was "doing everything possible to get on top of the problem of helping the new government." This help would be directed at encouraging the Brazilian leaders to follow economic policies deemed appropriate in Washington. In a memo to Gordon on April 2, Mann explained that the United States should consider new aid packages focused on PL480, development of the northeast, agrarian reform, and effective use of U.S. loans. To Mann, concerned about who would take power, the suggestion of massive U.S. aid programs would be a way, and perhaps the best way, to ensure that the new government promoted economic policies that Washington thought prudent.[72]

Each time in previous military interventions, the Brazilian generals allowed civilians to assume the presidency, and in each case, from their perspective, it had not led to permanent stability. Thus, a faction within the military, which became dominant after the coup, suggested that returning power to civilians was a mistake. The military leadership, led by forceful young officers, decided to stay in power and "fix" Brazilian politics once and for all. In a series of *institutional acts*, the military declared a state of siege, cut the power of the congress, and deprived citizenship to anyone who was a threat to national security.[73]

Within days the congress, "encouraged" by the military, selected Castelo Branco as national president. Brazil did not turn into a harsh and repressive military dictatorship overnight. Castelo Branco's government allowed elections to continue, but increasingly began to control their outcomes. Initially, a set of 1965 laws only barred politicians who had served under Goulart from competing in elections. Later laws would eliminate all political parties.[74]

The United States welcomed Castelo Branco's assumption of power even though Gordon initially admitted to "considerable dismay" over the course of the political changes in Brazil. But Gordon understood that the United States had gained in the coup—or as the military called it, in the true fashion of political doublespeak, the "democratic revolution"—a more amenable government with which to move forward on shared political and economic goals. This was not simply U.S. policy in private. Mann explained in an interview with a leading Brazilian newspaper that as long as the new government supported a stabilization program and moved forward with self-help, the United States would make considerable funds available.[75]

Shortly after the coup, AID offered Castelo Branco a $50 million loan to help with the severe economic problems Goulart had left behind. In return, the new Brazilian government promised it would develop a threefold program to contain inflation, to build infrastructure, and to pursue reform. Castelo Branco insisted that his plan would be "entirely in line with [the] charter of Punta del Este."[76] The loan of $50 million was not enough though, and by August 1964, Lincoln Gordon made a pitch to the

State Department for a massive and unprecedented aid package. Upset at the small amount of the initial loan offer, Gordon argued, "After years of frustration watching [the] economy being mismanaged and country being subverted, [the] U.S. suddenly finds a . . . [government of Brazil] genuinely working in full spirit of [the] charter of Punta del Este." Therefore, Washington had to do more. Gordon recommended a program of between $600 million and $700 million each year for the foreseeable future. Of this money, $250 million would come from AID, and the rest would come from PL480, IADB, the World Bank, and private investors. European nations and Japan would also be encouraged to offer support.[77]

The U.S. government, Gordon suggested, had something of a responsibility toward Castelo Branco; having opposed Goulart and helped to guide plots against him, the new Brazilian leadership deserved special attention. Gordon claimed that as a result of the coup, the Brazilian government was now committed to real partnership and reform. In December 1964, because of this pressure, State Department officials decided to offer $250 million in aid; $100 million of this money would be in project lending, and the rest would be a program loan.[78]

Castelo Branco proved to be an excellent friend to the United States. Almost immediately his government broke relations with Cuba and took the lead in pushing for OAS action against Castro. Following the U.S. intervention in the Dominican Republic, the Brazilian government was active and conspicuous in its support. Though many Latin Americans opposed U.S. effort, the Brazilian military committed troops to join what became known as the Inter-American Police Force. These Brazilian troops allowed Johnson to argue that the occupation was an OAS operation. Without irony, Gordon wrote, "the new Brazilian government has now joined the free world."[79]

Overall, Washington was generally satisfied with Brazil. In a secret analysis the CIA explained, "the Castelo Branco government has provided responsible and effective leadership, reversing the movements toward chaos of the Goulart period and making an impressive start toward reasonable solutions of Brazil's many problems." But the CIA noted that the United States could not stop helping Brazil because of the country's economic problems. Hyperinflation had made growth impossible, and though Castelo Branco was trying, he was unable to reverse economic trends. The CIA report suggested that this could lead to more political chaos in Brazil.[80]

Johnson approved another program loan of $150 million in December 1965. Again, Gordon made the case that Castelo Branco was making progress toward economic stability and keeping Brazil secure. Mann argued in a memo for President Johnson that we have an "important stake . . . in the policies of Castelo Branco," a man who had an "outstanding record of self-help" and was under attack at home from both left and right-wing extremists." Mann continued, "Brazil is the keystone of our interests on the continent of South America. If we shave our assistance too close now we risk being penny wise and pound foolish." There was some discussion in the White House about only offering $100 million, but Dean Rusk pushed Johnson to support the full $150 million. He suggested that the United States could offer less in the new set of loans in an effort to be a little tougher with the Brazilians, but that this idea was not necessarily a good one. A smaller loan might look like the United States was punishing Brazil, and he wanted to avoid this at all costs. Castelo Branco seemed to be a leader the United States could work with. He came across as a man of dignity, and given his reputation as a legalist, as a man of honor. This perception remained, even though a CIA report on the Brazilian situation noted that there was no progress toward constitutional normalcy and that Castelo Branco had assumed for himself essentially unlimited powers.[81]

The United States did hope for some kind of consideration in return for its economic aid largesse. In late 1965 the Vietnam War was becoming an obsession for the Johnson administration. Policymakers in the United States decided to ask Castelo Branco for a suitable military contribution. In a meeting in mid-December 1965, Gordon told Castelo Branco about the $150 million loan, and at the same time made a pitch for Brazil to send troops to Vietnam. Though Gordon had been careful about being too explicit (he did not want to offend Castelo Branco's pride and make it seem as if the loan was a bribe), he did want to make it clear that the United States thought Brazilian participation in the conflict was necessary. This tactic did not succeed. Even though Castelo Branco initially gave signs that he would help, Brazilian troops never went to Vietnam; his government only donated medical supplies and coffee to the U.S. effort. But the Brazilian lack of support had no impact on funding decisions.[82]

Aid to Brazil continued throughout the late 1960s. Johnson signed a $150 million program loan in 1966 and a $100 million program loan for 1967. These loan totals do not include additional money from project loans or funds provided through the PL480 program, IADB, or the Export-Import Bank. Total U.S. funding was $329 million for FY1966, $240 million for FY1967, and $280 million for FY1968.[83]

This funding flowed even though Castelo Branco became even more authoritarian. In July 1964, Castelo Branco had the congress cancel presidential elections for 1965 and extended his own term until March 1967. He intervened to remove opposition leaders and manipulated state legislatures to guarantee that his allies would become governors. He then authorized a new constitution that made military dominance permanent. Following March 1967, conditions became even more repressive as General Artur

Costa e Silva, the war minister, assumed the presidency. Whereas Castelo Branco had been a moderate within the military, Costa e Silva had been among the most strident in calling for action against Goulart. It was a sign that human rights conditions would worsen over time.[84]

The Drift to Repression and the Final Aid Failure in Brazil

There was little U.S. criticism of the trend toward repressive dictatorship. Some U.S. policymakers were concerned, but they were careful to express their disappointment in an indirect way. For example, in a speech about the Alliance for Progress in November 1966, Vice President Hubert Humphrey deplored, without mentioning Brazil by name, the curtailment of democratic reforms in Latin America. More typical of the U.S. approach was an effort to invite Costa e Silva to Washington in January 1967 so Johnson could develop a personal relationship with him.[85]

The Brazilian military, after beginning economic reform, backed away from movements toward what might be considered self-help. In March 1967 the United States signed a major agreement with Costa e Silva to modernize the national education system. When the program faced criticism in Brazil, he abandoned it. The United States also tried to get the armed forces to pursue agrarian and labor reforms, but without success. The Brazilian military also failed to follow through on commitments made in the early 1960s. The United States had helped build two housing projects in Rio de Janeiro—Vila Kennedy and Vila Aliança. These communities turned into failures because the government did not provide them enough access to transportation networks and charged high rents. Efforts to build schools in the northeast also failed. Though the United States had hoped to build almost 16,000 new classrooms, just under 3,000 were actually completed. The Brazilian military had not committed itself to internal reform nor to the developmentalist ideals of the Alliance for Progress.[86] (see Figure I.10 following page 148.)

There was some discussion within the U.S. government in mid-1967 about confronting the Brazilian government with its lack of effective economic reform and withholding funds as a result. This was standard procedure in Alliance for Progress loans elsewhere. Yet in Brazil, fears about instability and a desire to see the Costa e Silva government succeed ensured that U.S. policymakers would continue to provide funding. The U.S. ambassador in Brazil following Gordon, John Tuthill, wrote in a telling memo to White House and State Department officials in June 1967, "There is no question that a number of steps which the new government [of Costa e Silva] has taken are ill-advised. There is also no doubt that they have failed so far to comply with important [Alliance for Progress] goals."

He continued, "[it is] almost inexcusable that Costa e Silva . . . [has not] developed an economic program." But Tuthill found an excuse. He suggested that the political problems of governance were so complex that trying to create stability was far more important. He argued, successfully, that the United States should not even confront Costa e Silva with the idea that failure to comply with loan criteria would lead to curtailment of aid programs. Confronting the Brazilians with an ultimatum would lead to a more conflict-prone relationship, which would ultimately limit U.S. influence and likely weaken Costa e Silva.[87]

There were no real attempts to guide Brazil toward more democracy, and in December 1968 the Brazilian military under Costa e Silva decided to increase its power even more.[88] To limit dissent the military closed the Brazilian congress permanently, suspended the rights of habeas corpus, and took complete control of the national and state governments. Individuals lost all rights to work, property, or free speech. Media censorship and control of education became routine and opponents of the regime, and even those who simply wanted to work toward aims different from the regime, were imprisoned. By the end of 1969, the United Nations International Commission of Jurists concluded that torture was being "systematically used against political prisoners."[89]

Only at this point did Washington halt aid programs. Brazil had received $280.7 million in FY1968, but only $29.2 million in FY1969. The turn toward repression was extremely disheartening to U.S. officials, partially because there was little they could do, and partially because they realized the situation in Brazil indicated a failure of U.S. policy. They had wanted an anti-Communist government, and could even tolerate a military one, but it was hard to accept a repressive military regime. The United States could protest privately, and even suggest publicly that they hoped the military would step back from repression, but because of the long ties with the military, completely walking away would have been quite embarrassing. As Ruth Leacock, a historian of U.S.–Brazilian relations explains, Washington got caught up in the semantic doublespeak of the Brazilian military. Castelo Branco had called his movement a democratic response to Goulart's actions and explained that his control over the political process was done in the interests of defending democracy. Because U.S. policymakers had not done an effective enough job of divorcing themselves from these fallacies, they had failed to come to terms with the fact that Brazil was, over time, becoming more authoritarian than democratic. The United States continually overestimated the Brazilian military's desire to return to real democracy.[90]

Final Thoughts

By the end of the 1960s the situation in Brazil mattered little to Washington officials. The Alliance for Progress had been designed as a means to exert influence on Brazil, but that policy failed and there was little the United States could do. The policy had, in reality, failed much earlier. The United States had been unable, and unwilling, to engage Quadros or Goulart in ways that suggested real partnership. In this case the Brazilian leaders share much of the blame. Their desire to have it both ways, to gain U.S. support but retain an independent line, was unrealistic and destined to create antagonism.

Support for the military seemed like the best option, and the only one after the coup. Continuing to provide funds throughout the later part of the decade was the only way to justify earlier actions and to try, in vain, to influence change. By the end of the 1960s the turn toward repression was a convenient excuse for extricating the United States from a distasteful situation. The kinds of politicians the U.S. supported in Brazil were very different from the ones backed in Chile, but the end result was the same. In Brazil, foreign aid did not buy all that much.

At the start of the 1960s the Alliance for Progress in Brazil was a way to encourage resistant left-leaning politicians to accept U.S. leadership. When this failed, it became a way to undermine Goulart's government. Finally, after the coup, it became a way to reward a pro-U.S. military government for achieving political stability. None of these strategies had much to do with the Charter of Punta del Este. Kennedy's initial vision was that the Alliance for Progress was to be a partnership between the United States and Latin American nations committed to reform and improving material conditions. This obviously did not happen in Brazil. At least in Chile, U.S. policymakers thought promoting reform should be a top priority, though not always in the short term. In Brazil, because of concerns about Quadros and Goulart, it actually became a tool to undermine the political system. This does not mean U.S. policymakers completely failed to encourage self-help and reform, only that they did so to weaken a democratic government. Metaphorically speaking, if the Alliance for Progress was a lever in Chile, it was a stick in Brazil. This changed when the military took over; then it became a present.

CHAPTER **6**

The Dominican Republic and the Alliance for Progress

Using Aid to Clean Up the Post-Trujillo and Postintervention Messes

From FY1962 to FY1969 (July 1, 1961 to June 30, 1969), the Dominican Republic received $402.3 million in U.S. economic aid. (see Table 6.1) This made the country the fourth highest recipient of Alliance for Progress funding.[1] As with other aid recipients, the timing of aid to the Dominican Republic followed a pattern closely connected to political events. The United States did not offer funding to Rafael Trujillo, an odious military dictator, but following his assassination, his family's exile, and the creation of a democratic regime, the United States began to offer tentative but substantial support. However, the bulk of aid sent to the Dominican Republic came during, and in the aftermath of, the military intervention in 1965. After determining that it was necessary to send soldiers to ensure political stability, it made sense to send money to ensure that economic systems would also be stable.

Often there was little connection between aid to the Dominican Republic and Alliance for Progress mechanisms, yet as with Chile and Brazil, this case demonstrates how the United States attempted to use aid for political purposes in Latin America during the 1960s. Policymakers in the United States imagined that aid could change the political landscape in Chile and Brazil, but in the Dominican Republic, political conditions were far more precarious. Aid became a way to help create effective systems rather than to influence existing systems. It also illustrates how aid programs

Table 6.1 U.S. Economic Assistance Loans and Grants to the Dominican Republic, FY1962–FY1969 (in millions of U.S. dollars; data not adjusted for inflation)

Year	FY1962 7/1/61– 6/30/62	FY1963 7/1/62– 6/30/63	FY1964 7/1/63– 6/30/64	FY1965 7/1/64– 6/30/65	FY1966 7/1/65– 6/30/66	FY1967 7/1/66– 6/30/67	FY1968 7/1/67– 6/30/68	FY1969 7/1/68– 6/30/69
Loans and Grants	27	50.2	14.5	66.2	100.6	58.8	58.7	26.3

Source: United States Agency for International Development website, The Greenbook (http://qesdb.cdie.org/gbk).

intersected with other types of foreign policy actions. In Chile and Brazil, aid programs were usually the most important bilateral issue. This was not the case in the Dominican Republic. The United States employed military intervention and a host of diplomatic maneuvers to influence political change. These other tools often defined the relationship. The Alliance for Progress had an important supporting role, but it was just that—a means to support other ways of affecting Dominican politics.

Trujillo's Megalomaniacal Leadership

The Dominican Republic is situated on the eastern half of the island of Hispaniola, which it shares with Haiti. It is a small country of only 18,704 square miles and containing, in 1960, just over 3 million people.[2] Through the nineteenth and most of the twentieth centuries, the country had great difficultly developing an effective government. Howard Wiarda, a scholar of Dominican history, calculated that between 1844 and 1930 there "were fifty presidents (one every 1.7 years) and thirty revolutions (one every 2.9 years)," and "With the exception of Venezuela, the Dominican Republic had more constitutions (twenty-two) than any other country in the world."[3]

The country had a difficult time achieving independence in the first place. Only in 1865, after struggles against Haiti and a war with Spain, the country finally became permanently independent. It was, however, not a particularly deep sovereignty. Decades of internal conflict among corrupt military leaders kept effective political systems from emerging. Political leaders usually proved to be inept and corrupt financial managers, borrowing far more than they had the ability to repay. When inevitable loan defaults occurred, foreign governments, most notably the United States, became involved in local politics. In 1905 the United States took control of Dominican custom houses and used the income to pay off the nation's creditors. U.S. involvement increased as disorder continued and a civil war developed. To protect its interests, the United States intervened in 1916 and occupied the country until 1924. As part of an effort to create stability in the wake of the invasion, U.S. Marines organized and trained a national police force, which would become the national army. Following withdrawal of U.S. forces, a popular officer, Rafael Leonidas Trujillo Molina, used this new army to seize power.[4]

Trujillo was keenly aware that good relations with Washington were vital to his security. He also knew that during the years of occupation the Dominican economy had become inexorably linked to the United States, especially through the sugar trade. He became an exceptionally strong supporter of U.S. international positions, and throughout most of his tenure, U.S. leaders believed he was as a reliable ally who had brought peace to a poor country.

Trujillo treated the country as his personal property, even going as far as renaming Santo Domingo, the capital city, *Ciudad Trujillo* (Trujillo City). As part of his domination, Trujillo came to control the economic life of the country. By 1960 Trujillo personally owned about two-thirds of the nation's total productive capacity, more than half its farmland, and most of the nation's sugar-refining facilities. Central to Trujillo's power was his ability to use the armed forces, a secret police force, and a vast network of informers to terrorize the people. He also controlled the education system, creating an official "cult" which taught students about Trujillo's virtues. All good things, and even many ordinary things, that the government gave the people were Trujillo's gifts. Yet the dictator was always careful to give his regime the appearance of democracy. After serving as president at the beginning of his tenure, he allowed others to win crafted elections and occupy the position.[5]

By the late 1950s the megalomaniacal Trujillo had become something of a pariah in the region as other military dictators lost power. Between 1956 and 1959, repressive leaders fell in Honduras, Colombia, Venezuela, and Cuba. New democratic leaders, most notably Rómulo Betancourt of Venezuela, became committed to helping encourage change in the Dominican Republic. In response, Trujillo sponsored anti-Betancourt groups and ultimately an assassination attempt against the Venezuelan. As a result of his actions, an Organization of American States (OAS) meeting of Foreign Ministers in San Jose, Costa Rica, in August 1960 condemned the Dominican government and called on all member states to break relations with it. Five months later the OAS voted to impose limited economic sanctions on the Dominican Republic, encouraging member nations to cut all oil, truck, and spare part shipments.[6]

Getting Rid of the Trujillo Family

Following the OAS decisions, Eisenhower limited Dominican sugar sales in the United States and prohibited trade in key goods with the country. The international pressure emboldened domestic opposition and assassination plots abounded. Despite these actions, U.S. diplomats were not sure that anything would happen, even though they estimated that from 80 to 90 percent of all literate people in the country hoped that Trujillo would be overthrown and some groups had approached U.S. officials asking for weapons.[7]

Because Trujillo was so loathsome, it was impossible to offer him any Alliance for Progress money. As McGeorge Bundy, Kennedy's special assistant for national security affairs explained, "there can be little doubt that the whole concept of the Alliance for Progress would be gravely shadowed in the eyes of Latin Americans if we were to move to anything like a policy of 'friendly guidance' toward Trujillo." Any connections with Trujillo or any efforts to help him would undercut Kennedy's attempt to be seen as a liberal leader in Latin America.[8]

In light of the experience with Batista in Cuba, U.S. policymakers worried about what might happen if Trujillo lost control, especially abruptly, because it could cause a vacuum of power that Communists could fill. Therefore, while Kennedy opposed Trujillo, his ouster was not necessarily the best option for the United States. Washington needed to encourage change, but in a controlled way. This led, in May 1961, to the creation of contingency plans for dealing with post-Trujillo regimes. Policymakers in the United States were aware of rebels in Cuba and Venezuela who hoped to overthrow Trujillo, but reasoned that these groups were unlikely to be amenable to U.S. influence. More attractive were a series of anti-Trujillo moderate leaders who had been in close contact with the U.S. Consulate in Ciudad Trujillo. But it became hard to determine who would be successful. It certainly was possible that in the wake of a coup d'état, radical or Communist elements might be able to seize power. To guard against this eventuality, Kennedy ordered the military to prepare to invade the Dominican Republic, just in case.[9]

The coup U.S. policymakers expected happened in late May. Three cars ambushed Trujillo's limousine, and using CIA-supplied weapons, eight assailants fired more than 70 rounds of ammunition into it. Trujillo's death ended his more than thirty-year rule. This did not mean the end of the Trujillo dictatorship, however, because no mass uprising or military revolts followed. Trujillo's handpicked president, Joaquín Balaguer, remained in office, but more significantly, Trujillo's son, Ramfis, moved quickly to gain control of the armed forces. Ramfis had been groomed from a young age to eventually take power. He had been made a full colonel in the army at age four and a brigadier general at nine. All was not an easy path for Ramfis, who had developed a reputation as a playboy. He had also flunked out of the U.S. Army War College at Fort Leavenworth, Kansas. Nevertheless, Ramfis's ability to control the armed forces gave him effective control over the political system.[10]

The anarchy that Kennedy expected and had planned for did not develop. To pacify the United States, Ramfis promised limited reforms and there was a slight opening of the political system. Yet he was unable to dominate political structures as his father had, and by September 1961 many segments of the Dominican population began calling for him to leave. Even Balaguer, a loyal Trujillo ally, began distancing himself. Kennedy was concerned about the situation, but largely in the context of what would come next. He is reported to have mused, "There are three possibilities in descending order of preference: a decent democratic regime, a continuation of the Trujillo regime, or a Castro regime. We ought to aim for the first, but we can't really renounce the second until we are sure that we can avoid the third." That is, Kennedy hoped that the Dominican Republic would begin a reform process, but if there was any chance of that reform leading to a Communist government, Ramfis would have to stay.[11]

To understand what was going on in the Dominican Republic and to push Ramfis and the rest of the Trujillo clan to leave in an orderly way, Kennedy sent John Bartlow Martin on a mission to the country. Martin was a writer who had experience in the country and he had worked on the 1960 Kennedy election. Martin recognized that the Trujillo family had great power and that even steps toward democratization would still mean that Ramfis would control most of the country. He recommended, as a solution, that Ramfis be encouraged to sell, at reasonable prices, much of his family property. While he would still be allowed to dominate the armed forces, some kind of free election would be necessary. Martin suggested that if the Dominicans took these steps the United States could reward the government with aid and prod it to continue to move toward real democracy. Based on Martin's arguments, White House aide Richard Goodwin penned a memo to Kennedy arguing that if the government did make serious changes, the United States should send "a series of missions to the Dominican Republic—economic development, agriculture, organization of public administration, even a constitutional government mission—to help re-establish a viable society." Goodwin concluded, "The presence of these missions and their work is the surest short-term guarantee of some sort of stability." While he did not mention the Alliance for Progress, the implication was that economic aid through the program would be a reward for any political reform.[12]

By November 1961, pressure on Ramfis convinced him, and the rest of his family, that they should leave the Dominican Republic voluntarily. While Ramfis had considerable support in the armed forces, U.S. officials made it clear that they would not lift sanctions associated with the OAS declarations while the Trujillo family was in power. This meant that the Dominican Republic could not sell sugar to the United States and its economy would have great difficulty in functioning. To help get the Trujillo family to leave and to make sure the transition was a peaceful one in which U.S. interests were assured, Kennedy sent a series of naval vessels to Dominican waters and Air Force jets buzzed the capital. Balaguer, who had come to believe that he could consolidate power himself if Ramfis left, was informed that U.S. troops would be happy to arrange a "courtesy visit" to Ciudad Trujillo. These tactics worked. The appearance of U.S. ships and encouragement from U.S. diplomats was enough to encourage leaders in the armed forces to renounce support for Ramfis and pledge loyalty to Balaguer. Ramfis wisely determined that the end was near and escaped on his yacht. He understood that escaping as a wealthy man was better than ending up as his father had.[13]

Aid to Help Bolster the Council of State

The demise of the Trujillo regime did not mean an immediate turn to representative democracy in the Dominican Republic as Balaguer, who had a long history of collaboration with Trujillo, remained president. Kennedy hoped that immediately after Ramfis left the country Balaguer would announce elections. He did not. Washington had considerable resources to pressure Balaguer, however, including refusal to lift economic sanctions or allow sugar exports into the United States. On the other hand, U.S. policymakers promised "the extension of the Alliance for Progress to the Dominican people" if he resigned. This tactic was successful and Balaguer agreed in January 1962 to step down. An interim Council of State took over with the goal of running the government until legislative elections in August 1962 and presidential elections four months later.[14]

In January 1962, to help the interim government stabilize the country, the Kennedy administration offered a $25 million Alliance for Progress loan to deal with a difficult balance-of-payments problem. The money also went to the creation of planning agencies, efforts to create an agricultural bank for small farmers, and the restructuring of the formerly Trujillo-dominated sugar industry. Kennedy also reopened the sugar trade and released $22 million from shipments to the United States that had not been paid because of the boycott. As they would again after the 1965 intervention, U.S. officials recognized that they had an interest in helping promote short-term economic stability in the Dominican Republic. They consistently feared that the country would descend into chaos and that the Communists might somehow take power. The loss of sugar income due to the sanctions, plus the looting of the economy by the Trujillo family and the need to restructure the economy after their departure, meant that the Dominican Republic could have faced severe economic upheaval, which could have played into the hands of pro-Castro Dominican elements. The Alliance for Progress, in this case, acted as an anti-chaos mechanism.[15]

A Department of State policy directive on the Dominican Republic issued in May 1962 reinforced many of these points. The United States, the paper suggested, should remain committed to aid programs in the country as long as the Council of State, which was led by members of the armed forces, proceeded with elections on schedule. The United States should also, according to the policy statement, encourage the Council of State and the two leading parties that had emerged, the National Civil Union/*Unión Cívica Nacional* (UCN) and the Dominican Revolutionary Party/*Partido Revolucionario Dominicana* (PRD), to develop agreements about "the principle of agrarian reform" and "specific economic and social projects under the Alliance for Progress." Aid would also be a way for the United States to help the Dominican government "finance a thorough inventory and analysis, by a first-class U.S. management group, of all the Trujillo properties." Through AID, the United States could also "help the Dominican Government in obtaining technical assistance to operate the properties efficiently." The State Department also hoped to "Expand, coordinate and improve the technical assistance and training programs of the Alliance organizations in the economic and financial agencies of the Dominican Government, as the priority element of a public administration program." It would "Provide AID financing for a privately prepared and presented 'political literacy' course to teach, through radio and television, the basic principles and procedures of democratic government."[16]

Manipulating Sugar Quotas to Help the Dominican Economy

How much money the United States would send to the Dominican Republic was a key issue. But beyond direct financial support, the country's economic health was tied to the United States because of the importance of sugar. Roughly 50 percent of all government foreign exchange revenues came from sugar and 60 percent of sugar sales came from formerly Trujillo-owned, but now government-owned, firms.

A U.S. quota determined the amount of Dominican sugar exports. The U.S. government offered each sugar-exporting nation a set fraction of the total market. Manipulating that share, or even threatening to manipulate that share, could have an incredible impact on the Dominican economy.[17]

The Dominican Republic benefited from its generous sugar quota, but in mid-1962 this situation began to change. The Kennedy administration and Congress moved to eliminate the national quotas in favor of a single quota for all sugar imports into the United States. That is, instead of assigning quotas for specific countries, the United States would only assign a percentage of the total market to foreign producers. This step was supposed to protect the domestic sugar industry and lower what many in Washington thought was an artificially high price for sugar. Kennedy's announcement that he would support this legislation created a storm of protest in the Dominican Republic. The Council of State threatened to immediately cancel all AID agreements and suspend the Alliance for Progress in the Dominican Republic.[18] This appeared to punish the Dominican Republic, not the United States, but it would seriously limit U.S. efforts to influence the country.

The withdrawal of the sugar quota was a blow to U.S.–Dominican relations. While not necessarily an aid question, sugar sales were to be the primary means by which the Dominican government would finance economic development. Kennedy promised to help the Dominican Republic develop stability, but the new sugar legislation signaled that the promise might be meaningless. Thus, the sugar issue was not just economic, it was also psychological and political. John Bartlow Martin, who had become the U.S. ambassador in March 1962, wrote,

> The Council of State has staked everything on US support. Now that that support has, in the Dominican view, been suddenly withdrawn, some Councilors instinctively feel that [the] Council can save [it]self only by setting its face against US and going it alone. Others do not go so far, but feel [the] need to somehow disentangle [the] Council from [the] U[nited] S[tates]. Councilors therefore propose to shut the sugar mills, cut wages, tighten belts, and go it alone. They propose to stop—and in fact have already stopped—spending any more of the $25 million US loan made in January on ground[s] they cannot obligate future government[s] to debt it cannot pay since its sugar quota is cut. . . . This stops [the] Alliance dead. It threatens suicide of [the] Council, since if [the] Council tries to go it alone, it will probably fail. [An] austerity—isolation policy can bring only more unemployment, misery and unrest. [It also] will open [the] door to left, and if left rises, [the] military right probably would take over. So ends moderate democracy here. Of course, if AID had gotten off [the] ground and projects were already actually employing people, [the] Council

would have difficulty stopping them. But AID has not. So Dominican pressure to continue [the] program (which might be termed by critics only a pile of papers anyway) is likely to be minimal.

Martin believed that the Dominican decision was not some kind of attempt to blackmail Congress, but came from a real fear that without sugar income the Dominican Republic would never be able to repay its loans. In a country with a history of financial problems that had even faced an intervention by U.S. Marines to control the customshouse because of debt, the Council of State was understandably scared.[19]

Martin's argument encouraged Kennedy administration officials to push for a bill that retained the Dominican Republic's full quota. This did not get much support in Congress. As an alternative, Kennedy supported legislation to allow the Dominican Republic a much smaller special quota (190,000 tons of sugar as opposed to its earlier quota of 900,000). To get the Dominican government to accept this change, the Kennedy administration agreed to set up a special $30 million aid package to make up the difference in the expected loss of income over a three-year period. This move helped convince the Dominican leadership to resume Alliance for Progress projects. The Kennedy administration shifted another special quota allocated for Cuba, but obviously not being spent, to the Dominican Republic. Finally, an amendment to the bill also allowed Kennedy discretion in distributing an additional special quota of 225,000 tons. Initially about half, but ultimately the bulk of this quota, went to the Dominican Republic as well.[20]

Attempting to Tie Bosch to U.S. Aid, But without Much Enthusiasm

Once the sugar crisis passed, Dominican politics shifted to focus on presidential elections in December 1962. Juan Bosch, the left-leaning PRD candidate, established himself as the early favorite. In exile for 26 years, Bosch had been a powerful anti-Trujillo voice calling for democratic reform. During this time he also developed close ties with a group of important Latin American anti-Communist leftist leaders including José Figueres of Costa Rica, Victor Raúl Haya de la Torre of Peru, and Romulo Betancourt of Venezuela. No other candidate had such stature, and as a result he won by more than a two-to-one margin over his closest competitor.[21]

The United States had aggressively supported the elections, and Bosch understood that Washington's interests in promoting democracy and stability in his country could lead to greater aid programs. Bosch visited Washington in late 1962 to make the case that his country needed more help. In meetings with Kennedy, he indicated his strong support for the

Alliance for Progress and explained that his country faced serious problems as "a result of unemployment, under-investment, a lack of farm-to-market roads and inefficient and slow production." He hoped that a $35 or $40 million Alliance for Progress loan would solve many of these issues. Bosch also pushed Kennedy for help in developing a program that would provide loans to small farmers. Kennedy, understanding how difficult conditions were, and hoping that Bosch would succeed, was amenable to offering assistance. The people of the Dominican Republic needed to see that, in some way Bosch's government was going to make life better. Economic development would create stability and ensure that radical leftists would not gain a foothold. Kennedy believed that this kind of program was exactly what the Alliance for Progress should be doing.[22]

Though Bosch won the election, like President João Goulart in Brazil, he did not necessarily have a great deal of control over the machinery of power. The UCN, which had become the party representing the economic elite, was extremely hostile to his calls for reform. More importantly, Bosch did not have the support of the military or the national police led by Antonio Imbert. As a member of the Council of State, Imbert had orchestrated a massive increase in the size of the police force, whose members were loyal to him.[23]

Bosch's power was also limited by the fact that John Bartlow Martin, the U.S. ambassador, really did not trust him. Even before Bosch took power, Martin suggested that the odds of Bosch being successful were slim. This was not due to the steep challenge of creating stability or growth, but because Martin thought he might be "a deep-cover communist." The solution, to Martin, was to "hang onto the military," and to save Imbert "as an ace in the hole." Martin argued in a memo on Bosch's prospects that the United States should "do all the nice things to build for the future and strengthen democratic institutions," but do these in a way that goes "over the head of the government to the people themselves." Martin did suggest that the United States "should, of course, support Bosch until he goes wrong," but he continued, "if he ever goes wrong—and I mean if his basic loyalties ever belong to another country than his own—we had better have the military on our side and, if it happens soon, Imbert . . . as well. That might pit us against the people, and the results would not be pretty to contemplate. But we can have no new Castro in the Caribbean."[24]

According to Martin, the way to help Bosch and ensure that he would be agreeable with respect to U.S. interests, was to use aid to "tie him so closely to us that he cannot wriggle loose." Martin continued in a memo on aid policy, "At the same time . . . we should try to avoid tying ourselves too tightly to him—should not build him up too much, should not bet on him too heavily, should not propagate the idea that the Alliance is sure to succeed here if anywhere. The prospects here seem dazzling—but we must not be bedazzled, for the inherent difficulties are still enormous." Martin believed that the United States needed to help, however. He explained, "during the months ahead the emphasis of our work will shift from the political to the economic. Alongside Bosch, the *Alianza* [Alliance for Progress] should do better than alongside the Council of State—the Council was a semi-caretaker, and its oligarchs shrank from some *Alianza* goals." Nevertheless, Bosch was not to be trusted completely.[25]

According to Martin, Bosch failed to provide effective leadership almost immediately on taking power. He was consistently frustrated and confused by Bosch's efforts and thought he was obstinate and naive. Martin's beliefs came from Bosch's unwillingness to follow U.S. direction. Like Goulart, Bosch wanted to pursue an independent foreign policy and allow Communists to participate in national politics. It baffled Martin, for example, that Bosch allowed a pro-Castro exile, Maximo López Molina, to return to the country. It suggested that Bosch was not reliable.[26]

Through 1963 Martin's frustrations grew. By September he was advocating a radically interventionist policy. He suggested in a memo to Washington:

> I believe that we should recognize Bosch is not much of a president, that we should recognize most of his opposition is almost equally incompetent, and that we should attempt to take his government away from him, insofar as possible. This involves what amounts to an extension of activist diplomacy. That is to say, we should woo his own supporters, ministers, and advisors ardently; use every means—or almost every means—to get rid of those whom we cannot control; exert every pressure to put our own people close to him and the other levers of power and, to the extent possible, though these people run his government without his knowing it.

Some of this would take additional funds, and Martin encouraged AID to make more money available for the country.[27]

According to Piero Gliejeses, a historian of U.S.–Dominican relations, U.S. opposition to supporting Bosch suggests a persistent "imperial behavior" in Latin America. He wrote that although the United States supported some democratic leftist reformers, "in order to belong to the circle of 'good boys' a Latin American leader had to prove his qualifications according to the narrow and arbitrary criteria set by the Kennedy administration." In other words, while the United States wanted democratic leftist reformers to take power in Latin America, it did not want them to be too leftist or democratic enough that they would allow radical leftists to participate in the political process.[28]

The Willingness to Send Aid to the Triumvirate

Martin's plan was not put into place because on September 25, 1963 the military overthrew Bosch. They claimed he was incompetent and allowing Communists to flourish. To run the country, and to serve as a front for military leadership, the leading generals created a three-man civilian junta, the Triumvirate. There is no good evidence that the United States was behind the coup, although military leaders did understand that Washington would not be particularly upset about an end to Bosch's tenure. Yet, while Martin was happy to see Bosch fall, the return to military rule was a problem, at least symbolically. In the Alliance for Progress the United States had committed to promoting democracy, therefore the Kennedy administration felt it had little choice but to suspended diplomatic relations and recall Martin.[29]

Given the difficult transition from the Trujillo dictatorship, U.S. policymakers could not publically embrace a return to military rule. The Dominican situation was complicated by the fact that in the preceeding months governments in Peru, Guatemala, and Ecuador were all overthrown, and there was another coup in Honduras shortly afterwards. These coups suggested that the Alliance for Progress was failing. Latin American governments seemed to be regressing towards dictatorship and away from progressive reformist leadership. Thus, while there was little unhappiness about seeing Bosch go, Kennedy administration officials argued that it was absolutely necessary to limit economic support in the Dominican Republic to send the message that the United States rejected the return of militarism.[30]

The plan to avoid supporting the military changed quickly though. A memo from the State Department in October 1963 argued that the Dominican people should not suffer from the misdeeds of their leaders. It suggested that programs such as PL480 and the Peace Corps continue. At the same time, some U.S. policymakers began strategizing about ways to encourage the military to move back to constitutional government and to proceed with Alliance for Progress reforms.[31]

Changes in Washington were also important in encouraging a closer relationship with the Dominican armed forces. As Johnson replaced Kennedy and Thomas Mann became assistant secretary of state for inter-American affairs, promoting stability became more important than democracy and reform. The Mann Doctrine maintained that moral judgments about particular governments were less important than practical considerations. This change suggested that military rule was not an obstacle, but useful in advancing U.S. interests. A more favorable attitude toward the Triumvirate also came from its scheduling of elections for 1965. The elections gave U.S.

policymakers a clear objective: the improvement of economic conditions to ensure the return of democracy. To meet this goal, they developed new Alliance for Progress programs. In May 1964, they authorized a $4 million Export-Import Bank loan for road maintenance equipment and 1,500 new housing units. These small efforts, and others such as a $1.1 million loan for education programs, were supposed to prove that the United States was a friend of the Dominican people. They were not technically impact projects, but they operated as such.[32]

Reflecting a new sensibility about aid to the military, the new U.S. ambassador in Santo Domingo, W. Tapley Bennett, who served as Martin's replacement, called for an aggressive aid program to help the Triumvirate. He noted that the Dominican political system was a mess, and this was causing the poor, who were the bulk of the population, to shift their sympathies leftward. The unrest in the country suggested to him that the United States must redevelop a full-scale Alliance for Progress program. If this did not happen, it was possible that the Dominican public might go Communist.[33]

Donald Reid Cabral, the leader of the Triumvirate, was willing to work with the United States, but he did not intend to play the role of supplicant. In public speeches, he claimed that Alliance for Progress money would help build a series of projects, including development of new port facilities. Reid also told the Dominican press that the United States would pay for roads and hospitals in the country. That is, instead of waiting for the United States to use aid to manipulate him, he made speeches explaining, erroneously, that Washington had committed to specific projects. This, he hoped, would force the United States' hand. Policymakers in the United States, while rejecting most of Reid's ideas, did appreciate his reform efforts. They had determined that Bosch had not been able to tackle the economic system, but calculated that Reid seemed willing to do so. Nevertheless, they pushed Reid toward accepting a more realistic and more U.S.-directed approach.[34]

In large part, objections came from the nature of the things Reid wanted. Concerned about productive capacity, the United States was not interested in funding port facilities, hospitals, or roads, but instead wanted to focus on supporting agricultural growth and improvements in education. As it would be most everywhere, Washington was also concerned with inflation. In July 1964, U.S. policymakers pushed Reid to accept IMF limitations on government spending to keep inflation down. The quid pro quo, for Reid, was a statement from the United States that it would give the Dominican Republic an aid program of "generous proportions." This meant, to the Dominicans, something on the order of $50 million. Although this was too large for the Johnson administration to contemplate, the U.S. embassy did consider a $25 million loan that would be under strict controls. While

$25 million or even $50 million would not have been considered a sizeable loan in other target countries, given the size of the Dominican Republic, and the history of offering aid there, the sums were significant.[35] But the State Department rejected the idea of a massive loan; there were just too many concerns about Reid and the Dominican Republic. Officials in the United States insisted that loans should follow definitive signs that a reform program had begun. This was not a rejection of aid to Reid's government, only a concern about spending money wisely.[36]

In late 1964 Reid began to pursue an economic stabilization program written in large part by the State Department, and promised the IMF that he would institute an austerity program to cut government spending to fix the government's deep balance-of-payments problem. Meanwhile, the Reid government also made progress toward curbing imports and improving tax collection, partially through being more aggressive in training tax collectors and hounding tax evaders. The IMF was pleased about this, along with the successful efforts to cut imports. While the country still faced massive budget problems, and according to the IMF imports were still excessive, there was hope for the economic future. As a result, by October 1964, the United States was working on a $15 million aid program and an additional $10 million loan in January 1965. These loans would support growth in agricultural productivity, economic stabilization, impact projects, and some food imports under the PL480 program.[37]

Drifting Toward Civil War

The real problem for Reid was not economic, it was political. The former presidents, Bosch and Balaguer, who were in exile, both worked to increase their influence in the country and challenged Reid's authority. Bosch, who claimed he was still the legitimate president and had become more radical in exile, was the greater threat. He retained a great deal of support throughout Dominican society.[38]

On April 24, 1965 a group of young pro-Bosch military officers staged a revolt. They hoped Bosch's return would break up the command structure, which had changed little since Trujillo's assassination. Quickly seizing the initiative, the rebels took control of most of Santo Domingo, and began preparing to fight the rest of the armed forces. Pro-Bosch civilians joined the rebellious soldiers as well. Reid decided that given the conflict within the military, which had created the Triumvirate in the first place, he should resign. Many military leaders, especially the senior commanders, found the revolt, the participation of civilians, and the idea of bringing Bosch back appalling. They vowed to fight and the country drifted toward civil war.[39]

President Johnson, in consultation with Mann, decided to send in a force of 400 Marines to evacuate U.S. citizens caught in the midst of the conflict. While this action was initially about the evacuation, Mann expressed a fear that Bosch might take power again and hoped that U.S. Marines might play some role in stopping this. As Mann explained in a telephone conversation with Johnson as the civil war was emerging, "we do not think this fellow Bosch understands the Communist danger. We do not think he is a Communist but what we are afraid of is that if he gets back in, he will have so many of them around him; and they are so much smarter than he is, that before you know it, they'd begin to take over." Mann obviously had little respect for Bosch's capabilities and explained that Bosch was "kind of a literary man. He writes books but he is the most impractical fellow in the world —sort of an idealist floating around on cloud nine type."[40]

During the first days of fighting it appeared the pro-Bosch forces were winning. To help stabilize the situation and help the anti-Bosch forces, Johnson decided to send an additional 1,200 troops to Santo Domingo. The fact that U.S. citizens remained in the city seemed to provide a reasonable pretext for more involvement. Far more important in encouraging the intervention were reports that some of leaders of the pro-Bosch movement were, in the words of the CIA Director William Raborn, "hard-core, Castro-trained guerrillas that . . . pushed aside the Bosch people and took command of the forces."[41]

On April 30, a second group of U.S. Marines landed in the city and two battalions went to the headquarters of the anti-Bosch forces outside Santo Domingo.[42] While some U.S. officials doubted the infiltration of Communists into the pro-Bosch forces, Johnson believed it and therefore thought intervention was appropriate. In a meeting with his top foreign policy advisors, he argued that the United States had fought Communism all over the world, and that it was reasonable and necessary to fight it somewhere so close to home. Johnson's understanding of the rebels stretched the available evidence. There was no good intelligence that the pro-Bosch rebel group was either dominated by Communists or that if they were victorious, Communists might be able to take power. This mattered little to Johnson, who seemed to have developed a gut feeling about the rebels, even if the evidence suggested otherwise.[43]

As troops were arriving, the Johnson administration began an effort to shift diplomatic responsibility for managing the crisis to the OAS, while still retaining control. The intervention was extremely unpopular in Latin America, not because of any love for Bosch, but because of traditional concerns with aggressive and unilateral U.S. action. Much like the first decades of the twentieth century, many Latin Americans saw that U.S. policymakers still assumed that "might made right." The intervention also was particularly damaging to the Alliance for Progress ideal of U.S.-Latin American partnership. By pushing the OAS to take the lead, Johnson was able to claim that the United States was working in concert with its regional partners to solve the problem. An OAS team helped broker a cease-fire between the two forces in Santo Domingo, and in Washington, the OAS council voted to send a peace commission to help restore order.[44]

Johnson quickly increased the number of troops on the ground in Santo Domingo to 6,200, and then to 14,000. U.S. officials convinced enough states to support an OAS resolution calling for the creation of the Inter-American Police Force (IAPF) for the Dominican Republic. Though the United States expected that at least ten countries would help, only six nations, five of which were dictatorships, contributed to the efforts. The total force was composed of 1,152 Brazilian, 250 Honduran, 184 Paraguayan, 159 Nicaraguan, 21 Costa Rican, and 3 El Salvadoran troops. There were also 23,000 U.S. soldiers in the IAPF. In theory, the IAPF was acting as a peacekeeping force, but it was actually providing support and equipment (including tanks, cannon, and communications devices) to the anti-Bosch forces. Peacekeeping forces also kept pro-Bosch supporters from advancing as part of an effort to maintain the cease-fire, yet they looked the other way when anti-Bosch forces hoped to advance.[45]

The Alliance for Progress as Emergency Aid

The complete resolution of what became known as the Dominican Crisis would ultimately take months, during which time the pro-Bosch forces gradually lost power and the anti-Bosch forces, with the support of the U.S. government and IAPF units, were able to ensure their primacy. In early May, the anti-Bosch forces created what they called the Government of National Reconstruction/*Gobierno de Reconstrucción Nacional* (GRN). The Johnson administration dedicated itself to helping the GRN gain effective control of the nation. A key part of this project was military. But, as importantly, there was an economic aspect; aid programs helped the GRN establish its legitimacy.[46]

In the first month of fighting, the United States sent $5 million in aid to the Dominican Republic for food and other emergency relief.[47] By the end of May, Washington began to undertake a second effort: payment of government salaries through the OAS. In total, the OAS distributed almost $8 million. Of this, $6.7 million came from the United States. In June, Washington transferred $17 million to the OAS to spend on salaries for June and July. Other U.S. funds went to support the social security system, government-owned businesses, universities and local schools, the foreign service, hospitals, fire departments, health centers, and an anti-Malaria program.[48] The United States also guaranteed payment to private companies, most notably those in the oil industry, worried about sending goods into a country with no effective government. The final short-term step was taking control of the Central Bank. Management of the Central Bank was important because U.S. policymakers believed it was vital in creating financial stability, but also because it could be used to pressure the GRN, or other Dominican forces, to follow U.S. advice.[49]

In mid-June 1965, in a wide-ranging meeting on policy in the Dominican Republic, Johnson suggested taking all the unobligated Alliance for Progress funds for the year, approximately $20 to $30 million, and sending them to the Dominican Republic. He further suggested that the bulk of unobligated AID funds in total, not just those for Latin America, should be sent to the country. In this meeting Johnson estimated that the Dominican Republic aid effort would ultimately end up costing something on the order of $250 million. The U.S. embassy in Santo Domingo concurred and argued that without a significant influx of money the economy would fail and disorder would continue. The lack of economic activity had cut consumption drastically, leading to factory shutdowns. It also forced reductions in the prices of agricultural goods, which hurt farmers.[50]

In addition to simply keeping the Dominican economy functioning, U.S. policymakers began considering impact projects. One initial idea was to earmark $5 million for a road-building program. This effort, which would take place in urban and rural areas, would demonstrate U.S. commitment to ordinary Dominicans. It would also hopefully do something about the growing unemployment problem created by the crisis. U.S. policymakers estimated that they could employ more than 6,000 people in the project.[51]

The Johnson administration dispensed with most ordinary procedures for sending funds. Rather than going through elaborate loan or grant negotiations, AID simply deposited money in the Central Bank (which the United States controlled). By early August 1965, the United States sent $42 million to help improve economic conditions. Washington also sent an additional $5.5 million to pay for food shipments. Most of this money did not come from Alliance for Progress funds. The money for the Dominican Republic in the first months of the crisis came from a foreign aid contingency fund. This distinction was technical, however. Policymakers in the United States could not move Alliance for Progress money as quickly as the contingency funds, and Johnson administration officials thought of their aid spending as part of the Alliance for Progress.[52]

Economic aid was key to the reestablishment of normal life in Santo Domingo. In September 1965, the United States sent the OAS an additional $20 million to deposit in the Central Bank. Discussions between the

OAS and U.S. policymakers then determined exactly how to spend these funds. They decided to spend $350,000 to repair schools, $60,000 for cleaning buildings in Santo Domingo, and $75,000 to repair streets. The United States, through the OAS, also committed to making loans to private businesses, cleaning the port, and developing a rat eradication program.[53]

Propping Up the Interim Government with the Alliance for Progress

By early September, the pro-Bosch, anti-Bosch, and GRN leaders had agreed to the creation of a provisional government led by Hector García-Godoy, a former diplomat. In announcing the recognition of the new provisional government, the Johnson administration committed to developing large new economic aid programs. Beyond the projects that had been under way before the intervention, Johnson promised an immediate Alliance for Progress loan of $20 million for reconstruction and implied that this was just the beginning of U.S. support. The assumption of power by García-Godoy effectively ended the military conflict; it did not end U.S. economic involvement.[54]

New loan discussions began in November 1965. The Johnson administration committed $50 million in Alliance for Progress assistance during FY1966 for the purpose of, in the words of State Department officials, reducing "political and economic pressures so that we can move toward the installation of an elected government and our withdrawal." Although this effort would be extremely important in helping the country, the United States would not provide this money in grants or without strings. As with other nations, the Dominican government would have to commit to a requirement that 50 percent of all goods paid for with aid funds be shipped on U.S.-flagged vessels. The United States, as was typical, also made it clear that it would only send all the money if the provisional government acted in a fiscally responsible way. In this package, roughly half ($25.4 million) was sent immediately on the signing of the loan. The smallest part, $600,000, went to charitable organizations. More significantly, $19.8 million went to budgetary support and $5 million went toward development projects.[55]

The U.S. embassy in Santo Domingo, under U.S. Ambassador to the OAS Elsworth Bunker's control, was adamant in suggesting that, at the minimum, the first half of this money should be in grants, not loans. García-Godoy's provisional government was extremely sensitive about increasing the national debt and passing on problems to elected governments, just as previous administrations had been. From Washington's perspective, anything that would strengthen the provisional government was a good thing. The provisional government used some of the money creatively. One early project included reestablishing the media. García-Godoy had funds transferred to two newspapers to reopen their businesses in the hope that their publishing once again would signify that life was returning to normal in Santo Domingo.[56]

Focusing on the 1966 Elections

In early 1966, the Johnson administration began considering how to approach a transition from the provisional government to a more permanent government. In elections called for June 1, 1966, Bosch ran against Balaguer in a rematch of the 1962 election. The U.S. National Security Council's special group, also known as the 303 Committee, argued early on that "The presidential election in the Dominican Republic simply must be won by the candidate favored by the U.S. government." There was little point in developing a massive military intervention and a significant aid program if an anti-U.S. candidate would then take control of the country. The 303 Committee determined, understandably, that Balaguer was the only "visible candidate to support." As with the Chilean election in 1964, the 303 Committee committed itself to providing covert support to assist the Balaguer campaign. This included providing funding directly to Balaguer's party, giving of advice to Balaguer through trusted intermediaries, and developing media that would support his candidacy. Exactly how much the United States spent on this campaign, or how that money was spent, is unknown. The amounts remain classified.[57]

Ironically, though U.S. policymakers had no interest in seeing Bosch win the election, it was vital to have him compete. Bosch, who in the early months of 1966 threatened to withdraw his candidacy, had to participate to ensure that Dominicans saw the election as fair. If he repudiated the election, and Balaguer ran without competition from the left, Balaguer, the hoped-for winner, would not enjoy legitimacy and Bosch would continue to be a problem. Thus, U.S. policymakers considered a series of methods of influencing Bosch, including asking his friends to pressure him to stay in the race. In a meeting of U.S. officials in March 1965, Bunker even proposed paying Bosch.[58]

The idea of helping Bosch may have come from Bunker's feeling that as president for a second time, Bosch might not be so bad. Bunker argued that having learned the hard way, Bosch would likely work out a better relationship with the military and act in a more appropriate way. While he obviously wanted Balaguer to win the election, Bunker's argument suggested that the United States might have continued to help in Dominican economic development programs had Bosch won. Indeed, in a conversation with Bosch in March 1965, Bunker told the ex-president that it was "the policy of the United States Government . . . that it will recognize and support a freely elected government." Immediately after saying this, however, he proceeded to tell Bosch an outright lie, that, "the United States had no favorite among the presidential candidates."[59] Bosch was appropriately suspicious of U.S. motives. According to Charge d'Affairs John Crimmins, who would become the new Ambassador, Bosch said that he had "no faith in U.S. policies and assurances; no faith in the ability of the U.S. to understand the enormously complex Dominican political life; [and] no faith that the U.S. government could maintain consistent policies over a prolonged period."[60]

While the United States provided funds to the Balaguer campaign, some of the effort, as in Chile, went to improving general economic conditions. The Johnson administration could never publicly suggest its support for Balaguer, but U.S. officials were confident that Dominicans understood that the United States was behind him. If Dominicans saw the U.S. relationship as beneficial, they would be more likely to vote against Bosch. Thus, expanding Alliance for Progress programs and their visibility became a priority.[61]

Money from the United States flowed into the Dominican Republic as the election campaign moved ahead. Beyond the rest of the $50 million loan in November 1965, U.S. policymakers sent $17.9 million to help businesses rebuild and $5 million to give government workers Christmas bonuses. There were other projects as well, some for distribution of food and others for infrastructure construction.[62]

Generous Aid to Guarantee Balaguer's Success

Balaguer won an easy victory with roughly 57 percent of the vote. Dominicans seemed to be wary that electing Bosch might again lead to turmoil. As with the 1964 presidential election in Chile, it is not clear what impact, if any, U.S. funding had on the race.

Having committed to the Dominican Republic, enjoying the Balaguer victory, and hoping for stability, the Johnson administration remained engaged. Even before the victory was official, U.S. policymakers sent a memo to guide Crimmins in his initial meeting with Balaguer. The key point he was to make was that the United States would continue to fund generous aid programs. State Department officials wanted him to "offer to lend our cooperation if he [Balaguer] wishes to utilize it, or any part of it, in his planning." In talks with Balaguer, Crimmins committed to a minimum of $70 million for FY1966 and FY1967. In addition to this amount, the United States would consider additional loans of between $10 million and $25 million. The goal was, quite simply, to enable the Balaguer administration to begin investing immediately.[63]

At the same time, some U.S. policymakers recognized that creating development in the Dominican Republic would be extremely difficult and take a great deal of time given the extant poverty. Policymakers, such as Assistant Secretary of State for Economic Affairs Anthony Solomon, recommended emphasizing programs that would give Dominicans an immediate "sense of progress." They probably would not see any improvement in their own lives, he understood, but they had to come to believe that "their children's lives will be better than their own." Solomon felt the United States should focus on style over substance. Rather than filling the AID mission with specialists on technical assistance, the United States should focus on "highly visible regional projects." To that end, he supported a loan through the Export-Import Bank, which the State Department pointedly called an "Alliance for Progress loan," of just under $9 million for the purchase of a 53.3-megawatt thermal power plant and transmission lines.[64]

The United States also developed a series of initiatives designed to promote education. Among these was a program created for the Autonomous University of Santo Domingo and the National University Pedro Henriquez Urena. This effort, which was to cost $400,000 annually for five years, would bring U.S. academics to the Santo Domingo universities to counter the strength of Communist faculty members. In June 1968, Johnson approved negotiation of another education program, a $12 million loan to improve and expand primary and secondary educational opportunities by building schools and training and hiring teachers. The ambitious goal of this loan was to triple the number of high school graduates and double the number of college graduates by 1972.[65]

The commitment to Balaguer remained serious through FY1967 and FY1968. Ultimately the United States would spend $58.8 million on economic aid in the Dominican Republic in FY1967 and $58.7 million in FY1968. In large part, support for the Dominican Republic had more to do with appearances than with economics. Economic aid programs for the Dominican Republic were vital, not necessarily as a means to actually change conditions in the country, but as a public symbol that the United States was behind Balaguer. The opposition to Balaguer, as well as the Dominican press, tended to read aid policy statements in the Dominican Republic as they would read tea leaves, attempting to divine some larger meaning from them. U.S. embassy officials in Santo Domingo worried that any statement that funding for the country would drop would have a disastrous impact. Thus, even though overall U.S. funding to Latin America was falling precipitously in the late 1960s, there was more consistency in approach when dealing with the Dominican Republic.[66] The United States could push Balaguer toward self-help, but could not force the development of policies that might negatively impact his unstable government. That is,

Washington needed to shore up the Balaguer government, but needed to be careful not to help push it over as a result of its pressure.

The Dominican government suffered from many of the same problems that other Latin American countries had. Most notable of these was a balance-of-payments problem. Import earnings simply were not able to keep up with expenditures. Aid from the United States could help in this respect in the short term, but U.S. policymakers hoped that the Dominicans would be willing to make changes in their financial systems that would keep this from being a long-term problem. To work out these problems and ensure that extant aid programs moved forward, Balaguer and Crimmins took the extraordinary step of having weekly meetings to track aid programs.[67]

Far more than in other major recipient countries, the United States developed a series of smaller loans to achieve specific goals. In April 1967, the United States proposed a $5 million loan to help address the problem of unemployment in Santo Domingo. In a rare moment of explaining and appreciating exactly what they were doing, aid officials wrote to Johnson, "The justification for this loan is purely political. Ambassador Crimmins reports that growing unemployment in Santo Domingo and increasing political activity by the leftist opposition have created political tensions which threaten the stability of the Balaguer regime. The purpose of the loan is to reduce the possibility of a political explosion in Santo Domingo." The problem had its roots in the firing of 2,700 city workers due to budget problems, and the loan would employ roughly the same number for street and sewage projects. The United States made this loan even though, as the memo to Johnson explained, "President Balaguer does not regard the problem in Santo Domingo as seriously as does Ambassador Crimmins."[68]

The Johnson administration developed other imaginative strategies to help the Balaguer government. Heavily reliant on sugar exports, the quota system still limited Dominican sales in the United States. The Johnson administration was able to creatively increase the amount of Dominican sugar exports by limiting sugar exports from other nations. This increased the Dominican export earnings, which U.S. officials expected would strengthen the Balaguer government. The Johnson administration also encouraged private U.S. firms to consider joint ventures in the Dominican Republic or to invest directly in manufacturing plants or the tourist trade.[69]

The United States sent aid even though the Dominican government was incredibly far away from either financial stability or growth. The revolution against Trujillo, the necessary reorientation of the economy, and dependence on sugar threw the economy into disarray in the early 1960s. As it began to recover, the U.S. intervention in 1965 had the practical effect of stopping economic activity. U.S. policymakers understood that the prospects for growth and recovery were slim. Nevertheless they persisted in developing aid programs that in essence funded the vast majority of Dominican government expenditures.[70]

Back to Business as Usual with Aid Policy

By the beginning of 1968, Washington was trying to handle the Dominican Republic in a fashion similar to other key Alliance for Progress recipients. The United States began to use aid money to induce the Dominican government to make dramatic changes in its fiscal policies, and to ensure that U.S. businesses would have unfettered access to local markets. In January 1968 the United States entered into negotiations with the Dominican government for a multipart economic aid package. Officials in the United States were prepared to offer a $16 million loan for budgetary support and a $14 million PL480 program. In addition to these loans, the United States would commit almost $30 million to a series of specific development projects for hydroelectric power, for sewer and water systems, and for expansion of health systems. A large part of the loans, $23 million, would cover the financing of the Tavera Dam project, an eighty-megawatt dam project on the Yaque del Norte River. In return for these loans, U.S. policymakers expected movement toward self-help. By the late 1960s, as elsewhere, self-help had come to mean the development of fiscal policies that would stimulate trade and cut government spending.[71]

Balaguer was fearful of the inflationary impact created by economic stabilization programs U.S. advisors pushed, and reluctant to open up Dominican markets. He wanted U.S. money, but did not want to follow Washington's guidance. So, just as they did in other countries, in the face of resistance U.S. policymakers refused to make payments on Dominican loans, at least initially. Yet because it had so much to lose in the Dominican Republic, and conditions were so bad, or at least potentially politically dangerous for Balaguer, the Johnson administration was inclined to be less rigid than elsewhere.[72] In the case of the Dominican Republic, political considerations (the need to help Balaguer and demonstrate that the United States was his ally) trumped concerns about the lack of economic reform.

These considerations were central in the negotiation for a new set of loans in late 1968 and early 1969. As Walt Rostow explained to Johnson in a memo requesting authorization to start negotiations on the 1968 loan, "Steady U.S. support for Balaguer has been one of his few solid bases; his chances of completing the constitutional term are relatively favorable so long as our support is unquestioned." However, a report on Dominican progress on the evolution of financial policies from January 1969 explained that the country was simply not meeting its goals or commitments. The government had agreed to hold imports down, but instead they grew; Central Bank borrowing was supposed to remain limited, but it grew; a new investment law was passed, but it was extremely weak. Still, given the hurdles and the stakes, the United States was inclined to accept Dominican explanations for each of these situations as legitimate. Policymakers in the United States pushed, got as much as they could, but had to accept that the Dominican Republic needed to be treated delicately.[73]

In the 1969 loan, Johnson faced an interesting issue. Beyond simply the question of whether to negotiate the loan, he had to decide whether to leave negotiation for the incoming Nixon administration. While it would have made sense to allow Nixon to determine where funds should go, making a decision to enter into negotiations in early 1969 effectively tied the United States to an aid program in the Dominican Republic for the first year and a half of the Nixon administration. Johnson used late-in-the-day negotiations to tie his successor to aid programs he believed were vital.[74]

Final Thoughts

The Dominican Republic was not initially an aid priority, yet the threat of instability led U.S. policymakers to imagine that the Alliance for Progress could be effective in advancing their goals. In part because the country was relatively small and extraordinarily poor, U.S. aid could be more effective than elsewhere. The stakes in this case were higher than elsewhere. Troops from the United States intervened in a burgeoning civil war, and while definitely playing favorites, managed to help stop that conflict and restore order. In their attempts to do this, aid proved important. The United States wanted stability, and only massive infusions of money could buy that stability. That said, this case does little to make a case for either the success or failure of the Alliance for Progress.

Looking at the Dominican Republic also provides a reminder that there are other foreign policy tools beyond aid. In this case the United States used economic sanctions, trade quotas, the threat of military action, and military action. Economic aid was at the heart of U.S.–Chilean and U.S.–Brazilian relationships. In the Dominican Republic it was often a way to reinforce other tools. The Alliance for Progress was important, but it was mostly a way to protect outcomes that other means had achieved.

U.S. policymakers worried about political change in both Chile and Brazil, but neither case had the immediacy of the Dominican Republic. Aid to the Dominican Republic again raises the question, what was the Alliance for Progress? In the Dominican case, especially following Bosch's ouster, there was very little connection between the U.S. program and the Charter of Punta del Este. It suggests that U.S. policymakers believed that any aid to Latin America was the Alliance for Progress. The case also demonstrates why this expanded definition may have been necessary. Calling aid to the Dominican Republic part of the Alliance for Progress justified it and made it meaningful. Policymakers in the United States and Latin America recognized that aid was a political tool, but referring to aid as the Alliance for Progress made it a good tool. More than in any other case, the Alliance for Progress terminology in the Dominican Republic was about style rather than substance.

CHAPTER 7

Colombia and the Alliance for Progress

*Pushing Reliable Allies to Demonstrate
That Aid Could Work*

From FY1962 to FY1969 (July 1, 1961 to June 30, 1969), Colombia received $761.9 million in U.S. economic aid. (see Table 7.1) This made the country the second highest aid recipient in Latin America during the period. Unlike Chile, Brazil, and the Dominican Republic, where U.S. aid peaked in the mid-1960s, aid to Colombia was more consistent. In seven out of the eight years between FY1964 and FY1971, Colombia received at least $100 million.[1] Explaining aid to Colombia is substantially more complex than explaining it in other counties. In Brazil, Chile, and the Dominican Republic, there were a series of episodes that pushed the United States' hand; this was not the case in Colombia. Relative stability, a sense that U.S. aid could really make a difference in promoting economic development, and extremely close ties between the two governments were all key reasons that Colombia became, and remained, a U.S. priority. There was never a fear that Communists or Communist-friendly leaders might gain power, yet Colombia became central to the Alliance for Progress anyway.

Why Colombia became an early focus, and remained important throughout the decade, is helpful in explaining the nature of the Alliance for Progress and suggesting caveats to the previous case studies. In Chile, the United States sent money to help Eduardo Frei win an election and to assist him afterward. In Brazil, aid was part of the effort to destabilize João Goulart and later to support the military. In the Dominican Republic, aid was central to rebuilding the country after U.S. intervention. In each case

149

Table 7.1 U.S. Economic Assistance Loans and Grants to Colombia, FY1962–FY1969 (in millions of U.S. dollars; data not adjusted for inflation)

Year	FY1962 7/1/61– 6/30/62)	FY1963 7/1/62– 6/30/63	FY1964 7/1/63– 6/30/64	FY1965 7/1/64– 6/30/65	FY1966 7/1/65– 6/30/66	FY1967 7/1/66– 6/30/67	FY1968 7/1/67– 6/30/68	FY1969 7/1/68– 6/30/69
Loans and Grants	39.6	77.6	121.6	105.7	27.2	101.6	117.3	100

Source: United States Agency for International Development website, The Greenbook (http://qesdb. cdie.org/gbk).

there were political factors that led U.S. policymakers to use aid to achieve immediate, or at least proximate, goals. In Colombia, aid also supported specific political leaders and agendas, but goals were broader. The highest U.S. priority was helping Colombia develop a healthy economy to justify the Alliance for Progress. By creating a successful Colombian "laboratory," Washington would prove that its aid program could work.

Colombia initially became a target country for a series of reasons: (1) its leadership at the start of the 1960s, and to a lesser extent throughout the rest of the decade, was committed to reform, (2) its government was consistently a good U.S. ally in that it was vehemently anti-Communist and a supporter of U.S. policy on Cuba, and (3) its serious economic problems seemed solvable. In addition, (4) no other major country was attractive as a model for the program in the early 1960s. Argentina and Peru had suffered coups d'etat in 1962 and therefore seemed unstable. The unpredictable Goulart led Brazil, and the conservative antireformist Jorge Alessandri led Chile. Because of petroleum wealth, Venezuela and Mexico did not seem to require much aid. Colombia seemed like the best place for notable Alliance for Progress successes.[2] Conditions were favorable in smaller countries, but U.S. policymakers thought success in a small country would not demonstrate the potential of the Alliance for Progress.

Colombian Conflicts and the Origins of the National Front

Colombian history has been tumultuous. Violence and instability associated with the international drug trade is only the latest manifestation of this history. During the nineteenth century there were eight civil wars, most of which pitted supporters of the Liberal Party against those of the Conservative Party. Though there were ideological differences about the power of the central government, the role of the church, and free trade, the parties were generally vehicles for individuals to gain community, regional, or national influence. The many civil wars led to the creation of a political culture that established the use of violent rebellion as a legitimate recourse for opposition politicians and kept the country from developing effective democratic institutions.[3] The final civil war of the nineteenth century, *La Guerra de los Mil Días*/The War of a Thousand Days, which lasted from July 1899 to June 1902, was the bloodiest of all. A Liberal Party attempt to unseat the Conservative Party government led to more than 100,000 deaths and destroyed the economy. This civil war especially, which had begun as a disagreement between elite groups seeking power, engulfed the poor and made them accessories to the party conflicts. As members of poor rural families died at the hands of armies representing the other party, they began to engage in vendetta killings that lasted well beyond the war.[4]

Recognizing that party conflicts were damaging to national prosperity and their own domination, elite leaders developed coalition governments in the first decades of the twentieth century to keep the peace. The coalition governments gave way to Liberal rule in 1930. Conflict did not abate, but during the first half of the century there were no civil wars. This period of relative calm ended in 1946 when Conservatives, because of fissures in the Liberal Party, won the presidential election. The transfer of power was not smooth as some Conservatives took advantage of their victory to steal Liberal-owned properties. In response, Liberals fought back and fighting began. Conflict accelerated following the assassination of the Liberal leader Jorge Eliécer Gaitán in April 1948 and continued into the 1950s and 1960s. Ultimately during this period, known simply as The Violence/*La Violencia*, roughly 200,000 Colombians died.[5]

In 1953, to deal with *La Violencia*, the army, led by Lieutenant General Gustavo Rojas Pinilla, removed the Conservative leadership and took power. His efforts did not completely end the fighting, but his offers of amnesty, willingness to use force against guerilla bands, and a series of reforms designed to improve the economy narrowed the dimensions of the internal conflict. Over time he became increasingly dictatorial though, and by 1957 it became obvious that he had no interest in relinquishing power or allowing elections. This drove the two parties together in the name of a return to democracy. The politicians hated each other, but they hated the idea of a military dictatorship more. They successfully encouraged other military officers to oust Rojas and schedule national elections. They also recognized that long-term party conflict made any kind of national peace or economic development impossible, and decided that it was time to try to change the system.[6]

In meetings during 1956 and 1957, leaders of the two parties created a power-sharing scheme they called the National Front/*Frente Nacional*. Under this arrangement, which started in 1958, the parties split seats in the legislature, state governorships, regional legislatures, and municipal councils. The parties agreed to divide all cabinet positions evenly, and most importantly, to rotate the presidency between themselves. In 1958, a Liberal, Alberto Lleras Camargo, became president. His successor in 1962 was the Conservative Guillermo Leon Valencia. Carlos Lleras Restrepo and Misael Pastrana Borrero, a Liberal and Conservative, respectively, followed. In agreeing to the National Front, both parties accepted the notion, given *La Violencia* and military rule, that they needed to act as partners. It was profoundly undemocratic as voters only had the choice of supporting or opposing the system, but it provided a much-needed respite from internal political conflict.[7]

Lleras Camargo as the Ideal Latin American Leader

The stability provided by the National Front led both parties to embrace reform agendas and ultimately the Alliance for Progress. Colombia, all agreed, had suffered badly because of internal conflict and needed to tackle severe economic and social problems. As a result, in the late 1950s and early 1960s there was no country in the region with a more unified political elite and a greater consensus about the need for change and pursuit of economic development. This should not be taken to mean that there were no political conflicts, or that the National Front succeeded on all levels, only that there was a general harmony about reform and a political system capable of managing that reform.

Colombians pursued Alliance for Progress–style reforms even before there was an entity known as such. In 1958, President Lleras Camargo's government established the Municipal Development Institute to build and maintain water and sewer facilities around the country, and in 1961 it created the Institute of Agricultural Reform to control land redistribution and improve production. To manage and coordinate these agencies and others, the government formed the National Council on Economic Policy and Planning.[8] In 1961, with wide bipartisan support, the policy and planning council unveiled an aggressive and comprehensive ten-year General Economic and Social Development Plan/*Plan General de Desarrollo Económico y Social* aimed at creating a 7.6 percent increase in industrial production, a 10.2 percent increase in construction, and similar levels of growth in electric power generation, transportation infrastructure, and communications technology. It was exactly the type of self-help program that the United States had hoped for throughout Latin America. A sophisticated and complex document, the Colombians developed their goals well before most countries even had planning departments established.[9]

Not only did the Colombian government issue an ambitious plan, it began to implement it. Lleras Camargo's government instituted a major tax reform that increased rates on the wealthy and altered the tax code to promote savings and investment for individuals and corporations. The land reform agency, with the assistance of the National University, trained agricultural experts and began to implement legislation calling for distribution of public lands to individuals. In housing construction the Colombian government was similarly active. Between 1961 and 1963 it built 131,313 homes, half of which were specified for low-income families. The government also commenced work on a sewer and water project to serve 3 million people in medium- and small-sized cities.[10]

To connect with rural Colombians, Lleras Camargo created the Community Action/*Acción Comunal* initiative. This program helped local communities by providing funds to sponsor projects they deemed necessary. The program provided financing only, expecting that local communities would take the lead in planning and construction. This program was not only about creating development projects. Lleras Camargo understood that somehow he needed to empower the Colombian people so they would back reform, and by extension his government.

A major problem with the National Front was that the lack of electoral competition eliminated the need for politicians to connect with the masses. Colombians of all regions and socioeconomic groups quickly became apathetic as National Front leaders made agreements among themselves. By setting up *Acción Comunal*, which lasted well into the 1960s, the Lleras Camargo government could attempt to reenergize the nation.[11]

These types of programs were, in effect, a challenge to the United States. In May 1962, the Colombian Finance Minister Jorge Mejía Palacio explained quite forthrightly that his country had moved forward on reform in part to increase the prospects for a large foreign aid program. "We are the Latin American country" Mejía noted, "that has totally fulfilled the requirements set by the Alliance for Progress as a condition for benefiting from it." Thus, Colombian actions were more than simply reforms; they were part of a marketing scheme, ultimately successful, in gaining Alliance for Progress funding.[12] The Kennedy administration, as a result of Colombian policies, decided to provide Colombia with roughly half of the $200 million in external support needed to implement its ten-year development plan.[13]

Colombian Support for U.S. Foreign Policy

With the possible exception of Rómulo Betancourt, the Venezuelan president in the early 1960s, Lleras Camargo was the most aggressively anti-Castro, anti-Communist, and pro-U.S. democratic leader in Latin America during this period. As Kennedy hoped to gather regional support for his Cuban policies, the Colombian government also tried to push other Latin

American governments to embrace U.S. goals. Colombian backing for U.S. foreign policy objectives increased Washington's willingness to offer substantial aid.[14]

Most notably, Lleras Camargo's help was evident in planning the January 1962 conference at Punta del Este dedicated to kicking Cuba out of the OAS. In April 1961 the State Department sent a fiery memo to all its Latin American embassies, which Kennedy personally cleared, explaining that the Cuban government had "crushed freedom in all aspects of Cuban life," that it was completely subservient to the Soviet Union, and that it constituted a "threat to the peace and security of the Americas." The memo instructed U.S. diplomats to speak with national leaders as soon as possible to convey this message. They were also told to push Latin American politicians to "condemn, isolate, and weaken [the] Castro regime." Kennedy hoped this would lead to an OAS resolution forcing all Latin American nations to break diplomatic relations with Cuba.[15] This policy met significant Latin American resistance. Brazilian, Mexican, and Argentine leaders failed to see Cuba as a threat, and Chile, Uruguay, Bolivia, and Ecuador showed little enthusiasm for U.S. efforts.[16]

Lleras Camargo, however, joined the U.S. campaign. He took the important step of calling for the OAS meeting because he recognized, at least symbolically, that it would be advantageous for a Latin American country to take the lead on this initiative. The effort was a success, but just barely. U.S. and Colombian delegates were able to pass a resolution that ousted Cuba from the OAS and called upon member nations to break diplomatic relations with Castro's government, but they were unable to sway six key nations to join them—Argentina, Brazil, Mexico, Bolivia, Chile, and Ecuador—a group that represented 60 percent of the total Latin American population. These six nations did vote in favor of resolutions that condemned Marxism-Leninism and suggested the Cuban government was incompatible with the inter-American system, but they refused to expel to Cuba from the OAS.[17] The lack of enthusiasm from other major countries ensured that the United States would continue to look favorably at Colombian requests for aid.

Selecting Colombia as a Model to Reflect Alliance for Progress Ideals

With a solid anti-Communist foreign policy and moves toward reform, Colombia became a target for the Alliance for Progress. As Chester Bowles, Kennedy's special representative and advisor on African, Asian, and Latin American affairs, explained in a 1962 speech in Colombia, the Alliance for Progress needed to focus on countries where U.S. funding would have an impact, and that had the proper environment for growth. Planning, a reformist atmosphere, and effective pro-U.S. leaders were all necessary. Bowles explained, Colombia "stands in the vanguard of the Alliance for Progress" because it had made the effort to remove local obstacles to growth and it had mustered its own resources. Other countries might do this in the future, Bowles suggested, and therefore become Alliance for Progress targets, but in 1962 the list of nations that appeared to be moving in the right direction was short, and perhaps included only Colombia.[18]

Policymakers in the United States understood that while Colombia met Alliance for Progress standards and deserved to become a major aid recipient, other less cooperative nations like Chile and Brazil still received a great deal of support. As the sole major country that received aid *and* met U.S. criteria, support for Colombia was thus exceptional and made an important statement about U.S. values. In a broad planning document from 1963, U.S. policymakers in the State Department wrote:

> Colombia has been singled out as a leading country in the Alliance because of basic strengths that appear to make it possible for large-scale foreign technical and capital assistance to help this medium per-capita income country to a high rate of self-sustaining economic growth which will be relatively widely shared. In this respect Colombia represents a new departure for U.S. foreign aid policy; it is not a country immediately threatened by direct or indirect aggression such as Korea or Taiwan where massive U.S. economic aid is a corollary of military aid; it is not a country with a historically strong economy which needs reconstruction such as Europe after the war. It is most like India – a country whose development is a world example because of its large population and relatively democratic institutions. The foreign assistance proposed for Colombia is larger than that proposed for much poorer India on a per-capita basis. Thus this foreign promoted development in Colombia is part of a proposition new to economic history; foreign promoted development of a country not because it has some natural resource or production which is demanded abroad or for immediate security reasons but merely for the long run aim of helping to build the country into a prosperous, independent and democratic member of the Western Community. If this effort succeeds in Colombia, it will serve as an outstanding example for other countries and thus stimulate self-help efforts elsewhere and demonstrate that firm association with the Western World can offer a path to the rapidly improving living standards desired in most underdeveloped countries.[19]

Colombia was a perfect country for such an experiment, according to U.S. policymakers, because of the favorable "political and social atmosphere" reflected in "real conviction of the leaders of both major parties . . . that rapid economic change and progress widely shared are first priority goals." Colombia also had good environment for growth. Again, as U.S. policymakers commented,

> First, its natural resource base, geographic location, and land–man ratio are favorable for rapid economic development by bringing into production presently unused or under-used natural and human resources. Second, and more important, the political, economic, and social development of Colombia has reached a stage where upward mobility is substantial, where the middle class is already beginning to surpass the upper class in economic importance (partly because there are few real giants in wealth among the upper class), where a sizeable group of effective and dynamic entrepreneurs already exists, [and] where the social conscience of the wealthy and middle classes has already been fairly well developed.[20]

These comments are significant and worth reproducing at length because they are rare examples of U.S. policymakers consciously thinking about what they were doing in the largest terms with aid programs. In considering other countries U.S. policymakers similarly wrote memos about foreign aid programs, but they did not have the self-reflective quality evident in the Colombian reports. Justifying aid to Colombia was more complex and required nuanced thought. In Chile, Brazil, and the Dominican Republic, the justification was generally political; there was instability or a fear of Communists taking power. In Colombia, aid was certainly political, but also idealistic and symbolic.

Valencia Embraces the Alliance

As Colombia became a priority for the United States in 1961 and 1962, Lleras Camargo's presidential term was ending. He had been the most aggressive pro–Alliance for Progress leader in Latin America and was a key reason that the United States found working with Colombia appealing. His successor, the Conservative Guillermo Leon Valencia, was also inclined to support the United States and the Alliance for Progress. This ensured continuity in U.S. policy toward Colombia. Yet while Valencia, who took office in August 1962, was a pro–Alliance for Progress reformer, he was not as ambitious as Lleras Camargo. The Colombian economist Carlos Díaz-Alejandro would later write that while President Valencia was "a remarkable man of talent and courage," he was "not particularly interested in economics, just at a time when the inherited situation called for a chief executive with an appetite for financial matters."[21] Not all Colombians shared this vision of Valencia as capable but disengaged. Often he appeared to have little control over his cabinet ministers and seemed to overlook vital issues. For example, he failed to appoint an ambassador to the United States for more than a year after his inauguration. Robert Dix, a scholar writing in the late 1960s claimed, "From the start of his administration, and even before, critics representing almost every shade of political opinion censured Valencia for maladroitness, lack of firmness, and a fuzzily romantic approach to the problems of the country." Valencia, in contrast to the serious Lleras Camargo, was also given to undisciplined flowery rhetoric and had a rather odd, dandyish style.[22]

In part, Valencia's problems stemmed from the fact that he had less power due to a weakening of the National Front. Under Lleras Camargo, all sides had recognized that unity was necessary to ensure the National Front system would be successful. As the embodiment of the system, no leader would ever be as powerful, and perhaps as popular with the people, as Lleras Camargo. By the time Valencia took power, Colombian politicians had become more restive. Though Liberals and Conservatives were still supportive of the system, they were increasingly critical of each other. The National Front system was also challenged by the development of political forces outside the two parties. Rojas, the former military dictator, led a new party that made governance more complex for Valencia. Rather than having a free hand to legislate without consideration of public opinion, Valencia actually needed to worry about elections and congressional votes.[23] It took U.S. policymakers time to understand Valencia's political problems and personal weaknesses and to discover that achieving Alliance for Progress successes would be difficult. They had assumed that helping Colombia would be easy. This was not the case.

As with Lleras Camargo, Valencia knew that maintaining consistent pro-U.S. international policies helped smooth aid relationships. Frei in Chile, Goulart in Brazil, and Juan Bosch in the Dominican Republic all failed to appreciate this simple idea. They wanted to maintain independent foreign policies and also receive aid. The Colombians, generally, had no such ambitions. In meetings in June 1962 in Washington, Valencia, then still only the president-elect, told Kennedy administration officials that "he considered that Colombia had a permanent alliance with the United States, and that it would follow this country [the United States] in defending the causes of justice and freedom anywhere in the world." Like Lleras Camargo, Valencia expressed his support because he truly felt Cuba and Communism represented threats, but lurking behind his rhetoric was the notion that Colombia was the most reliable U.S. ally in Latin America and deserved more financial aid. It only made sense, Valencia said, that the United States should develop greater economic cooperation with its loyal friends.[24]

In Washington, Valencia worked with the Kennedy administration on a $21 million loan to build health centers and sewage plants in Cali and Medellín and a pilot program for bringing private investments to Latin America. Valencia wanted to focus, at least initially, on tangible development projects that would help the Colombian people feel the impact of the Alliance for Progress. While in the United States he visited the Tennessee Valley Authority electric generation facilities built as part of President Franklin D. Roosevelt's New Deal in the 1930s. He reported to Chester Bowles that he was impressed by these plants and hoped to build similar Colombian electrical capacity to promote a more sophisticated economy.[25]

This concern for specific projects faded in late 1962 as U.S. policymakers came to recognize the extent of Colombia's broader fiscal problems. Declining coffee prices exacerbated a growing balance-of-payments deficit that made government expenditures difficult, limited the possibilities for reform, and ultimately appeared likely to bankrupt the government. Between 1957 and 1962, coffee amounted to more than 65 percent of total national exports. However, world coffee prices on the open market fell consistently from a post–World War II high of nearly eighty cents per pound in 1954 to just under forty cents in 1963. In part, this drop was a function of increasing global supply caused by the expansion of coffee production in Asia and Africa. Falling prices hit Colombia harder than other exporting nations. Most of its competitors had preferential trade agreements with importing nations. For example, in 1962 the U.S. government paid coffee producers in its commonwealth, Puerto Rico, forty-eight cents per pound. Colombian coffee, at the same time, cost between forty and forty-three cents per pound. Similarly, European nations had special arrangements with their African and Asian colonies and former colonies.

As prices for its key export fell, the Colombian government was busy starting national development programs. These programs required foreign goods, further straining the balance-of-payments problem. Finally, there were also debts to pay off. In efforts to end *La Violencia*, previous governments had borrowed heavily, and the need to repay these debts worsened the balance-of-payments problem.[26]

In response, the Lleras Camargo government had attempted two solutions, borrowing money and manipulating exchange rates. For loans, as early as 1958 the Colombian government began seeking out the U.S. government. Although the United States provided little assistance in the late 1950s, the IMF was willing and able to help the Colombian financial situation. The Alliance for Progress changed the United States' approach. From mid-1960 to mid-1962 the United States made $117.2 million in loans to Colombia to fund rural housing projects, public health programs, and other development projects. This capital inflow reduced the balance-of-payments problem significantly, but only in the short term.[27]

Beyond taking loans to finance imports, the Colombian government also tried to control its balance-of-payments situation by manipulating currency exchange rates. By creating artificially high currency exchange rates, and even higher separate rates for coffee, the government could attempt to make Colombian goods more expensive on world markets. It would also, at the same time, reduce the cost of imported goods in Colombia.[28]

The weakness of the Colombian financial position is important to keep in mind as a factor driving Lleras Camargo and Valencia to embrace the Alliance for Progress. Colombia desperately needed financial aid to avert a major crisis. While the Colombians wanted to fund development projects, the much larger issue was instability created by the balance-of-payments problem. This transformed the Alliance for Progress from a development program to a stabilization one. As Carlos Sanz de Santamaria, the Colombian ambassador in Washington during the Lleras Camargo administration, and later the minister of finance, argued in 1962, Kennedy needed to "arrive at the conviction that our [Colombia's] economic crisis is more a crisis in the terms of trade than one of internal economy." Kennedy needed to "decide to cooperate in financing deficits in the balance-of-payments for a reasonable time," during which Colombia could diversify its economy and increase exports. For Colombia, this would mean "a great step toward the success of the Alliance for Progress."[29]

Shifting to Fiscal Stability and Following U.S. Advice

Obtaining money through loans to continue to fund its balance-of-payments deficit was the priority for the Colombians, but U.S. policymakers believed that manipulation of exchange rates was the larger problem. They believed that as fixed currency exchange rates diverged from a theoretical market rate, economic activity would slow. If Colombia devalued its currency, trade would increase and foreigners would be more inclined to invest. The resultant expansion of commercial activity would eventually reduce the need for imports and loans, and would promote a more diversified export industry. It would mean short-term problems, however. To the extent the country relied on imports, inflation would develop because of rising prices for imported goods. Policymakers in the United States believed that in the long run, this shock was necessary. Espousal of these policies was not without self-interest. Greater openness in the economy would improve the prospects for U.S. companies hoping to invest or sell products in Colombia and for U.S. consumers hoping to purchase Colombian goods.[30]

Given Valencia's precarious fiscal position, following U.S. advice was his only option; his government devalued its currency in December 1962. The decision was not popular because most Colombians understandably opposed policies that would create inflation. Poorer Colombians were especially worried because, as they argued, inflation would have a disproportionately negative impact on them. The rich would suffer, but they would still be able to purchase necessities and had protection because they owned property and tangible goods that would also increase in value. Further, there would be a lag between the time prices for ordinary goods rose and when wages increased. This would benefit employers at the expense of employees. Inflation was also unpopular because many Colombians held the position that the potency of their currency was a marker of their national strength. Devaluing the national currency appeared tantamount to devaluing the nation.[31]

As a reward for following through with the devaluation, the State Department negotiated a $60 million loan in December 1962. The next month the IMF offered an additional $30 million. These loans operated as they did elsewhere in Latin America. The United States committed money both because it recognized a country warranted aid and to spur additional reform programs. While U.S. policymakers wanted to make Colombia a priority and thought that aiding Valencia was vital, it did not mean the United States would make new loans or disburse signed ones without seeing evidence of a continuing process of reform. In this case, the December 1962 loan was contingent on the continuing monetary stabilization programs.[32]

Sticking with Valencia in the Face of Colombian Problems

In the first months of 1963, the shock of currency deflation led to rising inflation, industrial recession, and increasing unemployment. In the six months following the deflation, the cost of living rose 27.5 percent and wholesale prices jumped 23.7 percent. This was dramatic because from 1960 to 1962 the Colombian economy only averaged a 5.6 percent annual increase in the cost of living and a 4.4 percent annual increase in wholesale prices. Rather than taking austerity measures that would have pushed the economy to adjust on its own, Valencia raised wages for government workers and lowered taxes on coffee producers. His policies increased spending and cut government income, and largely undid the potential benefits of the currency devaluation. Valencia proved unwilling to continue to make the tough fiscal policy decisions encouraged by the United States and international financial organizations.[33]

The Valencia government also began to respond to domestic conflict repressively. It crushed labor groups that had become critical of the government because of the economic conditions. Some of these protests centered on U.S. companies. A major strike on the U.S.-owned Colombian Petroleum Company led to a complete shutdown of operations, use of the army to maintain control, and ultimately to a series of bombings in Bogotá. As disturbingly, in the words of Carlos Díaz-Alejandro, the 10-year development program was "quietly ignored by the Valencia administration."[34]

During 1963, the U.S. government felt it had little choice but to continue making Colombia a priority. Rather than back off, Fulton Freeman, the U.S. ambassador in Bogotá, argued for a "redoubled effort." Colombia had a wealth of resources, a stable political situation, and aggressively pro-U.S. leaders. Because it offered such a fertile ground for the program, it was important for demonstrating that the Alliance for Progress was working, and could work.[35] In aiding Colombia despite the turn to repression, failure to stick with the devaluation, and abandonment of the development program, aid to Colombia began to resemble other Alliance for Progress situations. Having committed to Valencia, it mattered little what he actually did. The Colombian change is interesting because Freeman advocated abandoning Alliance for Progress ideals (notably self-help) to save the Alliance for Progress.[36]

Valencia understood U.S. policy, however, and knew he needed additional funds to solve his country's balance-of-payments problem. He recognized that he could probably get away with the wage increase, but he would have to comply with at least some U.S. advice about creating a better investment climate through cutting inflation and government budgets. To do this he limited spending for infrastructure programs that had been an early Alliance for Progress priority.[37] In 1963, the Colombian government spent 30 percent less on development projects than the year before, and 45 percent less than in 1961. As elsewhere, U.S. policymakers cared less about social programs or construction projects and more about creating an attractive investment climate as the 1960s progressed. Here, the Colombian program was similar to other Alliance for Progress efforts. In each of the target countries helping individuals and focusing on improvement in social conditions became less important than inflation and balance-of-payments problems.

Valencia's economic policies led to some successes. Reductions in government spending, even with the wage increases, seemed to be limiting inflation. In late 1963 the economy began to grow rapidly, and Colombian estimates suggested that the government might actually run a budget surplus in 1964.[38] The Colombian financial position continued to improve in 1964 as coffee prices temporarily increased. In part to reward the Colombian government for its actions, and in part to develop more leverage over Valencia's economic policies, U.S. policymakers began contemplating another loan in February 1964.[39]

In the early period of Valencia's administration there was also enthusiasm about a gradual decline in violence. While determining exactly how much violence existed is difficult, Robert Dix estimated that during Lleras Camargo's administration about two to three thousand people were killed each year, and that this number dropped significantly during the first part of the Valencia administration. Part of the reason for declining levels of violence was, to the United States, an acceleration of Alliance for Progress–style reforms and the implementation of *Acción Cívica Militar*.[40]

Managed by General Alfredo Ruiz Novoa, Valencia's minister of war, the *Acción Cívica Militar* program assumed that the military was the only institution capable of managing reform programs in remote areas. The military built roads to isolated communities and developed programs to improve sanitation, extend electrical power service, and bring basic education to the people. Among the most ambitious programs was Operation Marquetalia, a $30 million U.S.-funded program designed to reclaim an area dominated by guerilla leaders in Tolima province. The rebels supposedly had received arms from Castro, and upon capture seemed well equipped with Communist propaganda. The central problem for this program was the lack of training soldiers had in civic action programs. James Henderson, a historian of *La Violencia* notes, "Soldiers were sent into the countryside with paper, pencils, and other implements of instruction to teach grizzled *campesinos* who only recently had fought [against them]. . . . In places no soldier had dared enter a few years before, the populace witnessed the incongruous spectacle of seventeen-year-old recruits nervously clutching M-1 rifles while attempting to teach *primeras letras* to equally uncomfortable *campesinos*."[41] (see Figure I.12 following page 148.)

Fighting Crisis in Colombia with Aid

While the Colombian government seemed in better shape in early 1964 because of the influx of foreign aid money and higher coffee prices, economic stability was difficult to maintain. Loans from the United States had helped the Valencia government avoid crisis and major reforms, but by mid-1964 the problems with exchange rates once more led to a dangerous situation. A *New York Times* headline from January 1964 had accurately noted, "Massive Aid Wins Time for Colombia." The article explained that the United States hoped that, "by maintaining a strong level of external support for two or three more years, Colombia will be able to overcome the hurdle" of creating lasting stability. The article also implied that U.S. aid was giving Valencia an opportunity to fix underlying fiscal and currency problems, but that he did not want to do so.[42]

Hoping to push Valencia to again focus on the economy, the United States considered withholding the disbursement of $45 million. This tactic was standard practice for the Alliance for Progress. When governments did not follow through on reforms, U.S. policymakers reserved the right to hold back promised funds. The problem, in the case of Colombia, was that the Valencia government had actually done a good job in moving forward with the particular self-help goals specified in the loan agreements, especially on cutting government spending, and in implementing reforms through programs such as *Acción Cívica Militar*. The Valencia government had not, however, done well with fiscal and currency policies. Washington understood that disbursement of U.S. money in 1964 would simply go to plugging a hole in the currency problem, not toward overall or lasting reform of the system.[43]

Cutting funds however, given the interest in making Colombia a model for the Alliance for Progress, was difficult. Officials in the United States understood that no matter what kinds of economic policies the Valencia government followed, the United States might have to make loans. As Covey T. Oliver, Fulton Freeman's replacement as U.S. ambassador in Bogotá argued, the U.S. had little choice but to "consider AID on a bail-out basis" to help "uphold constitutional government" and "a country of law and a worth-while model of economic development."[44]

Throughout 1963 and 1964 the Colombian peso again became overvalued relative to the dollar. The increasingly more expensive peso put pressure on imports, and given the lack of confidence in the system, created capital flight and the erosion of Colombia's foreign reserves. It certainly did not help that coffee prices dropped toward the end of 1964 and into 1965.[45] Ambassador Oliver was sympathetic to Valencia's plight and urged that because of the rapidly deteriorating situation the United States should speed already promised money to Colombia to ensure that the economic system would not collapse and the government would not run out of cash. Accepting the notion that this was an emergency, AID approved a special transfer of $15 million to Colombia in November 1964 and allowed the Colombians, in an unusual move, to borrow an additional $30 million directly from the U.S. Federal Reserve System in December. This did little to alleviate the crisis as the Colombian foreign reserves continued to fall. The obvious answer to the problem, at least in the short term, was devaluation, but fearing the inflationary impact of this move, Valencia publicly repudiated that option, going so far as to take a public pledge that he would not attempt one. From Valencia's perspective, the currency devaluation encouraged by the United States, as well as the IMF and World Bank, like the 1962 devaluation, would create even more inflation. This inflation would further exacerbate the crisis.[46]

From December 1964 to mid-July 1965, Colombia was in a state of constant emergency as inflation continued to leap higher. The government tried a series of solutions to the economic problems in January 1965, including adjusting sales taxes, fixing prices for basic goods, and creating new regulations on imports and exports. Opposition to these policies, especially the new taxes, led to political instability. Major unions took the lead in protesting the greater cost of living and threatened a massive national general strike. Faced with this prospect, Valencia withdrew the new taxes. This action, though perhaps unavoidable, made the president seem weak and emboldened his critics. The minister of public works resigned in December 1964 and the minister of war quit in January 1965. The Valencia government was falling apart.[47]

As economic and political stability disintegrated, the trends of diminishing violence reversed. In December 1964, the leading Bogotá newspaper commented that the country was witnessing a surge in political conflict. An attack in early January in which 100 bandits entered the town of Simacota in Santander province and killed 5 soldiers shocked the nation for its brazenness. While Valencia promised a tough line against the renewed violence, his government could do little as rebel activity increased and the size of rural bandit armies seemed to be growing. In March, a wave of kidnappings of prominent Colombians, including a former minister of development who was eventually killed, further weakened public confidence in the government. By June there were even bandits engaged in prolonged street fights with the military in Bogotá. In some areas of the country, especially in the more affluent neighborhoods, self-defense groups formed to keep the peace. Student strikes, some directed against the growing violence and others driven by anger about U.S. intervention in the Dominican Republic, further shook the country.[48]

Violence, and political and economic failures, led to new concerns that the National Front might fail. Challenges from inside the two parties, and from politicians who opted out of the system, began to become more intense. Leaders associated with General Rojas had done extremely well against a combined slate of Liberals and Conservatives in the March 1964 congressional elections and seemed, through 1964 and 1965, to be gaining strength.[49] Factions within the parties also had become more powerful and destabilized the system. Guaranteeing an equal number of representatives in congress had not eliminated political competition, it simply moved it to the intra-party level, and as Valencia faltered, factions within each party became increasingly critical and less supportive of his government.[50]

By mid-1965, U.S. policymakers had little confidence in Valencia and the National Front. An analysis of prospects for Colombia prepared by the CIA, Departments of State and Defense, and the National Security Council suggested that Valencia had been a dismal failure. There had been no improvement in the Colombian fiscal position, the Congress refused to even pass the limited and questionable stabilization programs he proposed, and he had no choice but to legislate by decree in order to try to improve the government's financial position.[51]

In a way, the acceptance that Valencia had failed and that Colombia needed stronger leadership was quite useful. Although in June 1964 Johnson proposed that the United States "shore-up" Valencia and argued "it looked as if we ought to pour all the money we can in," the overwhelming sense of pointlessness in remaining committed freed the United States and its allies to take one final tough stand. The IMF and World Bank jointly announced that they would halt all assistance plans for Colombia. The United States also rebuffed a Colombian effort to negotiate new loans and refused to send $10 million from a loan approved in 1964. To fight for reversal of these policies, Valencia planned to send a high-level delegation to Washington to convince the Johnson administration that he needed more short-term loans, but faced with certain failure, the minister of finance, who was to lead the delegation, quit.[52] The U.S. government had been hesitant to take a tough line with Valencia for fear of sparking political turmoil, but given his failures to act decisively on currency stabilization and the unlikely chance that political instability would lead to a radical regime, pushing him made more sense. No U.S. policymaker imagined that even if Valencia was overthrown it would lead to an anti-U.S. state. This freed U.S. policymakers to move from carrots to sticks in its approach to the Colombian government. As Valencia was failing, the Alliance for Progress failed as well. This case was supposed to demonstrate U.S. ability to strengthen Latin America, but it seemed not to be working.

The Improving Colombian Context and How Aid Helped

Faced with the refusals of the United States, IMF, and World Bank to continue to fund the balance-of-payments deficit, Valencia had little choice but to relent in July 1965 to a massive economic reform package. To accelerate the changes, he appointed a new minister of finance, Joaquín Vallejo Arbeláez. In rapid order, Vallejo presided over a currency devaluation and increases in income and coffee taxes. Officials in the United States focused on the situation found the Colombian actions satisfactory. After spending months trying to get the Valencia government to accept outside advice, it finally changed its policies. This, along with written promises to AID, the

IMF, and the World Bank about continuing to move forward with self-help on economic stabilization led the United States to offer a $65 million loan in October 1965; the IMF and World Bank would provide $130 million.[53]

In approving the loan, U.S. Bureau of the Budget Director Charles Schultze noted that AID would only distribute the loan in four quarterly tranches. The first $20 million would be sent on signing of the loan, probably before the end of 1965, and additional amounts of $15 million would be released throughout 1966, if, and only if, the Colombian government continued its steps toward following U.S.-, IMF-, and World Bank–dictated economic policies. These included creation of a liberalized trade policy, noninflationary fiscal and monetary policies, increases in tax collection, an agricultural reform program, and an effort to expand locally financed primary education.[54]

Key members of the Johnson Administration, including McGeorge Bundy, Johnson's special presidential assistant for national security affairs, and Thomas Mann, who had become the undersecretary of state for economic affairs supported the loan. Mann explained, "if we fail to come through in a timely way with our end of the bargain, the progress which has made could begin to become unraveled . . ." Ambassador Oliver concurred that the program was the best tool the United States had to help create stability in Colombia. He argued, "A democratic, confident Colombia is of the greatest importance to our strategic and political national interests." Johnson authorized the loan but was concerned about prospects for success. He wrote that he was approving it only "with reluctance, reservations and considerable misgivings."[55] Given Valencia's poor record of accomplishment, Johnson was not sure he would follow through. He insisted on receiving monthly reports on Colombian progress toward implementing the conditions required in the loan. These monthly messages explained the changing political situation, financial trends, government compliance with the terms of the loan, and other self-help efforts Valencia was trying to pursue.[56]

Conditions in Colombia did improve, though exactly how much of this improvement was a result of the Valencia administration's efforts to follow U.S., IMF, and World Bank financial advice is unclear. In congressional elections in March 1966 the National Front withstood a challenge from opposition parties, including those affiliated with Rojas. Had opponents outside the National Front won enough seats in the legislature they could have destroyed the power-sharing system. Given perceptions of disappointment with Valencia, this was a victory for him. Even more heartening was the overwhelming victory of Carlos Lleras Restrepo in the presidential election in May 1966. Lleras Restrepo's only significant challenger was Gustavo Jaramillo Giraldo, a Rojas ally. The victory meant a greater likelihood of stability and an efficient progressive government in Colombia, continued good performance on loan agreements, and cooperation on major international issues.[57]

The Alliance for Progress in Colombia under Valencia seemed to be a roller coaster of ups and downs. At first he seemed to be the kind of leader U.S. policymakers could rely upon, then his reluctance to fully commit to economic stabilization programs led to frustrations. Economic problems seemed to get better in the middle of his four-year term, but they again worsened and started to undermine the National Front's future. Comparatively speaking, he was not a bad Alliance for Progress leader (like Alessandri or Goulart), but he was not a good one either. Policymakers in the United States hoped Lleras Restrepo would do better, but Colombian politics and economics continued their vacillations.

Seeing Success through Alliance for Progress Loans

As president, Lleras Restrepo reenergized development initiatives in Colombia. He enlarged planning agencies and sought to insulate them from political changes. As importantly, he focused his attention on solving the exchange rate issue. By September 1966, U.S. policymakers were quite pleased with developments in Colombia. Some of this had to do with Lleras Restrepo, but a big part came from their understanding of how the $65 million loan made in 1965 had pushed Valencia to change.

Special Assistant for National Security Affairs Walt Rostow, in a memo to Johnson he titled "Colombia: What We Achieved with Our Program Loan," explained that conditions in mid-1965 seemed, in his words, "grim." The Colombian budget faced serious deficits, inflation seemed likely, foreign exchange reserves were depleted, exchange rates were seriously overvalued, and public confidence in the National Front seemed to be waning. But following the work with AID, the IMF, and World Bank, and the $65 million loan, Colombia was in excellent shape. There was a budget surplus, inflation appeared under control, the nation had dramatically improved its foreign exchange reserves, and trade liberalization had moved forward. As a result, there was increased confidence in the government, both within and outside Colombia. This led in part to a strengthened National Front and greater stability. Rostow concluded, "Much remains to be done, of course, but our investment in this important Latin American country during the past 12 months has paid off."[58]

This memo was part of the preparation for a new aid package for Colombia. Confident that the $65 million 1966 loan had been so successful, officials at AID and the Department of State, as well as within the White House, pushed for a larger, $100 million loan. The United States, again, would work with the IMF and World Bank, who would be providing $165 million on their own. The new loan would serve in part as a reward for doing well with the last one. But part of the logic came from the idea that although Valencia had been successful on internal reform, Lleras Restrepo, a Liberal who had been trained as an economist, would go even further. Rostow, in a memo to Johnson requesting approval to begin negotiation of the loan, explained that the Colombian government needed money to launch a "development program while continuing stabilization measures." The United States would continue to limit releases of the money to ensure continuing compliance, but Colombia appeared to be at a critical point. Just as with Frei in Chile in 1964, the United States appeared in Colombia to have a government willing to pursue Alliance for Progress objectives with vigor. Rostow argued that Lleras Restrepo seemed to be part of the "new generation of democratic, progressive Latin American leaders" that Washington hoped to see succeed.[59]

Having struggled with Valencia, Rostow expected that with the new loan, Colombia could finally live up to its billing as the Alliance for Progress showcase. President Johnson was not necessarily skeptical about Lleras Restrepo, but seemed worried as he asked, "if we really want to blow that much on Colombia." He nevertheless approved moving forward with negotiations for the loan. The argument presented to him by Rostow and others was that the Alliance for Progress had been successful in Chile and Brazil, and now it was time to shift U.S. priorities to another country that needed help, deserved help, and would use help appropriately.[60]

Lleras Restrepo Learns About U.S. Aid and U.S. Demands

Although willing to help Lleras Restrepo, U.S. policymakers and their allies in the IMF pushed him hard to increase the pace of devaluation as a means of lowering domestic demand for imported products and increasing the chances that the country would develop the capability to earn enough foreign currency through its export trade. This position baffled Lleras Restrepo, who, like Valencia, recognized that these policies would be inflationary and lead to difficult economic conditions, at least in the short run. Development spending programs were his priority, and as he initially understood U.S. statements, he thought that they would be the focus of U.S. loans as well. He did not have experience in aid loan negotiations and did not know why the United States would be so demanding given its insistence that it wanted to back him and his understanding of the Alliance for Progress as a partnership.[61] As with debates over Chile in 1965 and 1966, the United States and the IMF rejected the ideas of local leaders about how to solve domestic financial problems. Lleras Restrepo hoped, in line with basic Alliance for Progress philosophy, to grow his way out of his nation's fiscal problems, but U.S. policymakers had different ideas.

Lleras Restrepo opted to make his conflict with the U.S. and IMF public. In part he saw this as an opportunity to shore up his political support. If he could demonstrate that foreigners were attempting to control the Colombian economy, opposition politicians both within and beyond the National Front would have to rally to his side. In late November 1965 he gave a speech on Colombian television that explained he was rejecting the demands of foreign creditors in connection with a proposed $100 million loan from the United States and a $60 million agreement with the IMF.[62] He then used emergency powers to freeze all dollar holdings in Colombian and foreign banks, and established a set of priorities through which Colombians would have access to foreign exchange to purchase imports. Shortly thereafter Lleras Restrepo issued a decree that gave the government exclusive control of the market for dollars within Colombia. Lleras Restrepo effectively portrayed these moves in a nationalistic fashion. The leading Bogotá daily, *El Tiempo*, in a rare banner headline declared, "Lleras Defends National Economic Independence," and in subsequent issues noted the popularity of Lleras Restrepo's stand throughout the country.[63]

The nationalistic stand against the IMF and United States strengthened Lleras Restrepo's hand in dealing with internal political forces, but he still needed external financial support. His economic steps played well at home, but did not get him any closer to being able to pursue development spending. Moreover, the violence that had been resurgent in the second half of the Valencia administration continued unabated. He felt he had little choice but to proclaim martial law to deal with the fighting. He had previously put the country on a state of alert, but the martial law decree of March 13, 1967 ensured that the government would call upon all its resources to fight violence.[64]

Yet Lleras Restrepo was a realist. He knew that he had to come to terms with the United States and the IMF to obtain loans. Thus, on March 22, 1967 he issued Decree 444 to develop a new series of exchange rates, which allowed his government to progressively devalue currency in order to better manage currency flows and promote exports. Under this new system, called a *crawling peg*, rates did not float freely, but could be (and were) regularly adjusted to encourage trade. This policy ultimately led to an increase in Colombian exports and the promotion of financial stability. To U.S. policymakers, the step indicated that although he might make a fuss in public, Lleras Restrepo could be counted on make the difficult decisions required to help the Colombian economy develop.[65]

Decree 444 represented a major shift in policy. Until this point, the Colombian government hoped to manipulate currency exchange rates in order to support import-substitution-industrialization (ISI) policies. The goal of ISI involved limiting imports, or at least making them expensive enough that local industry would develop to produce goods that would substitute for imported goods. In this way the nation would develop productive capacity. In the Colombian case, low coffee prices in the 1960s presented a major problem for ISI. Because of the weaknesses in the economy, Colombians had trouble buying any goods, foreign or domestic, leading the nation to actually develop excess industrial capacity. Under Lleras Restrepo and Decree 444, the Colombian government gradually, and often imperceptibly to the public at large, altered exchange rates so that local manufacturers could more easily export products. This ultimately led to a massive increase in manufacturing exports, and a substantially healthier Colombian economy. Exports of non-coffee products jumped from an average of $196 million annually between 1963 and 1966 to an average of $277 million annually between 1967 and 1970.[66]

The law transformed the Colombian economy by encouraging a shift away from coffee exportation to broader and more diversified trade. It meant giving up on ISI, but it had not worked. Ultimately, coffee would fall in importance and Colombians would begin to earn enough to solve their balance-of-payments problems. The control over dollars that was part of Decree 444 also had a significant impact. In practice it meant that any major private investment needed government approval. This command-like economic policy ensured, relatively effectively, that the nation did not develop excess production capacity, and more importantly that foreign investment did not drive Colombians out of business.[67] This is perhaps the best example of a clear economic success for U.S. policymakers. Their advice proved useful. Lleras Restrepo's decision to use a crawling peg method to slow the impact of exchange rate changes limited the shock of devaluation, but U.S. policymakers were right that making trade easier would go a long way toward fixing the Colombian economy. Notably, it was only in May 1967, after the passage of these laws, that U.S. policymakers approved the final agreements for the $100 million loan.[68]

In the larger context of the Alliance for Progress, it is important to mention that violence in Colombia had little to do with U.S. aid programs. Bloodshed was a part of life in Colombia throughout the decade. While U.S. policymakers were cognizant of this, it was not central to the process of deciding on loans. The United States was supportive of the Colombian efforts and did offer financial and material support to fight the rebels, but it did not impact larger aid decisions. Policymakers in the United States appeared to believe that Lleras Restrepo was particularly capable of fighting the insurgency, even though evidence of Cuban support for rebels had emerged.

Lleras Restrepo's response to the upsurge in violence was in line with Alliance for Progress ideology. Instead of seeing fighting as the solution to rural conflict, he suggested that agrarian reform would solve the problems of rural poverty and ensure future stability. He energized the land redistribution program in order to help peasants gain their own land and break up large landholdings. These programs were connected to initiatives to diversify crops and create rural peasant cooperative organizations. Ultimately these programs were unable to create lasting and deep change in the countryside and to eliminate the specter of rural violence.[69]

The Last Loans and Persistence in the U.S.
Approach to Push Lleras Restrepo

In the first months of 1968 the Johnson administration again took stock of Colombian economic achievement and the role of U.S. aid in helping that achievement. As in 1967, U.S. policymakers believed that in part because of the U.S. program loan, and in part because of the policies that the United States and IMF forced on Colombia, there was greater economic stability. They were proud to explain in April 1968 that Colombia had achieved 4.5 percent growth in GNP despite a drop in coffee prices. They noted that increased tax collections and management of spending had allowed a 42 percent increase in public investment, mostly in agriculture and education. Further, inflation continued to fall and exports continued to rise.[70]

Given such successes, Colombia continued to be an Alliance for Progress priority, even though far less money was allocated for Latin America in total. This is a testament to how much U.S. policymakers believed in Lleras Restrepo as a model. A memo from AID officials to Johnson explained, "President Lleras has reunited his Liberal Party, consolidated his position in Congress, surrounded himself with a dynamic group of executives, and laid the groundwork for further political and economic reforms." Lleras's successes were vital because in Colombia there were "no viable alternative political parties or groups, and the danger of political disintegration is considerable if the Lleras Administration founders significantly in its political and economic objectives."[71] More to the point, another document for Johnson explained simply, "President Lleras's very good performance with our aid last year was one of the brightest spots in our Alliance for Progress efforts."[72] These kinds of comments and rationale for making Colombia a priority were common, not only in private documents, but also in public ones. In statements before Congress, the AID mission director in Colombia explained that "leadership of top quality exists . . . ." He argued, "I think in Colombia today you have in the public sphere and to a great extent in the private sphere probably better managers, better policymakers, better leaders in general, than has been the case in many countries, and in Colombia, in some periods of the past."[73]

In February 1968 the Johnson Administration opened negotiations with Colombia for a new series of loans totaling $90 million. While the United States would have a smaller program loan than in past, it still would be a significant $58 million. Added to this loan, the United States also offered a $15 million loan to help agricultural development, a $14.5 million Food for Peace package, and smaller amounts for specific projects. In these loans, believing that their policies and judgments had been important in helping Colombian success, U.S. policymakers continued to press for more aggressive action. Rather than see the new loans as a reward for past reforms, or even to accept the fact that Lleras Restrepo had earned the benefit of the doubt, U.S. policymakers still pressed for performance targets. These actions again angered Lleras Restrepo, who like Frei in Chile, was uncomfortable with allowing the United States to control his economic policy.[74] Lleras Restrepo argued that because he had been an effective and trusted recipient of aid in the past, the United States should loan money to his government on faith.

This policy was unacceptable to the United States and its partners in the IMF and World Bank who insisted that the success in making reforms must not only continue, but that it needed to accelerate. The United States wanted more devaluation of exchange rates and more trade liberalization. When Lleras Restrepo balked, negotiations broke down. As a means of pressuring Lleras Restrepo, the United States even decided to halt payment of the final tranche of the 1967 loan. While both sides were able to find room to compromise, again the process of loan negotiation turned unpleasant. These steps repeated themselves in December 1968 as AID proposed $69 million in the final major loans for Colombia in the Johnson era.[75]

Assessment of these loan negotiations is remarkable because they seemed entirely divorced from the rest of U.S.–Colombian relations. The Colombians started to become less perfect allies. Lleras Restrepo, and others within his administration began to make negative remarks about U.S. foreign policy. In September 1967, for example, Colombian officials criticized the Vietnam War as unnecessary and destructive to U.S. global influence. Lleras Restrepo made a speech during the same month attacking the U.S. government, and wealthy countries in general, for their resistance to policies that would lead to fair pricing for items like coffee. He argued that as long as his country had to import expensive goods, and rich countries did not pay equal amounts for their imports from countries like Colombia, his country would always be poor.[76]

Still, Lleras Restrepo's economic reforms made him a reliable pro–Alliance for Progress leader. Only Frei in Chile was as committed to reform.

Yet at the same time there was always tension associated with loan negotiations. Though the United States wanted and needed Lleras Restrepo to succeed, it also needed to ensure that it was getting something for its money. That something may have been the Alliance for Progress, but as in other cases, by the end of the 1960s it becomes hard to say exactly what that meant.[77]

Final Thoughts

It is impossible to assess the exact impact of U.S. aid on overall economic change in Colombia during the 1960s or beyond. Other factors, most importantly fluctuating coffee prices, were more significant than any influx of economic aid could ever have been. Nevertheless, there was growth in non-coffee exports, which may be attributable to more realistic exchange rates. This helped improve the overall Colombian economic condition. Yet Colombia did not make a jump from an underdeveloped and poor country to an industrialized and rich country. Social inequality, poor government services, and mass poverty remained.

Examining aid to Colombia demonstrates that even in very good conditions, development of effective and cooperative relationships between U.S. leaders and those in recipient nations was difficult. U.S. aid programs, though designed to help foreign governments, generally created some antagonism as disputes over the appropriateness of economic policies emerged. In the Colombian case, even though Valencia agreed on the seriousness of his problem and understood the reasons for devaluation, he was hesitant to follow U.S. advice because of domestic political concerns. While these kinds of disputes existed elsewhere, the fact that they proved to be so serious in Colombia helps explain the central problem facing the Alliance for Progress. U.S. policymakers, even when willing to make significant loans, had limited power to compel foreign governments. This is probably a good thing, as a program designed to eliminate control of foreign governments over their own economies suggests imperialism. As Kennedy understood, the Alliance for Progress had to be a partnership, but in this partnership, compromise proved difficult.

This argument suggests that aid to Colombia was not completely different from aid to other major recipient nations during the 1960s. In practice, the Alliance for Progress was committed to creating stability. This was true in Colombia and in the countries that received aid for more political reasons. There may be a temptation to argue, especially given the political problems that existed in other countries (Salvador Allende's victory in Chile, the turn to repressive military dictatorship in Brazil, and Bosch's failure in the Dominican Republic), that aid in Colombia was more successful. Again though, it bears repeating that the successes the United States achieved in Colombia were a result of an often cooperative political class. No other country had a leadership as committed to following the United States at the beginning of the 1960s.[78] Kennedy had predicated the success of the Alliance for Progress on the concept of self-help. The wisdom of that decision appears to be borne out in the Colombian case.

CHAPTER **8**

The Alliance for Progress in the Late 1960s
The Slow Fade to Irrelevance

As the case studies suggest, the Alliance for Progress operated through-out the 1960s on national terms. Looking at Chile, Brazil, the Domini-can Republic, and Colombia alone, however, presents a view of U.S. aid policy in the mid- and late-1960s that overestimates U.S. involvement in the region as a whole. The four countries examined in the case studies were the highest priorities for Washington. In total they received 59.6 percent of all U.S. aid to the region from FY1962 to FY1969. As the 1960s wore on, these four received an even greater percentage of U.S. aid: 69.2 percent from FY1966 to FY1968.[1] Yet the cases also demonstrate a larger trend: the energy, enthusiasm, and idealism that existed at the start of the 1960s were no longer present.

Two factors ensured that interest in the program would wane by the mid-1960s. Following the 1964 presidential election, and into the first months of 1965, President Johnson increasingly focused on the war in Vietnam. This involvement drew his focus away from Latin America (as well as almost every other area of governance). Second, and linked to the first issue, the U.S. government faced a balance-of-payments crisis itself that made foreign aid programs particularly unattractive. There was not a conscious effort to neglect Latin America, but as bigger problems emerged elsewhere, and the region appeared stable, the Alliance for Progress fell down the list of U.S. priorities. While Latin American issues seemed to require urgent consideration in 1961, by the mid-1960s U.S. government officials, including Johnson, did not think they required much attention. The shifting focus away from Latin America suggests that whereas political concerns in Latin America guided the evolution of the Alliance for Progress in the early 1960s, political issues in the United States determined its course in the latter part of the decade.

Vietnam and the Alliance for Progress

In the 1950s and early 1960s, the United States supported France in its war to control Vietnam, and later it attempted to prop up the South Vietnamese state against Communist forces. Throughout this period, the Eisenhower and Kennedy administrations gradually increased foreign aid and the number of U.S. military advisors assigned to work with South Vietnamese forces. By the end of 1963 there were 15,000 U.S. troops in the country.[2]

When Johnson assumed the presidency, he needed to decide how to proceed with Vietnam. He was reluctant to increase U.S. involvement, not necessarily because he worried about the efficacy of U.S. efforts, but mostly because of the 1964 presidential election. Many moderate voters considered his opponent, Barry Goldwater, as aggressive and perhaps willing to use force in an irresponsible way. Johnson hoped to come across as the peace candidate, but remained alarmed about the situation. In early August 1964 his worries increased as U.S. naval vessels in the Gulf of Tonkin, off the coast of North Vietnam, appeared to come under attack by enemy ships. In response, and to gain broad support, Johnson sent Congress a request (the Gulf of Tonkin resolution) for authorization to "take all necessary steps, including the use of armed force" to aid South Vietnam. Passage of this resolution opened the door for rapid escalation of U.S. involvement.[3]

By early 1965, Johnson and his advisors had come to believe, or at least had convinced themselves, that an anti-Communist South Vietnam was an essential U.S. foreign policy objective. Defeat in Vietnam would demonstrate weakness and embolden the Soviets and Chinese to challenge anti-Communist regimes in other countries. However, U.S. aid had done little to stem the corruption and incompetence within the South Vietnamese government and military, which meant the United States would have to become more involved. By mid-1965 Johnson decided to send ground troops to Vietnam and felt it was necessary to do everything possible to win. To that end he repeatedly increased the number of U.S. forces on the ground. By the end of 1965 there were 185,000 U.S. soldiers in Vietnam. Two years later, in late 1967, this number had risen to 486,000.[4]

Johnson understood that victory on the battlefield was only one part of the war and that ensuring peace required functional political and economic systems. In a dramatic speech at Johns Hopkins University in April 1965, Johnson laid out what could be called an Alliance for Progress for Vietnam. He explained that disease, hunger, and death were part of everyday conditions and were the fundamental regional problems in Asia. The solution would be a billion dollar investment "to replace despair with hope, and terror with progress." He proposed a TVA-like project in the Mekong Delta—the spread of modern medicine, new schools, and assistance with agriculture. Vietnam may have pulled attention away from Latin America, but the tools the United States would use were similar.[5]

This short digression is necessary to place the Alliance for Progress in the mid- and late-1960s into a larger context. While President Kennedy thought Latin America appeared to be in imminent danger, Johnson believed Vietnam was in trouble. Spending so much time, energy, and political capital on the war, Johnson simply could not pay attention to Latin America. It is important to note that this did not mean the U.S. government gave up on the region. Johnson did follow developments and aid continued, but not to the same degree. The Alliance for Progress remained a priority lower in the bureaucratic chain. This was the case in part because the State Department was organized around regional bureaus. Starting with the assistant secretary of state for inter-American affairs, and down through the desk officers and embassy staffs, there were officials with the sole job of managing U.S.–Latin American relations. While these officials continued to write reports, develop recommendations, and ask for aid programs, the amount of attention and concern their memos received at the highest levels of the U.S. government clearly diminished.

Undersecretary of State George Ball would later write, "Vietnam constricted the American government's vision like a camera focused on a near object with little depth of field." His point was simply that as Vietnam became a bigger and bigger problem in the mid- and late-1960s, it became impossible for the U.S. government to deal effectively, let alone focus on, other situations.[6] This issue has been commented on by a series of scholars who have analyzed the Johnson administration. Nancy Bernkopf Tucker, a historian of U.S. foreign relations, wrote that during his time in office, "the weight of the Vietnam disaster precluded initiatives or accomplishments that would have made his place in history a positive rather than a negative chapter." Joseph Tulchin, a historian of U.S.–Latin American relations, similarly explained, "events in Asia, beginning with the Gulf of Tonkin episode, quickly took the attention of the U.S. administration away from the Western Hemisphere and skewed U.S. policy so as to redefine national security in terms of the experience in southeast Asia." More pointedly, Gaddis Smith, another historian of U.S. foreign relations argued, "Latin America fell off the mental map of high Washington officials in the late 1960s."[7]

Financing the War

While Vietnam pulled attention away from Latin America, it also pulled money away from the region. Making the situation even worse, the Vietnam War, and Johnson's handling of its financing, greatly hurt the U.S. economy. As the economy got worse, it became increasingly difficult to make the case that aid to Latin America should be a priority.

At the center of the struggles over macroeconomic policy in the Johnson administration were desires to continue to fund the Great Society programs dedicated to improving social conditions at home while also finding money to make possible an ever-increasing involvement in Vietnam. Economist John E. Ullmann, in an essay entitled "Lyndon Johnson and the Limits of American Resources," explains the problem: "During the Johnson administration, the United States reached the limits of the reach of its economy, of its foreign and military policy, and of its ability to cope with, let alone alleviate, its gathering domestic difficulties." This took time for Johnson to comprehend. In his 1966 state of the union address, he claimed, "This nation is mighty enough—its society is healthy enough—its people are strong enough—to pursue our goals in the rest of the world and build a great society here at home." He was incorrect, perhaps because he had no inkling that the annual costs of the Vietnam War would jump from $5.8 billion in 1966 to $28.8 billion in 1969. These ever-increasing war expenditures, paid for by the creation of debt, would lead to a federal budget deficit of well over $25 billion by 1968.[8]

One of Johnson's greatest failures in his management of the Vietnam War was an unwillingness to be honest with the American people about the costs of war or to suggest that Americans needed to pay more taxes. Kennedy had been quite successful in the early 1960s in using strategic tax cuts to spur economic activity. He was the first president to heed the advice of economic advisors that lower taxes might create growth and result in greater government revenues. These policies led to a $25 billion increase in the GNP (gross national product), and coupled with reductions in government spending, led the U.S. government to a budget surplus.[9]

Following on Kennedy's heels, raising taxes was politically difficult for Johnson. More significantly though, he did not want the public or Congress to know about the full monetary costs of the Vietnam War or the sacrifices that would be necessary. He did this, initially, because he was hopeful the war would be short, but he also recognized that the massive cost of the war would become an argument for Americans uneasy about the fighting. In an effort to hide the true cost of the war, Johnson's military advisors even misled his civilian economic staff. Economic planners assumed, based on estimates given to them by the military about the cost of the war, that the budget deficit in 1966 would be around $1.8 billion, in actuality the figure was closer to $9 billion.[10]

The costs of government spending and growing deficits had an impact throughout the economy. Perhaps most important, in late 1965 military expenditures increased domestic inflation and drove the economy toward what was perceived to be an unsustainable rate of growth. Government spending at the outset of World War II had been effective in ending the Depression and creating economic growth. But because the U.S. economy was in an extremely strong position during the early 1960s, the increased expenditures proved destabilizing. Johnson attempted to fight inflation caused by too much spending by trying to limit increases in prices of basic materials (copper, nickel, steel, and others) but he was ultimately unsuccessful.[11]

Johnson's advisors pushed for a tax increase in 1965, in part to pay for the war, but also to slow dangerously rapid economic growth and thereby limit inflation. But Johnson, understanding the unpopularity of a tax hike, hesitated until 1967. Instead, he continued to use the Kennedy economic strategy. He pushed Congress to pass a bill in February 1965 that cut personal tax rates by 21 percent over two years. The bill also cut corporate tax rates dramatically. With lower government revenues, Johnson had to begin to reduce government expenditures in nonmilitary areas. To that end, in late 1966 he announced planned cuts of $5.3 billion in federal programs, and during 1967 began to trim the U.S. federal budget. The administration called for a complete cancellation of spending on highway construction to save $1.1 billion, along with other smaller cuts from a host of government agencies.[12]

Foreign aid programs, including the Alliance for Progress, suffered large reductions. Economic aid spending in Latin America peaked at $888.6 million in FY1966, but in the following years the amounts of money the Johnson administration requested to fund the Alliance for Progress, and that Congress appropriated, shrank. Latin American specialists in the State Department protested the reductions in U.S. aid as both a tactical mistake and a repudiation of the Alliance for Progress, but to little avail. By 1969, the last year of the Johnson budgets, the United States had cut its total regional spending to just under $440 million. Development aid to Latin America was not the only casualty; other regions also suffered similar cuts.[13] (see Figure 8.1)

Johnson's Balance-of-Payments Problem

The budgetary issue was not the only thing that made foreign aid programs less appealing during the late Johnson years. A balance-of-payments problem began to emerge in the early 1960s as foreign nationals accumulated

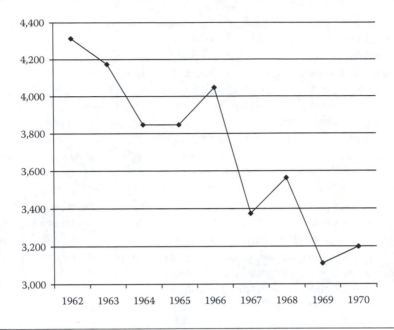

Figure 8.1 Total U.S. Economic Assistance FY1961 to FY1970 with Funding for Vietnam Removed (in millions of U.S. dollars; data not adjusted for inflation). From the United States Agency for International Development Web site, The Greenbook (http://qesdb.cdie.org/gbk).

large reserves of U.S. currency. Before the suspension of convertibility of dollars to gold in 1971, foreign holders of dollars could redeem their cash for gold at $35 per ounce. Because the U.S. economy was the strongest in the world in the years following World War II, foreign bankers attempted to obtain as many dollars as possible. By the late 1950s, however, there were so many dollars abroad that some foreigners became concerned and began to redeem them, leading to a depletion of U.S. gold stocks, and at least in theory, a draining of U.S. wealth. In addition, as European economies recovered in the 1950s, U.S. investors rushed to send money abroad in search of high growth rates. United States investment in Europe jumped from $1.7 billion in 1950 to $6.6 billion ten years later. This investment abroad continued in the 1960s and reached $12.2 billon by 1970. All this spending meant an outflow of dollars and a decrease in U.S. gold reserves, which fell from a post–World War II high of $24.5 billion in 1949 to a low of $10.2 billion in 1971.[14]

The Kennedy administration took a series of measures to improve the U.S. balance-of-payments situation. They instructed the military to buy as many supplies as possible within the United States, and convinced Western European governments, notably the French and West Germans, to swap their holdings of U.S. dollars for their own currencies. The Europeans did this, though it was against their immediate political and economic interests, because they accepted the argument that a weak U.S. economy would be bad for global security. The Kennedy tax cuts were a part of this effort as well. They aimed, in part, to increase foreign investment in the United States, which would further reduce the flow of currency out of the United States. This did not entirely solve the problem. Foreign investment in the United States did rise, from $6.9 billion in 1960 to $8.3 billion in 1964, but the growth was far slower than the rate of growth in U.S. investment abroad.[15]

Vietnam made the balance-of-payments problem worse. The fighting and the drain on the U.S. economy eroded global confidence in the United States, leading foreign holders of dollars to increasingly request gold exchanges. Economic aid programs, which sent dollars to other countries, simply served to increase the problem. The Johnson administration took steps to deal with the outflow of dollars, including setting up a voluntary program that encouraged U.S. corporations and financial institutions not to invest abroad. But an increased need to spend money in foreign markets for war goods made the balance-of-payments situation critical by late 1967. In response, during 1968 Johnson and the Treasury Department developed a more aggressive approach. This included a mandatory program to limit U.S. foreign investment abroad, steps to increase U.S. exports, and even a request to the American people to put off "all unessential travel" for two years. Given the problems, the reluctance to make new loans in the late 1960s is not surprising.[16]

It is worth noting the irony that especially in the mid-1960s, the U.S. government, in cooperation with the IMF and the World Bank, repeatedly counseled Latin American governments to tackle their balance-of-payments problems. The United States often made government spending cuts a requirement before more aid would be sent. At the same time this was happening, the United States faced its own balance-of-payments problem and was unable and unwilling to make the tough choices to fix the problem.

Regional Integration as the Last Big Idea

Vietnam distracted Johnson from Latin America. Although Kennedy had made three trips to the region in his presidency, Johnson did not make a trip until April 1967. Still, it would be inaccurate to suggest that he completely ignored the region or even failed to consider the Alliance for Progress as a worthwhile endeavor. A limited amount of time and money made focus on Latin American issues difficult, but at key moments Johnson did pay significant attention. The most notable effort to refocus interest on the Alliance for Progress came at a meeting of Latin American presidents in mid-April 1967 in Punta del Este.

By this point it had become obvious that the economics of the Alliance for Progress had not been effective, and that continued large-scale U.S. development aid was not possible. As a means to spur Latin American growth, U.S. policymakers fell back on regional integration as a method for addressing the problems of underdevelopment. The thinking was that while U.S. largesse had been unable to help spur economic growth, lowering trade barriers might allow Latin Americans to help each other. The idea of regional integration was not new in 1967. As U.S. policymakers were shifting their attention to Latin America in the early 1960s there was a push, connected to the development of the Alliance for Progress, to create the Latin American Free Trade Association (LAFTA).[17]

Economists at the United Nations Economic Commission for Latin America/*Comisión Económica para América Latina* (CEPAL) argued in the 1950s that industrial development was fundamental to growth, but that in many fields, markets had to be sufficiently large to make it feasible. Raúl Prebisch, the leading CEPAL economist, advocated a common market to solve this problem. In the United States, Walt Rostow aggressively pushed this idea as well. In a long briefing memo written prior to the 1967 conference, Rostow argued that Latin American firms, especially in heavy industry, were capable of growing rapidly, but only needed bigger markets. In this way, to Rostow, Latin America in the late 1960s was like Europe in the 1950s. A common market in Latin America would provide markets for growth as had the European Common Market.[18]

The countries that joined LAFTA (initially Argentina, Uruguay, Chile, Brazil, Paraguay, Peru, and Mexico, with Colombia and Ecuador joining later) had success in the mid-1960s in lowering tariffs and increasing interhemispheric trade. Between 1961 and 1963, trade among the LAFTA nations rose 41.2 percent, from $659 million to $931 million. Trade continued to rise to $1.6 billion by 1968.[19] LAFTA was not the only regional free trade agreement. In December 1960, four Central American Nations (El Salvador, Guatemala, Nicaragua, and Honduras) agreed to form the Central American Common Market (CACM), and were joined by Costa Rica in 1963. As with the larger LAFTA, there was a lowering of tariffs and a resultant increase in trade. Well before 1967, the United States made a series of loans to help these Central American nations with regional integration.[20]

Both the Central American Common Market and LAFTA faced significant problems. Bureaucratic hurdles and concerns of business elites in some countries slowed the process of integration, yet talks about improving efficiency and expansion continued. In 1966, representatives of five nations (Colombia, Chile, Venezuela, Peru, and Ecuador) jointly agreed to work together to create a more substantial integration agreement. Their 1966 Declaration of Bogotá was the initial step in the creation of the Andean Pact, a regional trade agreement they hoped would create a fully functioning and complete common market by 1985. These moves toward regional integration developed frameworks for the summit of the presidents held in Punta del Este, but until 1967 they were in the background of the Alliance for Progress. Indeed, technical experts had dominated discussions about regional integration, they only became political discussions at the conference.[21]

Strengthening these free trade agreements and making them central to the Alliance for Progress appeared to be an easy and potentially effective way of improving economic development in Latin America. It was also consistent with the idea of self-help and part of the Charter of Punta del Este. It had no link to the Kennedy ideals about social justice and reform that had driven the Alliance for Progress at the outset, but it was a way to create economic growth.[22]

To help Latin American countries move forward with organization and implementation of broader free trade agreements, Johnson proposed before the 1967 Punta del Este conference that the United States commit $300 million annually for five years to ease the costs associated with integration. This would be in addition to $900 million Johnson hoped to commit to agriculture and education programs.[23] These propositions faced difficulties early in the process. To strengthen his hand at Punta del Este and thereafter, Johnson requested that Congress pass a nonbinding resolution that offered support for the president's plans. The House of Representatives quickly approved a statement, but the Senate, led by Senator William Fulbright (D-AR), refused to give what he termed a "blank check" to the president. The Senate Foreign Relations Committee rewrote the resolution, explaining that as agreements are reached by the Latin American nations, the United States would "give due consideration to cooperation in such agreements." Fulbright had become a strong opponent of Johnson's foreign policy as a result of the Dominican intervention and Vietnam, and saw this as opportunity to reign him in.[24]

Limited by Congress, Johnson was unable to offer any dramatic gestures at Punta del Este. There were no big promises like those that Dillon had made in 1961. Johnson was able to offer only "a substantial contribution to a fund that will help ease the transition into an integrated regional economy," and a pledge to do all he could to help Latin Americans achieve the goals of the Alliance for Progress. Johnson also promised to support more funds for communications projects, to push for trade preferences for Latin American nations in the United States, to create new technical and educational programs, and to continue to fund development projects that would bring more medical facilities, roads, and schools to Latin America. The real work, however, as Johnson explained, had to come from the Latin Americans themselves.[25]

Echoing a theme that had been dominant since the earliest days of the Alliance for Progress, Johnson told the Latin American presidents, "All that has been dreamed of in the years since the Alliance started can only come to pass if your hearts and your minds are dedicated and committed to it." He explained, "The pace of change is not fast enough. It will remain too slow unless you join your energies, your skills and commitments, in a mighty effort that extends into the farthest reaches of the hemisphere."[26] These ideas about executing regional integration programs became a central focus of a document produced at the conference, the Declaration of the Presidents of America (see Appendix D). In its tone the declaration mirrored the Charter of Punta del Este; it imagined that the creation of a common market would be a panacea to create growth that could eventually lead to improved social conditions.[27]

Following the 1967 Summit, Chile, Colombia, Peru, Bolivia, Ecuador, and Venezuela continued with talks to establish a common market, and in May 1969 five of these six nations finally signed an agreement (Venezuela opted not to join until 1973). The Central American nations also moved forward on their own regional development bank.[28] The focus on regional free trade agreements should be seen as a lasting impact of the Alliance for Progress. Given the difficulty, if not the impossibility, of creating growth by giving external aid, it is reasonable to suggest that as the Alliance for Progress evolved under Johnson it became more realistic. Latin American economic problems would not disappear rapidly, but they could improve gradually. Further, by stressing regional integration, Johnson remained true to the ideal of Latin Americans helping each other. The United States would provide support, encouragement, and some financial help, but for all practical purposes, Latin Americans needed to be responsible for each other and themselves. Indeed, at the summit the United States maintained a distinctly low profile. Johnson spent much of the trip at a fashionable estate holding one-to-one meetings with Latin American presidents. In large part because he had no carrots to offer, he was reduced to listening. As the *New York Times* reported, "Latin Americans, to their surprise, found that the summit truly belonged to them." Johnson was "conspicuously inconspicuous."[29]

Johnson saw these Punta del Este meetings, at least initially, as a renewal of the Alliance for Progress. Following the summit he instructed the State Department to catalog the promises he had made at the meeting. Each month the assistant secretary of state for inter-American affairs, first Lincoln Gordon and then Covey T. Oliver, prepared an extensive report on what had been done about them. The 1967 trip to Punta del Este, however, did little to stem the long-term trend away from focus on Latin American aid programs. Without money, and with more pressing crises elsewhere in the world, and without the serious problems associated with Latin America in the early 1960s, the Alliance for Progress became far less vital. Indeed, the idea of regional integration as a new centerpiece of the Alliance for Progress consigned the United States to an external and limited role in regional economic development planning. The United States gave up its leadership role on economic matters.[30]

Nixon and the Alliance for Progress

During his successful 1968 presidential campaign, Richard Nixon offered a vision of U.S.–Latin American policy that focused on trade rather than aid. Given the declining interest and ability of the Johnson administration to offer significant aid packages, and their focus by 1967 on regional trade integration, this simply represented an extension of the Johnson administration's approach and echoed U.S. government policy in the 1950s when Nixon was Eisenhower's vice president.[31] (see Table 8.1) Beyond generalities, Nixon spoke little about the region. In 1967 he visited several Latin American countries and seemed to endorse some Alliance for Progress ideals, but he did not give many specifics about how he would act as president. When he was critical of the Alliance for Progress, it was mostly to accuse the Johnson administration of bureaucratic inefficiency. He promised to do better.[32]

Shortly after taking office, on February 17, 1969, Nixon commissioned a study to assess the state of Latin American affairs and to suggest what kinds of U.S. responses would be appropriate. Given the perceptions in the United States and Latin America that the Alliance for Progress had failed, this was entirely reasonable. It was also reasonable because the new administration had a responsibility to assess government programs to see what was working. To lead the study, Nixon appointed his most potent political rival within the Republican Party, New York State Governor Nelson Rockefeller.[33]

The poor relationship between the two Republicans suggested that Nixon's interest in the study would not be great, and in a larger way it set the tone for the low priority Latin America would hold in the late 1960s and early 1970s. Observers at the time understood that the mission was simply a way to buy time toward the development of a comprehensive Latin American policy while his administration considered bigger and more important issues elsewhere. Indeed, it took almost a year from the 1968

Table 8.1 U.S. Economic Aid to Latin America FY1962–FY1976 (in millions of U.S. dollars; data not adjusted for inflation)

Fiscal Year	Aid
FY1962	841.7
FY1963	864.2
FY1964	988.7
FY1965	820.1
FY1966	888.6
FY1967	671.9
FY1968	762.5
FY1969	439.7
FY1970	607.4
FY1971	463.5
FY1972	477.2
FY1973	436.0
FY1974	346.0
FY1975	427.7
FY1976	417.6

Source: The United States Agency for International Development website, The Greenbook (http://qesdb.cdie.org/gbk).

election for Nixon to even say anything substantial about Latin American policy. Through most of 1969, though he claimed Latin America would be his "highest priority," he also said it would be prudent to wait for the Rockefeller report to make any decisions.[34]

In response to Nixon's request, in early 1969 Rockefeller and a series of advisors made four study trips to Latin America. Most of the visits turned out to be an embarrassment, and suggested that real problems remained for the United States in Latin America. As they had during Nixon's 1958 trip, students protested and used violence as a means of keeping Rockefeller from continuing his travels. In Argentina and the Dominican Republic, large rallies turned violent, leading the Uruguayans to insist that Rockefeller visit the Punta del Este resort instead of Montevideo. The Peruvian government suggested that a visit would be "inconvenient," and dramatically, both the Chilean and Venezuelan governments asked that Rockefeller cancel visits to their countries. There were some friendly, uneventful visits, but the fact that Rockefeller was able to wave to cheering crowds from a balcony along with the brutal Haitian dictator, François "Papa Doc" Duvalier, was not much of a positive sign.[35]

In a letter to Nixon that served as a preface to his report, Rockefeller attempted to explain the negative response his mission evoked. He wrote,

> There is general frustration over the failure to achieve a more rapid improvement in standards of living. The United States, because of its identification with the failure of the Alliance for Progress to live up to expectations, is blamed. People in the countries concerned also used our visit as an opportunity to demonstrate their frustrations with the failure of their own governments to meet their needs . . . demonstrations that began over grievances were taken over and exacerbated by anti-US and subversive elements which sought to weaken the United States, and their own governments in the process.[36]

Latin America, according to the authors of the Rockefeller report, was facing serious problems. It suggested, "Everywhere in the hemisphere we see similar difficulties—problems of population and poverty, urbanization and unemployment, illiteracy and injustice, violence and disorder." Even worse, "Political and social instability, increased pressure for radical answers to the problems, and a growing tendency to nationalistic independence from the United States dominate the setting." These suggested a big problem because "The restless yearning of individuals for a better life . . . is chipping away at the very order and institutions by which society makes it possible for man to fulfill his personal dignity. The seeds of nihilism and anarchy are spreading throughout the hemisphere." This language echoed the concerns about Latin America in the late 1950s; little seemed to have changed, but given the failures of the Alliance for Progress, the solution had to be different.[37]

A major part of Rockefeller's suggestion was a reduction of U.S. involvement. In the body of the report he argued, "Our ability to affect or influence the course of events in other nations is limited," and "we must recognize that the specific forms or processes by which each nation moves toward a pluralistic system will vary with its own traditions and situation." In other words, "we, in the United States, cannot determine the internal political structure of any other nation." Given there was little the United States could or should do toward changing political behavior in other countries, it made no sense to attempt to use economic aid as a political tool. This understanding justified the reduction in economic aid toward the region.[38]

But the Rockefeller report did not completely call for the ending of U.S. aid programs to Latin America. Rockefeller devoted considerable energy to developing recommendations for creating more effective aid programs that would reduce some of the tensions inherent in the donor–recipient relationship. He also called for a new structure for the U.S.–Latin American policy apparatus to simplify decision making and give more power to a single individual responsible for the totality of Latin American policy.[39]

Part of Rockefeller's argument also suggested that the United States did not necessarily need to object to military and repressive governments if they emerged. In testimony before the House Committee on Foreign Affairs in March 1969, James R. Fowler, the acting coordinator of the Alliance for Progress explained this idea. He argued, "the regression in democratic institutions in specific instances here and there . . . is something which we do not approve of, and obviously wish wouldn't happen." But Fowler added that this should not be important in making aid decisions. He explained, "Governments change from time to time but the modernization and development process . . . should be measured in terms of decades and generations." He asked, "Should our assistance to that development process be stopped, or turned off and on, or rise and fall, simply because of these shorter term political manifestations, many of which seem to us to be retrogressive, many of which are disappointing if measured by the democratic norms which we establish?" He concluded by asking, "Can we maintain both a long-term development policy, looking toward long-term development objectives, and at the same time not appear to be condoning or supporting political movements which we all find highly disturbing[?]" The answer seemed to be yes. Governments would continue to receive U.S. funding, but reform, especially political reforms, were not necessary.[40]

Beyond the advice from Rockefeller, Latin Americans were aggressive in suggesting courses of action to Nixon. In two notable meetings, Latin American leaders argued that if the United States was serious about the idea of trade replacing aid, it needed to improve its complex and unfair trade practices. That is, the Latin Americans could accept the idea that trade was fundamental to U.S. development strategies, but that trade had to be among equals. In mid-June, Gabriel Valdés, the Chilean foreign minister, met with the president to deliver a statement crafted in Viña de Mar, Chile, by representatives of twenty-one Latin American nations. Valdés and the document he presented, which came to be known as "The Consenus of Viña del Mar" argued that the United States should open its market to Latin American goods. Washington aggressively pushed Latin Americans to open their markets to U.S. firms, but did not play fair by limiting the sale of Latin American goods in the United States. The United States, Valdés suggested, could become wealthy because of inter-American trade, but the same was not true of the Latin Americans.[41]

Valdés also raised the problem of regulations within aid loan contracts that limited Latin American trade. All loans stipulated that purchases of goods and services made with aid money had to occur in the United States, but because prices in the United States were often significantly higher than elsewhere, Latin Americans ended up paying premium prices, and in essence wasting aid money intended for development. In 1964 this problem got worse. The U.S. Congress imposed a device called *additionality* to loans. Under this policy, aid recipient nations had to purchase goods in the United States in amounts equal to those they had purchased before the development of aid programs. The goal was to keep recipient nations from shifting purchasing patterns away from U.S. companies to protect the U.S. balance-of-payments position. The policy seemed overly restrictive and demeaning to Latin Americans. In addition to the purchasing requirements, there were other concerns. Latin Americans who wanted to buy goods in the United States needed to give forty-five days notice to the Small Business Administration of their intent, and half of all the goods purchased with aid dollars needed to be shipped on U.S. vessels, even if lower freight rates were available elsewhere.[42]

Following the meeting with Valdés, Nixon saw Colombian President Carlos Lleras Restrepo in his first meeting with a Latin American head of state. Lleras Restrepo reinforced the points Valdés had made. He argued, as had Valdés, that the United States offered aid, but at the same time limited its utility with "fine print" clauses. Lleras Restrepo gave the example of Colombia's intention to export $4 million worth of rice in 1969 cultivated under a project developed with the assistance and encouragement of U.S. aid officials who encouraged crop diversification. He explained that if his country exported this rice, the U.S. government would have to cut off PL480 programs worth $15 million. The U.S. Congress had passed legislation that forbade exports of wheat in PL480 programs to countries that sold goods (rice in this case) that competed with U.S. agricultural exports. As a Colombian government official explained to the press, "The State Department tells us to diversify exports so as not to be dependent on aid," but "then the Department of Agriculture insists we must not compete with United States exports. It's crazy."[43]

Nixon's Speech

The sluggish development of Nixon's Latin American policy reflected the region's relative lack of importance and his unwillingness to offer any major policy initiatives on par with the Alliance for Progress. However, after the submission of the Rockefeller report, he had little choice but to say something about the region. At the end of October 1969 he made a major policy address setting out his plans. He began by being suitably and accurately critical of the Alliance for Progress. Nixon explained,

Often we in the United States had been charged with an overweening confidence in the rightness of our own prescriptions, and occasionally we've been guilty of the charge. I intend to correct that. . . . For years, we in the United States have pursued the illusion that we alone could remake continents. Conscious of our wealth and technology, seized by the force of good intentions, driven by our habitual impatience, remembering the dramatic success of the Marshall Plan in postwar Europe, we have sometimes imagined that we knew what was best for everyone else and that we could and should make it happen. Well, experience has taught us better. . . . What I hope we can achieve, therefore, is a more mature partnership in which all voices are heard and none is predominant—a partnership guided by a healthy awareness that give and take is better than take-it-or-leave-it.

Though he offered "no grandiose promises and no panaceas," Nixon claimed he would "offer action." He pledged to lead an effort "to reduce nontariff barriers to trade maintained by nearly all industrialized countries against products of particular interest to Latin America and other developing countries." This pledge included a commitment to "press for a liberal system of generalized tariff preferences for all developing countries, including Latin America." Further, Nixon pledged to eliminate the restrictions on the use of U.S. aid programs, as the consensus of Vina del Mar suggested. At the time of his speech, Nixon was working to eliminate the additionality restrictions to allow Latin Americans to spend aid dollars anywhere in the world. He also committed to "ordering that all other onerous conditions and restrictions on United States assistance loans be reviewed, with the objective of modifying or eliminating them." These actions were positive steps, though perhaps less meaningful given the sharp reductions in the actual sending of economic aid.[44]

Beyond responding to the criticism of Valdés and Lleras Restrepo, Nixon also addressed the question of nondemocratic states. Echoing the conclusions of the Rockefeller report, Nixon explained that the United States

lives by a democratic system which has preserved its form for nearly two centuries. It has its problems, but we are proud of the system. We are jealous of our liberties and we hope that eventually most, perhaps even all, of the world's people will share what we consider to be the blessings of a genuine democracy. . . . Nevertheless, we recognize that enormous, sometimes explosive, forces for change are operating in Latin America. These create instabilities; they bring changes in governments. On the diplomatic level we must deal realistically with governments in the inter-American system as they are.

In his most aggressive sloganeering of the entire speech, Nixon called for the 1970s to be a decade of "action for progress," though he did not define what this meant in practice or its connection to the Alliance for Progress. Responding to claims that the United States had abandoned Latin America he said, "We do care. I care."[45]

Critics of Nixon's policies in Latin America contend that the Rockefeller report and the October 1969 speech did not set policy. That is, they were rhetoric only. This is an unfair assessment. Nixon was true to his word in arguing that the United States would not consider aid as the sole means for developing Latin America, and he most certainly accepted governments, including brutal and repressive military dictatorships, as they were.[46]

It would also be unfair to suggest that Nixon did not believe in foreign aid. Upon coming into office, Nixon was supportive of foreign aid programs and attempted to strengthen U.S. efforts as a sign of commitment to developing nations. In a National Security Council meeting in early April 1969 attended by key members of the administration, Nixon approved a series of documents that guided the U.S. government to insist on a substantial foreign aid program. According to the text of the minutes, the president explained, "since Congressional sentiment tends to be increasingly isolationist, it will be necessary to justify new programs in a more meaningful way. The humanitarian aspect should be emphasized in justifying economic aid (other than war-related programs in Southeast Asia); the long-run economic benefit to the United States of a higher level of economic development elsewhere is also important. The aid should not be built on expectations of immediate political returns to the United States." Nixon also "decided that the requested authorization for foreign assistance in FY1970 should be on the generous side as an early indication of the Administration's attitude toward foreign assistance."[47]

Although speeches may have been for public consumption, that Nixon would say these things in private to top policymakers is significant. In this meeting Nixon also approved policy documents that called for larger requests to Congress for foreign aid. He agreed with the logic that "only a major program . . . would enable the US to again provide decisive leadership in the economic development process." This would "make virtually certain economic progress in the Subcontinent [i.e., India and Pakistan], enhance greatly the Alliance for Progress, assure a major Southeast Asia postwar development program, and give . . . flexibility to respond to new opportunities in Asia."[48]

Just as Kennedy and Johnson had, Nixon faced a reluctant and resistant Congress. For 1970, Nixon had submitted a request for $2.63 billion in aid, but the House of Representatives foreign aid appropriations committee reduced the bill to $2.18 billion. Nixon had to become involved in pressuring Louisiana Congressman Otto Passman to abandon $400 million in further cuts in November 1969.[49] As with Johnson and Kennedy, it is important to remember that although the executive had the ability to set agendas and suggest priorities and AID budgeting, those decisions were ultimately subject to the declining will of Congress.

A complete study of Nixon administration aid policy toward Latin America is beyond the scope of this work, but this short review suggests consistency with late Johnson administration policies. To push trade, Nixon supported the Inter-American Development Bank and the creation of the Overseas Private Investment Corporation (OPIC). This entity, created in the Foreign Assistance Act of 1969, provided support to U.S. companies interested in international investments by giving financial assistance, insurance, and guidance about local conditions.[50]

This is not to suggest that Nixon's foreign policy toward Latin America should be seen as wholly innocuous or even positive, only that there was not a dramatic transformation in aid policy through the last years of the Johnson administration to that of Nixon. Beyond aid, the Nixon administration demonstrated an unwillingness to accept Latin American realities or engage in Latin American change in a constructive way. Most notably, this problem is visible in U.S. policy toward Chile in the early 1970s.

In 1970 the Chilean people elected the Marxist Salvador Allende as president. Although there was no evidence that Allende intended to export revolution, this turn of events greatly distressed Nixon and his chief foreign policy advisor, Henry Kissinger. The CIA worked hard to stop Allende from taking office and orchestrated the assassination of a military leader who was thought to be standing in the way of a coup d'etat. Once Allende was in office, Nixon pushed for an economic blockade that destroyed the Chilean economy and was a key factor in encouraging its military to intervene in 1973. The Chilean case suggests that the Nixon administration had not given up on the idea that the United States could have an impact on Latin American political processes. It suggests only abandonment of the idea that aid could be used as a tool for change.

The CIA, guided by top officials in the Nixon administration, pursued engagement on the cheap throughout the Allende term. While there was no interest in a comprehensive aid program for Chile, the Nixon staff was willing to spend money for a propaganda campaign to do precisely what Rockefeller had suggested was not possible—have an impact on Latin American political processes.[51] It is easy to be critical of U.S. policy toward Chile and the use of the CIA in the early 1970s, yet this type of action was not unprecedented. The U.S. government had used the CIA to attempt to destabilize Cuba in the 1960s, and its agents had been active in many other countries, including Chile, during the Kennedy and Johnson administrations. Nixon administration officials may have overstepped some moral line, but they were not the first to do so.

It is certainly reasonable to suggest, from a U.S. perspective, that a focus on Latin America in 1969 made far less sense than it had in 1961. Latin American nations, if not democratic, were at least stable. The warnings of doom and concern about an imminent Communist takeover, with the exception of Chile, had proved to be mistaken. While Communist parties did exist, and in some places were powerful, the notion that Latin America might be consumed by Castro-like revolutions was easy to dismiss. The Soviet Union had shown little interest in funding rebel groups, and Cuban efforts to extend revolution had failed pitifully.[52]

The Nixon administration had fewer qualms about working with anti-Communist, nondemocratic totalitarian states. The Johnson administration was certainly willing to work with dictatorships, but the Nixon team actively embraced them. Even governments that the United States was happy about, however, did not receive extensive economic aid. Increases in military aid often became a way to balance drops in economic aid. For example, U.S. economic aid to Brazil in the 1970s dropped consistently from FY1970 to FY1976, but military aid grew during this same period, surpassing economic aid in FY1974, FY1975, and FY1976.[53] (see Table 8.2)

A lack of concern with democracy would ultimately be a key criticism of Nixon policy. Along with Henry Kissinger, his national security advisor, and after 1973 also the secretary of state, the United States developed warm relationships with brutal dictatorships in Latin America. Though unpleasant and ethically repugnant, these relationships should be seen in the con-

Table 8.2 Military and Economic Aid to Brazil, FY1971–FY1976 (in millions of U.S. dollars; data not adjusted for inflation)

Economic Aid						
FY1970	FY1971	FY1972	FY1973	FY1974	FY1975	FY1976
154	117.6	21	53.8	17.2	14.7	4

Military Aid						
FY1970	FY1971	FY1972	FY1973	FY1974	FY1975	FY1976
0.8	12.0	20.6	17.5	46.1	65.3	44.1

Source: United States Agency for International Development Web site, The Green-book (http://qesdb.cdie.org/gbk).

text of the global situation. It is important to repeat that while Communism appeared to be a minor threat in Latin America, it remained a big problem elsewhere. In Vietnam, Nixon's ascension to the presidency had solved little, and the larger struggle with the Soviet Union remained. In the calculus of global politics in the 1960s, Latin America could not be a priority. Thus, a less engaged policy made a great deal of sense.[54]

Conclusion
Aid to Latin America in Context

At the start of the Kennedy administration, the Alliance for Progress was the great hope of U.S. policymakers as the means to counter the rise of Communism in Latin America. Rather than use force or coercion to influence political change, the program would encourage leaders to pursue reform. Aid from the United States would be a way to help Latin American leaders help themselves create lasting economic growth and stability, and in doing so develop new, more cooperative and positive inter-American relationships. As Richard Nixon had found in 1958, and as Castro's success illustrated, many in the region resented U.S. power and arrogance, but Kennedy hoped to change all this and usher in a new age of collaboration and mutual respect.

The Alliance for Progress did not achieve these goals. In an effort to establish the program, the United States instructed Latin Americans on how to pursue reform. As the case studies demonstrate, they were rewarded when they cooperated and punished when they did not. The program therefore did not represent a partnership, but reinforced Latin American ideas about the overbearing United States. In developing the program, policymakers in the United States did not imagine, comprehensively or rationally, exactly how it would work; the mechanisms they developed were unwieldy, impractical, inefficient, and ignored. While there was an initial desire to allow Latin Americans an important role in determining how money was spent, blunt political considerations made that impossible. This meant that the Alliance for Progress devolved into a U.S. foreign aid program that retained little of its dramatic and revolutionary content. It became simply a way to help friends, hurt enemies, and promote a set of theories about how to best create economic stability. It was not an *alliance*, and it was not even always about economic *progress*.

Initially, Kennedy stressed that the Alliance for Progress would reject the notion of imperial hubris—the idea that the United States, as the strong and wealthy power, and with great ability to influence change, knew what was best for Latin America. Kennedy wanted Latin Americans to believe that the United States wanted to help because it was the right thing to do and that he cared about their problems. In terms of rhetoric, Kennedy was successful. Latin Americans saw him as a great leader dedicated to progressive change. The reality is that, however unfortunately, his policies and those of his successors did not live up to the initial ideals. Faced with political and economic instability and the threat of anti-American politicians taking power, U.S. policymakers felt they had little choice but to use the tools available, including the Alliance for Progress, to create conditions favorable to their own interests. To expect them to have acted otherwise ignores the overwhelming and larger context of the Cold War, which informed their understandings of the world and the reality of their power relative to Latin Americans.

The application of foreign programs as a way to manipulate foreign nations was at one level necessary and obvious, but on a second level clearly counter to the best traditions of American democracy. In a remarkable address at the University of Denver in August 1966, Johnson explained that "the overriding rule" for U.S. foreign policy was that it "must always be an extension of . . . domestic policy." He argued, "our safest guide to what we do abroad is always to take a good look at what we are doing at home." One application of this "rule" in Johnson's mind was that "in the United States we do not like being told what to do. We like even less being told what to think." Thus, in international relations, "The United States has no mandate to interfere wherever government falls short of our specifications." Unfortunately, these dictums did not guide policy. Rather, U.S. policy was the exact opposite of what Johnson professed.[1]

Had the policy actually worked effectively it would be possible to make an argument that interference was a good idea, but U.S. political successes were few. In Brazil, U.S. foreign aid programs had minimal effect on the political orientation of the Goulart government, and were unable to influence the military government in important ways. In Chile, the massive aid in the pre-1964 era had little impact on Frei's victory, and thereafter served mostly as an irritant that drove Chilean leaders toward anti-American positions. Most dramatically, nine and one-half years after Kennedy announced his ten-year commitment to Latin America, Salvador Allende won his country's presidential election. In the Dominican Republic the ledger may be significantly more positive. It is unlikely that U.S. aid programs had much impact on political changes during the first half of the decade, but they did create stability in the postintervention era. Finally, in Colombia, aid may have had a marginal effect in strengthening the governments of the National Front; it allowed them to avoid tough decisions, and to spend, essentially, beyond their means.

Understanding the political logic of the Alliance for Progress helps in developing a perspective about U.S.–Latin American relations during the 1960s. Throughout the decade, U.S. policymakers continually looked to the program as a catchall solution to the problems they faced. This should not suggest that the Alliance for Progress was central to every piece of the relationships, only that it was a way of manipulating them to U.S. advantage. With the notable exception of policy toward Cuba, decisions about economic aid programs were part of every major U.S. action in the region. The U.S. government was willing to use the CIA to engage in covert actions, to use Marines to invade the Dominican Republic, to encourage military leaders to overthrow civilians, and to use its considerable power to help U.S. businesses. But in each one of these cases there was a connection to economic aid in an attempt to create stability, reward friends, or keep threats from emerging.

In broader terms, the Alliance for Progress also helps clarify how policy toward Latin America in the 1960s was consistent with earlier and later periods in inter-American relations. There is little debate in the scholarly community that the major theme in the history of U.S.–Latin American relations is the U.S. desire and ability to dominate the region.[2] This interest came from aspirations about increasing U.S. power, economic and otherwise, and it was usually justified by assumptions about Latin American cultural inferiority. The Alliance for Progress demonstrates that U.S. policy in the 1960s was, though different rhetorically from other eras, essentially similar in application. Kennedy talked about the Alliance for Progress as a partnership of equals and suggested that his goals were more moral and cooperative than his predecessors. The reality was more complicated. Though U.S. policymakers did hope to implement Kennedy's vision, the discrepancy in economic power, U.S. global interests, and assumptions about U.S. superiority meant that U.S. policy was not a repudiation of the past, but a continuation of it.

Appendix A

Address by President John F. Kennedy at the White House Reception for Members of the Diplomatic Corps of the Latin American Republics, March 13, 1961

It is a great pleasure for Mrs. Kennedy and me, for the Vice President and Mrs. Johnson, and for the members of Congress to welcome the ambassadorial corps of our hemisphere, our long-time friends, to the White House today. One hundred and thirty-nine years ago this week the United States, stirred by the historic struggle of its fellow Americans, urged the independence and recognition of the new Latin American republics. It was then, at the dawn of freedom through this hemisphere, that Bolívar spoke of his desire to see the Americas fashioned into the greatest region in the world, "greatest," he said, "not so much by virtue of her area and wealth as by her freedom and glory."

Never in the long history of our hemisphere has this dream been nearer to fulfillment, and never has it been in greater danger.

The genius of our scientists has given us the tools to bring abundance to our land, strength to our industry, and knowledge to our people. For the first time we have the capacity to strike off the remaining bonds of poverty and ignorance—to free our people for the spiritual and intellectual fulfillment which has always been the goal of our civilization.

Yet at this very moment of maximum opportunity, we confront the same forces which have imperiled America throughout its history—the alien forces which once again seek to impose the despotisms of the Old World on the people of the New.

I have asked you to come here today so that I might discuss these challenges and these dangers.

We meet together as firm and ancient friends, united by history and experience and by our determination to advance the values of American civilization. For this New World of ours is not a mere accident of geography. Our continents are bound together by a common history, the endless exploration of new frontiers. Our nations are the product of a common struggle, the revolt from colonial rule. And our people share a common heritage, the quest for the dignity and the freedom of man.

The revolutions which gave us birth ignited, in the words of Thomas Paine, "a spark never to be extinguished." And across vast, turbulent continents these American ideals still stir man's struggle for national independence and individual freedom. But as we welcome the spread of the American revolution to other lands, we must also remember that our own struggle—the revolution which began in Philadelphia in 1776, and in Caracas in 1811—is not yet finished. Our hemisphere's mission is not yet completed. For our unfulfilled task is to demonstrate to the entire world that man's unsatisfied aspiration for economic progress and social justice can best be achieved by free men working within a framework of democratic institutions. If we can do this in our own hemisphere, and for our own people, we may yet realize the prophecy of the great Mexican patriot, Benito Juarez, that "democracy is the destiny of future humanity."

As a citizen of the United States let me be the first to admit that we North Americans have not always grasped the significance of this common mission, just as it is also true that many in your own countries have not fully understood the urgency of the need to lift people from poverty and ignorance and despair. But we must turn from these mistakes—from the failures and the misunderstandings of the past—to a future full of peril, but bright with hope.

Throughout Latin America, a continent rich in resources and in the spiritual and cultural achievements of its people, millions of men and women suffer the daily degradations of poverty and hunger. They lack decent shelter or protection from disease. Their children are deprived of the education or the jobs which are the gateway to a better life. And each day the problems grow more urgent. Population growth is outpacing economic growth—low living standards are further endangered—and discontent—the discontent of a people who know that abundance and the tools of progress are at last within their reach—that discontent is growing. In the words of José Figueres, "once dormant peoples are struggling upward toward the sun, toward a better life."

If we are to meet a problem so staggering in its dimensions, our approach must itself be equally bold—an approach consistent with the majestic concept of Operation Pan America. Therefore I have called on all people of the hemisphere to join in a new Alliance for Progress—*Alianza para Progreso* [*sic*]—a vast cooperative effort, unparalleled in magnitude and nobility of purpose, to satisfy the basic needs of the American people for homes, work and land, health and schools—*techo, trabajo y tierra, salud y escuela*.

First, I propose that the American Republics begin on a vast new Ten Year Plan for the Americas, a plan to transform the 1960's into a historic decade of democratic progress.

These ten years will be the years of maximum progress, maximum effort, the years when the greatest obstacles must be overcome, the years when the need for assistance will be the greatest.

And if we are successful, if our effort is bold enough and determined enough, then the close of this decade will mark the beginning of a new era in the American experience. The living standards of every American family will be on the rise, basic education will be available to all, hunger will be a forgotten experience, the need for massive outside help will have passed, most nations will have entered a period of self-sustaining growth, and though there will be still much to do, every American Republic will be the master of its own revolution and its own hope and progress.

Let me stress that only the most determined efforts of the American nations themselves can bring success to this effort. They and they alone, can mobilize their resources, enlist the energies of their people, and modify their social patterns so that all, and not just a privileged few, share in the fruits of growth. If this effort is made, then outside assistance will give vital impetus to progress; without it, no amount of help will advance the welfare of the people.

Thus if the countries of Latin America are ready to do their part, and I am sure they are, then I believe the United States, for its part, should help provide resources of a scope and magnitude sufficient to make this bold development plan a success—just as we helped to provide, against equal odds nearly, the resources adequate to help rebuild the economies of Western Europe. For only an effort of towering dimensions can ensure fulfillment of our plan for a decade of progress.

Secondly, I will shortly request a ministerial meeting of the Inter-American Economic and Social Council, a meeting at which we can begin the massive planning effort which will be at the heart of the Alliance for Progress.

For if our Alliance is to succeed, each Latin nation must formulate long-range plans for its own development, plans which establish targets and priorities, ensure monetary stability, establish the machinery for vital social change, stimulate private activity and initiative, and provide for a maximum national effort. These plans will be the foundation of our development effort, and the basis for the allocation of outside resources.

A greatly strengthened IA-ECOSOC, working with the Economic Commission for Latin America and the Inter-American Development Bank, can assemble the leading economists and experts of the hemisphere to help each country develop its own development plan—and provide a continuing review of economic progress in this hemisphere.

Third, I have this evening signed a request to the Congress for $500 million as a first step in fulfilling the Act of Bogotá. This is the first large-scale Inter-American effort, instituted by my predecessor President Eisenhower, to attack the social barriers which block economic progress. The money will be used to combat illiteracy, improve the productivity and use of their land, wipe out disease, attack archaic tax and land tenure structures, provide educational opportunities, and offer a broad range of projects designed to make the benefits of increasing abundance available to all. We will begin to commit these funds as soon as they are appropriated.

Fourth, we must support all economic integration which is a genuine step toward larger markets and greater competitive opportunity. The fragmentation of Latin American economies is a serious barrier to industrial growth. Projects such as the Central American common market and free-trade areas in South America can help to remove these obstacles.

Fifth, the United States is ready to cooperate in serious, case-by-case examinations of commodity market problems. Frequent violent change in commodity prices seriously injure the economies of many Latin American countries, draining their resources and stultifying their growth. Together we must find practical methods of bringing an end to this pattern.

Sixth, we will immediately step up our Food for Peace emergency program, help establish food reserves in areas of recurrent drought, help provide school lunches for children, and offer feed grains for use in rural development. For hungry men and women cannot wait for economic discussions or diplomatic meetings—their need is urgent and their hunger rests heavily on the conscience of their fellow men.

Seventh, all the people of the hemisphere must be allowed to share in the expanding wonders of science—wonders which have captured man's imagination, challenged the powers of his mind, and given him the tools for rapid progress. I invite Latin American scientists to work with us in new projects in fields such as medicine and agriculture, physics and astronomy, and desalinization, to help plan for regional research laboratories in these and other fields, and to strengthen cooperation between American universities and laboratories.

We also intend to expand our science teacher training programs to include Latin American instructors, to assist in establishing such programs in other American countries, and translate and make available revolutionary new teaching materials in physics, chemistry, biology, and mathematics, so that the young of all nations may contribute their skills to the advance of science.

Eighth, we must rapidly expand the training of those needed to man the economies of rapidly developing countries. This means expanded technical training programs, for which the Peace Corps, for example, will be available when needed. It also means assistance to Latin American universities, graduate schools, and research institutes.

We welcome proposals in Central America for intimate cooperation in higher education—cooperation which can achieve a regional effort of increased effectiveness and excellence. We are ready to help fill the gap in trained manpower, realizing that our ultimate goal must be a basic education for all who wish to learn.

Ninth, we reaffirm our pledge to come to the defense of any American nation whose independence is endangered. As its confidence in the collective security system of the OAS spreads, it will be possible to devote to constructive use a major share of those resources now spent on the instruments of war. Even now, as the government of Chile has said, the time has come to take the first steps toward sensible limitations of arms. And the new generation of military leaders has shown an increasing awareness that armies cannot only defend their countries—they can, as we have learned through our own Corps of Engineers, help to build them.

Tenth, we invite our friends in Latin America to contribute to the enrichment of life and culture in the United States. We need teachers of your literature and history and tradition, opportunities for our young people to study in your universities, access to your music, your art, and the thought of your great philosophers. For we know we have much to learn.

In this way you can help bring a fuller spiritual and intellectual life to the people of the United States—and contribute to understanding and mutual respect among the nations of the hemisphere.

With steps such as these, we propose to complete the revolution of the Americas, to build a hemisphere where all men can hope for a suitable standard of living, and all can live out their lives in dignity and in freedom.

To achieve this goal political freedom must accompany material progress. Our Alliance for Progress is an alliance of free governments, and it must work to eliminate tyranny from a hemisphere in which it has no rightful place. Therefore let us express our special friendship to the people of Cuba and the Dominican Republic, and the hope they will soon rejoin the society of free men, uniting with us in common effort.

This political freedom must be accompanied by social change. For unless necessary social reforms, including land and tax reform, are freely made—unless we broaden the opportunity for all of our people—unless the great mass of Americans share in increasing prosperity—then our alliance, our revolution, our dream, and our freedom will fail. But we call for social change by free men—change in the spirit of Washington and Jefferson, of Bolívar and San Martin—not change which seeks to impose on men tyrannies which we cast out a century and a half ago. Our motto is what it has always been—progress yes, tyranny no—*progreso sí, tiranía no*!

But our greatest challenge comes from within—the task of creating an American civilization where spiritual and cultural values are strengthened by an ever-broadening base of material advance—where, within the rich diversity of its own traditions, each nation is free to follow its own path towards progress.

The completion of our task will, of course, require the efforts of all governments of our hemisphere. But the efforts of governments alone will never be enough. In the end, the people must choose and the people must help themselves.

And so I say to the men and women of the Americas—to the *campesino* in the fields, to the *obrero* in the cities, to the *estudiante* in the schools—prepare your mind and heart for the task ahead—call forth your strength and let each devote his energies to the betterment of all, so that your children and our children in this hemisphere can find an ever richer and a freer life.

Let us once again transform the American continent into a vast crucible of revolutionary ideas and efforts—a tribute to the power of the creative energies of free men and women, an example to all the world that liberty and progress walk hand in hand. Let us once again awaken our American revolution until it guides the struggle of people everywhere, not with an imperialism of force or fear, but the rule of courage and freedom and hope for the future of man.

Source: Public Papers of the Presidents of the United States: John F. Kennedy, 1961 (Washington, DC, 1962), 170–81.

Appendix B

The Charter of Punta Del Este:
Establishing an Alliance for Progress
within the Framework of Operation
Pan America, August 17, 1966

Preamble

We, the American Republics, hereby proclaim our decision to unite in a common effort to bring our people accelerated economic progress and broader social justice within the framework of personal dignity and political liberty.

Almost two hundred years ago we began in this Hemisphere the long struggle for freedom which now inspires people in all parts of the world. Today, in ancient lands, men moved to hope by the revolutions of your young nations search for liberty. Now we must give a new meaning to that revolutionary heritage. For America stands at a turning point in history. The men and women of our Hemisphere are reaching for the better life which today's skills have placed within their grasp. They are determined for themselves and their children to have decent and ever more abundant lives, to gain access to knowledge and equal opportunity for all, to end those conditions which benefit the few at the expense of the needs and dignity of the many. It is our inescapable task to fulfill these just desires—to demonstrate to the poor and forsaken of our countries, and of all lands, that the creative powers of free men hold the key to their progress and to the progress of future generations. And our certainty of ultimate success rests not alone on our faith in ourselves and in our nations but on the indomitable spirit of free man which has been the heritage of American civilization.

Inspired by these principles, and by the principles of Operation Pan America and the Act of Bogotá, the American Republics hereby resolve to adopt the following program of action to establish and carry forward an Alliance for Progress.

Title I: Objective of the Alliance for Progress

It is the purpose of the Alliance for Progress to enlist the full energies of the people and governments of the American republics in a great cooperative effort to accelerate the economic and social development of the participating countries of Latin America, so that they may achieve maximum levels of well-being, with equal opportunities for all, in democratic societies adapted to their own needs and desires.

The American Republics agree to work toward the achievement of the following fundamental goals in the present decade:

1. To achieve in the participating Latin American countries a substantial and sustained growth of per capita income at a rate designed to attain, at the earliest possible date, levels of income capable of assuring self-sustaining development, and sufficient to make Latin American income levels constantly larger in relation to the levels of the more industrialized nations. In this way the gap between the living standards of Latin America and those of the more developed countries can be narrowed. Similarly, presently existing differences in income levels among the Latin American countries will be reduced by accelerating the development of the relatively less developed countries and granting them maximum priority in the distribution of resources and in international cooperation in general. In evaluating the degree of relative development, account will be taken not only of average levels of real income and gross product per capita, but also of indices of infant mortality, illiteracy, and per capita daily caloric intake.

   It is recognized that, in order to reach these objectives within a reasonable time, the rate of economic growth in any country of Latin America should be not less than 2.5 percent per capita per year, and that each participating country should determine its own growth target in the light of its stage of social and economic evolution, resource endowment, and ability to mobilize national efforts for development.

2. To make the benefits of economic progress available to all citizens of all economic and social groups through a more equitable distribution of national income, raising more rapidly the income and standard of living of the needier sectors of the population, at the same time that a higher proportion of the national product is devoted to investment.

3. To achieve balanced diversification in national economic structures, both regional and functional, making them increasingly free from dependence on the export of a limited number of primary products and the importation of capital goods while attaining stability in the prices of exports or in income derived from exports.

4. To accelerate the process of rational industrialization so as to increase the productivity of the economy as a whole, taking full advantage of the talents and energies of all; the private and public sectors, utilizing the natural resources of the country and providing productive and remunerative employment for unemployed or part-time workers. Within this process of industrialization, special attention should be given to the establishment and development of capital-goods industries.

5. To raise greatly the level of agricultural productivity and output and to improve related storage, transportation, and marketing services.

6. To encourage, in accordance with the characteristics of each country, programs of comprehensive agrarian reform leading to the effective transformation, where required, of unjust structures and systems of land tenure and use, with a view to replacing latifundia and dwarf holdings by an equitable system of land tenure so that, with the help of timely and adequate credit, technical assistance and facilities for the marketing and distribution of products, the land will become for the man who works it the basis of his economic stability, the foundation of his increasing welfare, and the guarantee of his freedom and dignity.

7. To eliminate adult illiteracy and by 1970 to assure, as a minimum, access to 6 years of primary education for each school-age child in Latin America; to modernize and expand vocational, secondary and higher educational and training facilities, to strengthen the capacity for basic and applied research; and to provide the competent personnel required in rapidly-growing societies.

8. To increase life expectancy at birth by a minimum of 5 years, and to increase the ability to learn and produce, by improving individual and public health. To attain this goal it will be necessary,

among other measures, to provide adequate potable water supply and sewage disposal to not less than 70 percent of the urban and 50 percent of the rural population; to reduce the mortality rate of children less than 5 years of age by at least one-half; to control the more serious communicable diseases, according to their importance as a cause of sickness, disability, and death; to eradicate those illnesses, especially malaria, for which effective techniques are known; to improve nutrition; to train medical and health personnel to meet at least minimum requirements; to improve basic health services at national and local levels; and to intensify scientific research and apply its results more fully and effectively to the prevention and cure of illness.

9. To increase the construction of low-cost houses for low-income families in order to replace inadequate and deficient housing and to reduce housing shortages; and to provide necessary public services to both urban and rural centers of population.

10. To maintain stable price levels, avoiding inflation or deflation and the consequent social hardships and maldistribution of resources, always bearing in mind the necessity of maintaining an adequate rate of economic growth.

11. To strengthen existing agreements on economic integration, with a view to the ultimate fulfillment of aspirations for a Latin American common market that will expand and diversify trade among the Latin American countries and thus contribute to the economic growth of the region.

12. To develop cooperative programs designed to prevent the harmful effects of excessive fluctuations in the foreign exchange earnings derived from exports of primary products, which are of vital importance to economic and social development; and to adopt the measures necessary to facilitate the access of Latin American exports to international markets.

Title II: Economic and Social Development

Chapter I. Basic Requirements for Economic and Social Development

The American Republics recognize that to achieve the foregoing goals it will be necessary:

1. That comprehensive and well-conceived national programs of economic and social development, aimed at the achievement of self-sustaining growth, be carried out in accordance with democratic principles.
2. That national programs of economic and social development be based on the principle of self-help—as established in the Act of Bogotá—and on the maximum use of domestic resources, taking into account the special conditions of each country.
3. That in the preparation and execution of plans for economic and social development, women should be placed on an equal footing with men.
4. That the Latin American countries obtain sufficient external financial assistance, a substantial portion of which should be extended on flexible conditions with respect to periods and terms of repayment and forms of utilization, in order to supplement domestic capital formation and reinforce their import capacity; and that, in support of well-conceived programs, which include the necessary structural reforms and measures for the mobilization of internal resources, a supply of capital from all external sources during the coming 10 years of at least 20 billion dollars be made available to the Latin American countries, with priority to the relatively less developed countries. The greater part of this sum should be in public funds.
5. That institutions in both the public and private sectors, including labor organizations, cooperatives, and commercial, industrial, and financial institutions, be strengthened and improved for the increasing and effective use of domestic resources, and that the social reforms necessary to permit a fair distribution of the fruits of economic and social progress be carried out.

Chapter II. National Development Programs

1. Participating Latin American countries agree to introduce or strengthen systems for the preparation, execution, and periodic revision of national programs for economic and social development consistent with the principles, objectives, and requirements contained in this document. Participating Latin American countries should formulate, if possible within the next eighteen months, long-term development programs. Such programs should embrace, according to the characteristics of each country, the ele-

ments outlined in the Appendix.

2. National development programs should incorporate self-help efforts directed to:

a. Improvement of human resources and widening of opportunities by raising general standards of education and health; improving and extending technical education and professional training with emphasis on science and technology; providing adequate remuneration for work performed, encouraging the talents of managers, entrepreneurs, and wage earners; providing more productive employment for underemployed manpower; establishing effective systems of labor relations, and procedures for consultation and collaboration among public authorities, employer associations, and labor organizations; promoting the establishment and expansion of local institutions for basic and applied research; and improving the standards of public administration.

b. Wider development and more efficient use of natural resources, especially those which are now idle or under-utilized, including measures for the processing of raw materials.

c. The strengthening of the agricultural base, progressively, extending the benefits of the land to those who work it, and ensuring in countries with Indian populations the integration of these populations into the economic, social, and cultural processes of modern life. To carry out these aims, measures should be adopted, among others, to establish or improve, as the case may be, the following services: extension, credit, technical assistance, agricultural research and mechanization; health and education; storage and distribution; cooperatives and farmers' associations; and community development.

d. More effective, rational and equitable mobilization and use of financial resources through the reform of tax structures, including fair and adequate taxation of large incomes and real estate, and the strict application of measures to improve fiscal administration. Development programs should include the adaptation of budget expenditures to development needs, measures for the maintenance of price stability, the creation of essential credit facilities at reasonable rates of interest, and the encouragement of private savings.

e. Promotion through appropriate measures, including the signing of agreements for the purpose of reducing or eliminating double taxation, of conditions that will encourage the flow of foreign investments and help to increase the capital resources of participating countries in need of capital.

f. Improvement of systems distribution and sales in order to make markets more competitive and prevent monopolistic practices.

Chapter III. Immediate and Short-Term Action Measures

1. Recognizing that a number of Latin American countries, despite their best efforts, may require emergency financial assistance, the United States will provide assistance from the funds which are or may be established for such purposes. The United States stands ready to take prompt action on applications for such assistance. Applications relating to existing situations should be submitted within the next 60 days.

2. Participating Latin American countries should, in addition to creating or strengthening machinery for long-term development programming, immediately increase their efforts to accelerate their development by giving special emphasis to the following objectives:

    a. The completion of projects already underway and the initiation of projects for which the basic studies have been made, in order to accelerate their financing and execution.

    b. The implementation of new projects which are designed: (1) To meet the most pressing social needs and benefit directly the greatest number of people; (2) To concentrate efforts within each country in the less developed or more depressed areas in which particularly serious social problems exist; (3) To utilize idle capacity or resources, particularly under-employed manpower; and (4) To survey and assess natural resources.

    c. The facilitation of the preparation and execution of long-term programs through measures designed: (1) To train teachers, technicians, and specialists; (2) To provide accelerated training to workers and farmers; (3) To improve basic statistics; (4) To establish needed credit and marketing facilities; and (5) To improve services and administration.

3. The United States will assist in carrying out these short-term measures with a view to achieving concrete results from the Alliance for Progress at the earliest possible moment. In connection with the measures set forth above, and in accordance with the statement of President Kennedy, the United States will provide assis-

tance under the Alliance, including assistance for the financing of short-term measures, totaling more than one billion dollars in the year ending March 1962.

Chapter IV. External Assistance in Support of
National Development Programs

1. The economic and social development of Latin America will require a large amount of additional public and private financial assistance on the part of capital-exporting countries, including the members of the Development Assistance Group and international lending agencies. The measures provided for in the Act of Bogotá and the new measures provided for in this Charter, are designed to create a framework within which such additional assistance can be provided and effectively utilized.

2. The United States will assist those participating countries whose development programs establish self-help measures and economic and social policies and programs consistent with the goals and principles of this Charter. To supplement the domestic efforts of such countries, the United States is prepared to allocate resources which, along with those anticipated from other external sources, will be of a scope and magnitude adequate to realize the goals envisaged in this Charter. Such assistance will be allocated to both social and economic development and, where appropriate, will take the form of grants or loans on flexible terms and conditions. The participating countries will request the assistance of other capital-exporting countries and appropriate institutions so that they may provide assistance for the attainment of these objectives.

3. The United States will assist in the financing of technical assistance projects proposed by a participating country or by the General Secretariat of the Organization of American States for the purpose of:

   a. Providing experts contracted in agreement with governments to work under their direction and to assist them in the preparation of specific investment projects and the strengthening of national mechanisms for preparing projects, using specialized engineering firms where appropriate;

   b. Carrying out, pursuant to existing agreements for cooperation among the General Secretariat of the Organization of American States, the Economic Commission for Latin America, and the Inter-American Development Bank, field investigations and studies, including those relating to development problems, the organization of national planning agencies and the preparation of development programs, agrarian reform and rural development, health, cooperatives, housing, education and professional training, and taxation and tax administration; and

c. Convening meetings of experts and officials on development and related problems.

The governments or above mentioned organizations should, when appropriate, seek the cooperation of the United Nations and its specialized agencies in the execution of these activities.

4. The participating Latin American countries recognize that each has in varying degree a capacity to assist fellow republics by providing technical and financial assistance. They recognize that this capacity will increase as their economies grow. They therefore affirm their intention to assist fellow republics increasingly as their individual circumstances permit.

Chapter V. Organization and Procedures

1. In order to provide technical assistance for the formulation of development programs, as may be requested by participating nations, the Organization of American States, the Economic Commission for Latin America, and the Inter-American Development Bank will continue and strengthen their agreements for coordination in this field in order to have available a group of programming experts whose service can be used to facilitate the implementation of this Charter. The participating countries will also seek an intensification of technical assistance from the specialized agencies of the United Nations for the same purpose.

2. The Inter-American Economic and Social Council, on the joint nomination of the Secretary General of the Organization of American States, the President of the Inter-American Development Bank, and the Executive Secretary of the United Nations Economic Commission for Latin America, will appoint a panel of nine high-level experts, exclusively on the basis of their experience, technical ability, and competence in the various aspects of economic and social development. The experts may be of any nationality, though if of Latin American origin an appropriate geographical distribution will be sought. They will be attached to the Inter-American Economic and Social Council, but will nev-

ertheless enjoy complete autonomy in the performance of their duties. For administrative purposes and the purposes of better organization of its work, the secretary general of the Organization of American States and the coordinator shall conclude the agreements of a technical or administrative nature necessary for operations.

Four, at most, of the nine members may hold other remunerative positions that in the judgment of the officials who propose them do not conflict with their responsibilities as independent experts. The coordinator may not hold any other remunerative position. When not serving as members of ad hoc committees, the experts may be requested by the coordinator to perform high-level tasks in connection with planning, the evaluation of plans, and execution of such plans. The panel may also be requested to perform other high level, specific tasks in its advisory capacity to the Inter-American Committee on the Alliance for Progress by the chairman of that committee, through the coordinator of the panel, provided such tasks are not incompatible with the functions set forth in paragraph 4. In the performance of such tasks the experts shall enjoy unquestioned autonomy in judgments, evaluations, and recommendations that they make.

The experts who perform their duties during only part of the year shall do so for a minimum of 110 days per year and shall receive a standard lump-sum payment in proportion to the annual remuneration, emoluments, and benefits of other members of the panel.

That proportion shall be set by the secretary general within the authorizations provided in the budget of the OAS.

Each time the coordinator requires the services of the members of the panel, they shall begin to provide them within a reasonable period.

The appointment of the members of the panel will be for a period of at least one and not more than three years, and may be renewed.

3. Each government, if it so wishes, may present its program for economic and social development for consideration by an ad hoc committee, composed of no more than three members drawn from the panel of experts referred to in the preceding paragraph together with an equal number of experts not on the panel. The experts who compose the ad hoc committee will be appointed by the Secretary General of the Organization of American States at the request of the interested government and with its consent.

4. The committee will study the development program, exchange opinions with the interested government as to possible modifications and, with the consent of the governments report its conclusions to the Inter-American Development Bank and to other governments and institutions that may be prepared to extend external financial and technical assistance in connection with the execution of the program.

5. In considering a development program presented to it, the ad hoc committee will examine the consistency of the program with the principles of the Act of Bogotá and of this Charter, taking into account the elements in the Appendix.

6. The General Secretariat of the Organization of American States will provide the personnel needed by the experts referred to in paragraphs 2 and 3 of this Chapter in order to fulfill their tasks. Such personnel may be employed specifically for this purpose or may be made available from the permanent staffs of the Organization of American States, the Economic Commission for Latin America, and the Inter-American Development Bank, in accordance with the present liaison arrangements between the three organizations. The General Secretariat of the Organization of American States may seek arrangements with the United Nations Secretariat, its specialized agencies and the Inter-American Specialized Organizations, for the temporary assignment of necessary personnel.

7. A government whose development program has been the object of recommendations made by the ad hoc committee with respect to external financing requirements may submit the program to the Inter-American Development Bank so that the Bank may undertake the negotiations required to obtain such financing, including the organization of a consortium of credit institutions and governments disposed to contribute to the continuing and systematic financing, on appropriate terms, of the development program. However, the government will have full freedom to resort through any other channels to all sources of financing, for the purpose of obtaining, in full or in part, the required resources.

   The ad hoc committee shall not interfere with the right of each government to formulate its own goals, priorities, and reforms in its national development programs.

   The recommendations of the ad hoc committee will be of great importance in determining the distribution of public funds under the Alliance for Progress which contribute to the external financing of such programs. These recommendations shall give special consideration of Title I.1.

The participating governments will also use their good offices to the end that these recommendations may be accepted as a factor of great importance in the decisions taken, for the same purpose, by inter-American credit institutions, other international credit agencies, and other friendly governments which may be potential sources of capital.

8. The Inter-American Economic and Social Council will review annually the progress achieved in the formulation, national implementation and international financing of development programs and will submit to the Council of the Organization of American States such recommendations as it deems pertinent.

Appendix. Elements of National Development Programs

1. The establishment of mutually consistent targets to be aimed at over the program period in expending productive capacity in industry, agriculture, mining, transport, power and communications, and in improving conditions of urban and rural life, including better housing, education and health.
2. The assignment of priorities and the description of methods to achieve the targets, including specific measures and major projects. Specific development projects should be justified in terms of their relative costs and benefits, including their contribution to social productivity.
3. The measures which will be adopted to direct the operations of the public sector and to encourage private action in support of the development program.
4. The estimated cost, in national and foreign currency, of major projects and of the development program as a whole, year by year over the program period.
5. The internal resources, public and private, estimated to become available for the execution of the programs.
6. The direct and indirect effects of the programs on the balance of payments, and the external financing, public and private, estimated to be required for the execution of the program.
7. The basic fiscal and monetary policies to be followed in order to permit implementation of the program within a framework of price stability.
8. The machinery of public administration—including relationships with local governments, decentralized agencies and non-govern-

mental organizations, such as labor organizations, cooperatives, business and industrial organizations—to be used in carrying out the program, adapting it to changing circumstances and evaluating the progress made.

Title III: Economic Integration of Latin America

The American Republics consider that the broadening of present national markets in Latin America is essential to accelerate the process of economic development in the hemisphere. It is also an appropriate means for obtaining greater productivity through specialized and complementary industrial production which will, in turn, facilitate the attainment of greater social benefits for the inhabitants of the various regions of Latin America. The broadening of markets will also make possible the better use of resources under the Alliance for Progress. Consequently, the American Republics recognize that:

1. The Montevideo Treaty (because of its flexibility and because it is open to adherence of all of the Latin American nations) and the Central American Treaty of Economic Integration are appropriate instruments for the attainment of these objectives, as was recognized in Resolution No. 11 (III) of the Ninth Session of the Economic Commission for Latin America.

2. The integration process can be intensified and accelerated not only by the specialization resulting from the broadening of markets through the liberalization of trade but also through the use of such instruments as the agreements of complementary production within economic sectors provided for in the Montevideo Treaty.

3. In order to assure the balanced and complementary economic expansion of all of the countries involved, the integration process should take into account, on a flexible basis, the condition of countries at a relatively advanced stage of economic development, permitting them to be granted special, fair, and equitable treatment.

4. In order to facilitate economic integration in Latin America, it is advisable to establish effective relationships between the Latin American Free Trade Association and the group of countries adhering to the Central American Economic Integration Treaty, as well as between either of these groups and other Latin American countries. These arrangements should be established within the limits determined by these instruments.

5. The Latin American countries should coordinate their actions to meet the unfavorable treatment accorded to their foreign trade in world markets, particularly those resulting from certain restrictive and discriminatory policies of extra-continental countries and economic groups.

6. In the application of resources under the Alliance for Progress, special attention should be given not only to investments for multinational projects that will contribute to strengthening the integration process in all its aspects, but also to the necessary financing of industrial production, and to the growing expansion of trade in industrial products within Latin America.

7. In order to facilitate the participation of countries at a relatively lower stage of economic development in multinational Latin American economic cooperation programs, and in order to promote the balanced and harmonious development of the Latin American integration process, special attention should be given to the needs of these countries in the administration of financial resources provided under the Alliance for Progress, particularly in connection with infrastructure programs and the promotion of new lines of production.

8. The economic integration process implies a need for additional investment in various fields of economic activity and funds provided under the Alliance for Progress should cover these needs as well as those required for the financing of national development programs.

9. When groups of Latin American countries have their own institutions for financing economic integration, the financing referred to in the preceding paragraph should preferably be channeled through these institutions. With respect to regional financing designed to further the purposes of existing regional integration instruments, the cooperation of the Inter-American Development Bank should be sought in channeling extra-regional contributions which may be granted for these purposes.

10. One of the possible means for making effective a policy for the financing of Latin American integration would be to approach the International Monetary Fund and other financial sources with a view to providing a means for solving temporary balance-of-payments problems that may occur in countries participating in economic integration arrangements.

11. The promotion and coordination of transportation and communications systems is an effective way to accelerate the integration process. In order to counteract abusive practices in relation to

freight rates and tariffs, it is advisable to encourage the establishment of multinational transport and communication enterprises in the Latin American countries, or to find other appropriate solutions.

12. In working toward economic integration and complementary economies, efforts should be made to achieve an appropriate coordination of national plans, or to engage in joint planning for various economies through the existing regional integration organizations. Efforts should also be made to promote an investment policy directed to the progressive elimination of unequal growth rates in the different geographic areas, particularly in the case of countries which are relatively less developed.

13. It is necessary to promote the development of national Latin American enterprises, in order that they may compete on an equal footing with foreign enterprises.

14. The active participation of the private sector is essential to economic integration and development, and except in those countries in which free enterprise does not exist, development planning by the pertinent national public agencies, far from hindering such participation, can facilitate and guide it, thus opening new perspectives for the benefit of the community.

15. As the countries of the Hemisphere still under colonial domination achieve their independence, they should be invited to participate in Latin American economic integration programs.

Title IV: Basic Export Commodities

The American Republics recognize that the economic development of Latin America requires expansion of its trade, a simultaneous and corresponding increase in foreign exchange incomes received from exports, a lessening of cyclical or seasonal fluctuations in the incomes of those countries that still depend heavily on the export of raw materials, and the correction of the secular deterioration in their terms of trade.

They therefore agree that the following measures should be taken:

Chapter I. National Measures

National measures affecting commerce in primary products should be directed and applied in order to:

1. Avoid undue obstacles to the expansion of trade in these products;
2. Avoid market instability;

3. Improve the efficiency of international plans and mechanisms for stabilization; and

4. Increase their present markets and expand their area of trade at a rate compatible with rapid development.

Therefore:

A. Importing member countries should reduce and if possible eliminate, as soon as feasible, all restrictions and discriminatory practices affecting the consumption and importation of primary products, including those with the highest possible degree of processing in the country of origin, except when these restrictions are imposed temporarily for purposes of economic diversification, to hasten the economic development of less developed nations, or to establish basic national reserves. Importing countries should also be ready to support, by adequate regulations, stabilization programs for primary products that may be agreed upon with producing countries.

B. Industrialized countries should give special attention to the need for hastening economic development of less developed countries. Therefore, they should make maximum efforts to create conditions, compatible with their international obligations, through which they may extend advantages to less developed countries so as to permit the rapid expansion of their markets. In view of the great need for this rapid development, industrialized countries should also study ways in which to modify, wherever possible, international commitments which prevent the achievement of this objective.

C. Producing member countries should formulate their plans for production and export, taking account of their effect on world markets and of the necessity of supporting and improving the effectiveness of international stabilization programs and mechanisms. Similarly they should try to avoid increasing the uneconomic production of goods which can be obtained under better conditions in the less developed countries of the Continent, in which the production of these goods is an important source of employment.

D. Member countries should adopt all necessary measures to direct technological studies toward finding new uses and byproducts of those primary commodities that are most important to their economies.

E. Member countries should try to reduce, and, if possible, eliminate within a reasonable time export subsidies and other measures which create instability in the markets for basic commodities and excessive fluctuations in prices and income.

Chapter II. International Cooperation Measures

1. Member countries should make coordinated, and if possible, joint efforts designed:
   a. To eliminate as soon as possible undue protection of the production of basic products;
   b. To eliminate taxes and reduce excessive domestic prices which discourage the consumption of imported basic products;
   c. To seek to end preferential agreements and other measures which limit world consumption of Latin American basic products and their access to international markets, especially the markets of Western European countries in process of economic integration, and of countries with centrally planned economies; and
   d. To adopt the necessary consultation mechanisms so that their marketing policies will not have damaging effects on the stability of the markets for basic commodities.
2. Industrialized countries should give maximum cooperation to less developed countries so that their raw material exports will have the greatest degree of processing that is economic.
3. Through their representation in international financial organizations, member countries should suggest that these organizations, when considering loans for the promotion of production for export, take into account the effect of such loans on products which are in surplus in world markets.
4. Member countries should support the efforts being made by international commodity study groups and by the Commission on International Commodity Trade of the United Nations. In this connection, it should be considered that producing and consuming nations bear a joint responsibility for taking national and international steps to reduce market instability.
5. The Secretary General of the Organization of American States shall convene a group of experts appointed by their respective Governments to meet before November 30, 1961 and to report, not later than March 31, 1962 on measures to provide an adequate and effective means of offsetting the effects of fluctuations in the volume and prices of exports of basic products. The experts shall:
   a. Consider the questions regarding compensatory financing raised during the present meeting;

    b. Analyze the proposal for establishing an international fund for the stabilization of export receipts contained in the Report of the Group of Experts to the Special Meeting of the Inter-American Economic and Social Council, as well as any other alternative proposals;

    c. Prepare a draft plan for the creation of mechanisms for compensatory financing. This draft plan should be circulated among the member Governments and their opinions obtained well in advance of the next meeting of the Commission on International Commodity Trade.

6. Member countries should support the efforts under way to improve and strengthen international commodity agreements and should be prepared to cooperate in the solution of specific commodity problems. Furthermore they should endeavor to adopt adequate solutions for the short- and long-term problems affecting markets for such commodities so that the economic interests of producers and consumers are equally safeguarded.

7. Member countries should request other producer and consumer countries to cooperate in stabilization programs, bearing in mind that the raw materials of the Western Hemisphere are also produced and consumed in other parts of the world.

8. Member countries recognize that the disposal of accumulated reserves and surpluses can be a means of achieving the goals outlined in the first chapter of this Title, provided that, along with the generation of local resources, the consumption of essential products in the receiving countries is immediately increased. The disposal of surpluses and reserves should be carried out in an orderly manner, in order to:

    a. Avoid disturbing existing commercial markets in member countries; and

    b. Encourage expansion of the sale of their products to other markets.

However, it is recognized that:

    a. The disposal of surpluses should not displace commercial sales of identical products traditionally carried out by other countries; and

    b. Such disposal cannot substitute for large scale financial and technical assistance programs.

IN WITNESS WHEREOF this charter is signed in Punta del Este, Uruguay, on the seventeenth day of August, nineteen hundred sixty-one.

The original texts shall be deposited in the archives of the Pan American Union, through the Secretary General of the Special Meeting, in order that certified copies may be sent to the Governments of the Member States of the Organization of American States.

Source: "The Charter of Punta del Este" Alliance for Progress: Official Documents Emanating from the Special Meeting of the Inter-American Economic and Social Council at the Ministerial Level Held in Punta del Este, Uruguay, from August 5 to 17 (Washington DC, 1961).

Appendix C

President Lyndon B. Johnson's Remarks on the Alliance for Progress to Representatives of the Countries of Latin America, November 26, 1963

I have asked you to come here today because this is, in a very special sense, a family gathering, for nothing in President Kennedy's public career meant more to him than the ties which united this country and yours.

A little less than three years ago, here in the White House, in this very room, President Kennedy met with you, the representatives of the countries of Latin America. In the first full-scale foreign policy address of his administration, he called for an Alliance for Progress among the nations of the Americas.

Today among you in this same room I have come to reaffirm that Alliance, and pledge all the energies of my Government to our common goals.

I know from personal experience that the future of this hemisphere, the relations between the United States and Latin America must be among the highest concerns of my Government.

I have lived my life together with many who proudly claim descent from Latin America. The sound of the Spanish tongue and the signs of your rich, cultural traditions were among my earliest and my most enduring impressions.

I began my Government service in Washington under President Franklin D. Roosevelt. And from him I learned that nothing is more important to the country I now lead than its associations with our good neighbors to the south.

In October 1960 during the political campaign I reminded my fellow citizens of the United States that, and I quote, "We must support, morally and financially, the struggle of our Latin American friends against political, economic, and social injustice, not only to improve their standard of living but to foster the democratic way of life in every country."

To me, therefore, as it was to President Kennedy, the Alliance for Progress is part of a long and deeply rooted tradition. That alliance contains the basic principles of the new society which we are building, principles agreed to by all our countries in the Charter of Punta del Este.

The first of these agreed principles is the right of every American nation to govern itself free from outside dictation or coercion from any quarter. None among us can tell another how to organize its society or how to conduct its foreign affairs.

The second of these agreed principles is the right to human freedom, the right of each person to freely speak his views, worship God in his own way, participate in the political life of his nation. History and circumstances have created restraints on democracy in some of our nations. But we must never forget that our task will not be completed until every American lives in the dignity of freedom.

The third of these agreed principles is the right to social justice. The right of every citizen to share in the progress of his nation. We have called for land for the landless, education for those denied education, and an end to the unjust privilege of a few at the expense of the needs of the many.

The fourth of these agreed principles is dedication to economic progress. To this end we have embarked upon a cooperative program in which the nations of Latin America have agreed to dedicate their resources, bear fresh sacrifice, and expect hard labor. And the United States has pledged itself and will carry out its own commitments. And it is to these principles that we have pledged ourselves.

So I reaffirm the pledge which President Kennedy made last week to improve and strengthen the role of the United States in the Alliance for Progress. We all know that there have been problems within the Alliance for Progress, but the accomplishments of the past 3 years have proven the soundness of our principles. The accomplishments of the years to come will vindicate our faith in the capacity of free men to meet the challenges of a new day. And it was in the spirit of the principles that we have worked together that President Kennedy launched the Alliance for Progress in this very room. Inspired by his memory and in that same spirit, we will carry on the job.

Let the Alliance for Progress be his living memorial.

Source: *Public Papers of the Presidents of the United States: Lyndon B. Johnson, 1963-1964* (Washington, 1965), 8-9.

Appendix D

Declaration of the Presidents of America, Punta del Este, Uruguay, April 14, 1967

The Presidents of the American States and the Prime Minister of Trinidad and Tobago Meeting in Punta del Este, Uruguay

RESOLVED to give more dynamic and concrete expression to the ideals of Latin American unity and of solidarity among the peoples of America, which inspired the founders of their countries;

DETERMINED to make this goal a reality within their own generation, in keeping with the economic, social and cultural aspirations of their peoples;

INSPIRED by the principles underlying the inter-American system, especially those contained in the Charter of Punta del Este, the Economic and Social Act of Rio de Janeiro, and the Protocol of Buenos Aires amending the Charter of the Organization of American States;

CONSCIOUS that the attainment of national and regional development objectives in Latin America is based essentially on self-help;

CONVINCED, however, that the achievement of those objectives requires determined collaboration by all their countries, complementary support through mutual aid, and expansion of external cooperation;

PLEDGED to give vigorous impetus to the Alliance for Progress and to emphasize its multilateral character, with a view to encouraging balanced development of the region at a pace substantially faster than attained thus far;

UNITED in the intent to strengthen democratic institutions, to raise the living standards of their peoples and to assure their increased participation in the development process, creating for these purposes suitable conditions in the political, economic and social as well as labor fields;

RESOLVED to maintain a harmony of fraternal relations in the Americas, in which racial equality must be effective;

PROCLAIM the solidarity of the countries they represent and their decision to achieve to the fullest measure the free, just, and democratic order demanded by the peoples of the Hemisphere.

I: Latin America will create a common market

THE PRESIDENTS OF THE LATIN AMERICAN REPUBLICS resolve to create progressively, beginning in 1970, the Latin American Common Market, which shall be substantially in operation in a period of no more than fifteen years. The Latin American Common Market will be based on the complete development and progressive convergence of the Latin American Free Trade Association and of the Central American Common Market, taking into account the interests of Latin American countries not yet affiliated these systems. This great task will reinforce historic bonds, will promote industrial development and the strengthening of Latin American industrial enterprises, as well as more efficient production and new opportunities for employment, and will permit the region to play its deservedly significant role in world affairs. The ties of friendship among the peoples of the Continent will thus be strengthened.

THE PRESIDENT OF THE UNITED STATES OF AMERICA, for his part, declares his firm support for this promising Latin American initiative.

THE UNDERSIGNED PRESIDENTS AFFIRM THAT:

We will lay the physical foundations for Latin American economic integration through multinational projects.

Economic integration demands a major sustained effort to build a land transportation network and to improve transportation systems of all kinds so as to open the way for the movement of both people and goods throughout the Continent; to establish an adequate and efficient telecommunications system; to install inter-connected power systems; and to develop jointly international river basins, frontier regions, and economic areas which include the territory of two or more countries.

We will join in efforts to increase substantially Latin-American foreign-trade earnings.

To increase substantially Latin American foreign-trade earnings, individual and joint efforts shall be directed toward facilitating nondiscriminatory access of Latin American products in world markets, toward increasing Latin American earnings from traditional exports, toward avoiding frequent fluctuations in income from such commodities, and, finally, toward adopting measures that will stimulate exports of Latin American manufactured products.

We will modernize the living conditions of our rural populations, raise agricultural productivity in general, and increase food production for the benefit of both Latin America and the rest of the world.

The living conditions of the rural workers and farmers of Latin America will be transformed, to guarantee their full participation in economic and social progress. For that purpose, integrated programs of modernization, land settlement, and agrarian reform will be carried out as the countries so require. Similarly, productivity will be improved and agricultural production diversified. Furthermore, recognizing that the Continent's capacity for food production entails a dual responsibility, a special effort will be made to produce sufficient food for the growing needs of their own peoples and to contribute toward feeding the peoples of other regions.

We will vigorously promote education for development.

To give a decisive impetus to education for development, literacy campaigns will be intensified, education at all levels will be greatly expanded, and its quality improved so that the rich human potential of their peoples may make their maximum contribution to the economic, social, and cultural development of Latin America. Educational systems will be modernized taking full advantage of educational innovations, and exchanges of teachers and students will be increased.

We will harness science and technology for the service of our peoples.

Latin America will share in the benefits of current scientific and technological progress so as to reduce the widening gap between it and the highly industrialized nations in the areas of production techniques and of living conditions. National scientific and technological programs will be developed and strengthened and a regional program will be started; multinational institutes for advanced training and research will be established; existing institutes of this kind in Latin America will at the same time be strengthened and contributions will be made to the exchange and advancement of technological knowledge.

We will expand programs for improving the health of the American peoples.

The fundamental role of health in the economic and social development of Latin America demands that the prevention and control of communicable diseases be intensified and that measures be taken to eradicate those which can be completely eliminated by existing techniques. Also programs to supply drinking water and other services essential to urban and rural environmental sanitation will be speeded up.

Latin America will eliminate unnecessary military expenditures.

THE PRESIDENTS OF THE LATIN AMERICAN COUNTRIES, conscious of the importance of armed forces to the maintenance of security, recognize at the same time that the demands of economic development and social progress make it necessary to devote to those purposes the maximum resources available in Latin America.

Therefore, they express their intention to limit military expenditures in proportion to the actual demands of national security in accordance with each country's constitutional provisions, avoiding those expenditures that are not indispensable for the performance of the specific duties of the armed forces and, where pertinent, of international commitments that obligate their respective governments. With regard to the Treaty on the Banning of Nuclear Arms in Latin America, they express the hope that it may enter into force as soon as possible, once the requirements established by the Treaty are fulfilled.

IN FACING THE PROBLEMS CONSIDERED IN THIS MEETING which constitute a challenge to the will of the American governments and peoples, the Presidents proclaim their faith in the basic purpose of the inter-American system; to promote in the Americas free and democratic societies, existing under the rule of law whose dynamic economies, reinforced by growing technological capabilities, will allow them to serve with ever-increasing effectiveness the peoples of the Continent, to whom they announce the following program.

II. Action Program

Chapter 1. Latin American Economic Integration and Industrial Development

1. Principles, objectives, and goals
Economic integration is a collective instrument for accelerating Latin American development and should constitute one of the policy goals of each of the countries of the region. The greatest possible efforts should be made to bring it about, as a necessary complement to national development plans. At the same time, the different levels of development and economic and market conditions of the various Latin American countries must be borne in mind, in order that the integration process may promote their harmonious and balanced growth. In this respect, the countries of relatively less economic development and, to the extent required, those of insufficient market, will have preferential treatment in matters of trade and of technical and financial cooperation.

Integration must be fully at the service of Latin America. This requires the strengthening of Latin American enterprise through vigorous financial and technical support that will permit it to develop and supply the regional market efficiently. Foreign private enterprise will be able to fill an important function in assuring achievement of the objectives of integration within the pertinent policies of each of the countries of Latin America.

Adequate financing is required to facilitate the economic restructuring and adjustments called for by the urgent need to accelerate integration.

It is necessary to adopt all measures that will lead to the completion of Latin American integration, above all those that will bring about, in the shortest time possible, monetary stability and the elimination of all restrictions, including administrative, financial, and exchange restrictions, that obstruct the trade of the products of the area.

To these ends, the Latin American Presidents agree to take action on the following points:

 a. Beginning in 1970, to establish progressively the Latin American Common Market, which should be substantially in operation within a period of no more than fifteen years.
 b. The Latin American Common Market will be based on the improvement of the two existing integration systems: the Latin American Free Trade Association (LAFTA) and the Central American Common Market (CACM). The two systems will initiate simultaneously a process of convergence by stages of cooperation, closer ties, and integration, taking into account the interest of the Latin American countries not yet associated with these systems, in order to provide their access to one of them.
 c. To encourage the incorporation of other countries of the Latin American region into the existing integration systems.

2. Measures with regard to the Latin American Free Trade Association
The Presidents of the member states of LAFTA instruct their respective Ministers of Foreign Affairs, who will participate in the next meeting of the Council of Ministers of LAFTA, to be held in 1968, to adopt the measures necessary to implement the following decisions:

 a. To accelerate the process of converting LAFTA into a common market. To this end, starting in 1970, and to be completed in a period of not more than fifteen years, LAFTA will put into effect a system of programmed elimination of duties and all other nontariff restrictions, and also a system of tariff harmonization, in order to establish progressively a common external tariff at levels that will promote efficiency and productivity, as well as the expansion of trade.
 b. To coordinate progressively economic policies and instruments and to harmonize national laws to the extent required for

integration. These measures will be adopted simultaneously with the improvement of the integration process.

c. To promote the conclusion of sectoral agreements for industrial complementation, endeavoring to obtain the participation of the countries of relatively less economic development.

d. To promote the conclusion of temporary subregional agreements, with provision for reducing tariffs within the subregions and harmonizing treatments toward third nations more rapidly than in the general agreements, in keeping with the objectives of regional integration. Subregional tariff reductions will not be extended to countries that are not parties to the subregional agreement, nor will they create special obligations for them.

Participation of the countries of relatively less economic development in all stages of the integration process and in the formation of the Latin American Common Market will be based in the provisions of the Treaty of Montevideo and its complementary resolutions, and these countries will be given the greatest possible advantages, so that balanced development of the region may be achieved.

To this same end, they have decided to promote immediate action to facilitate free access of products of the LAFTA member countries of relatively less economic development to the market of the other LAFTA countries, and to promote the installation and financing in the former countries of industries intended for the enlarged market.

The countries of relatively less economic development will have the right to participate and to obtain preferential conditions in the subregional agreements in which they have an interest.

The situation of countries characterized as being of insufficient market shall be taken into account in temporary preferential treatments established to the extent necessary to achieve a harmonious development in the integration process.

It is understood that all the provisions set forth in this section fall within or are based upon the Treaty of Montevideo.

3. Measures with regard to the Central American economic integration programs
The Presidents of the member states of the Central American Common Market commit themselves:

a. To carry out an action program that will include the following measures, among others.
  1. Improvement of the customs union and establishment of a Central American monetary union;

2. Completion of the regional network of infrastructure;
3. Promotion of a common foreign-trade policy;
4. Improvement of the common market in agricultural products and implementation of a joint, coordinated industrial policy
5. Acceleration of the process of free movement of manpower and capital within the area;
6. Harmonization of the basic legislation required for economic integration.

b. To apply, in the implementation of the foregoing measures, and when pertinent, the temporary preferential treatment already established or that may be established, in accordance with the principle of balanced development among countries.

c. To foster closer ties between Panama and the Central American Common Market, as well as rapid expansion of trade and investment relations with neighboring countries of the Central American and Caribbean region taking advantage, to this end, of their geographic proximity and of the possibilities for economic complementation; also, to seek conclusion of subregional agreements and agreements of industrial complementation between Central America and other Latin American countries.

4. Measures common to Latin American Countries
The Latin American presidents commit themselves:

a. Not to establish new restrictions on trade among Latin American countries, except in special cases, such as those arising from equalization of tariffs and other instruments of trade policy, as well as from the need to assure the initiation or expansion of certain productive activities in countries of relatively less economic development.

b. To establish, by a tariff cut or other equivalent measures, a margin of preference within the region for all products originating in Latin American countries, taking into account the different degrees of development of the countries.

c. To have the measures in the two preceding paragraphs applied immediately among the member countries of LAFTA, in harmony with the other measures referring to this organization contained in the present chapter and, insofar as possible, to extend them to non-member countries in a manner compatible with existing international commitments, inviting the latter countries to extend similar preferences to the members of LAFTA, with the same qualification.

    d. To ensure that application of the foregoing measures shall not hinder internal readjustments designed to rationalize the instruments of trade policy made necessary in order to carry out national development plans and to achieve the goals of integration.

    e. To promote acceleration of the studies already initiated regarding preferences that LAFTA countries might grant to imports from the Latin American countries that are not members of the Association.

    f. To have studies made of the possibility of concluding agreements of industrial complementation in which all Latin American countries may participate, as well as temporary subregional economic integration agreements between the CACM and member countries of LAFTA.

    g. To have a committee established composed of the executive organs of LAFTA and the CACM to coordinate implementation of the foregoing points. To this end, the committee will encourage meetings at the ministerial level, in order to ensure that Latin American integration will proceed as rapidly as possible, and, in due course, initiate negotiation of a general treaty or the protocols required to create the Latin American Common Market. Latin American countries that are not members shall be invited to send representatives to these meetings and to those of the committee of the executive organs of LAFTA and the CACM.

    h. To give special attention to industrial development within integration, and particularly to the strengthening of Latin American industrial firms. In this regard, we reiterate that development must be balanced between investments for economic ends and investments for social ends.

5. *Measures common to member countries of the Organization of American States (OAS)*
The Presidents of the member states of the OAS agree:

    a. To mobilize financial and technical resources within and without the hemisphere to contribute to the solution of problems in connection with the balance of payments, industrial readjustments, and retraining of the labor force that may arise from a rapid reduction of trade barriers during the period of transition toward the common market, as well as to increase the sums available for export credits in intra-Latin American trade. The Inter-American Development Bank and the organs of both existing integration systems should participate in the mobilization of such resources.

    b. To mobilize public and private resources within and without the hemisphere to encourage industrial development as part of the integration process and of national development plans.

c. To mobilize financial and technical resources to undertake specific feasibility studies on multinational projects for Latin American industrial firms, as well as to aid in carrying out these projects.

d. To accelerate the studies being conducted by various inter-American agencies to promote strengthening of capital markets and the possible establishment of a Latin American stock market.

e. To make available to Central America within the Alliance for Progress, adequate technical and financial resources including those required for strengthening and expanding the existing Central American Economic Integration Fund for the purpose of accelerating the Central American economic integration program.

f. To make available, within the Alliance for Progress and pursuant to the provisions of the Charter of Punta del Este, the technical and financial resources needed to accelerate the preparatory studies and work involved in converting LAFTA into a common market.

Chapter 2. Multinational Action for Infrastructure Projects

The economic integration of Latin America demands a vigorous and sustained effort to complete and modernize the physical infrastructure of the region. It is necessary to build a land transport network and improve all types of transport systems to facilitate the movement of persons and goods throughout the hemisphere; to establish an adequate and efficient telecommunications system and interconnected power systems; and jointly to develop international watersheds, frontier regions and economic areas that include the territory of two or more countries. In Latin America there are in existence projects in all these fields, at different stages of preparation or implementation, but in many cases of the completion of prior studies, financial resources, or merely the coordination of efforts and the decision to bring them to fruition are lacking.

The Presidents of the member states of the OAS agree to engage in determined action to undertake or accelerate the construction of the infrastructure required for the development and integration of Latin America and to make better use thereof. In so doing, it is essential that the groups of interested countries or multinational institutions determine criteria for assigning priorities, in view of the amount of human and material resources needed for the task.

As one basis for the criteria, which will be determined with precision upon consideration of the specific cases submitted for study, they stress the fundamental need to give preferential attention to those projects that benefit the countries of the region that are at a relatively lower level of economic development.

Priority should also be given to the mobilization of financial and technical resources for the preparation and implementation of infrastructure projects that will facilitate the participation of landlocked countries in regional and international trade.

In consequence, they adopt the following decisions for immediate implementation:

1. To complete the studies and conclude the agreements necessary to accelerate the construction of an inter-American telecommunications network.

2. To expedite the agreements necessary to complete the Pan American Highway, to accelerate the construction of the Bolivarian Highway (Carretera Marginal de la Selva) and its interaction with the Trans Chaco Highway and to support the studies and agreements designed to bring into being the new highway systems that will join groups of countries of continental and insular Latin America, as well as the basic works required to develop water and airborne transport of a multinational nature and the corresponding systems of operation. As a complement to these agreements, negotiations should be undertaken for the purpose of eliminating or reducing to a minimum the restrictions on international traffic and of promoting, technical and administrative cooperation among land, water and air transport enterprises and the establishment of multinational transport services.

3. To sponsor studies for preparing joint projects in connection with watersheds, such as the studies commented on the development of the River Plate basin, and that relating to the Gulf of Fonseca.

4. To allocate sufficient resources to the Preinvestment Fund for Latin American Integration of the IDB for conducting studies that will make it possible to identify and prepare multinational projects in all fields that may he of importance in promoting regional integration. In order that the aforesaid Fund may carry out an effective promotion effort, it is necessary that an adequate part of the resources allocated may be used without reimbursement or with reimbursement conditioned on the execution of the corresponding projects.

5. To mobilize within and outside the hemisphere, resources in addition to those that will continue to be placed at the disposal

of the countries to support national economic development programs, such resources to be devoted especially to the implementation of multinational infrastructure projects that can represent important advances in the Latin American economic integration process. In this regard, the IDB should have additional resources in order to participate actively in the attainment of this objective.

Chapter 3. Measures to Improve International Trade Conditions in Latin America

The economic development of Latin America is seriously affected by the adverse conditions in which its international trade is carried out. Market structures, financial conditions, and actions that prejudice exports and other income from outside Latin America are impeding its growth and retarding the integration process. All this causes particular concern in view of the serious and growing imbalance between the standard of living in Latin American countries and that of the industrialized nations and, at the same time, calls for definite decisions and adequate instruments to implement the decisions.

Individual and joint efforts of the member states of the OAS are essential to increase the incomes of Latin American countries derived from, and to avoid frequent fluctuations in, traditional exports, as well as to promote new exports. Such efforts are also essential to reduce any adverse effects on the external earnings of Latin American countries that may be caused by measures which may be taken by industrialized countries for balance of payments reasons.

The Charter of Punta del Este, the Economic and Social Act of Rio de Janeiro and the new provisions of the Charter of the OAS reflect a hemispheric agreement with regard to these problems, which needs to be effectively implemented; therefore, the Presidents of the member states of the OAS agree:

1. To act in coordination in multilateral negotiations to achieve, without the more highly developed countries expecting reciprocity, the greatest possible reduction or the elimination of tariffs and other restrictions that impede the access of Latin American products to world markets. The Government of the United States intends to make efforts for the purpose of liberalizing the conditions directing exports of basic products of special interest to Latin American countries, in accordance with the provision of Article 37(a) of the Protocol of Buenos Aires.
2. To consider together possible systems of general nonreciprocal preferential treatment for exports of manufactures and semiman-

ufactures of the developing countries, with a view to improving the condition of the Latin American export trade.

3. To undertake a joint effort in all international institutions and organizations to eliminate discriminatory preferences against Latin American exports.

4. To strengthen the system of intergovernmental consultations and carry them out sufficiently in advance, so as to render them effective and ensure that programs for placing and selling surpluses and reserves that affect exports of the developing countries take into account the interests of the Latin American countries.

5. To ensure compliance with international commitments to refrain from introducing or increasing tariff and nontariff barriers that affect exports of the developing countries, taking into account the interests of Latin America.

6. To combine efforts to strengthen and perfect existing international agreements, particularly the International Coffee Agreement, to obtain favorable conditions for trade in basic products of interest to Latin America and to explore all possibilities for the development of new agreements.

7. To support the financing and prompt initiation of the activities of the Coffee Diversification Fund, and consider in due course the creation of other funds to make it possible to control the production of basic products of interest to Latin America in which there is a chronic imbalance between supply and demand.

8. To adopt measures to make Latin American export products more competitive in world markets.

9. To put in operation as soon as possible an inter-American agency for export promotion that will help to identify and develop new export lines and to strengthen the placing of Latin American products in international markets, and to improve national and regional agencies designed for the same purpose.

10. To initiate such individual or joint action on the part of the member states of the OAS as may be required to ensure effective and timely execution of the foregoing agreements, as well as those that may be required to continue the execution of the agreements contained in the Charter of Punta del Este, in particular those relating to foreign trade.

With regard to joint action, the Inter-American Committee on the Alliance for Progress (CIAP) and other agencies in the region shall submit to the Inter-American Economic and Social Council (IA-ECOSOC), for

consideration at its next meeting, the means, instruments, and action program for initiating execution thereof.

At its annual meetings, IA-ECOSOC shall examine the progress of the
programs under way with the object of considering such action as may
ensure compliance with the agreements concluded, inasmuch as a substantial improvement in the international conditions in which Latin American
foreign trade is carried on is a basic prerequisite to the acceleration of economic development.

*Chapter 4. Modernization of Rural Life and Increase of
Agricultural Productivity, Principally of Food*

In order to promote a rise in the standard of living of farmers and an
improvement in the condition of the Latin American rural people and
their full participation in economic and social life, it is necessary to give
greater dynamism to agriculture in Latin America, through comprehensive programs of modernization, land settlement, and agrarian reform
when required by the countries.

To achieve these objectives and to carry out these programs, contained
in the Charter of Punta del Este, it is necessary to intensify internal efforts
and to provide additional external resources.

Such programs will be oriented toward increasing food production in
the Latin American countries in sufficient volume and quality to provide
adequately for their population and to meet world needs for food to an
ever-increasing extent, as well as toward improving agricultural productivity and toward a diversification of crops, which will assure the best possible competitive conditions for such production.

All these development efforts in agriculture must be related to the overall development of the national economics in order to harmonize the supply of agricultural products and the labor that could be freed as a result
of the increase in farm productivity with the increase in demand for such
products and with the need for labor in the economy as a whole.

This modernization of agricultural activities will furthermore create conditions for a development more in balance with the effort toward
industrialization.

To achieve these goals, the Latin American presidents undertake:

1. To improve the formulation and execution of agricultural policies
   and to ensure the carrying out of plans, programs, and projects
   for preinvestment, agricultural development, agrarian reform,
   and land settlement, adequately coordinated with national economic development plans, in order to intensify internal efforts
   and to facilitate obtaining and utilizing external financing.

2. To improve credit systems, including those earmarked for the resettlement of rural workers who are beneficiaries of agrarian reform, and for increased productivity, and to create facilities for the production, marketing, storage, transportation, and distribution of agricultural products.

3. To provide adequate incentive, including price incentives, to promote agricultural production under economic conditions.

4. To foster and to finance the acquisition and intensive use of those agricultural inputs which contribute to the improvement of productivity, as well as the establishment and expansion of Latin American industries producing agricultural inputs, particularly fertilizers, pesticides, and agricultural machinery.

5. To ensure the adequacy of tax systems that affect the agricultural sector, so that they may contribute to the increase of productivity and better land distribution.

6. To expand substantially programs of specialized education and research and of agricultural extension, in order to improve the training of the rural worker and the education of technical and professional personnel, and, also, to intensify animal and plant sanitation campaigns.

7. To provide incentives and to make available financial resources for the industrialization of agricultural production, especially through the development of small and medium industry and the promotion of exports of processed agricultural products.

8. To facilitate the establishment of multinational or international programs that will make it possible for Latin America to supply a larger proportion of world food needs.

9. To foster national programs of community development and of self-help for small-scale farmers, and to promote the creation and strengthening of agricultural cooperatives.

By recognizing the importance of the state objectives, goals and means, the Presidents of the members state of the OAS undertake, within the spirit of the Alliance for Progress, to combine intensified internal efforts with additional external support especially earmarked for such measures.

They call upon CIAP, when analyzing the agricultural sector as included in national development plans, to bear in mind the objectives and measures indicated herein, giving due attention to agrarian reform programs in those countries that consider these programs an important basis for their agricultural progress and economic and social developments.

Chapter 5. Educational, Technological, and Scientific
Development and Intensification of Health Programs

A. Education and Culture
Education is a sector of high priority in the overall development policy of Latin American nations.

The Presidents of the member states of the OAS recognize that, during the past decade, there has been development of educational services in Latin America unparalleled in any other period of the history of their countries.

Nevertheless it must be admitted that:

a. It is necessary to increase the effectiveness of national efforts in the field of education;
b. Educational systems should be more adequately adjusted to the demands of economic, social, and cultural development;
c. International cooperation in educational matters should be considerably intensified in accordance with the new standards of the Charter of the OAS.

To these ends, they agree to improve educational, administrative and planning systems; to raise the quality of education so as to stimulate the creativity of each pupil; to accelerate expansion of educational systems at all levels; and to assign priority to the following activities related to economic, social, and cultural development:

1. Orientation and, when necessary, reorganization of educational systems, in accordance with the needs and possibilities of each country, in order to achieve:
   a. The expansion and progressive improvement of preschool education and extension of the period of general education;
   b. An increase in the capacity of secondary schools and the improvement of their curricula;
   c. An increase in opportunities following general education, including opportunities for learning a trade or a specialty or for continuing general education;
   d. The general elimination of barriers between vocational and general education;
   e. The expansion and diversification of university courses, so that they will include the new professions essential to economic and social development;
   f. The establishment or expansion of graduate courses through professional schools;

    g. The establishment of refresher courses in all branches and types of education, so that graduates may keep their knowledge up to date in this era of rapid scientific and technological progress;

    h. The strengthening and expansion of adult education programs;

    i. The promotion of special education for exceptional students.

2. Promotion of basic and advanced training for teachers and administrative personnel; development of educational research and experimentation, and adequate expansion of school building programs.

3. Broadening of the use of educational television and other modern teaching techniques.

4. Improvement of rural elementary schools to achieve a level of quality equal to that of urban elementary schools, with a view to assuring equal educational opportunities to the rural population.

5. Reorganization of vocational education, when necessary, taking into account the structure of the labor force and the foreseeable manpower needs of each country's development plan.

6. An increase in private financing of education.

7. Encouragement of local and regional communities to take an active part in the construction of school buildings and in civic support for educational development.

8. A substantial increase in national scholarship and student loan and aid programs.

9. Establishment or expansion of extension services and services for preserving the cultural heritage and encouraging intellectual and artistic activity.

10. Strengthening of education for international understanding and Latin American integration.

Multinational Efforts

1. Increasing international resources for the purposes set forth in this chapter.

2. Instructing the appropriate agencies of the OAS to:

    a. Provide technical assistance to the countries that so request:

      i. In educational research, experimentation, and innovation;

      ii. For training of specialized personnel;

      iii. In educational television. It is recommended that a study be made of the advisability of establishing a multinational training center in this field;

b. Organize meetings of experts to recommend measures to bring national curricula into harmony with Latin American integration goals;

c. Organize regional volunteer teacher programs;

d. Extend inter-American cooperation to the preservation and use of archeological, historic and artistic monuments.

3. Expansion of OAS programs for fellowships, student loans, and teacher exchange.

National educational and cultural development efforts will be evaluated in coordination by CIAP and the Inter-American Council for Education, Science, and Culture (now the Inter-American Cultural Council).

B. Science and Technology

Advances in scientific and technological knowledge are changing the economic and social structure of many nations. Science and technology offer infinite possibilities for providing the people with the well-being that they seek. But in Latin American countries the potentialities that this wealth of the modern world offers have by no means been realized to the degree and extent necessary. Science and technology offer genuine instruments for Latin American progress and must be given an unprecedented impetus at this time. This effort calls for inter-American cooperation, in view of the magnitude of the investments required and the level attained in such knowledge. In the same way, their organization and implementation in each country cannot be effected without a properly planned scientific and technological policy within the general framework of development.

For the above reasons the Presidents of the member states of the OAS agree upon the following measures:

Internal Efforts

Establishment, in accordance with the needs and possibilities of each country, of national policies in the field of science and technology, with the necessary machinery and funds, the main elements of which shall be:

1. Promotion of professional training for scientists and technicians and an increase in their numbers.

2. Establishment of conditions favoring full utilization of the scientific and technological potential for solving the economic and social problems of Latin America, and to prevent the exodus of persons qualified in these fields.

3. Encouragement of increased private financial contributions for scientific and technological research and teaching.

Multinational Efforts

1. Establishment of a Regional Scientific and Technological Development Program designed to advance science and technology to a degree that they will contribute substantially to accelerating the economic development and well-being of their peoples and make it feasible to engage in pure and applied scientific research of the highest possible quality. This Program shall complement Latin American national programs in the area of science and technology and shall take special account of the characteristics of each of the countries.

2. The Program shall be oriented toward the adoption of measures to promote scientific and technological research, teaching, and information; basic and advanced training of scientific personnel; and exchange of information. It shall promote intensively the transfer to, and adaptation by, the Latin American countries of knowledge and technologies originating in their regions.

3. The Program shall be conducted through national agencies responsible for scientific and technological policy, through institutions national or international, public or private—either now existing or to be established in the future.

4. As part of the Program, they propose that multinational technological and scientific training and research institutions at the postgraduate level be established, and that institutions of this nature already existing in Latin America be strengthened. A group, composed of high-ranking, qualified persons, experienced in science, technology, and university education, shall be established to make recommendations to the Inter-American Council for Education, Science, and Culture (now the Inter-American Cultural Council) on the nature of such multinational institutions, including such matters as their organization, the characteristics of their multinational administration, financing, location, coordination of their activities among themselves and with those of pertinent national institutions, and on the other aspects of their operation. The aforementioned group, selected and convoked by the Inter-American Council for Education, Science, and Culture (now the Inter-American Cultural Council) or, failing this, by CIAP, shall meet within 120 days after the close of this meeting.

5. In order to encourage the training of scientific and technological personnel at the higher academic levels, they resolve that an Inter-American Fund for Scientific and Technological Training shall be established as part of the Program, so that scientists and research

workers from Latin American countries may pursue advanced scientific and technological studies, with the obligation to engage in a period of scientific work in Latin America.

6. The Program shall be promoted by the Inter-American Council for Education, Science, and Culture (now the Inter-American Cultural Council), in cooperation with CIAP. They shall coordinate their activities with similar activities of the United Nations and other interested organizations.

7. The Program may be financed by contributions of the member states of the inter-American system, inter-American or international institutions, technologically advanced countries, universities, foundations, and private individuals.

C. Health

Improvement of health conditions is fundamental to the economic and social development of Latin America. Available scientific knowledge makes it possible to obtain specific results, which, in accordance with the needs of each country and the provisions of the Charter of Punta del Este, should be utilized to attain the following objectives:

a. Control of communicable diseases and eradication of those for which methods for total elimination exist. Pertinent programs shall receive international coordination when necessary.

b. Acceleration of programs for providing drinking-water supplies, sewage, and other services essential to environmental sanitation in rural and urban areas, giving preference to lower income groups. On the basis of studies carried out and with the cooperation of international financing agencies, national revolving fund systems shall be used to assure the continuity of such programs.

c. Greater and more rapid progress in improving nutrition of the neediest groups of the population, taking advantage of all possibilities offered by national effort and international cooperation.

d. Promotion of intensive mother and child welfare programs and of educational programs on overall family guidance methods.

e. Priority for basic and advanced training of professional, technical, administrative, and auxiliary personnel, and support of operational and administrative research in the field of health.

f. Incorporation, as early as the preinvestment phase, of national and regional health programs into general development plans.

The Presidents of the member states of the OAS, therefore, decide:

1. To expand, within the framework of general planning, the preparation and implementation of national plans that will strengthen infrastructure in the field of health.
2. To mobilize internal and external resources to meet the needs for financing these plans. In this connection, to call upon CIAP, when analyzing the health sector in national development programs, to take into account the objectives and needs indicated.
3. To call upon the Pan American Health Organization to cooperate with the governments in the preparation of specific programs relating to these objectives.

Chapter 6. Elimination of Unnecessary Military Expenditures

The Latin American Presidents, conscious of the importance of the armed forces in maintaining security, at the same time recognize that the demands of economic development and social progress make it necessary to apply the maximum resources available in Latin America to these ends.

Consequently, they express their intention to limit military expenditures in proportion to the actual demands of national security, in accordance with each country's constitutional provisions, avoiding those expenditures that are not indispensable for the performance of the specific duties of the armed forces and, where pertinent, of international commitments that obligate their respective governments.

With regard to the Treaty on the Banning of Nuclear Arms in Latin America they express the hope that it may enter into force as soon as possible, once the requirements established by the Treaty are met.

DONE at Punta del Este, Uruguay. in the English, French, Portuguese, and Spanish languages, this Pan American Day the fourteenth of April of the year one thousand nine hundred sixty-seven, the seventy-seventh anniversary of the founding of the inter-American system.

Source: Barry Sklar and Virginia Hagen, *Inter-American Relations: A Collection of Documents, Legislation, Descriptions of Inter-American Organizations, and Other Material Pertaining to Inter-American Affairs* (Washington, 1972).

Appendix E

Key Officials in the Alliance for Progress Era

Assistant Secretary of State for Inter-American Affairs[a]

Robert F. Woodward (July 14, 1961–March 17, 1962)
Edwin M. Martin (May 12, 1962–January 2, 1964)
Thomas C. Mann[b] (December 21, 1963–March 17, 1965)
Jack Hood Vaughn (March 11, 1965–February 28, 1966)
Lincoln Gordon (February 25, 1966–June 30, 1967)
Covey T. Oliver (June 9, 1967–December 31, 1968)
Charles A. Meyer (March 28, 1969–March 2, 1973)

U.S. Coordinator of the Alliance for Progress[b]

Teodoro Moscoso (November 21, 1961–December 21, 1963)

Administrator of the Agency for International Development[a]

Fowler Hamilton (September 30, 1961-December 7, 1962)
David Elliot Bell (December 17, 1962–July 31, 1966)
William S. Gaud (August 1, 1966–January 10, 1969)

President of Chile

Jorge Alessandri (November 3, 1958–November 3, 1964)
Eduardo Frei (November 3, 1964–November 3, 1970)
Salvador Allende (November 3, 1970–September 11, 1973)

U.S. Ambassador to Chile[a]

Robert F. Woodward (April 18, 1961–July 6, 1961)
Charles W. Cole (September 23, 1961–September 27, 1964)
Ralph A. Dungan (November 24, 1964–August 2, 1967)
Edward M. Korry (August 23, 1967–October 12, 1971)

President of Brazil

Juscelino Kubitschek (January 31, 1956–January 31, 1961)
Jânio Quadros (January 31, 1961–August 25, 1961)
João Goulart (September 7, 1961–April 1, 1964)
Humberto Castelo Branco (April 15,1964–March 15, 1967)
Artur da Costa e Silva (March 15, 1967–August 31, 1969)

U.S. Ambassador to Brazil[a]

John M. Cabot (May 28, 1959–August 17, 1961)
Lincoln Gordon (September 18, 1961–February 25, 1966)
John W. Tuthill (May 27, 1966–January 9, 1969)

President of the Dominican Republic (or other head of state)

Joaquín Balaguer (August 3, 1960–January 16, 1962)
Council of State (January 16, 1962–February 27, 1963)
Juan Bosch (February 27, 1963–September 25, 1963)
Donald Reid Cabral/Triumvirate (September 26, 1963–April 25, 1965)
Héctor García Godoy/Provisional Government (September 3, 1965–July 1, 1966)
Joaquín Balaguer (July 1, 1966–August 16, 1978)

U.S Ambassador to Dominican Republic[a]

John Bartlow Martin (March 2, 1962–September 28, 1963)
W. Tapley Bennett, Jr. (March 4, 1964–April 13, 1966)
John Hugh Crimmins (June 27, 1966–16 April 16, 1969)

President of Colombia

Alberto Lleras Camargo (August 7, 1958–August 7, 1962)
Guillermo León Valencia (August 7, 1962–August 7, 1966)
Carlos Lleras Restrepo (August 7, 1966–August 7, 1970)

U.S. Ambassador to Colombia[a]

Fulton Freeman (May 4, 1961–March 14, 1964)
Covey T. Oliver (May 1, 1964–August 29, 1966)
Reynold E. Carlson (September 16, 1966–June 2, 1969)

---

[a] Dates for U.S. officials indicate appointment to last day at the post.
[b] Starting with Thomas C. Mann, the Assistant Secretary of State for Inter-American Affairs was also the U.S. Coordinator of the Alliance for Progress.

Endnotes

Introduction

1. *U.S. Overseas Loans and Grants 2004*—The Greenbook (Washington, 2005). All *Greenbook* data is available at the United States Agency for International Development website at: qesdb.usaid.gov.
2. The Greenbook. If funds that are not specified as targeted toward a single country are removed from the total spending, the percentages become significantly larger.
3. Political scientists have commented extensively on this theme. A limited sample includes Hans Morgenthau, "A Political Theory of Foreign Aid," *American Political Science Review* 56, no. 2 (1972): 301–309; Earl Conteh-Morgan, *American Foreign Aid and Global Power Projection* (Brookfield, VT, 1990); Robert McKinlay and Richard Little, "A Foreign Policy Model of U.S. Bilateral Aid Allocation," *World Politics* 30, no. 1 (1979): 58–86; William Easterly, *The White Man's Burden: Why the West's Efforts to Aid the Rest of the World Have Done So Much Ill and So Little Good* (New York, 2006); Glenn Palmer, Scott B. Wohlander, and T. Clifton Morgan, "Give or Take: Foreign Aid and Foreign Policy Sustainability," *Journal of Peace Research* 39, no. 1 (2002): 5–26; Steven W. Hook, *National Interest and Foreign Aid* (Boulder, 1995); David Arase, *Buying Power: The Political Economy of Japan's Foreign Aid* (Boulder, 1995); Robert A. Packenham, *Liberal America and the Third World: Political Development Ideas in Foreign Aid and Social Science* (Princeton, 1973); David A. Baldwin, *Economic Statecraft* (Princeton, 1985); and David A. Baldwin, *Economic Development and American Foreign Policy, 1942–1963* (Chicago, 1966).
4. Larry Diamond et al., *Foreign Assistance in the National Interest: Promoting Freedom, Security, and Opportunity* (Washington, 2003), 1.
5. Samuel Hale Butterfield, *U.S. Development Aid— An Historic First: Achievements and Failures in the Twentieth Century* (Westport, CT, 2004); *America's Helping Hand: Paving the Way to Globalization* (New York, 2005); Charles

Kimber Pearce, *Rostow, Kennedy, and the Rhetoric of Foreign Aid* (East Lansing, 2001); John F. O'Conor, *Cold War and Liberation: A Challenge of Aid to the Subject Peoples* (New York, 1961); Simon Payaslian, *U.S. Foreign Economic and Military Aid: The Reagan and Bush Administrations* (Lanham, MD, 1996); Robert F. Zimmerman, *Dollars, Diplomacy, and Dependency: Dilemmas of U.S. Economic Aid* (Boulder, 1993); Sergei Shenin, *The United States and the Third World: The Origins of Postwar Relations and the Point Four Program* (Huntington, NY, 2000).

6. John Agnew and J. Nicholas Entrikin, "Introduction: The Marshall Plan as Model and Metaphor," in *The Marshall Plan: Model and Metaphor*, ed. John Agnew and J. Nicholas Entrikin, 1–22 (London, 2004); Alan Milward, *The Reconstruction of Western Europe, 1945–1951* (Los Angeles, 1984); Michael J. Hogan, *The Marshall Plan: America, Britain, and the Reconstructing of Western Europe, 1947–1952* (Cambridge, U.K., 1987); Barry Eichengreen, *Europe's Postwar Recovery* (Cambridge, 1995).

7. Packenham, *Liberal America*, 111–160.

8. Elizabeth Cobbs Hoffman, *All You Need Is Love: The Peace Corps and the Spirit of the 1960s* (Cambridge, 1988), 3–38.

9. The United Nations set a goal for developed countries at .7 percent of Gross Domestic Product in 1970. Only Denmark, Norway, the Netherlands, Sweden, and Luxembourg have met that goal recently. Bilal Siddiqi, "Picture This: Aiding Development," *Finance and Development, A Quarterly Magazine of the IMF* 42, no. 3 (2005), www.imf.org/external/pubs/ft/fandd/2005/09/picture.htm; International foreign aid statistics are also available from the Center for Global Development at www.cgdev.org and the UN Millennium Project at www.unmillenniumproject.org.

10. Barbara Crossette, "Hurting the World's Poor in Morality's Name," *World Policy Journal* 21, no. 4 (winter 2004–2005): 57–62; "Study Challenges Abstinence as Crucial to AIDS Strategy," *New York Times* (hereafter *NYT*), February 24, 2005; "U.S. Focus on Abstinence Weakens AIDS Fight, Agency Finds," *NYT*, April 5, 2006; "Bush, A Friend of Africa," *NYT*, July, 5 2005; "Panel Reverses Bush Cuts in Family Planning Aid," *NYT*, May 20, 2006; Memorandum for the USAID Administrator on Restoration of the Mexico City Policy from President George W. Bush, January 22, 2001, available at www.whitehouse.gov/news/releases/20010123-5.html; U.S. Agency for International Development, "Mexico City Policy" available at www.usaid.gov/our_work/global_health/pop/mcpolicy.html; Susan A. Cohen, "Abortion Politics and U.S. Population Aid: Coping with a Complex New Law," *International Family Planning Perspectives* 26, no. 3 (2000): 137–145; also see, John B. Sharpless, "World Population Growth, Family Planning and American Foreign Policy," *Journal of Policy History* 7 (1995): 72–102.

11. A 1961 dollar is equivalent to 5.08 dollars in 2004 according to AID. See The Greenbook.

12. This is a description of modernization theory, an idea that will be discussed in the next chapter. See, Michael E. Latham, *Modernization as Ideology: American Social Science and "Nation Building" in the Kennedy Era* (Chapel Hill, 2000), 1–19.

13. The Greenbook.

14. United States Senate, Select Committee to Study Governmental Operations

with Respect to Intelligence Activities, *Covert Action in Chile, 1963–1973*; *Staff Report of the Select Committee to Study Governmental Operations with Respect to Intelligence Activities* (Washington, 1975).

15. For examples, see Jerome Levinson and Juan de Onís, *The Alliance That Lost Its Way: A Critical Report on the Alliance for Progress* (Chicago, 1970); L. Ronald Scheman, "The Alliance for Progress: Concept and Creativity," in *The Alliance for Progress: A Retrospective*, ed. L. Ronald Scheman, 3–62 (New York, 1988); William D. Rogers, *The Twilight Struggle: The Alliance for Progress and the Politics of Dependence in Latin America* (New York, 1967); Stephen G. Rabe, *The Most Dangerous Area in the World: John F. Kennedy Confronts Communist Revolution in Latin America* (Chapel Hill, 1999); Robert M. Smetherman and Bobbie Smetherman, "The Alliance for Progress: Promises Unfulfilled," *American Journal of Economics and Sociology* 31, no 1. (1972): 79–86.

16. Rabe, *Most Dangerous Area*, 173–175; Arthur M. Schlesinger Jr., "The Alliance for Progress: A Retrospective," in *Latin America: The Search for a New Institutional Role*, ed. Ronald G. Raskin and Bernard Fall, 57–92 (New York, 1975); Arthur M. Schlesinger Jr., "Myth and Reality" in Scheman, ed., 67–72; Eduardo Frei Montalva, "The Alliance That Lost Its Way," *Foreign Affairs* 45, no. 3 (1964): 389–404; Alberto Lleras Camargo, "The Alliance for Progress: Aims, Distortions, Obstacles," *Foreign Affairs* 42, no. 4 (1963): 639–646; Edwin Guthman and Jeffrey Shulman, eds. *Robert Kennedy in His Own Words: The Unpublished Recollections of the Kennedy Years* (New York, 1988), 408.

Chapter 1

1. "President Gives 10-Year Aid Plan to Latin America," *NYT*, March 14, 1961; Rabe, *Most Dangerous Area*, 9–10.

2. "The Unfinished Revolution," *Washington Post*, March 14, 1961.

3. Morris H. Morley, *Imperial State and Revolution: The United States and Cuba, 1952–1986* (Cambridge, 1987); Alan Luxenberg, "A Backward Look at U.S. Latin American Policy: Did Eisenhower Push Castro into the Arms of the Soviets?" *Journal of Interamerican Studies and World Affairs* 30, no. 1 (1988): 37–64.

4. *Public Papers of the Presidents of the United States: John F. Kennedy, 1961* (Washington, 1962), 170–175.

5. Michael Gambone, *Capturing the Revolution: The United States, Central America, and Nicaragua, 1961–1972* (Westport, CT, 2001), 27–31; Stephen G. Rabe, *Eisenhower and Latin America: The Foreign Policy of Anticommunism* (Chapel Hill, 1988); Harvey S. Perloff, *Alliance for Progress: A Social Invention in the Making* (Baltimore, 1969), 7–18; Milton S. Eisenhower, *The Wine Is Bitter: The United States and Latin America* (Garden City, NY, 1963).

6. Burton Kaufman, *Trade and Aid: Eisenhower's Foreign Economic Policy* (Baltimore, 1982), 12–55; David A. Baldwin, *Economic Development*, 117–190; Rabe, *Eisenhower and Latin America*, 64–83; William O. Walker, "Mixing the Sweet with the Sour: Kennedy, Johnson, and Latin America," in *The Diplomacy of the Crucial Decade: American Foreign Relations during the 1960s*, ed. Diane Kunz, 43–44. (New York, 1994).

7. FY1954 through FY1958, a period representing July 1, 1953 to June 30, 1958, does not correspond exactly with Eisenhower's term, but it generally reflects the budgets that the policies in question created. There was always a time lag between policy and shifts in spending. See The Greenbook. Also see Office of Statistics and Reports, Bureau for Program and Policy Coordination, Agency for International Development, *U.S. Overseas Loans and Grants and Assistance from International Organizations, Obligations and Loan Authorizations, July 1, 1945–June 30, 1971* (Washington, 1972). The Eisenhower policy was not entirely new, but rather a continuation of policies developed in the Truman years. See Chester Pach, "Containment of U.S. Military Aid to Latin America, 1944–1949," *Diplomatic History* 6, no. 3 (1982): 225–241.

8. Rabe, *Eisenhower and Latin America*, 31–34, the quote is from page 32.

9. Robert J. McMahon, "The Illusion of Vulnerability: American Reassessments of the Soviet Threat, 1955–1956," *International History Review* 18, no. 3 (August 1996): 591–619; Dennis Merrill, *Bread and the Ballot: The United States and India's Economic Development, 1947-1963* (Chapel Hill, 1990), 123; Harry Hanak, "Foreign Policy," in *Khrushchev and Khrushchevism*, ed. Martin McCauley, 180–193 (Bloomington, 1987).

10. Rabe, *Eisenhower and Latin America*, 84–99.

11. Rabe, *Eisenhower and Latin America*, 90, 92; McMahon, "The Illusion of Vulnerability," 608–609.

12. Richard M. Nixon, *Six Crises* (Garden City, NY, 1962), 183; James F. Siekmeier, *Aid, Nationalism, and Inter-American Relations: Guatemala, Bolivia, and the United States* (Lewiston, NY, 1999).

13. Alan McPherson, *Yankee No!: Anti-Americanism in U.S.-Latin American Relations* (Cambridge, 2003), 27; Marvin R. Zahniser and W. Michael Weis, "A Diplomatic Pearl Harbor?: Richard Nixon's Goodwill Mission to Latin America in 1958," *Diplomatic History* 13 (1989): 163–191.

14. McPherson, *Yankee No!*, 27–28.

15. Nixon quote in Nixon, 219; Russ Olson, "You Can't Spit on a Foreign Policy," *Passport: The Society for Historians of American Foreign Relations Newsletter* 31, no. 3 (2000): 28–39; Zahniser and Weis, 184–185.

16. McPherson, *Yankee No!*, 11.

17. Kaufman, 168, 171; McPherson, *Yankee No!*, 30–31.

18. Kaufman, 164–165.

19. Quoted in Rabe, *Eisenhower and Latin America*, 110.

20. W. Michael Weis, *Cold Warriors and Coups d'Etat: Brazilian-American Relations, 1945-1964* (Albuquerque, 1993), 113–127; Rabe, *Eisenhower and Latin America*, 113–115. Victor Wallis, "Brazil's Experiment with an Independent Foreign Policy," in *Contemporary Inter-American Relations: A Reader in Theory and Issues*, ed. Yale Ferguson, 35–50 (Englewood Cliffs, NJ, 1972).

21. Eisenhower, 248, 329.

22. John Bell to Rubottom, July 5, 1960, Policy 1960, Box 2, Lots 64D418 and 64D15, Bureau of Inter-American Affairs, Subject Files of the Assistant Secretary, 1959–1962, Record Group (hereafter RG) 59, National Archives and Records Administration, College Park, MD (hereafter NA); Rabe, *Eisenhower and Latin America*, 110, 141–144; Devine to Rubottom through Mallory, June 17, 1960, Latin American Aid Program 1960, Box 5, Lot 64D24,

Bureau of Inter-American Affairs, Records of the Special Assistant on Communism, 1958–1961, RG 59, NA; Achillies to Smith, July 5, 1960, Latin American Aid Program 1960, Box 5, Lot 64D24, Bureau of Inter-American Affairs, Records of the Special Assistant on Communism, 1958–1961, RG 59, NA; Devine to Rubottom through Mallory, July 15, 1960, Latin American Aid Program 1960, Box 5, Lot 64D24, Bureau of Inter-American Affairs, Records of the Special Assistant on Communism, 1958–1961, RG 59, NA; Macy to Mann, July 18, 1960, Latin American Aid Program 1960, Box 5, Lot 64D24, Bureau of Inter-American Affairs, Records of the Special Assistant on Communism, 1958–1961, RG 59, NA; Mann to Macy, July 19, 1960, Latin American Aid Program 1960, Box 5, Lot 64D24, Bureau of Inter-American Affairs, Records of the Special Assistant on Communism, 1958–1961, RG 59, NA; Devine to Rosenson, July 21, 1960, Latin American Aid Program 1960, Box 5, Lot 64D24, Bureau of Inter-American Affairs, Records of the Special Assistant on Communism, 1958–1961, RG 59, NA; Devine to Rubottom, July 25, 1960, Latin American Aid Program 1960, Box 5, Lot 64D24, Bureau of Inter-American Affairs, Records of the Special Assistant on Communism, 1958–1961, RG 59, NA; Phillips to Mann through Mallory, September 13, 1960; Latin American Aid Program 1960, Box 5, Lot 64D24, Bureau of Inter-American Affairs, Records of the Special Assistant on Communism, 1958–1961, RG 59, NA; United States Senate, Committee on Foreign Relations, *Hearings on a Bill to Provide for the Assistance in the Development of Latin America and in the Reconstruction of Chile, and for Other Purposes* (Washington, 1960).

23. Devine to Rubottom through Mallory, June 17, 1960, Latin American Aid Program 1960, Box 5, Lot 64D24, Bureau of Inter-American Affairs, Records of the Special Assistant on Communism, 1958–1961, RG 59, NA.

24. Organization of American States, *Act of Bogotá; Measures for Social Improvement and Economic Development within the framework of Operation Pan America* (Washington, 1961).

25. The Greenbook.

26. Nils Gilman, "Paving the World with Good Intentions: The Genesis of Modernization Theory, 1945–1965" (Ph.D. dissertation, University of California, Berkeley, 2000), 205–233; Walt W. Rostow, *Eisenhower, Kennedy, and Foreign Aid* (Austin, 1985), 42.

27. Rostow, *Eisenhower, Kennedy, and Foreign Aid*, 197.

28. Max Millikan, *A Proposal: Key to an Effective Foreign Policy* (New York, 1957), the quote is on page 25; Gilman, "Paving the World," 233–244; Nick Cullather, "Development: It's History," *Diplomatic History* 24, no. 4 (2000): 641–653.

29. Nils Gilman, *Mandarins of the Future: Modernization Theory in Cold War America* (Baltimore, 2003), 4–5.

30. Latham, 1–19.

31. Walt W. Rostow, *The Stages of Economic Growth: A Non-Communist Manifesto* (Cambridge, U.K., 1960), 4–9, 17–53; Gilman, "Paving the World," 261–275.

32. Rostow quotes in Rostow to Kennedy, February 28, 1961, Foreign Aid 2/24/61–2/28/61, Staff Memoranda, Walt W. Rostow, Box 324, Meetings and Memoranda File, National Security File (hereafter NSF), John F. Kennedy

Library, Boston, MA (hereafter JFKL); Memorandum on a New Organization for the U.S. Foreign Aid Program, Foreign Aid 1–10/61, Staff Memoranda, Walt W. Rostow, Box 324, Meetings and Memoranda File, NSF, JFKL. Interestingly, perhaps because he was not explicitly involved with Latin America, only in general aid policy, Rostow later claimed that he was not connected to the early stages of the Alliance for Progress. See, Walt W. Rostow Oral History, April 11, 1964, Interviewer: Richard Neustadt, JFKL.

33. Richard N. Goodwin, *Remembering America: A Voice from the 1960s* (Boston, 1988), 146–159; Lincoln Gordon Oral History, May 30, 1964, Interviewer: Dennis O'Brien, JFKL; On Berle and the rest of the task force, see Levinson and Onís, 52–56. Most task force plans came directly from the ideas of an informal organization of academics working at MIT and Harvard with close connections to the CENIS group, and with scholars such as Arthur Schlesinger. In late 1960 this Latin American group, composed of Harvard faculty members Lincoln Gordon and William Barnes, and also a Washington attorney, Peter Nehemkis, came together at the Harvard Faculty Club and developed a plan for a more active aid policy in Latin America. Though this group was unofficial, Kennedy appointed one of the Harvard group's members, Gordon, to the task force, thus bringing the ideas of the informal group into the government; Willard Beaulac, *The Fractured Continent: Latin America in Close-Up* (Stanford, 1988), 28–29.

34. Draft Memorandum from the Consultant to the Task Force on Latin America (Gordon) to the President's Assistant Special Counsel (Goodwin), March 6, 1961, Doc. 6, *Foreign Relations of the United States* (hereafter *FRUS) 1961–1963*, Vol. XII.

35. *Public Papers, Kennedy, 1961*, 170–175.

36. *Public Papers, Kennedy, 1961*, 1–3.

37. Victor Lasky, *J.F.K.: The Man and the Myth* (New York, 1963), 3–16; David Burner, *John F. Kennedy and a New Generation* (Glenville, IL, 1988), 57–71; David Halberstam, *The Best and The Brightest* (New York, 1969).

38. Rostow, *Eisenhower and Latin America*, 58. The program was called Point Four because it was the fourth point Truman made about U.S. foreign policy objectives in a January 1949 speech.

39. *Congressional Record*, 82nd Cong., 2nd sess., Vol. 98, pt. 7, 8492–8493; Herbert S. Parmet, *Jack: The Struggles of John F. Kennedy* (New York, 1980), 226–228; Merrill, 30, 66–67.

40. Parmet, 226; John F. Kennedy, *The Strategy of Peace* (New York, 1960), 57–61.

41. Kennedy, *The Strategy of Peace*, 66–81; Parmet, 399–407; Kennedy quote in *Congressional Record*, 85th Cong., 1st sess., Vol. 103, pt. 8, 10781.

42. Kennedy, *The Strategy of Peace*, 63–64; Rostow, *Eisenhower and Latin America*, 61–62.

43. John F. Kennedy, "A Democrat Looks at Foreign Policy," *Foreign Affairs* 36, no. 1 (1957): 53.

44. Merrill, 146–147; Rostow, *Eisenhower and Latin America*, 6–7; Kennedy quote in *Congressional Record*, 85th Cong., 2nd sess., Vol. 104, pt. 4, 5246–5253.

45. Rabe, *Eisenhower and Latin America*, 162, 173. Thomas G. Paterson, "Fixation with Cuba: The Bay of Pigs, Missile Crisis, and Covert War against Fidel

Castro," in *Kennedy's Quest for Victory: American Foreign Policy, 1961–1963*, ed. Thomas G. Paterson, 123–124, 130 (New York, 1989).

46. Paterson, "Fixation with Cuba," 127–131.
47. Thomas G. Paterson, *Contesting Castro: The United States and the Triumph of the Cuban Revolution* (New York, 1994), 258; Karl Meyer and Tad Szulc, *The Cuban Invasion* (New York, 1962).
48. Rabe, *Most Dangerous Area*, 9–33, the quote is from page 19.

Chapter 2

1. The meetings were originally planned for the Uruguayan capital, Montevideo, but moved to Punta del Este, then among the most luxurious resort towns in South America. Because the meetings were in August, in the middle of the South American winter, Punta del Este was a quiet place to have sessions, yet well equipped with hotels. Memorandum from the Chairman of the Task Force on Latin America (Berle) to President Kennedy, April 25, 1961, Doc. 10, *FRUS 61–63*, Vol. XII.
2. Rostow quote in Rostow to Kennedy, March 2, 1961, Rostow 3/61–5/61, Staff Memoranda, Box 64A Presidential Office Files, Lyndon Baines Johnson Library, Austin, TX (hereafter LBJL); The United States, in the words of Chester Bowles, undersecretary of state, needed an anti-Communist consensus, but could not "expect to interpret the world to Latin Americans as if they were satellites." Proceedings of the Fourth Regional Operations Conference, Lima, Peru, October 9–11, 1961, Depts. and Agencies, State Department 10/61–12/61, Box 88, Presidential Office Files, JFKL; Michael R. Beschloss, *The Crisis Years: Kennedy and Khrushchev, 1960–1963* (New York, 1991), 100–125.
3. Goodwin quote in Goodwin, 190; *Public Papers, Kennedy, 1961*, 278: Ball to Martin, May 9, 1961, Alliance for Progress 1/61–12/61, Box 290, NSF, JFKL.
4. *Public Papers, Kennedy, 1961*, 228.
5. Memorandum from the President's Assistant Special Counsel (Goodwin) to President Kennedy, June 12, 1961, Doc. 12, *FRUS 61–63*, Vol. XII.
6. *Public Papers, Kennedy, 1961*, 415; Levinson and Onís, 61; At the UN, on the day of the Bay of Pigs invasion, Stevenson said, "The United States has committed no aggression against Cuba and no offensive has been launched from Florida or any other part of the United States." Of course, even if Stevenson had known the full details, it is hard to imagine that he would have been able to say anything else. "Soviet Urges U.N. to Assist Castro," *NYT*, April 19, 1961; "Opinion of the Week: At Home and Abroad, Stevenson's Mission," *NYT*, July 21, 1961; Adlai E. Stevenson, "The Alliance for Progress, a Road Map to New Achievements: Report to the Secretary of State by Ambassador Adlai E. Stevenson," *Department of State Bulletin* (August 21, 1961): 45.
7. Report From the Representative to the United Nations (Stevenson) to President Kennedy, June 27, 1961, Doc. 14, *FRUS 61–63*, Vol. XII.
8. Memorandum by the Acting Executive Secretary of the National Security Council (Smith), March 20, 1961, Doc. 9, *FRUS 61–63*, Vol. XII.
9. Dillon quote in Memorandum from Secretary of the Treasury Dillon to President Kennedy, August 1, 1961, Doc. 18, *FRUS 61–63*, Vol. XII. *Public*

Papers, Kennedy, 1961, 459; Memorandum from the Chairman of the Task Force on Latin America (Berle) to President Kennedy, April 25, 1961, Doc. 10, *FRUS 61–63*, Vol. XII.

10. Dillion quote in Memorandum from Secretary of the Treasury Dillon to President Kennedy, August 1, 1961, Doc. 18, *FRUS 61–63*, Vol. XII; Memorandum from the Chairman of the Task Force on Latin America (Berle) to President Kennedy, April 25, 1961, Doc. 10, *FRUS 61–63*, Vol. XII.

11. Memorandum from Secretary of the Treasury Dillon to President Kennedy, August 1, 1961, Doc. 18, *FRUS 61–63*, Vol. XII; Dillon quote in "Secretary Dillon's Speech to the Delegates at Punta del Este" *Department of State Bulletin* (August 28, 1961): 356–360; Though Dillon spoke of $20 billion, or $2 billion each year, throughout his presidency Kennedy spoke of $10 billion as a U.S. goal. In this he included not only AID spending, but also loans from the Export-Import Bank, the Inter-American Development Bank, and the Food for Peace program. See, for example, *Public Papers, Kennedy, 1962*, 216; Goodwin, 192.

12. Scheman in Scheman, ed., 3–66; quote from the Charter of Punta del Este, see Appendix B.

13. Charter of Punta del Este, see Appendix B.

14. Ibid.

15. There were differences at the conference about the organization of the Alliance for Progress. Among the most significant objections came from Argentina over the Wise Men concept. They suggested that this group, because it would judge development plans, would be a threat to national sovereignty. There was logic to this argument. The Argentines saw little reason to allow non-Argentines to comment on their internal planning. Part of this objection came from differences in development needs between Argentina and many other Latin American nations. Argentina had a relatively developed economy and did not need basic reforms. They wanted to focus on trade agreements, currency stabilization, and investment in industry in the Alliance for Progress. Given this, they were instrumental in pushing through language in the charter suggesting that the point of development was the creation of societies adapted to the particular needs of each nation. This would allow them, rather than the United States or the Wise Men, to make decisions about economic development programs. Though facing serious development problems in the northeast, the Brazilians, who also saw themselves as different, agreed with this critique. The Argentine vision of the nine Wise Men failed though, and Argentina and Brazil were unable to mold the Alliance for Progress to meet their own specific needs. The point of the Alliance for Progress was not to help the already wealthy, but to make sure the poor did not rebel. At the conference, Dillon suggested that the smaller countries reject Argentina's leadership, which easily solved the problem of Argentine opposition. In a conference dedicated to discussions of U.S. largesse, obviously the United States could expect to get its way. Telegram from the Embassy in Montevideo to the Department of State, August 12, 1961, Doc. 28, *FRUS 61–63*, Vol. XII. These divisions seemed important at the time, and certainly some antagonism remained, but they were not particularly significant in the grand scheme of things in large part because the nine Wise Men had little real power. Levinson and Onís, 68–70; Memorandum

from Secretary of the Treasury Dillon to President Kennedy, August 1, 1961, Doc. 18, *FRUS 61–63*, Vol. XII.

16. Telegram from the Embassy in Uruguay to the Department of State, August 12, 1961, Doc. 28, *FRUS 61–63*, Vol. XII; Levinson and Onís, 70–71.

17. "Dillon and Guevara in Uruguay for Americas Parley," *NYT*, August 5, 1961; "Cuban a Cynosure at Uruguay Talks," *NYT*, August 6, 1961; "U.S. Aides at Uruguay Parley Shunning Clash with Cubans" *NYT*, August 10, 1961.

18. Guevara quote in "Castro Foes Riot at Uruguay Talk as Cuban Speaks," *NYT*, August 9, 1961; Ernesto "Che" Guevara, *Cuba en Punta del Este* (Havana, 1961).

19. The Argentine visit was a bit more troublesome than the Brazilian one. In protest, Frondizi's secretary of war resigned, leading the commanders of the armed forces to demand the resignation of the foreign minister. "Argentine Chief Rebuffs Guevara," *NYT*, August 19, 1961; "Top Frondizi Aide Quits under Fire," *NYT*, August 29, 1961; Telegram from the Embassy in Uruguay to the Department of State, August 16, 1961, Doc. 28, *FRUS 61–63*, Vol. XII; Rabe, *Most Dangerous Area*, 58.

20. Telegram from the Embassy in Uruguay to the Department of State, August 11, 1961, Doc. 26, *FRUS 61–63*, Vol. XII; Telegram from the Department of State to the Embassy in Uruguay, August 12, 1961, Doc. 27, *FRUS 61–63*, Vol. XII.

21. Goodwin, 196–205; Memorandum from the President's Assistant Special Counsel (Goodwin) to President Kennedy, August 22, 1961, Doc. 257, *FRUS 61–63*, Vol. X.

22. Memorandum from the President's Assistant Special Counsel (Goodwin) to President Kennedy, August 22, 1961, Doc. 257, *FRUS 61–63*, Vol. X.

23. Levinson and Onís, 110–112; Goodwin, who operated as Kennedy's assistant on Latin American issues, had hoped for others. Memorandum of Conversation, February 26, 1962, Doc. 41, *FRUS 61–63*, Vol. XII; *Public Papers, Kennedy, 1961*, 718–719.

24. A. W. Maldonado, *Teodoro Moscoso and Puerto Rico's Operation Bootstrap* (Gainesville, 1997), 3–159.

25. Edwin Martin, *Kennedy and Latin America* (Lanham, MD, 1994).

26. Maldonado, 173–176.

27. Edwin Martin claimed that in part, the Wise Men were set up in such a way that they would not agree. This meant that when decisions needed to be made, he, Moscoso, or Kennedy could make them. Martin, 86–87.

28. Maldonado, 177.

29. Martin, 91.

30. Maldonado, 177–179; Rabe, *Most Dangerous Area*, 150.

31. "U.S. Weighs the Latin Attitudes," *NYT*, September 2, 1962; Moscoso quote in "Alliance Hoping to End Its Siesta," *NYT*, April 8, 1963; Levinson and Onís, 111; Memorandum from the Deputy Assistant Secretary for Inter-American Affairs (Goodwin) to President Kennedy, March 14, 1962, Doc. 43, *FRUS 61–63*, Vol. XII.

32. Levinson and Onís, 111.

33. Edward Anthony Duane, "Congress and Inter-American Relations, 1961–1965" (Ph.D. dissertation, University of Pennsylvania, Philadelphia, 1969); *Public Papers, Kennedy, 1962*, 12, 29, 216; Levinson and Onís, 114–115; Ran-

dolph Jones, "Otto Passman and Foreign Aid: The Early Years," *Louisiana History* 26 (1985): 53–62.

34. Baldwin, *Economic Development and American Foreign Policy*, 217.

35. Burton I. Kaufman, "Foreign Aid and the Balance-of-Payments Problem: Vietnam and Johnson's Foreign Economic Policy," in *The Johnson Years, Volume Two: Vietnam, the Environment, and Science*, ed. Robert A. Divine, 82 (Lawrence, KS, 1987).

36. Kennedy quotes in *Public Papers, Kennedy, 1962*, 689–690; Bell Press Statement, August 24, 1963, Foreign Aid 5/24/63, Box 297, NSF, JFKL; Baldwin, *Economic Development and American Foreign Policy*, 217–218.

37. Coffin memo, April 6, 1962, AID 1/62–6/62, Box 68, Presidential Office Files, JFKL.

38. *Public Papers, Kennedy, 1963*, 684–685.

39. USAID Press Release, June 26, 1962, AID 1/62–6/62, Box 68, Presidential Office Files, JFKL.

40. Arturo Morales-Carrion memo: Political and Ideological Force, April 9, 1962, Alliance for Progress 4/62–6/62, Box 290, NSF, JFKL.

41. *Public Papers, Kennedy, 1962*, 476; Arturo Morales-Carrion memo: Political and Ideological Force, April 9, 1962, Alliance for Progress 4/62–6/62, Box 290, NSF, JFKL.

42. Lleras Camargo, "Aims, Distortions, Obstacles," 25–37. Throughout the text Alberto Lleras Camargo is referred to as Lleras Camargo instead of simply Lleras. This will make it easier to distinguish between him and his relative, Carlos Lleras Restrepo, who served as president of Colombia in the late 1960s.

43. USIA did not only focus on the Alliance for Progress in their efforts in Latin America. As in other parts of the world, they produced a stream of anti-Soviet propaganda as well as producing materials on U.S. culture and society. Proceedings of the Fourth Regional Operations Conference, Lima, Peru, October 9–11, 1961, State Department 10/61–12/61, Box 88, Presidential Office Files, JFKL; Memorandum from the Attorney General's Administrative Assistant (Symington) to the President's Special Assistant (Schlesinger), March 13, 1963, Doc. 57, *FRUS 61–63*, Vol. XII.

44. Cartoons collected by the author at the USIA library in Washington, DC, from unprocessed files in March 1998.

45. From an as yet unpublished manuscript graciously shared with the author by Nicholas Cull.

46. *Partners of the Alliance/Compañeros de la Alianza: The Grass Roots Approach to the Alliance for Progress*, No Date, Alliance for Progress Vol. I. [1 of 2], Box 4, Agency File-Alliance for Progress, NSF, LBJL, also on file Operational Files, Latin America-CIAP, Central Files, World Bank Group Archives (hereafter WBGA), Washington, DC; "U.S., Latin American Citizens Work Together in Division of Alliance Program Headed by Mr. Jim Boren," *Congressional Record* 110, no. 50 (March 18, 1964); Charles W. Cole Oral History, April 26, 1969, Interviewer: Dennis O'Brien, JFKL.

47. Telegram from Secretary of State Rusk to the Department of State, March 19, 1963, Doc. 59, *FRUS 61–63*, Vol. XII; *Public Papers, Kennedy 1963*, 270; *Public Papers, Kennedy, 1961*, 805–806; *Public Papers, Kennedy, 1962*, 525; Telegram from the Embassy in Mexico to the Department of State, October

19, 1961, Doc. 34, *FRUS 61–63*, Vol. XII; Summary Minutes of Meetings, November 29, 1961, Doc. 35, *FRUS 61–63*, Vol. XII, 70–74.

Chapter 3

1. Highlights of the First Meeting of the Working Group on Problems of the Alliance for Progress, January 16, 1962, Doc. 37, *FRUS 61–63*, Vol. XII; Edwin Martin tried to see this from the Latin American perspective; he explained, "the label 'revolution' Kennedy gave to the 'powerful change' that we saw as the heart of the AFP [Alliance for Progress] was not always interpreted in our sense. It frightened many Latin Americans, especially those whose cooperation was needed if there were to be" movement on the Alliance. Martin, 89; See also, Teodoro Moscoso, *Address to the National Press Club, February 15, 1962* (Washington, 1962); *Public Papers, Kennedy, 1963*, 296.

2. Highlights of the First Meeting of the Working Group on Problems of the Alliance for Progress, January 16, 1962, Doc. 37, *FRUS 61–63*, Vol. XII; Memorandum from the President's Special Assistant (Schlesinger) to the President's Special Assistant (Dungan), October 15, 1962, Doc. 47, *FRUS 61–63*, Vol. XII; Morales-Carrion to Martin, June 20, 1963, AID (Alliance for Progress) 1/63, Box 3294, CFPF 63, RG 59, NA.

3. Kennedy quote in *Public Papers, Kennedy, 1963*, 17; State Department quotes in Highlights of Discussion at the Secretary of State's Policy Planning Committee Meeting, February 13, 1963, Doc. 40, *FRUS 61–63*, Vol. XII, 91–93; Rabe, *Most Dangerous Area*, 156–157.

4. Martin, 83.

5. Research Memorandum from the Director of the Bureau of Intelligence and Research (Hughes) to the Assistant Secretary of State for Inter-American Affairs (Woodward), January 19, 1962, Doc. 39, *FRUS 61–63*, Vol. XII; Alliance for Progress Clearinghouse for Information, *Periodical Report: Public Opinion and the Alliance for Progress* 1 (Washington, 1962), E-1. The loan to the Honduran railway union, the Sindicato de Trabajadores of the Tela Railway Company, is curious because the railway was an affiliate of the U.S.–owned, and quite powerful United Fruit Company. According to the terms of the loan, United Fruit would donate twenty five acres of land to the union and provide $45,000 for streets, paving, water, electricity, and sewage systems. The total value of the company contribution was estimated to be $155,000. In Brazil, AIFLD would run three-month seminars for labor leaders, and would often invite top students to visit the United States for another three months. Ruth Leacock, *Requiem for Revolution: The United States and Brazil, 1961–1969* (Kent, OH, 1990), 186–187.

6. Research Memorandum Prepared in the Bureau of Intelligence and Research, January 17, 1962, Doc. 38, *FRUS 61–63*, Vol. XII.

7. Taylor to Bundy, December 5, 1961, National Security Action Memorandum 118, Joint Chiefs of Staff Proposal and Summary Tab B Appendix A, Meetings and Memorandum File, Box 324, NSF, JFKL. National Security Action Memorandum 118 is also available at www.jfklibrary.org/images/nsam118.jpg; Daniel M. Masterson, *Militarism and Politics in Latin America: Peru from Sanchez Cerro to Sendero Luminoso* (New York, 1991), 147.

8. Inter-American Economic and Social Council, *The Alliance for Progress: Its First Year, 1961–1962* (Washington, 1963).

9. Ibid.

10. Ibid.

11. Ibid. Not all countries made self-reports, though this does not suggest that they did not pursue any reform or development programs, only that they chose not to make a report to the meetings; Rabe, *Most Dangerous Area*, 162.

12. Alliance for Progress Clearinghouse for Information, *The Alliance for Progress: A Weekly Report on Activities and Public Opinion 19, January 7, 1963* (Washington: Pan American Union); see also volumes 20–25 (January 14, 1963, January 21, 1963, January 28, 1963, February 4, 1963, February 11, 1963, February 18, 1963).

13. Memorandum from the Deputy Assistant Secretary of State for Inter-American Affairs (May) to the Assistant Secretary for Inter-American Affairs (Martin), August 13, 1962, Doc. 46, *FRUS 61–63*, Vol. XII.

14. Biweekly Summary Report on the Alliance for Progress, No Date, Doc. 49, *FRUS 61–63*, Vol. XII; Airgram from the Department of State to All Posts in the American Republics, November 10, 1962, Doc. 50, *FRUS 61–63*, Vol. XII.

15. Quotes from Memorandum of Conversation, December 13, 1962, Doc. 52, *FRUS 61–63*, Vol. XII; Martin, 87.

16. Harriman quote in USIA News Policy Note, October 25, 1963, Doc. 67, *FRUS 61–63*, Vol. XII; Martin, 88–89.

17. State to ARA Posts, June 27, 1963, AID (Alliance for Progress), Box 3294, CFPF 63, RG 59, NA; State to ARA Posts, June 19, 1963, AID (Alliance for Progress) 1/63, Box 3294, CFPF 63, RG 59, NA. "U.S. Dominance in the Alliance for Progress," *NYT*, May 8, 1966; Levinson and Onís, 128–129.

18 Levinson and Onís, 128–129; Raúl Sáez S. "The Nine Wise Men and the Alliance for Progress: Background of Economic Relations within the Inter-American System," *International Organization* 22, no. 1 (1968): 244–269.

19. Memorandum from the Assistant Secretary of State for Inter-American Affairs (Martin) to Secretary of State Rusk, November 27, 1963, Doc. 71. *FRUS 61–63*, Vol. XII.

20. *Public Papers, Johnson, 1963–1964* (Washington, D.C., 1965), 6–7.

21. Memorandum from President Kennedy to Secretary of State Rusk, October 29, 1963, Doc. 68, *FRUS 61–63*, Vol. XII.

22. Editorial Note, Doc. 1, *FRUS 64–68*, Vol. XXXI; *Public Papers, Johnson, 1963–1964*; Aid memo: Notes on the Alliance for Progress, April 6, 1962, Subjects: Alliance for Progress 4/62–6/62, Box 290, NSF, JFKL; "Latins Concerned About U.S. Role in Alliance," *NYT*, December 29, 1963; McCone to Johnson, December 3, 1963, Alliance for Progress [Vol. 1], Box 4, Agency File—Alliance for Progress, NSF, LBJL.

23. "What Is the Mann Doctrine?," *NYT*, March 21, 1964; Levinson and Onís, 87, 88; Walter LaFeber, "Latin American Policy," in *The Johnson Years, Volume One: Foreign Policy, the Great Society, and the White House*, ed., Robert A. Divine, 64 (Lawrence, 1987).

24. William O. Walker III, "The Struggle for the Americas: The Johnson Administration and Cuba," in *The Foreign Policies of Lyndon Johnson:*

Beyond Vietnam, ed., H. W. Brands, 72 (College Station, 1999); Walker in Kunz, ed., 60; "One Mann & 20 Problems," *Time*, January 13, 1964; Gambone, 101.

25. Goodwin, 245; Schlesinger in Raskin and Fall, eds., 57–92; Schlesinger in Scheman, ed., 67–72; Rabe, *Most Dangerous Area*, 173–179.
26. LaFeber in Divine, 64. See Appendix E.
27. Mann and Rostow circular memo, March 21, 1964, Alliance for Progress [Vol. 1], Box 4, Agency File—Alliance for Progress, NSF, LBJL; Chase to Bundy, May 12, 1964, Alliance for Progress [Vol. 1], Box 4, Agency File—Alliance for Progress, NSF, LBJL; Rogers quote in Chase to Bundy, May 7, 1964, Alliance for Progress [Vol. 1], Box 4, Agency File—Alliance for Progress, NSF, LBJL.
28. *Public Papers, Johnson, 1965*, 615.
29. Bowdler to Bundy, July 28, 1964, Alliance for Progress [Vol. 2], Box 5, Agency File—Alliance for Progress, NSF, LBJL; Bowdler to Valenti, March 15, 1966, Alliance for Progress [Vol. 2], Box 5, Agency File—Alliance for Progress, NSF, LBJL.
30. Rabe, *Most Dangerous Area*, 181–182.
31. Sternfeld to Mann and Rostow, March 31, 1966, Alliance for Progress [Vol. 2], Box 5, Agency File—Alliance for Progress, NSF, LBJL.
32. Ibid; Inter-American Development Bank, *Social Progress Trust Fund Annual Report, 1965* (Washington, 1966), 84; James W. Wilkie, *Statistical Abstract of Latin America*, 38th ed. (Los Angeles, 2002), 206.
33. Buenos Aires Action Program quote in Moyers to Rostow (Gordon Report), April 4, 1966, Alliance for Progress [Vol. 2], Box 5, Agency File—Alliance for Progress, NSF, LBJL; "National Efforts By Latins Urged," *NYT*, March 26, 1966; "Action Plan Is Set by Latin Alliance," *NYT*, April 1, 1966.
34. Barall to Linowitz, March 22, 1967, Alliance for Progress [Vol. 3], Box 5, Agency File—Alliance for Progress, NSF, LBJL.
35. Bell to Johnson, October 21, 1965, Alliance for Progress [Vol. 2], Box 5, Agency File—Alliance for Progress, NSF, LBJL.
36. Rostow to Bell, January 24, 1967, Brazil Vol. VI Memos, Box 11, Country File (hereafter CF), NSF, LBJL.

Chapter 4

1. The Greenbook.
2. Brian Loveman, *Chile: The Legacy of Hispanic Capitalism* (New York, 1979), 9–41, 263; C. Paul Roberts, *Statistical Abstract of Latin America*, 12th ed. (Los Angeles, 1969), 48.
3. Armando de Ramón, *Breve Historia de Chile: Desde La Invasion Incaica Hasta Nuestros Dias, 1500–2000* (Buenos Aires, 2001), 63–109; Sergio Villalobos R., *Chile y Su Historia* (Santiago, 2001); Markos Mamalakis, *The Growth and Structure of the Chilean Economy: From Independence to Allende* (New Haven, CT, 1976); Loveman, *Chile*, 116–212.
4. Villalobos, 359–392; Loveman, *Chile*, 213–302.
5. Michael Fleet, *The Rise and Fall of Chilean Christian Democracy* (Princeton, NJ, 1985); Carmelo Furci, *The Chilean Communist Party and the Road to Socialism* (London, 1984); Federico G. Gil, *El Sistema Politico de Chile* (San-

tiago, 1969); Francisco Javier Gonzalez Errazuriz, *El Partido Democrata Cristiano: La Lucha por Definirse* (Valpariso, Chile, 1989); Larissa Adler Lomnitz and Ana Melnick, *La Cultura Politica Chilena y los Partidos de Centro: Una Explicacion Antropologica* (Santiago, 1998); Leopoldo Benavides, "La Formacion de la Izquierda Chilena: Relaciones Entre el Partido Communista y el Partido Socialista, Los Antecedentes Historicos," *FLASCO (Facultad Latinoamericana de Ciencias Sociales) Working Paper 389* (Santiago, 1988); Paul W. Drake, *Socialism and Populism in Chile, 1932–1952* (Urbana, IL, 1978); Julio Faundez, *Marxism and Democracy in Chile: From 1932 to the Fall of Allende* (New Haven, CT, 1988); Tomas Moulian, *La Forja de Ilusiones: El Sistema de Partidos, 1932–1973* (Santiago, 1993); Benny Pollack and Hernan Rosenkranz, *Revolutionary Social Democracy: The Chilean Socialist Party* (New York, 1986); Timothy R. Scully, *Rethinking the Center: Party Politics in Nineteenth- and Twentieth-Century Chile* (Stanford, CA, 1992); Cesar Caviades, *The Politics of Chile: A Sociogeographical Assessment* (Boulder, CO, 1979).

6. Jeffrey F. Taffet, "Alliance for What?: U.S. Development Assistance in Chile during the 1960s" (Ph.D. dissertation, Georgetown University, 2001), 63–76.

7. See Jon V. Kofas, *The Sword of Damocles: U.S. Financial Hegemony in Colombia and Chile, 1950-1970* (Westport, CT, 2002), 131–152 for a fine analysis of Alessandri's fiscal policies and the U.S. response; *Pensamiento Politico de Don Jorge Alessandri* (Santiago, 1970), 57; Alberto Cardemil, *El Camino de la Utopia: Alessandri, Frei, Allende—Pensamiento, Obra* (Santiago, 1997), 22–54.

8. Briefing Paper for use of the Secretary in Testifying on the Hill: "Aid to Chile for Reconstruction Purposes from U.S. Government and Other U.S. Sources," August 8, 1960, Jan–June Credits, Box 5, Lot 63D85, Records Relating to Chile, 1957–1964, RG 59, NA; Rubottom to Dillon, June 29, 1960, $100 Million Earthquake Loan, Box 3, Lot 64D4, Records Relating to Chile, 1957–1964, RG 59; Memorandum of Conversation: Dillon—Mueller—Schneider—Phillips, June 29, 1960, $100 Million Earthquake Loan, Box 3, Lot 64D4, Records Relating to Chile, 1957–1964, RG 59, NA; Statement of Douglas Dillon to House Foreign Affairs Committee, August 23, 1960, Mr. Dillon's Briefing Book, Box 5, Lot 61D288, Office Files of the Deputy Director for Program Planning (Special Assistant for Mutual Security Coordination), John O. Bell, 1957–1961, RG 59, NA; Coerr to Rusk, July 12, 1961, 825.10/1-1961, Central Decimal File (hereafter CDF) 60–63, RG 59, NA; Favell to Richardson, August 3, 1961, Untitled Folder, Box 3, Lot 64D4, Records Relating to Chile, 1957–1964, RG 59, NA.

9. Favell to State, August 11, 1961, 825.00/8-1161, CDF 1960–1963, RG 59, NA; Cole to State, October 24, 1961, 825.00/10-2061, CDF 1960–1963, RG 59, NA.

10. Faundez, 110–115; Favell to State, September 13, 1962, 825.00/9-1362, CDF 1960–1963, RG 59, NA.

11. Richard R. Nelson, T. Paul Schultz, and Robert L. Slighton, *Structural Change in a Developing Economy: Colombia's Problems and Prospects* (Princeton, NJ, 1971), 248–257.

12. Chile: Department of State Guidelines, March 1962, Chile General 5/1/62–5/21/62, Box 391, Ralph Dungan File, NSF, JFKL.

13. Cole quote in Cole to Woodward, January 15, 1962, Ambassadors, Box 4, Lot 64D573, Records Relating to Chile 1957–1964, RG 59, NA; Cole to Belcher, January 5, 1961, Foreign Exchange and Balance of Payments, Box 4, Lot 64D573, Records Relating to Chile 1957–1964, RG 59, NA.

14. *Memoria del Ministerio de Relaciones Exteriores* (Santiago, 1962), 127–131; Memorandum of Conversation: Moscoso, Goodwin, Cole, Alessandri, Sotomayor, Mackenna, Mueller, Escobar, et al., March 5, 1962, 725.11/3-562, CDF 1960–1963, RG 59, NA; Moscoso and Goodwin to Hamilton and Woodward, March 9, 1962, 825.10/3-862, CDF 1960–1963, RG 59, NA.

15. Robichek to Jacobson, March 13, 1962, C/Chile/1760 Stand-by Arrangements 1962–March 1963, Chile Files, International Monetary Fund Archive (hereafter IMFA), Washington, DC; Del Canto to Jacobson, May 1, 1962, C/Chile/810 Visit Del Canto April 1962, Chile Files, IMFA; Trezise to Martin and Moscoso, March 27, 1962, 825.00/3-2762, CDF 1960–1963, RG 59, NA (Memo from Frank A. Southard of the IMF to State attached to Trezise memo).

16. Quote in Martin to Cole, May 1, 1962, Letters to Embassy, Box 4, Lot 64D573, Records Relating to Chile, 1957–1963, RG 59, NA; Cole to Martin, May 9, 1962, Letters from Embassy, Box 4, Lot 64D573, Records Relating to Chile, 1957–1963, RG 59, NA; Martin to Rusk and Cole, May 28, 1962, IMF, Box 4, Lot 64D573IMF, Records Relating to Chile, 1960–1963, RG 59, NA.

17. Quotes in Cole to Martin, July 23, 1962, Letters from Embassy Santiago 1962, Box 4, Lot 64D573, Records Relating to Chile, 1957–1964, RG 59, NA; Belcher to Martin through Goodwin, July 25, 1962, 725.00/6-62, CDF 1960–1963, RG 59, NA; Edwin Martin to Charles Cole, July 20, 1962, 825.00/5-762, CDF 1960–1963, RG 59, NA; Cole to Woodward, January 15, 1962, 825.10/1-162, CDF 1960–1963, RG 59, NA.

18. Quote in Rostow to Dungan, May 25, 1962, Chile-General 5/22/62–5/31/62, Box 391, Ralph Dungan File, NSF, JFKL; Fried to Rostow, May 22, 1962, Chile-General 5/22/62–5/31/62, Box 391, Ralph Dungan File, NSF, JFKL.

19. Quotes in Cole to Richardson, June 22, 1962, Box 4, Lot 64D573, Records Relating to Chile, 1957–1963, RG 59, NA; also see the extensive Review of Chilean Political Situation Two Years before Presidential Election, July 11, 1962, 725.00/7-1162, CDF 1960–1963, RG 59, NA; Chile: Department of State Guidelines, March 1962, Chile General 5/1/62–5/21/62, Box 391, Ralph Dungan File, NSF, JFKL; Jester to State, February 8, 1963, E 2-2 Chile, CFPF 64-66, RG 59, NA; Richardson to Cole, February 11, 1963, Chron Embassy, Box 5, Lot 65D264, Records Relating to Chile 1957–1964, RG 59, NA; Policy Considerations Relating to U.S. Assistance for Chile, AID staff paper, January 9, 1963, Box 5, Lot 65D264, Records Relating to Chile 1957–1964, RG 59, NA.

20. Brian Loveman, *Struggle in the Countryside: Politics and Rural Labor in Chile, 1919–1973* (Bloomington, IN, 1976), 223–240; Robert R. Kaufman, *The Politics of Land Reform in Chile, 1950–1970: Public Policy, Political Institutions, and Social Change* (Cambridge, 1972), 45–76.

21. Memorandum of Conversation: Kennedy, Cole, Martin, Dungan, August 3, 1962, 825.00/8-362, CDF 1960–1963, RG 59, NA; Briefing Paper for Presi-

dent [Kennedy]: Visit of President Alessandri, 725.11/12-1162, CDF 1960–
1963, RG 59, NA; Belcher to U.S. Embassy Santiago, 725.11/12-1462, CDF
1960–1963, RG 59, NA; Memorandum of Conversation: Alessandri, Marti-
nez, Mackenna, Faivovich, Mueller, Molina, Kennedy, Cole, Martin, Moscoso, May, and Dungan, 725.00/12-1162, CDF 1960–1963, RG 59, NA.

22. Quote in Brubeck to Dungan through Bundy, October 19, 1962, Chile-
General 12/62, Box 391, Ralph Dungan File, NSF, JFKL; Frey to Dungan,
December 3, 1962, Chile-General 12/62, Box 391, Ralph Dungan File, NSF,
JFKL. Korican to Frey, October 16, 1962, Chile-General 12/62, Box 391,
Ralph Dungan File, NSF, JFKL; Martin does not deal with this issue in
Kennedy and Latin America, though he does note that President Kennedy
was clearly interested in the 1964 Chilean election as early as January 1963,
320–322.

23. Based on 1963 municipal elections in early April, the Christian Democratic
Party/*Partido Demócrata Cristiano* (PDC) had become the largest party in
Chile, surpassing the Radical Party/*Partido Radical* (PR), but the Radical
coalition with the Liberals and Conservatives was significantly larger than
the PDC. The PDC polled 22 percent of the vote, followed by the PR with
20.8 percent. The other major parties gained the following amounts: Liberal Party (PL), 12.6 percent, Communist Party (PC), 12.4 percent, Socialist
Party (PS), 11.1 percent, and Conservative Party (PCU), 11.0 percent. Ofi-
cina de Informaciones, *Estadisticas Electorales, 1925–1969* (Santiago, 1969),
63; Clift (Stevenson) to State, April 21, 1963, Pol 2-1 Chile, CFPF 63, RG
59, NA; Thompson to Martin, June 14, 1963, Political Reports, Box 7, Lot
65D264, Records Relating to Chile 1957–1963, RG 59, NA; Kardas (Stevenson) to State, February 1, 1963, Pol 2-1 Chile, CFPF 63, RG 59, NA.

24. Faundez, 122–123; Ernst Halperin, *Nationalism and Communism in
Chile* (Cambridge, 1965), 203–205.

25. Agency for International Development, *Economic Assistance Programs
Administered by the Agency for International Development and Predeces-
sor Agencies, April 3, 1948–June 30, 1971* (Washington: Agency for Interna-
tional Development, Office of Statistics and Reports, 1971); "Auyda a Chile,"
PEC, August 16, 1966. On the planning of these programs, see Stevenson to
State, December 12, 1962, Chile General 10/6/62–11/30/62, Box 391, Ralph
Dungan File, NSF, JFKL.

26. Mann to Jova, April 27, 1964, Aid-Aid Chile, CFPF 64-66, RG 59, NA;
Mann to Rusk, May 7, 1964, Pol Chile, CFPF 64-66, RG 59, NA.

27. Cole, however, deliberately returned to the U.S. during the campaign on
leave to show the U.S. disengagement from the campaign. Charles W. Cole
Oral History, April 26, 1969, Interviewer: Dennis O'Brien, JFKL, 38.

28. Quotes in USIS (United States Information Service)-Santiago to USIS-
Washington, November 25, 1964, Aid (Afp) Chile, CFPF 64-66, RG 59, NA;
Ray to State, August 12, 1964, Aid (Afp) Chile, CFPF 64-66, RG 59, NA;
Ray to State, June 25, 1964, Aid (Afp) Chile, CFPF 64-66, RG 59, NA; Cole
to State, August 28, 1964, Aid (U.S.) 8 Grants—Technical Assistance, CFPF
64-66, RG 59, NA.

29. Senate, *Covert Action,* 204–209.

30. Caviades, 224.

31. Tad Szulc, "Johnson Says Chilean Election Augurs a 'Very Bright Future,'"
NYT, September 6, 1964.

32. Caviades, 224, "Election in Chile Bouys the Alliance," *NYT*, September 13, 1964.

33. "Frei Interview with Jules Dubois," in Oscar Pinochet de la Barra, ed., *El Pensamiento de Eduardo Frei* (Santiago, 1982), 155.

34. "Frei Inaugural Speech," reproduced in *Eduardo Frei M. Obras Escogidas*, ed. Oscar Pinochet de la Barra, 299–305 (Santiago, 1993).

35. Ben G. Burnett, *Political Groups in Chile: The Dialogue between Order and Change* (Austin, 1970), 12–13.

36. Frei, "Mi Programa de Gobierno," *Poltica y Espiritu* 18 (June–August 1964): 3–21; Loveman, *Chile*, 279–287; John A. King, "Cooperation or Conflict?: Relations between Chile and the United States during the 1960s (Ph.D. Dissertation, Vanderbilt University, 1998), 145, 168–169; See also report on Sergio Molina speech in *El Mercurio*, November 25, 1964; James R. Whelan, *Out of the Ashes: Life, Death, and Transfiguration of Democracy in Chile 1833–1988* (Washington, 1989), 144–145; Thomas L. Edwards, *Economic Development and Reform in Chile: Progress under Frei, 1964–1970* (East Lansing, MI, 1972), 5–11; Faundez, 137–139; Arturo Aldunate Fontaine, *Todos Querían La Revolución: Chile 1964–1973* (Santiago, 1999), 44–45.

37. See Kofas, 153–173 for discussion of Frei economic policies and the U.S. response; "Auyda a Chile," *PEC*, January 1, 1963.

38. Briefing Memo for Mann, May 15, 1964, Pol Aff & Rel Chile-U.S., Box 2030, CFPF 64-66, RG 59, NA; Memorandum of Conversation, Mann, Solomon, Rogers, Tomic, Molina, Ahumada, Pinera, Favell, Robinson, Dentzer, Lunn, October 12, 1964, Pol 7, Box 2026, CFPF 64-66, RG 59, NA; "Chileans Open Talks with U.S. on Aid for Development Plans," *NYT*, October 13, 1964.

39. Dentzer to Santiago, October 17, 1964, Pol 7, CFPF 64-66, RG 59, NA. Memorandum of Conversation, Mann, Solomon, Tomic, Molina, Valdes, Pinera, Zabala, Dentzer, October 17, 1964, Pol Chile-U.S., Box 2030, CFPF 64-66, RG 59, NA; Memorandum of Conversation, Rusk, Mann, Solomon, Rogers, Tomic, Molina, Ahumada, Valdes, Pinera, Zabala, and Dentzer, October 14, 1964, Pol Chile-U.S., Box 2030, CFPF 64-66, RG 59, NA; Memorandum of Conversation, Mann, Solomon, Tomic, Molina, Valdes, Pinera, Zabala, Dentzer, October 17, 1964, Pol Chile-U.S., Box 2030, CFPF 64-66, RG 59, NA; Rostow to Mann, October 16, 1964, Pol Chile-U.S., Box 2030, CFPF 64-66, RG 59, NA.

40. Dungan to Bell, Vaughn, Rogers, Sternfield, Dentzer, and Robinson, April 21, 1965, E 2-2, CFPF 64-66, RG 59, NA.

41. Vaughn to Mann, April 21, 1965, AID (U.S.) 9, CFPF 64-66, RG 59, NA.

42. Palmer (Vaughn) to Ambassador, November 3, 1965, Aid (U.S.) 9, CFPF 64-66, RG 59, NA; Dungan to Vaughn, November 3, 1965, Aid (U.S.) 9, CFPF 64-66, RG 59, NA; Dungan to Vaughn, November 9, 1965, Aid (U.S.) 9, CFPF 64-66, RG 59, NA.

43. Mann to Bundy, November 10, 1965, Chile Vol. IV Memos 10/65–7/67, Box 13, CF, NSF, LBJL.

44. Bowdler to Bundy, November 10, 1965, Chile Vol. IV Memos 10/65–7/67, Box 13, CF, NSF, LBJL.

45. Quote in Bell to Johnson, November 6, 1965, Chile Vol. IV Memos 10/65–7/67, Box 13, CF, NSF, LBJL; See also, Schultze to Johnson, November 10, 1965, CF Oversize Attachments, [Materials on Copper], 1 of 2, Box 161, WHCF, LBJL.

46. Ackley to Attorney General, November 14, 1965, Chile Copper 11/12/65–11/17/65 Legislative Background Copper Price Increases Nov 1965, Box 1, CF, NSF, LBJL.

47. Dungan to State, October 20, 1965, Inco-Copper Chile, CFPF 64-66, RG 59, NA; Dungan to State, October 25, 1965, Inco-Copper Chile, CFPF 64-66, RG 59, NA.

48. Mann to Johnson, November 13, 1965, Chile Copper—After 11/17/65 Folder II Legislative Background Copper Price Increases Nov 1965, Box 1, CF, NSF, LBJL.

49. Editorial Note [Johnson/Mansfield Telephone Conversation], Doc. 297, *FRUS, 64-68,* Vol. IX.

50. Bundy to Dungan, November 12, 1965, Copper Problems, Box 7, Subject File, NSF, LBJL; an earlier draft of the memo can be found at CF Oversize Attachments [Materials on Copper] 1 of 2, Box 161, WHCF, LBJL.

51. Dungan to Bundy, November 13, 1965, Copper Problems, Box 7, Subject File, NSF, LBJL.

52. Harriman to Johnson, Ball, McNamara, Califano, and Bundy, November 15, 1965, Copper Problems, Box 7, Subject File, NSF, LBJL.

53. Harriman to Johnson, Ball, Mann, McNamara, Califano, November 19, 1965, Trips and Missions: Latin America File, Box 547, W. Averell Harriman Papers, Manuscript Division, Library of Congress (hereafter LC), Washington, DC; Califano to Johnson, November 21, 1965, Folder of Material Sent by Califano, [2 of 2], Box 161, WHCF Oversize Attachments, LBJL. On the $10 million loan, see Palmer to Solomon, March 8, 1966, Copper File, Box 2, Papers of Anthony M. Solomon, LBJL.

54. Harriman to Johnson, November 19, 1965, Trips and Missions: Latin America File, Box 547, W. Averell Harriman Papers, LC.

55. Interview by the author with William Rogers, June 24, 2005, Washington, DC. Walt Rostow, although in general a supporter of IMF-style stabilization programs, criticized U.S. reliance on the IMF and a lack of effective coordination between developmentalist and structural programs. See, Rostow Memo: "Stabilization and Economic Development," February 21, 1963, E1-1 Braz, Box 692, CFPF 64-66, RG 59, NA; These polices, and the IMF view of the world, are clarified in Garritsen de Vries, *The IMF in a Changing World, 1945–1985* (Washington, 1986) and Harold James, *International Monetary Cooperation since Bretton Woods* (New York, 1996).

56. Alter to Wright, Chile-Meeting with the IMF and the U.S. government, October 13, 1965, Chile-General Negotiations 9, WBGA; Reitter to Alter, December 22, 1965, Chile-AID, WBGA; Vera to Managing Director, December 1, 1965, C/Chile/810 Mission-Vera and Staff, November 1965, IMFA.

57. Dungan to State, November 27, 1965, FN 1-1 Chile, CFPF 64-66, RG 59, NA.

58. Dungan to Vaughn, November 30, 1965, FN 1-1 Chile, CFPF 64-66, RG 59, NA; Memorandum of Conversation, Vaughn, Tomic, Bronheim, Sternfield, Morris, Bloomfield, December 10, 1965, Aid (U.S.) 9 Chile, CFPF 64-66, RG 59, NA.

59. Dungan to State, Commerce, Treasury, and Federal Reserve, December 4, 1965, Aid (U.S.) 9 Chile, CFPF 64-66, RG 59, NA.

60. Tomic quotes in Memorandum of Conversation, Vaughn, Tomic, Bronheim,

Sternfield, Morris, Bloomfield, December 10, 1965, Aid (U.S.) 9 Chile, CFPF 64-66, RG 59, NA; Dungan to State, December 9, 1965, Aid (U.S.) 9 Chile, CFPF 64-66, RG 59, NA.

61. Frei quotes in Dungan to State, January 14, 1966, Inco-Copper Chile, CFPF 64-66, RG 59, NA; Dungan to State, January 19, 1966, Aid (U.S.) 9 Chile, CFPF 64-66, RG 59, NA; Palmer to Santiago, January 17, 1966, Inco-Copper Chile, CFPF 64-66, RG 59, NA.

62. "Frei en Rancagua," *La Nacion*, December 22, 1966; Massad to Schweitzer, December 22, 1966, C/Chile/1760, IMFA; Frei speech cited in Dean to State, December 28, 1966, Pol 1 Chile, CFPF 64-66, RG 59, NA.

63. Frei, "The Alliance that Lost Its Way," 427–448. Frei's article provided the inspiration and title for Jerome Levinson and Juan de Onis's *The Alliance That Lost Its Way*.

64. Taffet, 330–334.

65. Gaud to Johnson, November 16, 1966, Chile Vol. IV Memos 10/65–7/67, Box 13, CF, NSF, LBJL.

66. Dungan to State, March 16, 1966, Inco-Copper-Chile, CFPF 67-69, RG 59, NA; State to Santiago, March 12, 1967, Inco-Copper-Chile, CFPF 67-69, RG 59, NA; Dean to State, August 22, 1967, Inco-Copper-Chile, CFPF 67-69, RG 59, NA; Taffet, 334–335.

67. Korry to State, June 19, 1969, FN 12 Chile, CFPF 67-69, RG 59, NA.

68. Korry to State, June 27, 1969, Aid (U.S.) Chile 9, CFPF 67-69, RG 59, NA.

69. Oliver to Korry, July 2, 1968, Aid (U.S.) 9 Chile, CFPF 67-69, RG 59, NA.

70. Korry to State, July 9, 1968, Aid (U.S.) 9 Chile, CFPF 67-69, RG 59, NA; Korry (Moskowitz, Weintraub, Morehead, Johnson, et al.) to State, May 1, 1968, Pol 1 Chile-U.S., CFPF 67-69, RG 59, NA.

71. Quote in Korry (Skogstad, Weintraub) to State, July 13, 1968, Pol 1 Chile-U.S., CFPF 67-69, RG 59, NA.

72. Gaud to Johnson, attached to Palmer to Korry, July 19, 1968, Aid (U.S.) 9 Chile, CFPF 67-69, RG 59, NA.

73. Korry to Johnson, January 15, 1969, Aid (U.S.) Chile, CFPF 67-69, RG 59, NA.

74. Korry to Rostow, January 15, 1969, Aid (U.S.) Chile, CFPF 67-69, RG 59, NA.

75. Korry to Rusk, January 17, 1969, Pol Chile-U.S., CFPF 67-69, RG 59, NA.

Chapter 5

1. The Greenbook.

2. Boris Fausto, *A Concise History of Brazil* (Cambridge, U.K., 1999); Robert M. Levine and John J. Crocitti, eds., *The Brazil Reader: History, Culture, Politics* (Durham, 1999); E. Bradford Burns, *A History of Brazil*, 3rd ed. (New York, 1993); Stuart B. Schwartz, *Sugar Plantations in the Formation of Brazilian Society: Bahia, 1550–1835* (Cambridge, U.K., 1985); Thomas E. Skidmore, *Brazil: Five Centuries of Change* (Oxford, 1999); Robert M Levine, *The History of Brazil* (Westport, CT, 1999); Ronald M. Schneider, *Order and Progress: A Political History of Brazil* (Boulder, 1991); Daryle Williams, *Culture*

Wars in Brazil: The First Vargas Regime, 1930–1945 (Durham, 2001); Colin M. MacLachlan, *A History of Modern Brazil: The Past against the Future* (Wilmington, DE, 2003); Michael L. Conniff, *Urban Politics in Brazil: The Rise of Populism, 1925–1945* (Pittsburgh, 1981); Thomas E. Skidmore, *Politics in Brazil, 1930–1964: An Experiment in Democracy* (New York, 1967); Thomas E. Skidmore, *The Politics of Military Rule in Brazil, 1964–85* (New York, 1988).

3. Skidmore, *Politics*, 163–186; Phyllis R. Parker, *Brazil and the Quiet Intervention, 1964* (Austin, 1979), 14; Robert Jackson Alexander, *Juscelino Kubitschek and the Development of Brazil* (Athens, OH, 1991); "Special National Intelligence Estimate: The Character of the Goulart Regime in Brazil," February 27, 1963, Doc. 234, *FRUS 61–63*, Vol. XII.

4. Leacock, 2; Parker 14; Skidmore, *Politics*, 187–190, 194–197.

5. Jânio Quadros, "Brazil's New Foreign Policy," *Foreign Affairs* 40, no. 1 (1961); Victor Wallis, "Brazil's Experiment with an Independent Foreign Policy," in *Contemporary Inter-American Relations: A Reader in Theory and Issues*, ed. Yale Ferguson, 35–50 (Englewood Cliffs, NJ, 1972); Ralph G. Santos, "Brazilian Foreign Policy and the Dominican Crisis: The Impact of History and Events," *The Americas* 29, no. 1 (1972): 62–67; Weis, 137; The Brazilian government did negotiate trade agreements with the USSR and Eastern European states. See, Rio to State, May 22, 1963, E4 Braz-Czech, Box 3368, CFPF 63, RG 59, NA; Burns, 425–427.

6. Paper by the Operations Coordinating Board: Establishing Relations with New Brazilian Administration, February 1, 1961, Doc. 203, *FRUS 61–63*, Vol. XII; Telegram from the Department of State to the Embassy in Brazil, February 3, 1961, Doc. 204, *FRUS 61–63*, Vol. XII.

7. Rabe, *Most Dangerous Area*, 65.

8. Leacock, 21–22; Santos, 65; Weis, 145–147; Telegram from the Embassy in Brazil to the Department of State, March 3, 1961, Doc. 205, *FRUS 61–63*, Vol. XII, 426–427; Jan Knippers Black, *United States Penetration of Brazil* (Philadelphia, 1977), 39.

9. Weis, 146; Telegram from the Embassy in Brazil to the Department of State, May 31, 1961, Doc. 210, *FRUS 61–63*, Vol. XII, 437–438.

10. Weis, 148.

11. Parker, 6; Burns, 429; Schneider 203–209; Leacock, 53–56; Skidmore, *Politics*, 129–131, 200–208; Bryan McCann, "Carlos Lacerda: The Rise and Fall of a Middle-Class Populist in 1950s Brazil," *Hispanic American Historical Review* 83, no 4. (2003): 661–696.

12. Weis, 148; Telegram from the Embassy in Brazil to the Department of State, April 12, 1961, Doc. 207, *FRUS 61–63*, Vol. XII; Leacock, 34–52; Burns, 431–432; Skidmore, *Politics*, 209–215.

13. Weis, 149; Burns, 432; Quote in Telegram from the Embassy in Brazil to the Department of State, September 8, 1961, Doc. 214, *FRUS 61–63*, Vol. XII.

14. Parker, 7–8; Leacock, 47–48.

15. Telegram from the Embassy in Brazil to the Department of State, October 21, 1961, Doc. 217, *FRUS 61–63*, Vol. XII; Memorandum From Secretary of the Treasury Dillon to President Kennedy, April 3, 1962, Doc. 222, *FRUS 61–63*, Vol. XII; Parker, 14.

16. Weis, 149; Telegram from the Embassy in Brazil to the Department of State, October 21, 1961, Doc. 217, *FRUS 61–63*, Vol. XII.

17. Parker, 12–13, Leacock, 103; Burns, 432.

18. Quote in Letter from the Deputy Assistant Secretary of Defense for International Security Affairs (Williams) to the Assistant Secretary of State for Inter-American Affairs (Woodward), November 7, 1961, Doc. 218, *FRUS 61–63*, Vol. XII; Memorandum of Conversation: Rusk, Campos, et al., February 19, 1962, Doc. 221, *FRUS 61–63*, Vol. XII.

19. Special National Intelligence Estimate: Short-Term Prospects for Brazil under Goulart, December 7, 1961, Doc. 219, *FRUS 61–63*, Vol. XII.

20. Schneider, 220–221; Burns, 437.

21. Rio to State, March 24, 1962, 611.32, Box 1217, CDF 60-63, RG 59, NA. Woodward to State, March 3, 1962, 732.11, Box 1217, CDF 60-63, RG 59, NA. Joyce Carol Townsend, *Bureaucratic Politics in American Decision Making: Impact on Brazil* (Washington, 1982), 98–99; Parker, 16–17; Leacock, 86–89, 93–94.

22. Leacock, 52–53; Schneider, 220; Gordon to Martin, September 2, 1963, Pol U.S.-Braz, Box 3839, CFPF 63, RG 59, NA.

23. The Greenbook; Goodwin quoted in Parker, 12, Goodwin to Bundy, February 7, 1962, Brazil Vol. 2, Box 12 and 13, NSF, JFKL; Memorandum from Secretary of the Treasury Dillon to President Kennedy, April 3, 1962, Doc. 222, *FRUS 61–63*, Vol. XII; Memorandum from the Administrator of the Agency for International Development (Hamilton) to President Kennedy, February 9, 1962, Doc. 220, *FRUS 61–63*, Vol. XII.

24. Parker, 15–19; Memorandum of Conversation: Goulart and Kennedy, April 3, 1962, Doc. 223, *FRUS 61–63*, Vol. XII.

25. Superintendência do Desenvolvimento do Nordeste, *The Brazilian Northeast: SUDENE and Its First Guiding Plan* (Recife, 1962), 4–5; Riordan Roett, *The Politics of Foreign Aid in the Brazilian Northeast* (Nashville, 1972), ix, 7, 11–13.

26. Roett, 31–39; Albert O. Hirshman, *Journeys toward Progress: Studies of Economic Policy-Making in Latin America* (New York, 1973), 66–86; Superintendência do Desenvolvimento do Nordeste, 24.

27. Roett, 69–71, 87–90; National Intelligence Estimate: The Outlook for Brazil, August 8, 1961, Doc. 212, *FRUS 61–63*, Vol. XII; Hirshman, 88; Burns, 438–439.

28. Memorandum of Conversation: Martin and Goulart, April 4, 1962, 611.32, Box 1217, CDF 60-63, RG 59, NA; Parker, 17; Ministerio das Relações Exteriors, *Viagem do Presidente João Goulart aos Estados Unidos da América e ao México* (Rio de Janeiro, 1962).

29. Senate Committee on Foreign Relations, *A Decade of American Foreign Policy: Basic Documents, 1941–49* (Washington, 1950); Parker, 22–23; Memorandum of Discussion with Secretary Rusk, April 10, 1962, Doc. 226, *FRUS 61–63*, Vol. XII; Weis, 154.

30. Quote in Memorandum of Discussion with Secretary Rusk, April 10, 1962, Doc. 226, *FRUS 61–63*, Vol. XII.

31. These kinds of opinions mirrored the ideas of U.S. business leaders in Brazil. One important U.S. businessman suggested that "the United States government should force the economic collapse of Brazil by cutting off all aid to the

Goulart administration and thereby bringing about the downfall of Goulart himself." Leacock, 126; Quotes in Memorandum of Discussion with Secretary Rusk, April 10, 1962, Doc. 226, *FRUS 61–63*, Vol. XII.

32. Quote in Memorandum from the Executive Secretary of the Department of State (Brubeck) to the President's Special Assistant for National Security Affairs (Bundy), November 30, 1962, Doc. 229, *FRUS 61–63*, Vol. XII; Goulart was helpful in the U.S. efforts to deal with Cuba, See C. James Hershberg, "The United States, Brazil, and the Cuban Missile Crisis, 1962 (Part 1) *Journal of Cold War Studies* 6, no. 2 (2004); C. James Hershberg, "The United States, Brazil, and the Cuban Missile Crisis, 1962 (Part 2) *Journal of Cold War Studies* 6, no. 3 (2004); Parker, 28–29.

33. Parker, 30–32; Leacock, 138–139; Rabe, *Most Dangerous Area*, 69.

34. Skidmore, *Politics*, 220–223, 234–243; State to Rio (Moscoso), March 13, 1963, E1–Brazil, Box 3367, CFPF 63, RG 59, NA; Weis, 159; Parker, 33–34; Schneider, 214.

35. Memorandum of Conversation (Pinto and Harriman), October 3, 1963, E1–Braz, Box 3367, RG 59, NA.

36. Quotes from Special National Intelligence Estimate: The Character of the Goulart Regime in Brazil, February 27, 1963, Doc. 234, *FRUS 61–63*, Vol. XII; Rio to State, February 18, 1963, E5-Braz/Three-Year Plan, Box 3368, CFPF 63, RG 59, NA.

37. Parker, 37; Goulart quote in Goulart to JFK, March 8, 1963, Brazil Security, Box 112, Presidential Office Files, JFKL; Leacock, 140.

38. *Time*, "Report on Aid," March 29, 1963; Parker, 35.

39. Special National Intelligence Estimate: The Character of the Goulart Regime in Brazil, February 27, 1963, Doc. 234, *FRUS 61–63*, Vol. XII; Gordon quote in Memorandum from the Ambassador to Brazil to President Kennedy, No Date, Doc. 235, *FRUS 61–63*, Vol. XII.

40. Martin Cover Memo, May 16, 1963, AID (U.S.) Braz, Box 3312, CFPF 63, RG 59, NA; May to Rusk, May 14, 1963, AID (U.S.) Braz, Box 3312, CFPF 63, RG 59, NA.

41. Dantas quote in Memo of Conversation, Dantas, Bell, et al., March 20, 1963, AID (U.S.) 9 Braz, Box 3312, CFPF 63, RG 59, NA; Parker, 39; Leacock, 144–154.

42. Parker, 39–40.

43. May to Rusk, June 11, 1963, AID (U.S.) Braz, Box 3312, CFPF 63, RG 59, NA; Leacock, 79–102, 145–146; Parker, 42; Skidmore, *Politics*, 244–245.

44. State to Rio, September 24, 1963, AID (U.S.) Braz, CFPF 63, RG 59, NA; Dutton to Bayh, October 18, 1963, E1-Braz, Box 3367, CFPF 63, RG 59, NA; Parker, 40–41; Gordon to State, May 1, 1963, FN 1-1, Box 3424, CFPF 63, RG 59, NA.

45. Kennedy to Goulart, May 18, 1963, FN1-1 Braz, Box 3424, CFPF 63, RG 59, NA.

46. Gordon to State, September 11, 1963, Pol Braz-U.S., Box 3839, CFPF 63, RG 59, NA; Weis, 160; Leacock 147; Rio to State, July 17, 1963, AID (U.S.) Braz, Box 3312, CFPF 63, RG 59, NA; Gordon to Bell, July 3, 1963, AID (U.S.) 9 Braz, Box 3312, CFPF 63, RG 59, NA; Rio to State, August 7, 1963, E1-Braz-U.S., Box 3368, CFPF 63, RG 59, NA.

47. Memorandum for the Officer in Charge of Brazilian Affairs (Burton) to the Assistant Secretary of State for Inter-American Affairs (Martin), May 14, 1963, Doc. 238, *FRUS 61–63*, Vol. XII; Martin quote in Martin to Gordon, August 16, 1963, Pol U.S.-Braz, Box 3839, CFPF 63, RG 59, NA

48. Gordon quote in Gordon to Martin, August 21, 1963, Pol U.S.-Braz, Box 3839, CFPF 63, RG 59, NA; Parker, 43; United States Senate, Committee on Foreign Relations, *Nomination of Lincoln Gordon of Massachusetts to Be Assistant Secretary of State for Inter-American Affairs* (Washington, 1966); Gordon to State, September 11, 1963, Pol U.S.-Braz, Box 3839, CFPF63, RG 59, NA; Gordon to State, September 10, 1963, Pol U.S.-Braz, Box 3839, RG 59, NA; Dantas quote in Gordon to Martin, August 21, 1963, Pol U.S.-Braz, Box 3839, CFPF 63, RG 59, NA.

49. Gaud to Staat, August 16, 1968, Brazil Memos Vol. VII-a, Box 12, CF, NSF, LBJL; Rio to State, July 5, 1963, AID (Alliance for Progress) Braz, Box 3312, CFPF 63, RG 59, NA; Weis, 160–161; Parker, 46–47, 93; Recife to State, August 13, 1963, AID (Alliance for Progress) Brazil, Box 3312, CFPF 63, RG 59, NA; Rio to State, July 3, 1963, AID (U.S.) Braz, Box 3312, CFPF 63, RG 59, NA; Gordon to Martin, September 2, 1963, Pol U.S.-Braz, Box 3839, CFPF 63, RG 59, NA; Gordon to Martin, August 21, 1963, Pol U.S.-Braz, Box 3839, CFPF 63, RG 59, NA.

50. Townsend, 101.

51. Amercian Consulate General in Recife to State, March 17, 1964, AID (U.S.) Braz, Box 537, CFPF 64–66, RG 59, NA; Memorandum of Conversation, Alves, Jon de Vos, et al., March 7, 1964, AID (U.S.) Braz, Box 537, CFPF 64–66, RG 59, NA.

52. Salvador to State, September 20, 1963, AID (U.S.) Braz, Box 3312, CFPF 63, RG 59, NA.

53. The United States, in early 1963, had about $5.4 million committed to Pernambucan projects. Brubeck to Bundy and Dungan, February 11, 1963, AID (U.S.) Braz, Box 3312, CFPF 63, RG 59, NA; Sao Paulo to State, June 7, 1963, AID (Alliance for Progress) Braz, CFPF 63, Box 3295, RG 59, NA; Andrew J. Kirkendall, "Paulo Freire and the Politics of the Brazilian Northwest, 1958–1964" *Luso-Brazilian Review* 41, no .1 (2004): 168–189; Roett, 116–126; Second U.S. officals quote in Rio to State, June 4, 1964, AID (U.S.) Braz, Box 3312, CFPF 63, RG 59, NA; Rio to State, April 12, 1963, AID (U.S.) Braz, Box 3312, CFPF 63, RG 59, NA; First U.S. officials quote in Recife to State, February 8, 1963, AID (U.S.) Braz, Box 3312. CFPF 63, RG 59, NA; Arreas quote in Delgado-Arias to State, February 9, 1963, Pol U.S.-Braz, Box 3839, CFPF 63, RG 59, NA; Recife to State, February 2, 1964, E5 Braz, Box 694, CFPF 64–66, RG 59, NA.

54. Telegram from the Department of State to the Embassy in Brazil, August 16, 1963, Doc. 239, *FRUS 61–63*, Vol. XII, 505–507; Gordon to Martin, August 21, 1963, Pol U.S.-Braz, Box 3839, CFPF 63, RG 59, NA; Gaud to Staat, August 16, 1968, Brazil Memos Vol. VII-a, Box 12, CF, NSF, LBJL.

55. Memorandum of Conversation, January 9, 1964, AID (U.S.) Braz, Box 537, CFPF 64–66, RG 59, NA; AID to Bahia, July 23, 1963, AID (Alliance for Progress) Braz, CFPF 63, Box 3294, RG 59, NA; Lomanto quote in Salvador to State, September 20, 1963, AID (U.S.) Braz, Box 3312, CFPF 63, RG 59, NA; Rio to State, June 29, 1963, AID (U.S.) 9 Braz, Box 3312, CFPF 63, RG

59, NA; Alves of Rio Grande do Norte also became similarly critical. Memorandum of Conversation, Alves, Jon de Vos, March 7, 1964, AID (U.S.) Braz, Box 537, CFPF 64–66, RG 59, NA; Parker, 48, 97.

56. Leacock, 191; Black, *Penetration*, 24–25.
57. Santos, 71; Gordon quote in Gordon to Martin, August 29, 1963, Pol U.S.-Braz, Box 3839, CFPF 63, RG 59, NA; Memorandum from the Director of the Office of Brazilian Affairs (Burton) to the Assistant Secretary of State for Inter-American Affairs (Mann), January 8, 1964, Doc. 181, *FRUS 64–68*, Vol. XXXI; Parker, 45–46; Black, *Penetration*, 43.
58. Memorandum from the Ambassador to Brazil to President Kennedy, No Date, Doc. 235, *FRUS 61–63*, Vol. XII; Parker, 27–28; Gordon quote in Gordon to Martin, September 2, 1963, Pol U.S.-Braz, Box 3839, CFPF 63, RG 59, NA.
59. Skidmore, *Politics*, 260–263; Gordon quote in Gordon to Martin, October 18, 1963, AID (U.S.) Braz, CFPF 63, RG 59, NA; Weis, 162.
60. Weis, 164; Parker, 49–50.
61. Parker, 52.
62. Goulart quote in Gordon to Rusk, January 18, 1964, Brazil Vol. 1, Box 9, CF, NSF, LBJL; Parker, 56; Weis, 165–166; Rio to State, February 5, 1964, FN 9 Braz, Box 832, CFPF 64–66, RG 59, NA; Dutton to Javits, February 26, 1964, FN 9 Braz, Box 832, CFPF 64–66, RG 59, NA.
63. Martin to Gordon, December 2, 1963, Pol Braz-U.S., Box 3839, CFPF 63, RG 59, NA.
64. Leacock, 64, 71–73, 149–171; Parker, 56; Skidmore, 284–295.
65. Youssef Cohen, "Democracy from Above: The Political Origins of Military Dictatorship in Brazil," *World Politics* 40, no. 1 (1987): 30–54; Memorandum from Gordon Chase of the National Security Council Staff to the President's Special Assistant for National Security Affairs (Bundy), March 19, 1964, Doc. 185, *FRUS 64–68*, Vol. XXXI; Leacock, 160.
66. Parker, 57–58; Leacock, 191.
67. Leacock, 192.
68. Skidmore, *Politics*, 284–293; Parker, 59–60, 69; Leacock, 172; Black, *Penetration*, 46; Schneider, 106–194; Burns, 440–441.
69. Alan McPherson, *Intimate Ties and Bitter Struggles: The United States and Latin America since 1945* (Washington, 2006), 62.
70. Rusk quote in Summary Record of the 526th Meeting of the National Security Council with the Congressional Leaders, April 3, 1964, Doc. 208, *FRUS 64–68*, Vol. XXXI; Weis, 166–167; Parker, 72–87.
71. Editorial Note, Doc. 196, *FRUS 64–68*, Vol. XXXI.
72. Johnson quote in Summary Record of the 526th Meeting of the National Security Council with the Congressional Leaders, April 3, 1964, Doc. 208, *FRUS 64–68*, Vol. XXXI; Mann to Gordon, April 2, 1964, AID (U.S.) Braz, Box 537, CFPF 64–66, RG 59, NA; Parker, 82; Gaud to Staat, August 16, 1968, Brazil Memos Vol. VII-a, Box 12, CF, NSF, LBJL.
73. Skidmore, 303–309; Gordon to Rusk, June 8, 1964, Brazil Cables Vol. IV 4/64–8/64, Box 10, CF, NSF, LBJL; Weis, 167.
74. Skidmore, 309–313.
75. Weis, 168; Summary Record of the 526th Meeting of the National Security Council with the Congressional Leaders, April 3, 1964, Doc. 208, *FRUS 64–68*, Vol. XXXI; Parker, 92–93; Leacock, 222.

76. Telegram from the Embassy in Brazil to the Department of State, April 20, 1964, Doc. 212, *FRUS 64–68*, Vol. XXXI; Special National Intelligence Estimate: The Political Situation in Brazil, Washington, May 27, 1964, Doc. 213, *FRUS 64–68*, Vol. XXXI; Castelo Branco quote in Telegram from the Embassy in Brazil to the Department of State, June 10, 1964, Doc. 214, *FRUS 64–68*, Vol. XXXI; Rogers to Mein, June 19, 1964, AID (U.S.) Braz, Box 537, CFPF 64–66, RG 59, NA; Solomon to Gordon, June 6, 1964, AID (U.S.) Braz, Box 537, CFPF 64–66, RG 59, NA.

77. Gordon quote in Gordon to Bell, Mann, Rogers, and Solomon, June 8, 1964, Brazil Vol. IV Cables 4/64–8/64, Box 10, CF, NSF, LBJL; Letter from the Ambassador to Brazil (Gordon) to the Assistant Secretary of State for Inter-American Affairs (Mann), August 10, 1964, Doc. 215, *FRUS 64–68*, Vol. XXXI; Black, *Penetration*, 49–50.

78. Memorandum from Robert M. Sayre of the National Security Council Staff to the President's Special Assistant for National Security Affairs (Bundy), September 30, 1964, Doc. 216, *FRUS 64–68*, Vol. XXXI; FN 3; Gordon to Mann, Bell, and Rogers, November 14, 1964, AID (U.S.) Braz, Box 537, CFPF 64–66, RG 59, NA; Bell to State, December 10, 1964, AID (U.S.) Braz, Box 537, CFPF 64–66, RG 59, NA.

79. Santos, 62–77; Gordon quote in Letter from the Ambassador to Brazil (Gordon) to the Assistant Secretary of State for Inter-American Affairs (Mann), August 10, 1964, Doc. 215, *FRUS 64–68*, Vol. XXXI; Leacock, 235–236; Black, *Penetration*, 51.

80. National Intelligence Estimate: Prospects for Brazil, May 12, 1965, Doc. 218, *FRUS 64–68*, Vol. XXXI.

81. Mann quote in Mann to Johnson, December 8, 1965, AID (U.S.) Braz, Box 537, CFPF 64–66, RG 59, NA; Rusk to Johnson, December 3, 1965, AID (U.S.) Braz, Box 537, CFPF 64–66, RG 59, NA; Bundy to Johnson, December 7, 1965, AID (U.S.) Braz, Box 537, CFPF 64–66, RG 59, NA. Fowler to Johnson, December 7, 1965, AID (U.S.) Braz, Box 537, CFPF 64–66, RG 59, NA; Leacock, 230; CIA Report: The Political Situation in Brazil, November 29, 1965, Brazil Memos Vol. VI 12/65–3/67, Box 11, CF, NSF, LBJL; Gordon to Rusk, December 6, 1965, Brazil Memos Vol. VI 12/65–3/67, Box 11, CF, NSF, LBJL.

82. Memorandum from Secretary of State Rusk to President Johnson in Texas, December 3, 1965, Doc. 224, *FRUS 64–68*, Vol. XXXI; Ball to Gordon, December 18, 1965, Brazil Cables Vol. VI 12/65–3/67, Box 11, CF, NSF, LBJL. Harriman to Gordon, December 11, 1965, Brazil Cables Vol. VI 12/65–3/67, Box 11, CF, NSF, LBJL; Gordon to State, December 17, 1965, Brazil Cables Vol. VI 12/65–3/67, Box 11, CF, NSF, LBJL; Price for a Brazilian Contribution in Vietnam, December 30, 1966, Brazil Vol. VI Memos, Box 11, CF, NSF, LBJL; Leacock, 235; Black, *Penetration*, 52; Tuthill to State, December 16, 1966, Brazil Vol. VI Memos, Box 11, CF, NSF, LBJL.

83. State to Rio, December 8, 1966, AID (U.S.) Braz 9, Box 537, CFPF 64–66, RG 59, NA; Rio to State, October 21, 1966, AID (U.S.) Braz 9, Box 537, CFPF 64–66, RG 59, NA; Rio to State, November 11, 1966, AID (U.S.) Braz 8, Box 537, CFPF 64–66, RG 59, NA; Rostow to Johnson, June 29, 1966, Brazil Vol. VI Memos, Box 11, CF, NSF, LBJL; Rostow to Johnson, December 6, 1966, Brazil Vol. VI Memos, Box 11, CF, NSF, LBJL.

84. Memorandum from the President's Special Assistant (Rostow) to President Johnson, December 5, 1967, Doc. 232, *FRUS 64–68*, Vol. XXXI; Action Memorandum from the President's Special Assistant (Rostow) to President Johnson in Texas, February 23, 1968, Doc. 234, *FRUS 64–68*, Vol. XXXI; Information Memorandum from the President's Special Assistant (Rostow) to President Johnson, February 16, 1968, Doc. 233, *FRUS 64–68*, Vol. XXXI; Leacock, 238–239; Burns, 450–451.
85. Gordon to Rusk, August 17, 1966, Pol Braz-U.S., Box 1945, CFPF 64–66, RG 59; Visit of Costa e Silva Background Paper, January 18, 1967, Brazil—Costa e Silva Visit [1 of 2], Box 9, CF, NSF, LBJL.
86. Leacock, 242–244.
87. Tuthill quote in Tuthill to State, June 20, 1967, Brazil Cables Vol. VII, Box 11, CF, NSF, LBJL; Sayre to Tuthill, June 22, 1967, Brazil Cables Vol. VII, Box 11, CF, NSF, LBJL; Gaud to Staat, August 15, 1968, Brazil Memos Vol. VII-a, Box 12, CF, LBJL; Rostow to Johnson, February 23, 1968, Brazil Memos Vol. VII-a, Box 12, CF, NSF, LBJL; Gaud to Johnson, November 30, 1967, Brazil Memos Vol. VII-a, Box 12, CF, NSF, LBJL.
88. Leacock, 249; Burns, 460.
89. United Nations International Commission of Jurists quoted in Black, *Penetration*, 33; Leacock, 249.
90. Leacock, 227.

Chapter 6

1. The Greenbook.
2. Roberts, 48.
3. Howard J. Wiarda, *The Dominican Republic: Nation in Transition* (New York, 1969), 33.
4. Jonathan Hartlyn, *The Struggle for Democratic Politics in the Dominican Republic* (Chapel Hill, 1988), 27–28, 37; Piero Gleijeses, *The Dominican Crisis: The 1965 Constitutionalist Revolt and American Intervention* (Baltimore, 1978), 1–20.
5. Rabe, *Most Dangerous Area*, 35; Hartlyn, 45–52; Gleijeses 23–25; Wiarda, 34–49; Editorial Note, Doc. 308, *FRUS 61–63*, Vol. XII; Ignacio López-Calvo, *God and Trujillo: Literary and Cultural Representations of the Dominican Dictator* (Gainsville, 2005); Jesús de Galíndez, *La Era de Trujillo* (Santo Domingo, 1991).
6. United States Senate, Committee on Foreign Relations, *Background Information Relating to the Dominican Republic* (Washington, 1965), 6; Gleijeses, 25; Stephen G. Rabe, "The Caribbean Triangle: Betancourt, Castro, and Trujillo and U.S. Foreign Policy, 1958–1963," in *Empire and Revolution: The United States and the Third World since 1945*, ed. Peter L. Hahn and Mary Ann Heiss (Columbus, 2001).
7. Rabe, *Most Dangerous Area*, 35; Hartlyn, 71–72; Telegram from the Consulate General in the Dominican Republic to the Department of State, January 4, 1961, Doc. 300, *FRUS 61–63*, Vol. XII; Airgram from the Consulate General in the Dominican Republic to the Department of State, March 22, 1961, Doc. 304, *FRUS 61–63*, Vol. XII.

8. Memorandum from the President's Special Assistant for National Security Affairs (Bundy) to President Kennedy, May 2, 1961, Doc. 306, *FRUS 61–63*, Vol. XII; also quoted in Rabe, *Most Dangerous Area*, 39.

9. Memorandum from the Cuban Task Force of the National Security Council to the President's Special Assistant for National Security Affairs (Bundy), May 15, 1961, Doc. 307, *FRUS 61–63*, Vol. XII; Rabe, *Most Dangerous Area*, 39.

10. Editorial Note, Doc. 308, *FRUS 61–63*, Vol. XII; Hartlyn, 69.

11. Rabe, *Most Dangerous Area*, 40; Special National Intelligence Estimate: The Dominican Situation, July 25, 1961, Doc. 317, *FRUS 61–63*, Vol. XII; Memorandum of Conversation: Balaguer, Ball, McGhee and Hill, October 3, 1961, Doc. 322, *FRUS 61–63*, Vol. XII; Kennedy quote in Schlesinger, *A Thousand Days: John F. Kennedy in the White House* (Boston, 1966), 769.

12. Memorandum from the President's Special Assistant (Goodwin) to President Kennedy, October 3, 1961, Doc. 323, *FRUS 61–63*, Vol. XII.

13. Telegram from the Department of State to the Consulate General in the Dominican Republic, November 18, 1961, Doc. 329, *FRUS 61–63*, Vol. XII; Rabe, *Most Dangerous Area*, 43; Wiarda, 50–53.

14. Quote from Telegram from the White House to the Department of State, December 16, 1961, Doc. 332, *FRUS 61–63*, Vol. XII; Editorial Note, Doc. 336, *FRUS 61–63*, Vol. XII.

15. Senate, *Background Information*, 10; Telegram from the Embassy in the Dominican Republic to the Department of State, March 4, 1962, Doc. 339, *FRUS 61–63*, Vol. XII; Memorandum of Conversation: Rusk, E. Martin, et al., April 2, 1962, Doc. 340, *FRUS 61–63*, Vol. XII; John B. Martin, *Overtaken by Events: The Dominican Crisis from the Fall of Trujillo to the Civil War* (New York, 1966), 8, 97.

16. Editorial Note, Doc. 345, *FRUS 61–63*, Vol. XII.

17. Richard Lee Turits, *Foundations of Despotism: Peasants, the Trujillo Regime, and Modernity in Dominican History* (Stanford, 2003); Michael R. Hall, *Sugar and Power in the Dominican Republic: Eisenhower, Kennedy, and the Trujillos* (Westport, CT, 2000).

18. Editorial Note, Doc. 345, *FRUS 61–63*, Vol. XII; "President to Seek End of Price Premiums on All Sugar Imports," *NYT*, January 20, 1962; "U.S. Producers Ask Bigger Sugar Quota," *NYT*, January 27, 1962; "Kennedy Proposals for Sugar Outlined," *NYT*, February 18, 1962; "New Sugar Plan Meets Opposition," *NYT*, March 13, 1962; "Sugar Legislation Battle," *NYT*, March 17, 1962; "Basic Shift Urged for Sugar Quotas," *NYT*, March 25, 1962; "Uncle Sam, Sugar Daddy," *NYT*, April 25, 1962; "Sugar Bill Voted by Unit of House," *NYT*, June 16, 1962; "Plea in U.S. Senate Set by Dominicans," *NYT*, June 21, 1962; "Dominican Crisis Tests U.S. Plans," *NYT*, June 26, 1962; "Dominicans Fear Crisis Over Sugar," *NYT*, July 2, 1962; "White House Drafts a Plan to Diversify Dominicans' Crops," *NYT*, July 5, 1962; "Dominicans Told of U.S. Aid Plans," *NYT*, July 6, 1962; "U.S. Struggles to Ease Its Problem over Sugar," *NYT*, July 8, 1962; "House Unit Backs Dominican Sugar," *NYT*, July 13, 1962; "Dominicans Glum Over Sugar Quota," *NYT*, August 26, 1962.

19. Telegram From the Embassy in the Dominican Republic to the Department of State, June 20, 1962, Doc. 346, *FRUS 61–63*, Vol. XII; J. Martin, 163–164.

20. Ibid., 168–173; *Agreement between the United States and the Dominican Republic Signed at Washington*, August 13, 1963 (Washington, 1963).
21. Telegram from the Embassy in the Dominican Republic to the Department of State, October 15, 1962, Doc. 348, *FRUS 61–63*, Vol. XII; Telegram from the Department of State to the Embassy in the Dominican Republic, October 17, 1962, Doc. 349, *FRUS 61–63*, Vol. XII; Airgram From the Embassy in the Dominican Republic to the Department of State, December 9, 1962, Doc. 351, *FRUS 61–63*, Vol. XII; Senate, *Background Information*, 11.
22. Quote from Memorandum of Conversation: Kennedy, Bosch, Dungan, E. Martin, et al., January 10, 1963, Doc. 353, *FRUS 61–63*, Vol. XII; Telegram from the Department of State to the Embassy in the Dominican Republic, January 19, 1963, Doc. 355, *FRUS 61–63*, Vol. XII; Rabe, *Most Dangerous Area*, 45; Wiarda, 59.
23. Memorandum from the President's Special Assistant (Dungan) to President Kennedy, January 10, 1963, Doc. 352, *FRUS 61–63*, Vol. XII.
24. Airgram from the Embassy in the Dominican Republic to the Department of State, January 13, 1963, Doc. 354, *FRUS 61–63*, Vol. XII.
25. Quote from Airgram from the Embassy in the Dominican Republic to the Department of State, January 13, 1963, Doc. 354, *FRUS 61–63*, Vol. XII; Rabe, *Most Dangerous Area*, 46; J. Martin 343–371.
26. Senate, *Background Information*, 12.
27. Airgram from the Embassy in the Dominican Republic to the Department of State, January 13, 1963, Doc. 354, *FRUS 61–63*, Vol. XII.
28. Gleijeses, 286.
29. Senate, *Background Information*, 13.
30. Telegram from the Department of State to the Embassy in the Dominican Republic, Doc. 361, October 17, 1963, *FRUS 61–63*, Vol. XII.
31. Telegram from the Department of State to the Embassy in the Dominican Republic, Doc. 359, October 4, 1963, *FRUS 61–63*, Vol. XII; Telegram From the Department of State to the Embassy in the Dominican Republic, Doc. 361, October 17, 1963, *FRUS 61–63*, Vol. XII.
32. Telegram from the Embassy in the Dominican Republic to the Department of State, May 21, 1964, Doc. 5, *FRUS 64–68*, Vol. XXXII.
33. Ibid.
34. Bennett to State, June 9, 1964, AID (U.S.) 8 Dom Rep 1/1/64, Box 547, CFPF 64-66, RG 59, NA.
35. Telegram from the Embassy in the Dominican Republic to the Department of State, June 5, 1964, Doc. 6, *FRUS 64–68*, Vol. XXXII; Telegram from the Department of State to the Embassy in the Dominican Republic, June 6, 1964, Doc. 7, *FRUS 64–68*, Vol. XXXII.
36. Telegram from the Embassy in the Dominican Republic to the Department of State, August 29, 1964, Doc. 14, *FRUS 64–68*, Vol. XXXII; Telegram from the Department of State to the Embassy in the Dominican Republic, July 23, 1964, Doc. 10, *FRUS 64–68*, Vol. XXXII.
37. Improvement of Dominican Agricultural Production, Memo of Conversation, October 16, 1965, AID (U.S.) 8 Dom Rep 1/1/64, Box 547, CFPF 64-66, RG 59, NA; Santo Domingo to State, April 25, 1965, AID (U.S.) 8 Dom Rep 1/1/64, Box 547, CFPF 64-66, RG 59, NA; State to Santo Domingo, January 23, 1965, AID (U.S.) 8 Dom Rep 1/1/64, Box 547, CFPF 64-66, RG 59, NA;

Santo Domingo to State, December 17, 1964, AID (U.S.) Braz, Box 537, CFPF 64–66, RG 59, NA; Memorandum from Robert M. Sayre of the National Security Council Staff to the President's Special Assistant (Dungan), October 15, 1964, Doc. 16, *FRUS 64–68*, Vol. XXXII; Airgram from the Embassy in the Dominican Republic to the Department of State, December 5, 1964, Doc. 17, *FRUS 64–68*, Vol. XXXII.

38. Letter from the Assistant Secretary of State for Inter-American Affairs (Mann) to the Ambassador to the Dominican Republic (Bennett), February 25, 1965, Doc. 19, *FRUS 64–68*, Vol. XXXII; Letter from the Ambassador to the Dominican Republic (Bennett) to the Assistant Secretary of State for Inter- American Affairs (Mann), February 2, 1965, Doc. 18, *FRUS 64–68*, Vol. XXXII.

39. Gleijeses, 135–217; Bruce Palmer, *Intervention in the Caribbean: The Dominican Crisis of 1965* (Lexington, KY, 1989), 18–29; Hartlyn, 89; Russell Crandall, *Gunboat Democracy: US interventions in the Dominican Republic, Grenada, and Panama* (Lanham, MD, 2006); Eric Thomas Chester, *Rag-Tags, Scum, Riff-Raff, and Commies: The US Intervention in the Dominican Republic, 1965–1966* (New York, 2001).

40. Telephone Conversation between the Undersecretary of State for Economic Affairs (Mann) and President Johnson, April 27, 1965, Doc. 23, *FRUS 64–68*, Vol. XXXII.

41. Telephone Conversation between Director of Central Intelligence Raborn and President Johnson, April 29, 1965, Doc. 39, *FRUS 64–68*, Vol. XXXII.

42. Senate, *Background Information*, 15–18; Telegram from the Embassy in the Dominican Republic to the Director of the National Security Agency (Carter), April 28, 1965, Doc. 29, *FRUS 64–68*, Vol. XXXII; Memorandum of Telephone Conversation (Mann, Johnson, Rusk, Bundy), April 28, 1965, Doc. 31, *FRUS 64–68*, Vol. XXXII; Telegram from the Embassy in the Dominican Republic to the Director of the National Security Agency (Carter), April 28, 1965, Doc. 32, *FRUS 64–68*, Vol. XXXII.

43. Transcript of Teleconference between the Department of State and the Embassy in the Dominican Republic, April 29, 1965, Doc. 41, *FRUS 64–68*, Vol. XXXII; Palmer, 5–6; Alan McPherson, "Misled by Himself: What the Johnson Tapes Reveal About the Dominican Intervention of 1965," *Latin American Research Review* 38, no. 2 (2003): 127–146.

44. Senate, *Background Information*, 19–20.

45. Senate, *Background Information*, 32; Santos, 62–77; Gleijeses, 262; National Intelligence Estimate: Prospects for Stability in the Dominican Republic, April 28, 1966, Doc. 171, *FRUS 64–68*, Vol. XXXIII.

46. Santo Domingo to State, May 13, 1965, AID (U.S.) Dom Rep 1/1/64, Box 546, CFPF 64-66, RG 59, NA.

47. Solomon to State, May 24, 1965, AID (U.S.) Dom Rep 1/1/64, Box 546, CFPF 64-66, RG 59, NA; Memorandum for the President: Dominican Situation, June 27, 1966, Dominican Republic Vol. XVI Memos and Misc. [2 of 2], Box 47, CF, NSF, LBJL.

48. Bennett to State, June 25, 1965, AID (U.S.) Dom Rep 1/1/64, Box 547, CFPF 64-66, RG 59, NA; Santo Domingo to State, August 10, 1965, AID (U.S.) Dom Rep 1/1/64, Box 547, CFPF 64-66, RG 59, NA; Bunker to State, June 30, 1965, AID (U.S.) 8 Dom Rep 1/1/64, Box 547, CFPF 64-66, RG 59,

NA; Santiago to State, June 30, 1965, AID (U.S.) 8 Dom Rep 1/1/64, Box 547, CFPF 64-66, RG 59, NA; Santo Domingo to State, May 29, 1965, AID (U.S.) Dom Rep 1/1/64, Box 546, CFPF 64-66, RG 59, NA; Long to King, June 2, 1965, AID (U.S.) Dom Rep 1/1/64, Box 546, CFPF 64-66, RG 59, NA; Bennett to State, July 9, 1965, AID (U.S.) Dom Rep 1/1/64, Box 547, CFPF 64-66, RG 59, NA.

49. Santiago to State, June 16, 1965, AID (U.S.) Dom Rep 1/1/64, Box 547, CFPF 64-66, RG 59, NA; Bennett to Yarmolinsky, June 1, 1965, AID (U.S.) Dom Rep 1/1/64, Box 546, CFPF 64-66, RG 59, NA; Kranz to Yarmolinsky, June 1, 1965, AID (U.S.) Dom Rep 1/1/64, Box 546, CFPF 64-66, RG 59, NA; Bunker to State, June 28, 1965, AID (U.S.) Dom Rep 1/1/64, Box 547, CFPF 64-66, RG 59, NA.

50. Memorandum for the Record (Meeting with Johnson, Mann, Sayre, Bundy, and Chase), June 14, 1965, Doc, 10, *FRUS 64–68*, Vol. XXXII.

51. Santo Domingo to State, June 28, 1965, AID (U.S.) Dom Rep 1/1/64, Box 547, CFPF 64-66, RG 59, NA.

52. Bunker to Bundy, August 4, 1965, AID (U.S.) Dom Rep 1/1/64, Box 546, CFPF 64-66, RG 59, NA; State to Bennett, Bunker, and Firfer, June 28, 1965, AID (U.S.) Dom Rep 1/1/64, Box 547, CFPF 64-66, RG 59, NA; State to Bunker, July 30, 1965, AID (U.S.) Dom Rep 1/1/64, Box 547, CFPF 64-66, RG 59, NA.

53. State to Santo Domingo, September 17, 1965, AID (U.S.) 8 Dom Rep 1/1/64, Box 547, CFPF 64-66, RG 59, NA; Bennett to State, November 17, 1965, AID (U.S.) 8 Dom Rep 1/1/64, Box 547, CFPF 64-66, RG 59, NA; Bennett to State, September 11, 1965, AID (U.S.) 8 Dom Rep 1/1/64, Box 547, CFPF 64-66, RG 59, NA;

54. *Public Papers, Johnson, 1965,* 483–484.

55. State to Bunker, November 16, 1965, AID (U.S.) Dom Rep 1/1/64, Box 547, CFPF 64-66, RG 59, NA; Bunker to Vaughn, November 18, 1965, AID (U.S.) 8 Dom Rep 1/1/64, Box 547, CFPF 64-66, RG 59, NA; Bunker to Vaughn, November 16, 1965, AID (U.S.) 8 Dom Rep 1/1/64, Box 547, CFPF 64-66, RG 59, NA.

56. State Department quote in Bunker to State, November 26, 1965, AID (U.S.) 8 Dom Rep 1/1/64, Box 547, CFPF 64-66, RG 59, NA; Bunker to State, November 20, 1965, AID (U.S.) 8 Dom Rep 1/1/64, Box 547, CFPF 64-66, RG 59, NA.

57. Quote in Memorandum Prepared for the 303 Committee: Presidential Election in the Dominican Republic, December 30, 1965, Doc. 152, *FRUS 64–68*, Vol. XXXII; Memorandum from the Deputy Director for Coordination of the Bureau of Intelligence and Research (Koren) to the Assistant Secretary of State for Inter-American Affairs (Vaughn), January 6, 1966, Doc. 155, *FRUS 64–68*, Vol. XXXII; Memorandum Prepared for the 303 Committee: Contingency Plans in the Dominican Republic, January 11, 1966, Doc. 157, *FRUS 64–68*, Vol. XXXII; Editorial Note, Doc. 150, *FRUS 64–68*, Vol. XXXII; Crimmins to Johnson, June 28, 1966, Dominican Republic Vol. XV Cables, Box 46, CF, NSF, LBJL; Memorandum Prepared for the 303 Committee, April 30, 1966, Doc. 172, *FRUS 64–68*, Vol. XXXII; Memorandum from the Acting Deputy Director for Coordination of the Bureau of Intelligence and Research, Department of State (McAfee) to the Assistant Sec-

retary of State for Inter-American Affairs (Gordon), May 9, 1966, Doc. 173, *FRUS 64–68*, Vol. XXXII.

58. Memorandum for the Record: Meeting between U. Johnson, Bunker, Gordon, Koren, Sayre, et al., March 12, 1966, Doc. 163, *FRUS 64–68*, Vol. XXXII.

59. Ibid.; Memorandum of Telephone Conversation (Bunker and Stewart), March 17, 1966, Doc. 164, *FRUS 64–68*, Vol. XXXII; Paper Prepared by the Undersecretary of State (Mann), April 26, 1966, Doc. 170, *FRUS 64–68*, Vol. XXXII.

60. Bosch quote in Memorandum of Conversation: Bosch, Crimmins, et al., April 19, 1966, Dominican Republic Vol. XV Memos and Misc., Box 46, CF, NSF, LBJL.

61. Paper Prepared by the Undersecretary of State (Mann), April 26, 1966, Doc. 170, *FRUS 64–68*, Vol. XXXII.

62. Santo Domingo to State, March 5, 1966, AID (U.S.) 9 Dom Rep 1/1/64, Box 547, CFPF 64-66, RG 59, NA; State to Santo Domingo, March 11, 1966, AID (U.S.) 9 Dom Rep 1/1/64, Box 547, CFPF 64-66, RG 59, NA; Santo Domingo to State, March 2, 1966, AID (U.S.) 9 Dom Rep 1/1/64, Box 547, CFPF 64-66, RG 59, NA; Memorandum from the Assistant Secretary of State for Economic Affairs (Solomon) to President Johnson, June 17, 1966, Doc. 179, *FRUS 64–68*, Vol. XXXII; Richard A. Haggerty, *Dominican Republic and Haiti: Country Studies* (Washington, 1991), 33; Rafael Grullón, *PLD y PRD: Entre La Noche y El Amanecer* (Santo Domingo, 1999), 104–106; Jan Knippers Black, *The Dominican Republic: Politics and Development in an Unsovereign State* (Boston, 1986), 39–42.

63. Rusk to Johnson, May 30, 1966, Dominican Republic Vol. XV Memos and Misc., Box 46, CF, NSF, LBJL.

64. State to Santo Domingo, June 25, 1966, AID (U.S.) 9 Dom Rep 1/1/64, Box 547, CFPF 64-66, RG 59, NA; State to Santo Domingo, June 29, 1966, AID (U.S.) 9 Dom Rep 1/1/64, Box 547, CFPF 64-66, RG 59, NA; Memorandum from the Assistant Secretary of State for Economic Affairs (Solomon) to President Johnson, June 17, 1966, Doc. 179, *FRUS 64–68*, Vol. XXXII; Crimmins to Johnson, June 28, 1966, Dominican Republic Vol. XV Cables, Box 46, CF, NSF, LBJL; State to Santo Domingo, July 15, 1966, AID (U.S.) 9 Dom Rep 1/1/64, Box 547, CFPF 64-66, RG 59, NA.

65. Crimmins to State, September 9, 1966, AID (U.S.) 8 Dom Rep 1/1/64, Box 547, CFPF 64-66, RG 59, NA; Santo Domingo to State, August 11, 1966, AID (U.S.) 8 Dom Rep 1/1/64, Box 547, CFPF 64-66, RG 59, NA; Santo Domingo to State; March 15, 1966, AID (U.S.) 8 Dom Rep 1/1/64, Box 547, CFPF 64-66, RG 59, NA; CIA Special Report: Problems Facing Balaguer's Dominican Government, August 5, 1966, Dominican Republic Vol. XVI Memos and Misc [1 of 2], Box 47, CF, NSF, LBJL.

66. Crimmins to State, November 11, 1967, AID (U.S.) 9 Dom Rep 1/1/67, CFPF 67–69, RG 59, NA.

67. State to Santo Domingo, Feb 25, 1967, AID (U.S.) 9 Dom Rep 1/1/67, Box 469, CFPF 67–69, RG 59, NA; Memorandum for the President: Present Situation in the Dominican Republic, September 9, 1966, Dominican Republic Vol. XVI Memos and Misc. [2 of 2], Box 47, CF, NSF, LBJL.

68. Rostow to Johnson, May 4, 1967, Dominican Republic Vol. XVII Memos and Misc. [1 of 2] 9/66–7/67, Box 47, CF, NSF, LBJL; Quotes in Schultze to Johnson, April 24, 1967, Dominican Republic Vol. XVII Memos and Misc. [1 of 2] 9/66–7/67, Box 47, CF, NSF, LBJL.
69. Crimmins to State, May 19, 1967, Dominican Republic Vol. XVII Memos and Misc. [1 of 2] 9/66–7/67, Box 47, CF, NSF, LBJL; Memorandum for the President: Special Sugar Quota for the Dominican Republic, May 11, 1967, Dominican Republic Vol. XVII Memos and Misc. [1 of 2] 9/66–7/67, Box 47, CF, NSF, LBJL; Rusk to Johnson, May 8, 1967, Dominican Republic Vol. XVII Memos and Misc. [1 of 2] 9/66–7/67, Box 47, CF, NSF, LBJL; Bundy to Rostow, July 16, 1967, Dominican Republic Vol. XVII Memos and Misc. [1 of 2] 9/66–7/67, Box 47, CF, NSF, LBJL; Memorandum for the President: Dominican Republic, May 19, 1967, Dominican Republic Vol. XVII Memos and Misc. [1 of 2] 9/66–7/67, Box 47, CF, NSF, LBJL.
70. Memorandum for the President: Need for Continuing Supporting Assistance in the Dominican Republic, June 16, 1966, Dominican Republic Vol. XVI Memos and Misc. [1 of 2], Box 47, CF, NSF, LBJL.
71. Memorandum for Walt W. Rostow: Reply to Cable from President Balaguer to President Johnson, April 5, 1968, AID (U.S.) 9 Dom Rep 1/1/68, Box 469, CFPF 67–69, RG 59, NA; Crimmins to State, January 11, 1968, AID (U.S.) 8 Dom Rep 1/1/67, Box 469, CFPF 67–69, RG 59, NA; Rostow to Johnson, April 28, 1968, Dominican Republic Vol. XVIII Cables 8/67–12/68 [2 of 2], Box 48, CF, NSF, LBJL; Rostow to Johnson, April 2, 1968, Dominican Republic Vol. XVIII Cables 8/67–12/68 [2 of 2], Box 48, CF, NSF, LBJL; Memorandum for the President: PL-480 and Supporting Assistance Program for the Dominican Republic, December 24, 1967, Dominican Republic Vol. XVIII Cables 8/67–12/68 [2 of 2], Box 48, CF, NSF, LBJL; Memorandum for the President: PL-480 and Supporting Assistance Program for the Dominican Republic, December 30, 1967, Dominican Republic Vol. XVIII Cables 8/67–12/68 [2 of 2], Box 48, CF, NSF, LBJL; Gaud to Johnson, December 26, 1967, Dominican Republic Vol. XVIII Memos and Misc. 8/67–12/68, Box 48, CF, NSF, LBJL; Memorandum for the President: PL-480 Program for the Dominican Republic, December 27, 1968, Dominican Republic Vol. XVIII Memos and Misc. 8/67–12/68, Box 48, CF, NSF, LBJL.
72. Rostow to Johnson, January 16, 1968, Dominican Republic Vol. XVIII Memos and Misc. 8/67–12/68, Box 48, CF, NSF, LBJL; Memorandum for the President: PL-480 Program for the Dominican Republic, December 27, 1968, Dominican Republic Vol. XVIII Memos and Misc. 8/67–12/68, Box 48, CF, NSF, LBJL.
73. Rostow quote in Memorandum for the President: PL-480 Program for the Dominican Republic, December 31, 1968, Dominican Republic Vol. XVIII Memos and Misc. 8/67–12/68, Box 48, CF, NSF, LBJL; Crimmins to State, January 23, 1969, AID (U.S.) 9 Dom Rep 1/1/68, Box 469, CFPF 67–69, RG 59, NA.
74. Memorandum for the President: PL-480 Program for the Dominican Republic, December 31, 1968, Dominican Republic Vol. XVIII Memos and Misc. 8/67–12/68, Box 48, CF, NSF, LBJL.

Chapter 7

1. The Greenbook.
2. United States Senate, Committee on Foreign Relations, *Survey of the Alliance for Progress: Colombia, A Case History of U.S. Aid* (Washington, 1969), 12.
3. James E. Sanders, *Contentious Republicans: Popular Politics, Race, and Class in Nineteenth Century Colombia* (Durham, 2004); Geoffrey L. Simons, *Colombia: A Brutal History* (London, 2004); David Bushnell, *The Making of Modern Colombia: A Nation in Spite of Itself* (Berkeley, 1993).
4. Alvaro Ponce Muriel, *De Clérigos y Generales: Crónicas Sobre la Guerra de los Mil Dias* (Bogotá, 2000); Alberto Abello, *El Laberinto de la Guerra: Intriga Internacional Contra Colombia* (Bucaramanga, Colombia, 2004); Helen Delpar, *Red against Blue: The Liberal Party in Colombian Politics, 1863–1899* (University, AL, 1981).
5. James D. Henderson writes, "Colombia's *Violencia* was eminently political, the fruit of a hundred-year struggle that pitted the nation's Conservative and Liberal parties in unending contention for dominance in national affairs. Through a process whose dynamics are still not completely understood, these parties came to enlist all Colombians, prominent and humble alike, in their ranks. So thoroughly were citizens polarized and set against one another that some people have referred to the monolithic corporations as systems of 'hereditary hatreds.' These hatreds, fanned to white heat by events of the 1940s, touched off *Violencia* . . ." *When Colombia Bled: A History of the Violencia in Tolima* (University, AL, 1985), 2.
6. María Angela Lasso Vega, *Gustavo Rojas Pinilla* (Bogotá, 2005).
7. Harvey F. Kline, *Colombia: Democracy under Assault* (Boulder, 1995), 30–53; Marcos Palacios and Frank Safford, *Colombia: País Fragmentado, Sociedad Dividida—Su Historia* (Bogotá, 2002); Robert H. Dix, *Colombia: The Political Dimensions of Change* (New Haven, 1967), 77–128.
8. Christopher Abel and Marco Palacios, "Colombia since 1958," in *The Cambridge History of Latin America*, Vol. 8, *Latin America since 1930: Spanish South America*, ed. Leslie Bethell, 637 (Cambridge, U.K., 1991); Stephen J. Randall, *Colombia and the United States: Hegemony and Interdependence* (Athens, GA, 1992), 232; Henderson, 233.
9. Perloff, 213; Senate, *Colombia*, 19.
10. Abel and Palacios, 641; Inter-American Development Bank, *Social Progress Trust Fund Annual Report 1964* (Washington, 1965), 18–19, 232–252.
11. Bruce Michael Bagley, "Colombia: National Front and Economic Development" in *Politics, Policies, and Economic Development in Latin America*, ed. Robert Wesson, 124–160 (Stanford, 1984); "22 Millones Para Acción Comunal," *El Tiempo*, July 6, 1965; Henderson, 231–232.
12. Abel and Palacios, 641; Mejia quoted in Senate, *Colombia*, 10.
13. Memorandum of Conversation, Alberto Lleras Camargo and Fulton Freeman, July 23, 1962, 611.21/2-162, Box 1211, Decimal Files 1960–1963, RG 59, NA.
14. Steven Schwartzberg, "Rómulo Betancourt: From a Communist Anti-Imperialist to a Social Democrat with U.S. Support," *Journal of Latin American Studies* 29, no. 3 (1997): 613–665.

15. Bowdler Circular, May 6, 1961, Ambassador Stevenson's Trip to Latin America 6/61, 5/1/61–6/9/61, Box 250, Trips and Conferences, NSF, JFKL.
16. Record of Actions at the 483rd Meeting of the National Security Council, May 5, 1961, Doc. 205, *FRUS 61–63*, Vol. X; Circular Telegram from the Department of State to All Posts in the American Republics, June 24, 1961 Doc. 114, *FRUS 61–63*, Vol. XII.
17. Victor Edward Wallis, "Brazil's Experiment with an Independent Foreign Policy," in *Contemporary Inter-American Relations: A Reader in Theory and Issues*, ed. Yale Ferguson, 35–50 (Englewood Cliffs, 1972); Randall, 232; Rabe, *Most Dangerous Area*, 51, 60.
18. Senate, *Colombia*, 11.
19. U.S. Embassy Bogotá to State: Thoughts and Suggestions Regarding U.S. Economic Policy and Strategy for Colombia 1963–1965, September 4, 1963, E-Economic Affairs (Gen) Col 2/1/63, Box 3373, CFPF 63, RG 59, NA.
20. Ibid.
21. Carlos F. Díaz-Alejandro, *Foreign Trade Regimes and Economic Development: Colombia* (New York, 1976), 23–25.
22. Dix, 159–160.
23. Abel and Palacios, 642.
24. Memorandum of Conversation, June 26, 1962, Johnson (Deputy Undersecretary of State), Martin, Moscoso, Valencia, Sanz de Santamaria, et al. 611.12/2-162, Decimal Files 1960–1963, RG 59, NA.
25. Ibid.; Memorandum of Conversation, Valencia and Bowles, September 12, 1962, 611.12/2-162, Decimal Files 1960–1963, RG 59, NA.
26. Díaz-Alejandro, 22; Dragoslav Avramovic, *Economic Growth of Colombia: Problems and Prospects, Report of a Mission Sent to Colombia in 1970 by the World Bank* (Baltimore, 1972), 265. The prices quoted on the open market are New York prices for Manizales coffee; Carlos Sanz de Santamaria to Alberto Lleras Camargo, March 8, 1962, FN-Finance Col, Box 3428, CFPF 63, RG 59, NA; Senate, *Colombia*, 9; for the larger picture of the role of coffee in Colombia, see Marcos Palacios, *El Café en Colombia, 1850–1970: Una Historia Económica, Social, y Politica* (Bogotá, 1979).
27. Kofas, 37-51.
28. The Greenbook; Díaz-Alejandro, 24.
29. Carlos Sanz de Santamaria to Alberto Lleras Camargo, March 8, 1962, FN-Finance Col, Box 3428, CFPF 63, RG 59, NA.
30. Senate, *Colombia*, 6.
31. Inter-American Development Bank, *Social Progress Trust Fund Annual Report 1965* (Washington, 1966), 239.
32. Freeman to State, August 22, 1963, AID (U.S.) 9 Loans 2/1/63, Box 3316, CFPF, 1963, RG 59, NA; Memorandum of Conversation, Walter Robichek-IMF, Eaton, and Bushnell, January 30, 1963, FN 15 Col, Box 3429, RG 59, NA; Senate, *Colombia*, 15.
33. Díaz-Alejandro, 190.
34. Abel and Valencia,. 642; Senate, *Colombia*, 16; Díaz-Alejandro, 23–25; Randall 234.
35. Freeman to Moscoso, February 20, 1963, AID (U.S.) 9 Loans 2/1/63, Box 3316, CFPF, 1963, RG 59, NA; Freeman to State, March 1, 1963, AID (U.S.) 9 Loans 2/1/63, Box 3316, CFPF, 1963, RG 59, NA; Díaz-Alejandro quote on page 25.

36. U.S. Embassy Bogotá to State, May 9, 1963, FN 12 Col, Box 3429, CFPF 63, RG 59, NA.

37. Dearborn to State, June 20, 1963, AID (U.S.) 9 Loans 2/1/63, Box 3316, CFPF, 1963, RG 59, NA; Dearborn to State, July 13, 1963, AID (U.S.) 9 Loans 2/1/63, Box 3316, CFPF, 1963, RG 59, NA; Senate, *Colombia*, 18.

38. McDaniels to State, December 20, 1963, FN 15 Col, Box 3429, CFPF 63, RG 59, NA.

39. Freeman to Mann, February 2, 1964, AID (U.S.) 9 Col, Box 545, CFPF 64-66, RG 59, NA.

40. Dix, 160.

41. Henderson quote on page 231; Ohmans to State, April 19, 1963, Pol 25 2/1/63, Box 3871, CFPF, 1963, RG 59, NA; "Colombia Opens Drive on Outlaw," *NYT*, May 31, 1964; Abel and Palacios, 644; Dix, 160; "El Senado Debate Sobre el General Ruiz Novoa," *El Tiempo*, December 16, 1964; "Las Fuerzas Armadas y La Politica," *El Tiempo*, December 13, 1964; "Ruiz No Puede Hacer Campaña Como Ministro," *El Tiempo*, December 13, 1964; Ruiz had long-standing conflicts with Colombian politicians. An argument on the Senate floor with Conservative Dario Marin Vanegas in 1962 about the role of the military in *La Violencia* led the two men to challenge each other to a duel, which was illegal under Colombian law and never fought.

42. "Massive Aid Wins Time for Colombia," *NYT*, January 17, 1964.

43. Kofas, 53-66.

44. Telegram from the Embassy in Peru to the Department of State, December 9, 1964, Doc. 311, *FRUS 64-68*, Vol. XXXI.

45. "El Dólar Libre," *El Tiempo*, December 10, 1964; "Crisis de Confianza," *El Tiempo*, December 11, 1964; Senate, *Colombia*, 31.

46. Memorandum from the Assistant Secretary of State for Inter-American Affairs (Vaughn) to Secretary of State Rusk, June 4, 1965, Doc. 314, *FRUS 64-68*, Vol. XXXI; Senate, *Colombia*, 29-30; Memorandum from the President's Special Assistant for National Security Affairs (Bundy) to President Johnson, June 30, 1965, Doc. 315, *FRUS 64-68*, Vol. XXXI; Inter-American Development Bank, *1965*, 239; Senate, *Colombia*, 26-28; "Colombia Moving on Price Controls," *NYT*, January 16, 1965; "Problem for Latins" *NYT*, December 14, 1964; Dix, 161; "Operación Estabiliadad" *El Tiempo*, December 17, 1964.

47. Senate, *Colombia*, 30-31; "El Impuesto De Renta," *El Tiempo*, January 5, 1965; "Precios Oficiales Para Alimentos," *El Tiempo*, January 6, 1965; "Salió la Reglamentatión," *El Tiempo*, December 18, 1964.

48. "De Nuevo La Violencia," *El Tiempo*, December 10, 1964; "La Nueva Violencia," *El Tiempo*, January 9, 1965; "100 Bandoleros Asaltan a Simacota, Santander: Acción Con Characteristicas Castro-Comunistas," *El Tiempo*, January 8, 1965; "Pacificado el Quindío," *El Tiempo*, March 1, 1965; "Muerto Efraín Gonzalez en Combate con el Ejército," *El Tiempo*, June 10, 1965; "Asesinados Saul Díaz y Su Esposa," *El Tiempo*, March 13, 1965; "Gran Desfile en Cali," *El Tiempo*, March 24, 1965; Telegram from the Department of State to the Embassy in Colombia, May 22, 1965, Doc. 313, *FRUS 64-68*, Vol. XXXI; Senate, *Colombia*, 31.

49. Dix 162; Senate, *Colombia*, 23 suggests abstentions were 70 to 75 percent; Díaz-Alejandro, 196.

50. Letter from the Ambassador to Colombia (Oliver) to the Assistant Secretary of State for Inter-American Affairs (Mann), November 18, 1964, Doc. 310, *FRUS 64–68*, Vol. XXXI.

51. Senate, *Colombia*, 33; "El Gobierno No Va a Retirar el 'Ponquem'" *El Tiempo*, June 2, 1965.

52. Bundy to Johnson, June 11, 1965, Colombia Vol. 1. Memos 12/63–7/65, Box 14, CF, NSF, LBJL; Vaughn to Rusk, June 9, 1965, Colombia Vol. 1. Memos 12/63–7/65, Box 14, CF, NSF, LBJL; Bogotá to State, June 11, 1965, AID (U.S.) Col, Box 544, CFPF 64-66, RG 59, NA; Memorandum of Conversation: Uribe and Hill, June 11, 1965, AID (U.S.) Col, Box 544, CFPF 64-66, RG 59, NA; Memorandum from the President's Special Assistant for National Security Affairs (Bundy) to President Johnson, June 30, 1965, Doc. 315, *FRUS 64–68*, Vol. XXXI; Memorandum from the Assistant Secretary of State for Inter-American Affairs (Vaughn) to Secretary of State Rusk, June 4, 1965, Doc. 314, *FRUS 64–68*, Vol. XXXI; Senate, *Colombia*, 52.

53. Senate, *Colombia*, 33–34; "Plataforma de Estabilización Anunció Vallejo al Posesionarse," *El Tiempo*, July 15, 1965; "Renace la Confianza," *El Tiempo*, July 16, 1965; "Retorno el Equilbro" *El Tiempo*, July 18, 1965.

54. Senate, *Colombia*, 33.

55. Memorandum from the President's Special Assistant for National Security Affairs (Bundy) to President Johnson, June 30, 1965, Doc. 315, *FRUS 64–68*, Vol. XXXI; Schultze to Johnson, February 18, 1966, Colombia Vol. II Memos [1 of 2] 8/65–9/66, Box 14, CF, NSF, LBJL; Read to Rostow, September 15, 1966, Colombia Vol. II Memos [1 of 2] 8/65–9/66, Box 14, CF, NSF, LBJL; Read to Rostow, June 11, 1966, Colombia Vol. II Memos [2 of 2] 8/65–9/66, Box 14, CF, NSF, LBJL; Read to Smith, March 8, 1966, Colombia Vol. II Memos [1 of 2] 8/65–9/66, Box 14, CF, NSF, LBJL; Read to Bundy, February 8, 1966, Colombia Vol. II Memos [1 of 2] 8/65–9/66, Box 14, CF, NSF, LBJL; Memorandum from the President's Special Assistant for National Security Affairs (Bundy) to President Johnson, June 30, 1965, Doc. 315, *FRUS 64–68*, Vol. XXXI.

56. Read to Rostow, September 15, 1966, Colombia Vol. II Memos [1 of 2] 8/65–9/66, Box 14, CF, NSF, LBJL; Read to Rostow, June 11, 1966, Colombia Vol. II Memos [1 of 2] 8/65–9/66, Box 14, CF, NSF, LBJL; Read to Smith, March 8, 1966, Colombia Vol. II Memos [1 of 2] 8/65–9/66, Box 14, CF, NSF, LBJL; Read to Bundy, February 8, 1966, Colombia Vol. II Memos [1 of 2] 8/65–9/66, Box 14, CF, NSF, LBJL; Read to Bundy, January 15, 1966, Colombia Vol. II Memos [1 of 2] 8/65–9/66, Box 14, CF, NSF, LBJL.

57. Lleras Restrepo got 1,639,000 votes, Giraldo got 519,000. Other candidates (a dissenting Liberal and a Conservative) got 352,000 and 334,000, respectively; Information Memorandum for the Assistant Secretary of State for Inter-American Affairs (Gordon) to Secretary of State Rusk, April 30, 1966, *FRUS 64–68*, Vol. XXXI, Doc. 320; Memorandum from William G. Bowdler of the National Security Council Staff to President Johnson, March 24, 1966, Doc. 318, *FRUS 64–68*, Vol. XXXI.

58. Information Memorandum for the Assistant Secretary of State for Inter-American Affairs (Gordon) to Secretary of State Rusk, April 30, 1966, Doc. 320, *FRUS 64–68*, Vol. XXXI.

59. Rostow quote in Memorandum from the President's Special Assistant (Rostow) to President Johnson, November 15, 1966, Doc. 322, FRUS 64-68, Vol, XXXI.

60. Rostow to Johnson, November 27, 1965, Colombia Vol. III Memos [2 of 2] 10/66–11/68, Box 15, CF, NSF, LBJL; Memorandum from the President's Special Assistant (Rostow) to President Johnson, November 15, 1966, Doc. 322, *FRUS 64–68*, Vol, XXXI.

61. Díaz-Alejandro, 203–205; Randall, 236.

62. Díaz-Alejandro, 28, 205.

63. "Lleras Defiende Autonomía Económica," *El Tiempo,* November 30, 1966; "Reafirmacion de un derecho y de una politica," *El Tiempo,* December 1, 1966; Randall, 236.

64. "Vasta Transformación Rural Anuncia Lleras en Córdoba," *El Tiempo,* March 2, 1967; "Tranquilidad en el País: Continúa Estado de Alerta," *El Tiempo,* March 12, 1967; "Aplicactión total de Ley Marcial," *El Tiempo,* March 14, 1967; "Respuesta Positiva del País a Lleras," *El Tiempo,* March 15, 1967.

65. Richard L. Maullin, "The Colombia-IMF Disagreement of November–December 1966: An Interpretation of Its Place in Colombian Politics" in *Contemporary Inter-American Relations: A Reader in Theory and Issues,* ed. Yale Ferguson, ed. (Englewood Cliffs, NJ, 1972); Kofas, 76–78; Abel and Palacios, 648; Kline, 100; Díaz-Alejandro, 28; "Partimos Hacia el Desarrolo Real," *El Tiempo,* March 23, 1967; "Fijadas Cuatro Tasas de Cambio para los Dólares," *El Tiempo,* March 26, 1967; "Ejecutivo Fuerte," *El Tiempo,* March 26, 1967.

66. The statistical increase is higher if petroleum products are excluded. Petroleum exports declined from an average of $79 million in the years 1963 through 1966 to an average of $53 million in the years 1967 through 1970. Díaz-Alejandro, 22; Bruce Michael Bagley, "Colombia: National Front and Economic Development" in *Politics, Policies, and Economic Development in Latin America,* ed. Robert Wesson, 124–160 (Stanford, 1984).

67. Kline, 99–100.

68. Bowdler to Rostow, May 5, 1967, Colombia Vol. III Memos [2 of 2] 10/66–11/68, Box 15, CF, NSF, LBJL; Rostow to Johnson, April 26, 1967, Colombia Vol. III Memos [2 of 2] 10/66–11/68, Box 15, CF, NSF, LBJL; Schultze to Johnson, April 24, 1967, Colombia Vol. III Memos [2 of 2] 10/66–11/68, Box 15, CF, NSF, LBJL; Gaud to Johnson, April 18, 1967, Colombia Vol. III Memos [2 of 2] 10/66–11/68, Box 15, CF, NSF, LBJL.

69. Abel and Palacios, 649; Kofas, 78-83.

70. Gaud to Johnson, February 15, 1968, Colombia Vol. III Memos [1 of 2 10/66–11/68, Box 15, CF, NSF, LBJL.

71. Ibid.

72. Rostow to Johnson, February 24, 1968, Colombia Vol. III Memos [1 of 2] 10/66–11/68, Box 15, CF, NSF, LBJL.

73. U.S. House of Representatives, Subcommittee on Foreign Operations and Government Information, Committee on Governmental Operations, *Testimony of Marvin Weissman, Mission Director, U.S. Aid Mission to Colombia, January 29, 1968: U.S. Aid Operations in Latin America under the Alliance for Progress* (Washington, 1969), 120.

74. Memorandum from William G. Bowdler of the National Security Council Staff to the President's Special Assistant (Rostow), April 19, 1968, Doc. 325, *FRUS 64–68*, Vol. XXXI.
75. Rostow to Johnson, December 31, 1968, Colombia [Filed by LBJ Library], Box 15, CF, NSF, LBJL.
76. Bowdler to Rostow, September 19, 1967, Colombia Vol. III Memos [1 of 2] 10/66–11/68, Box 15, CF, NSF, LBJL.
77. Gaud to Johnson, December 4, 1968, Colombia [Filed by LBJ Library], Box 15, CF, NSF, LBJL.
78. Eduardo Frei would commit to the Alliance for Progress upon winning the Chilean presidential election in late 1964.

Chapter 8

1. The Greenbook. Funding for the four countries dropped in FY1969 because the United States stopped aggressively funding the Brazilian military. FY1966 was the year in which the four countries received the highest combined total of U.S. aid, 72 percent.
2. Irving Bernstein, *Guns or Butter: The Presidency of Lyndon Johnson* (New York, 1996), 329; David Kaiser, *American Tragedy: Kennedy, Johnson, and the Origins of the Vietnam War* (Cambridge, 2000); David Halberstam, *The Best and the Brightest* (New York, 1972); Jeffrey Helsing, *Johnson's War/Johnson's Great Society: The Guns and Butter Trap* (Westport, CT, 2000).
3. Bernstein, 337–338; Ezra Siff, *Why The Senate Slept?: The Gulf of Tonkin Resolution and the Beginning of America's Vietnam War* (Westport, CT, 1999); Edwin Moise, *Tonkin Gulf and the Escalation of the Vietnam War* (Chapel Hill, 1996).
4. Bernstein, 349.
5. *Public Papers, Johnson, 1965*, 394–399.
6. George Ball, *The Past Has Another Pattern* (New York, 1982), 336.
7. Nancy Bernkopf Tucker, "Threats, Opportunities, and Frustrations in East Asia," in *Lyndon Johnson Confronts the World: American Foreign Policy, 1963–1968*, ed. Warren Cohen and Nancy Tucker, 99 (New York, 1994); Joseph S. Tulchin, "U.S. Relations with Latin America," in Cohen and Tucker, eds., 241; Gaddis Smith, *The Last Years of the Monroe Doctrine: 1945–1993* (New York, 1994), 129.
8. John E. Ullmann, "Lyndon Johnson and The Limits of American Resources," in *Lyndon Johnson and the Uses of Power*, ed. Bernard J. Firestone and Robert C. Vogt, 233–244, (New York, 1988), quote on page 234. See also, Robert Dallek, *Flawed Giant: Lyndon Johnson and His Times, 1961–1973* (New York, 1998), 392–399; Robert M. Collins, *More: The Politics of Economic Growth in Postwar America* (New York, 2000); The Johnson quote is in *Public Papers, Johnson, 1966*, 3.
9. Diane B. Kunz, *Butter and Guns: America's Cold War Economic Diplomacy* (New York, 1997).
10. Bernstein 359–360.
11. This concern drove the Harriman/Solomon mission in November 1965 discussed in the chapter on Chile.

12. Bernstein, 358–378; James E. Anderson and Jared E. Hazleton, *Managing Macroeconomic Policy: The Johnson Presidency* (Austin, 1986), 61–71.
13. Gordon to Gaud, December 6, 1966, Alliance for Progress [Vol. 3], Box 5, Agency File—Alliance for Progress, NSF, LBJL; On cuts in the Johnson programs, see Gaud to Johnson, July 29, 1967, *FRUS, 64–68, Volume IX,* 185–189; Memorandum from the President's Special Assistant (Rostow) to President Johnson, July 31, 1967, Doc. 67, *FRUS, 64–68, Volume IX*; Summary Notes of the 576th Meeting of the National Security Council, October 11, 1967, Doc. 68, *FRUS, 64–68, Volume IX*; Memorandum from Edward K. Hamilton of the National Security Council Staff to the President's Special Assistant (Rostow), May 27, 1968, Doc. 76, *FRUS, 64–68, Volume IX*; Draft Memorandum for President Johnson, May 21, 1968, Doc. 75, *FRUS, 64–68,* Volume IX; The Greenbook.
14. Francis J. Gavin, *Gold, Dollars, and Power: The Politics of International Monetary Relations, 1958–1971* (Chapel Hill, 2004); Kunz, *Butter and Guns,* 96–97, George Thomas Kurian, *Datapedia of the United States, 1790–2005* (Lanham, MD, 2001), 417.
15. Gavin, 73–88, 209; Kunz, 104; Kurian, 418.
16. Gavin, 165–185; Burton I. Kaufman, "Foreign Aid and the Balance-of-Payments Problem: Vietnam and Johnson's Foreign Economic Policy" in *The Johnson Years, Volume Two: Vietnam, the Environment, and Science,* ed. Robert A. Divine, 79–109 (Lawrence, KS, 1987); Anderson and Hazleton, 186–190. See, in general, *FRUS, 64–68,* Volume VIII, for more information about international monetary and trade policy.
17. "Common Market for Latins Ready," *NYT,* May 28, 1961.
18. Walter Krause and F. John Mathis, *Latin America and Economic Integration: Regional Planning for Development* (Iowa City, 1970), 4; Sidney Dell, *A Latin American Common Market?* (New York, 1966), 228–256; LaFeber in Divine, 85.
19. "Latin Countries Base Their Hope on Kennedy Plan," *NYT,* January 10, 1962; Krause and Mathis, 86.
20. *Public Papers, Johnson, 1965,* 810.
21. "Aqui No Se Habla Ingles," *NYT,* January 22, 1965; "The Presidents," *NYT,* April 16, 1967; "6 Nations Suspend Common Market Talks," *NYT,* August 12, 1968; David Morawetz, *The Andean Group: A Case Study in Economic Integration among Developing Countries* (Cambridge, 1974); *The Andean Common Market: Business International Corporation Research Report 70-5* (New York, 1970).
22. LaFeber in Divine, ed., 83; Walker in Brands, ed., 86.
23. "Message from President Johnson to the Congress, March 13, 1967," *Department of State Bulletin* (April 3, 1967): 540–545.
24. "Goals for the Alliance," *NYT,* April 4, 1967.
25. Johnson quote in "Austere Johnson Aid Policy Stirs Some Sympathy," *NYT,* April 14, 1967; LaFeber in Divine, ed., 84.
26. "Johnson Remarks to Public Session of Chiefs of State Conference, Punta del Este, April 13, 1967 *Department of State Bulletin* (May 8, 1967): 708–711.
27. "Declaration of the Presidents of America" Department of State Bulletin (May 8, 1967): 712–721; "Leaders Approve 'Action Program' for the Ameri-

cas," *NYT*, April 14, 1967; William O. Walker, "Mixing the Sweet with the Sour," in *Diplomacy of the Crucial Decade: American Foreign Relations during the 1960s*, ed. Diane Kunz, 68 (New York, 1994).

28. Kline 121; Krause and Mathis, 15–30; Rusk to Johnson, July 15, 1967, Latin America Vol. VI 6/67–9/67, Box 3, CF, NSF, Latin America, LBJL.
29. Quote in "Post-Mortem on the Summit," *NYT*, April 16, 1967; "Punta del Este: The Fertile Giant," *NYT*, April 16, 1967; *Public Papers, Johnson, 1967*, 446–449.
30. Tulchin in Cohen and Tucker, eds., 239.
31. "Nixon Says U.S. Leadership Declines under Johnson Policies," *NYT*, September 13, 1967.
32. "Nixon Urges Help for Latin Nations," *NYT*, October 15, 1968; "Nixon, in Wisconsin, Gives Latin American Policy," *NYT*, February 7, 1968.
33. "Rockefeller Hears Opinions on Peru," *NYT*, May 29, 1969; Kline, 121.
34. "Nixon Announces Rockefeller Will Make a Series of Trips to Latin America," *NYT*, February 18, 1969; "Nixon and Latin's Mood," *NYT*, October 31, 1969; "President Urges Latins Take Lead to Spur Progress," *NYT*, November 1, 1969.
35. "Rockefeller Is in Jamaica," *NYT*, July 4, 1969; Gregorio Selser, *Los Cuatro Viajes de Cristóbal Rockefeller: Con Su Informe al Presidente Nixon* (Buenos Aires, 1971).
36. Nelson A. Rockefeller, *The Rockefeller Report on the Americas: The Official Report of a United States Presidential Mission to the Western Hemisphere* (Chicago, IL, 1969), 57–58.
37. *Rockefeller Report*, 22, 24.
38. Ibid., 95–96.
39. Ibid., 43, 75, 85.
40. U.S. House, Committee on Foreign Affairs, Subcommittee on Inter-American Affairs, *Hearings. February 1969–May 1969, New Directions for the 1970s: Toward a Strategy of Inter-American Development* (Washington, 1969). Quote on page 141.
41. "The Latins State Their Case," *NYT*, June 15, 1969.
42. Ibid; Senate, *Colombia*, 7.
43. "U.S. and Latins: Nixon Is Told the 'Time Has Come for Action,'" *NYT*, June 15, 1969.
44. *Public Papers, Nixon, 1969*, 892–901. The long quote is on page 894.
45. "President Urges Latins Take Lead to Spur Progress," *NYT*, November 1, 1969; *Public Papers, Nixon, 1969*, 892–901. This did not include Cuba of course. Nixon said, "we cannot have a peaceful community of nations if one nation sponsors armed subversion in another's territory." Nations like Cuba, which the United States felt was engaged in this practice, would not be part of the community of American nations. The long quote is on page 900.
46. Gambone, 178.
47. Memorandum by the President's Special Assistant for National Security Affairs (Kissinger), April 3, 1969, Doc. 6, *FRUS 69–72*, Vol. IV.
48. Action Memorandum from the President's Assistant for National Security Affairs (Kissinger) to President Nixon, No Date, Doc. 5, *FRUS 69–72*, Vol. IV.

49. Action Memorandum from C. Fred Bergsten of the National Security Council Staff to the President's Assistant for National Security Affairs (Kissinger), December 2, 1969, Doc. 15, *FRUS 69–72*, Vol. IV; Memorandum from the President's Special Assistant for National Security Affairs (Kissinger) to the President's Assistant (Harlow), December 9, 1969, Doc. 16, *FRUS 69–72*, Vol. IV.
50. *Report to the Congress by the Comptroller General of the United States: U.S. Direct Investment in South America's Andean Common Market* (Washington, 1977), 27; Editorial Note, Doc. 25, *FRUS 69–72*, Vol. IV.
51. Senate, *Covert Action*, 19–23.
52. Abraham Lowenthal, "Alliance Rhetoric Versus Latin American Reality," *Foreign Affairs* 48, no. 3 (1970), 494–508.
53. The Greenbook.
54. Gambone, 177.

Conclusion

1. Remarks of President Johnson at the University of Denver, August 26, 1966, Latin America Vol. V 1/67–3/67, Box 3, CF, NSF, LBJL.
2. See for example, Lars Schoultz, *Beneath the United States: A History of U.S. Policy toward Latin America* (Cambridge, 1998); Frederick Pike, *The United States and Latin America: Myths and Stereotypes in Civilization and Nature* (Austin, 1992); Kyle Longley, *In the Eagle's Shadow: The United States and Latin America* (Wheeling, IL, 2002); Peter Smith, *Talons of the Eagle: Dynamics of U.S.-Latin American Relations* (New York, 1996); Mark Gilderhus, *The Second Century: U.S-Latin American Relations since 1889* (Wilmington, DE, 2000); and Lester Langley, *America and the Americas: The United States in the Western Hemisphere* (Athens, GA, 1989).

Index

A

Figure I.1 Washington, DC. President Kennedy introduces the Alliance for Progress at a reception for Latin American diplomats on March 13, 1961. The front row of the audience includes Mrs. Andrés Alvarado Puerto and Dr. Céleo Dávila of Honduras, Lady Bird Johnson and Vice-President Lyndon B. Johnson, Dr. Guillermo Sevilla-Sacasa of Nicaragua, Jacqueline Kennedy, Ambassador Fernando Berckemeyer and Mrs. Claribel Berckmeyer of Peru, and Ambassador Manuel G. Escalante and Mrs. Escalante of Costa Rica. (Photo AR6424I, Audiovisual Archives, John F. Kennedy Library, Boston, MA; Credit: Abbie Rowe, 1961)

Figure I.2 Southern Chile. A worker drives a new Ford tractor on a collective farm created by the Chilean land reform process. A new truck, also a Ford, is visible on the left. Alliance for Progress funds allowed the farmers to purchase these vehicles and ensured that they would be imported from the United States. (Record Group 286-CF-31-4, National Archives, College Park, MD; Credit: Agency for International Development, no date)

Figure I.3 An internal page from *Arriba Muchachos* collected by the author in March 1998 at the United States Information Agency library in Washington, DC, from unprocessed files.

Figure I.4 The cover of *El Despertar*. Collected by the author in March 1998 at the United States Information Agency library in Washington, DC, from unprocessed files.

Figure I.5 Techo, Colombia. President Kennedy and Colombian President Lleras Camargo dedicate a plaque in front of what will be school in a large housing project constructed with U.S. funds on December 17, 1961. A large map of the project for Ciudad Techo towers behind them. On Kennedy's three trips to Latin America he visited Alliance for Progress projects to publicize the program. (Photo ST-285-13-61, Audiovisual Archives, John F. Kennedy Library, Boston, MA; Credit: Cecil Stoughton, 1961)

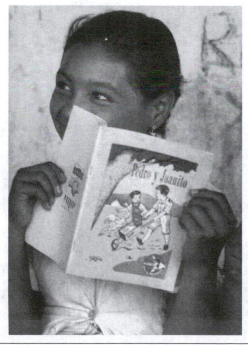

Figure I.6 La Maquina, Guatemala. A child reads from a textbook issued under a five-year free textbook program sponsored by the Alliance for Progress. Note the Alliance for Progress logo on the front of the book and the United States Agency for International Development logo on the back. (Photo 64-3257, Record Group 306, National, College Park, MD; Credit: Ken Heyman, 1964)

Figure I.7 Maine, Chile. Opening ceremonies for the community of Maine, a village constructed with U.S. aid as part of the earthquake reconstruction program. The bishop of Puerto Montt is flanked by Charles Henry Lee, a U.S. embassy officer and Charles Cole, the U.S. ambassador. The ceremonies were part of an effort to publicize the Alliance for Progress in the months preceding the 1964 Chilean presidential election. (Record Group 286-C, National Archives, College Park, MD; Credit: Agency for International Development, 1964)

Figure I.8 Santiago, Chile. A teacher training college in Santiago that received Alliance for Progress funding. (Record Group 286-CF-31-21, National Archives, College Park, MD; Credit: Agency for International Development, 1968)

Figure I.9 Alagoas, Brazil. Jack Kubish, the United States Agency for International Development mission director in Brazil, and his wife dedicate a plaque to honor President Kennedy at the opening of a housing project called Vila Kennedy funded by the Alliance for Progress. (Record Group 286-C, National Archives, College Park, MD; Credit: Servicio Photografico – SENEC, no date)

Figure I.10 Rio de Janeiro, Brazil. A family moving into a home in Vila Aliança, one of two major housing projects built with financial assistance from the Alliance for Progress in Rio de Janeiro. Residents of the community complained about poor access to transportation and high rents. (Photo 63-1389, Record Group 306, National Archives, College Park, MD; Credit: USIS/Rio de Janeiro. no date)

Figure I.11 Santo Domingo, Dominican Republic. Dominican civilians receive water from U.S. soldiers during the civil war on May 5, 1965. (Photo 65-136, Box 34, Record Group 306-PS, National Archives, College Park, MD; Credit: US Department of Defense, 1965)

Figure I.12 Marquetalia, Colombia. Part of a cache of Communist propaganda materials captured by the Colombian military in the stronghold of a local bandit leader in Marquetalia. Officials described the materials as the largest collection of evidence yet uncovered showing Cuban penetration in the country. This area was the focus of the Colombian Acción Cívica Militar program (Photo 64-2320, Box 34, Record Group, 306-PS, National Archives, College Park, MD; Credit: USIS-Bogotá, 1965)

Figure I.13 Fuquena, Colombia. Two workers push a loaded wheelbarrow through the mud toward the construction site of a new health center being built with the help of Alliance for Progress funds. The poster reads: Alliance for Progress, Health Center, another example of the cooperation between the people of Colombia and the United States. (Photo 62-4720, Record Group 306, National Archives, College Park, MD; Credit: Ken Heyman, 1964)

Figure I.14 Bogotá, Colombia. The U.S. ambassador to Colombia, Fulton Freeman, visits one of a number of low-income homes constructed by a community construction collective and funded, in part, by the Alliance for Progress. (Record Group 286-C, National Archives, College Park, MD; Credit: Agency for International Development, no date)

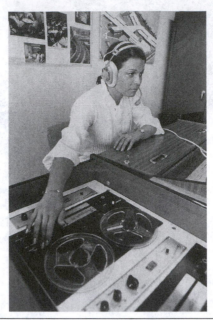

Figure I.15 Bogotá, Colombia. A woman identified as Maria Cristina Granada at the Santander School in Kennedy City. She uses U.S. made audio equipment to teach English. The United States Agency for International Development funded the school and classroom. (Record Group 286-CF-36-7, National Archives, College Park, MD; Credit: Agency for International Development, no date)

Figure I.16 San Salvador, El Salvador. Workers building a school funded by the Alliance for Progress. (Photo 63-1044, Record Group 306, National Archives, College Park, MD; Credit: Ken Heyman, 1962)